Andrea's Bio

Andrea is a full time personal trainer and nutrition & wellness consultant certified through CanFitPro. After losing over 50 lbs through a healthy and balanced diet combined with daily physical activity, she turned her new found knowledge and passion in to a career.

Now she owns her own 'Wholistic' Health & Wellness business 'Compass Fitness' and also writes on her popular food blog; 'Andrea's Blog' on www.compassfitnesskingston.com. This cookbook is a compilation of her favourite flavourful, nutritious and, of course, delicious recipes, that focuses on nourishing the body but also satisfying taste buds!

For more information on Andrea, to read the new recipes on her blog or to contact her please see her website: **www.compassfitnesskingston.com**

Thanks

This book is really all thanks to my mom, dad and grandparents for getting me cooking from a young age, to my boyfriend, business partner and general partner in crime Zach for being my recipe guinea pig and taste testing even the recipe failures. And to all of my friends, family and clients who are my taste testers, inspiration and motivation. If it wasn't for all of you I never would have make this book!

~ Andrea

Copyright © 2013

TABLE OF CONTENTS

My Story & Why I Made this Cookbook..3

How to Use This Cookbook..5

Portion Sizes...6

Eating Healthy on a Tight Budget...7

A Note on Exercise..11

Benefits of Exercise...12

Breakfast..13

Baking...24

Smoothies..40

Meats..44

Vegetarian...63

Hot Beverages..91

Desserts...96

MY STORY

Growing up, food and eating was a huge part of life. No matter what meal it was, if all four of us were home my family ate together - breakfast, lunch and dinner. In the kitchen and at the table is where we got ready for the day ahead and discussed everything that had happened throughout the day - the good and the bad. And oh how many life lessons were learned sitting at the kitchen table. Not surprisingly, the kitchen is still my favourite room in the house.

This love of food and eating did however lead to weight gain, making me overweight by the time I was in grade six. This wasn't because I was inactive; I played baseball, basketball and volleyball growing up, not to mention the daily chores like mucking horse stalls and taking care of the horses. And it wasn't because we ate unhealthy food. It was simply because my portions where too large because I love food! And so by the time I was 21 I was over 200lbs and out of shape.

Seeing pictures of myself on my 21st birthday I decided it was time to make some changes. I started watching my portions, researching and trying new and healthy recipes and working out regularly. And in time I lost over 50 lbs and got healthy - as you can see in my before and after picture!

After I lost the weight, I decided that I wanted to help other people get healthy too and became a personal trainer and with that got a certification in Nutrition & Wellness so I could be a well-rounded trainer. So now not only was I a food lover, I was a 'health nut' food lover who loved to cook! And the combination of those three things, I've found, is quite unique. And so with more and more of my clients asking for my recipes I started a simple little health and wellness blog focused on bringing healthy, yet still flavourful and delicious recipes to my clients and readers.

My focus with food is to make it easy to make and taste delicious while having each recipe contribute to your overall health. By swapping a few ingredients here and there, increasing one ingredient, leaving out another and adding new flavours you can change the nutritional content of any recipe without losing the flavour and feeling of satisfaction. After all you only live once, but I want you to live a long, healthy and active life as free of disease and illness as possible.

This cookbook is the consolidation and culmination of my nutrition knowledge, cooking experience, experimentation and of more than two years of food blogging, as well as the organization of all of my recipes in one place where they are easy to find. Let me show you that food doesn't have to be bad for you to taste delicious and that with a few small changes you can keep enjoying your favourite comfort foods while contributing to your health and well-being.

Enjoy! ☺

How to Use This Cookbook

Focus on Whole Natural Foods
Basically I want to encourage you to buy foods that don't have an ingredient list, foods that are as close to nature as possible and have been minimally processed. Fresh fruits and vegetables, lean meats, oats, rice and whole grains offer a huge variety of food and flavours without added sugar, salt, preservatives or chemicals that are harmful to our health.

Be Adventurous
I made this cookbook to put all of my recipes in to one place but also to challenge you to try new recipes, flavours and new twists on old favourites. There will be some foods, and combinations of foods, in the cookbook that you may look at and think 'No Way!' but trust me on this: you will like it. The number one rule with this cookbook is to try new things, experiment and enjoy!

Do Not Obsess Over Calories
One thing you may notice about this cookbook is that there is no calorie count or nutrient breakdown. This is because if you are filling you plate and your stomach with fresh whole vegetables, fruits and lean protein you don't need to obsess over calories which I find a lot of people (especially women) do. I want to move the focus from calories to fuelling your body for optimum health.

Get Your Body Moving
There is a small section on physical activity recommendations and benefits. Have a read through it and get moving!

Experiment!
Do not be afraid to experiment with these recipes and make them your own! Swap the vegetables, add meat to the vegetarian recipes, leave the meat out of the meat-atarian recipes, add different herbs and spices, the options are endless!

Great for Vegetarians & Meat-atarians Alike!
I've also added a few neat little symbols to help you out:

 Make is vegetarian: Every time you see this carrot you can make the recipe vegetarian!

 Make is meat-atarian: Every time you see this turkey you can add meat to a vegetarian dish for the meat lovers in the family or to add some extra protein!

PROPER PORTIONS

Nowadays it is so easy to over indulge especially with the huge portions we've gotten so used to. Portions weren't always the size they are now. For example, take the two bagels below. In the 1960's that bagel was about 3 inches in diameter and about 140 calories, now look at today's bagel, its 6 inches in diameter and closer to 350 calories! That's more than doubled! It's so important for you to know what proper portions are and how to measure them "on the fly" because this alone can make a huge impact on your overall health, fitness and weight.

| 1960's: 140 Calories | 2013: 350 Calories |

Below is a quick glance chart for helping you measure your portions without you actually having to measure them. Because really who has time for that? Use it to give yourself a rough estimate of your daily calories and become mindful of your portions.

Measurement	Foods	Calories
1 Fist	Pasta & Rice	200
1 Cup	Fruit	75
	Vegetables	40
Palm of Your Hand	Meat	160
3 Ounces / Deck of Cards	Fish	160
	Poultry	160
1 Handful	Nuts	170
1 Ounce / ¼ Cup	Raisins	85
2 Handfuls	Chips	150
1 Ounce	Popcorn	100
	Pretzels	100
Thumb	Peanut Butter	170
1 Ounce / 2 Tablespoons	Hard Cheese	100
Thumb Tip	Cooking Oil	40
1 Teaspoon	Butter, Mayo	35
	Sugar	15

HEALTHY EATING ON TIGHT BUDGET

"I want to eat healthier, but it's too expensive. I can't afford it." It's a phrase I hear almost every day. Now, I'll grant you that buying Rice Crispies is cheaper than buying organic Kashi cereal, there's no doubt about it: we live in a broken food culture where commercials constantly tell us to buy cheap, low-fat, fat-free, sugar-free processed foods that often contain less nutrition than a piece of cardboard and that, in the end, make us sick, fat, and depressed. It's not always easy to walk into a grocery store and choose salad greens and fish and ignore the miles of aisles filled with chemically-manufactured foods that are purposely designed to attract your attention and condition your taste buds to crave even more sugar, fat, and salt.

But this **does not** mean you can't make better food choices and eat healthy on a budget. Yes, it may mean changing your habits and priorities a bit, but I assure you the results will be worth it.

Here are my top six tips for eating healthy when you are on a tight budget. Follow them, and you'll find eating well is much easier, cheaper, and more delicious than you ever imagined.

TIP #1: HAVE A PLAN & PREPARE

This alone has can make the biggest difference in reducing your food costs and staying on track eating healthy foods. Meal planning allows you to make some foods ahead and have them available for lunches or to re-purpose for dinners. This also makes sure that you use up all of your food before it goes bad; there is nothing worse than wasting food because you didn't get to it in time when you're working so hard to buy healthy foods.

Set aside regular blocks of time for planning meals, making your grocery list and shopping, tasks that are most often short changed in food prep. Include healthy snack ideas, as well as main menu items and see how much easier it is to stay on track, on budget and reduce food waste.

Some examples of how to cook once and then use meats throughout the week:

- For turkey & chicken - leftover meat can be rolled in lettuce leaves for lunches, made into turkey enchiladas for dinners, added to soups, stews and casseroles, put in stir-frys etc. and the bones can be used for stock.

- For beef (roast, steaks, etc.) – leftover meat can be seasoned for fajitas, put in omelettes, made into barbecue, thrown in soups, made into omelette, quesadillas, etc. Bones can be used for broth/stock.

- For ham – Leftovers can be roasted with cauliflower for "ham and potatoes" dish, put in omelettes, wrap up in lettuce leaves, put on salads for lunch, or stir fry with cabbage for fast meal, etc.

You can also prepare large amounts of ground beef, chicken breasts or any other meat you have around and structure your meals for the week around it.

TIP #2: PRIORITIZE EATING HEALTHY

The fact of the matter is that most people don't make eating healthy a financial priority. I'm not going to tell you that you should give up all of your luxury purchases so you can buy better food. But I do think it's worth it for you to take a look at how you're spending your money and consider:

"Am I really supporting my health and meeting my personal goals this way?"

Many people spend lots of money on expensive coffee drinks, popcorn at the movies, convenience foods, chocolate bars, and more. I've had clients come in who are spending in excess of $15.00 a day on this kind of thing and then tell me they can't afford to eat healthy. That's just not true, they have the money to eat healthy, they simply choose not to.

How you spend your money is your business but at least take a look at how you're spending your hard-earned cash. I think you'll find there's more money in your budget for eating healthy that you initially realized.

There are other areas of a budget where you can save money to help buffer the food bill also. Here are some of the ways you can do it:

- Don't eat out, ever. I admit I love eating out, not because the food is good (it usually isn't) but because I don't have to cook and Zach doesn't have to clean for one whole meal. That being said, eating out even once a month can use up a lot of the food budget at once. Saving the money from eating out lets us have healthier options and we don't really miss it.

- Cut back on supplements: Unless you are taking a very specific supplement for a condition, chances are you can back off of some supplements when you start eating healthier. Supplements are meant to "supplement" a good diet anyway, and you can't out-supplement a bad diet.

- Do a Media Detox: If you've made the above changes and money is still tight, consider doing a media detox and cutting back on entertainment related expenses. We haven't had cable for more than a year and we don't even miss it. We can watch most things online and on Netflix ($7.99/Mo) which is significantly less expensive than a cable bill!

By making healthy eating a financial priority you can make small budget changes to find the money to invest in your own health and wellness.

TIP #3: USE FLYERS & COUPONS

If you're in the habit of trashing supermarket flyers or pages of coupons from the newspaper, you may want to rethink that impulse. Coupons are rising in popularity again and for good reason. Spending up to half an hour before you shop to scan flyers for weekly specials and look for coupons you can save a tune of money! Using the flyers you can also stock up on non-perishables and freezables (like meats, bread and bananas) while they are on sale.

TIP #4: BE A MINDFUL SHOPPER

We all sometimes get caught in "zombie shopping mode", it's the end of a long day, you just got off work and need to go pick up your kids from daycare, but first you have to stop by the store for some groceries. That trip to the market may be the only "down time" you get all day. So you walk in, and zone out. You head to the middle aisles of the supermarket, and like a zombie scoop items into your cart almost mindlessly.

If you want to eat healthy on a budget, I recommend you become a mindful shopper. Become fully aware of the dazzling display of foods around you. Realize that you are hunting and gathering the foods that are going to nourish the minds, bodies, and spirits of your entire family. Once you're in this mode, look around you and bring your critical mind to the act of shopping. Note which foods are good for you, the ones without long ingredient lists, and which are built by food engineers and marketing experts to draw your attention away from your health goals. Choose accordingly.

TIP #5: FOCUS ON A PLANT-BASED DIET

Veggies can vary tremendously in price, depending on the time of year and the source. Focusing on veggies that are in season will help cut costs. And vegetables like cabbage and sweet potatoes are inexpensive year round and can be great fillers and substitutes in recipes. You can stock up on things like these when they are in season; even buying several bags of sweet potatoes, potatoes and onions in the fall from farmers markets. And beans and lentils are pennies per serving.

TIP #6: STOCK UP ON THE ESSENTIALS

Stock your fridge and cupboards with items that are quick and easy to cook, kind to your wallet and often go on sale:

- **Beans and lentils:** Whether canned or dried, these guys make nutritious, hearty soups, and can be a main course with the addition of fresh vegetables or rice.

- **Basmati rice:** Is a great addition to leftover meat and veggies. Although basmati rice is slightly more expensive than plain white rice, the nutritional payoff is well worth it including the extra dose of protein not found in white rice.

- **Pasta:** Is quick and easy to prepare, and can be paired with veggies, meat, or a fresh salad. Have fun adding your own embellishments like vegetables, spices, and herbs. Choose whole-wheat pasta whenever available and a tomato based sauce.

- **Frozen vegetables and fruit:** You can also rely on frozen varieties as handy additions to last-minute meals. Veggies make great stir-fries and vegetable patties, while fruit is great as a quick nutritious snack and are great in smoothies.

- **Canned fish (in water):** Can be kept on hand for last-minute meals - try tuna or salmon, and then add dill, lemon juice, pepper and Greek yogurt to make it to a delicious sandwich filling or dip of whole wheat crackers, or serve it plain over a delicious green salad.

- **Condiments & spices:** Add flavour and interest to your dishes. Keep a selection of dried herbs, spices, curry powder, marinades, vinegars, tomato and soy sauces along with stock cubes, in your cupboard. Experiment with new flavours, such as sweet Thai chili sauce or roasted red pepper humus to keep food interesting.

By following these tips, you can eat healthy on a budget. And remember, when you shift away from highly-processed carbohydrates and sugar-filled foods toward healing vegetables and pastured meat, your appetite will naturally diminish. You will not be as hungry if you eat healthier, which means you'll eat less, save more money, and lose a few pounds in the process.

Paying attention to what you eat and how you spend your food dollars is worth it in every sense. You will have more energy and vitality, you'll heal your body naturally with the phytochemicals, healthy fats and proteins in these foods, and you may see your energy, mood, memory, and brain function improve as well.

A Note on Exercise

Being a personal trainer, I couldn't very well write a health focused cookbook without mentioning exercise! I won't get too deep in detail but here are some general guidelines for improved health and wellness, and I'll just remind you about the benefits in case you've forgotten.

For Eexercise, Health Canada Recommends:

- **250 Minutes per week of moderate intensity exercise or 125 minutes of vigorous exercise.** Moderate activity means you are sweating and your heart rate is elevated but you are still able to carry on a conversation. Examples are; vigorous walking, weight lifting, actively playing with children or biking. Vigorous exercise means you are really sweating and your blood is pumping, like when you play soccer or hockey, run or do a bootcamp. The most important thing? Make it enjoyable so you stick with it!

Your weekly exercise routine should include:

- **3-4 Days/Week Strength Training.** This can be any weight bearing exercise including weight lifting, body weight exercises, resistant band exercises or even swimming,

- **4-7 Days/Week Cardio.** walking, biking, hiking, playing with your kids. Whatever gets your heart rate elevated.

- **4-7 Days/Week Stretching.** Stretching is incredibly important and is often the first thing that goes if we're running short on time. But it helps us cool down after a workout, lengthens and loosens muscles to prevent injuries and makes our next workout that much better.

- **7 Days/Week Meditation.** I encourage all of my clients to practice daily meditation to calm the mind and relax the body. Try a 15 minute guided meditation on youtube and see the difference 15 minutes a day can make in your mood and mental outlook.

BENEFITS OF EXERCISE

Here is a list of some of the benefits of exercise. But most importantly it makes you feel great and lets you be able to do anything you want to do whether that's climbing a mountain or playing all afternoon with your kids:

- Improved body composition and weight control
- Improved cholesterol levels
- Improved blood pressure
- More energy
- Able to move freely and without pain
- Increased average lifespan
- Postpone age related illness
- Improved work performance
- Better sleep
- Stress relief
- Improved mood
- Improved mental health; exercise decreases symptoms of depression & anxiety
- Increased vitality

Decreases likelihood of:

- Cardiovascular disease
- Stroke
- Type 2 Diabetes
- Many cancers
- Osteoporosis
- Dependence in old age
- Limited range of motion
- Age related falls
- PREMATURE MORTALITY

BREAKFAST

Refrigerator Oatmeal

Makes 1, Total Time: 12 Hours

These super-easy, single-serve oatmeal cups are one of the best recipes for rushed mornings! You can make a week worth of these on Sunday all in a variety of flavours and have a hearty, healthy and yummy breakfast ready to go every morning. All you have to do is grab it out of the fridge, grab a spoon and go!

Base Ingredients

¼ Cup old fashioned oats, uncooked
1/3 Cup milk (or substitute)
¼ Cup plain Greek yogurt
1 Tbsp chia seeds

Nutella Banana

½ Large banana, sliced
1 Heaping tbsp nutella

Raspberry

¼ Cup raspberries
1 Tbsp honey

Espresso

1 Tbsp instant coffee
½ Tbsp cocoa powder
1 Tsp Organic sugar or honey

Directions

1. Mix all ingredients, put in a mason jar and put lid on tightly.

2. Let sit over night in the refridgerator.

3. In the morning, stir and enjoy on the go!

Apple Cinnamon

½ Small apple, diced
½ Tbsp maple syrup
Cinnamon to taste

Blueberry Maple

¼ Cup blueberries
1 Tbsp maple syrup

Breakfast Banana Split

Makes 1, Total Time: 10 Minutes

What better way to start a leisurely morning than by making a banana split! It tastes like dessert but has all of the ingredients of a healthy and filling breakfast: protein, fibre, fruit and chocolate!

Ingredients

1 Medium banana
½ Cup vanilla Greek yogurt
1 Tsp Chia seeds
½ Cup fresh berries
2 Tbsp granola
1 Tbsp chocolate chips

Directions

1. Peel banana and split in half length-wise, place on a plate or bowl.

2. Top with yogurt, then chia seeds, berries, granola and lastly chocolate chips

Berry Syrup

Makes ~1 Cup, Total Time: 20 Minutes

This delicious and easy-to-make berry syrup is perfect over pancakes and French toast! These flavours blend beautifully as the maple syrup brings out natural sweetness of the berries. Try it with my *'Overnight Stuffed French Toast' (pg. 16)* or *'Buckwheat Flour Pancakes' (pg. 17)* to add that little extra something special.

Ingredients

2 Cups frozen berries
¼ Cup pure maple syrup

Directions

1. Mix berries and syrup in a sauce pan, cover and turn to medium heat. Stir occasionally until berries are thawed and mixture begins to thicken slightly.

2. Remove from heat and let cool while you make your pancakes!

Overnight Stuffed French Toast

Serves 4-6, Total Time: 12 Hours

This is one of my favourite special occasion breakfasts. It's a little bit French toast, a little bit cheesecake and every bit delicious! You get fibre and healthy whole grains from the Ezekiel bread, protein from the cream cheese and eggs, a serving of fruit from the fresh berries and the combination of all of the above with pure maple syrup makes this taste absolutely decadent! Serve with maple syrup and fresh fruit or *'Berry Syrup' (pg. 15).*

Ingredients

1 Small tub light cream cheese, softened
2 ½ Tbsp Organic Sugar
1 Tsp nutmeg
8 Slices Ezekiel cinnamon raisin bread
4 Eggs
½ Cup skim milk
Fresh strawberries, sliced
Fresh blueberries
Maple syrup

Directions

1. Mix cream cheese and sugar until well blended, spread on to the bread.

2. Place 4 pieces of bread, cream cheese side up, in a baking dish. Then cover with other 4 pieces of bread cream cheese side down.

3. Whisk eggs, milk and nutmeg until well blended, pour over bread. Refrigerate over night.

4. Heat oven to 350*F. Bake uncovered for 30-35 minutes or until centre is set and top is slightly browned.

Buckwheat Pancakes

Makes 8 Pancakes, Total Time: 20 Minutes

My grandmother used to make these pancakes first for my dad and his seven siblings and then for my sister and I when we were growing up, so the delicious earthy taste always takes me back to my grandparents warm and welcoming kitchen. Serve these delicious pancakes with fresh fruit and maple syrup, or with my *'Berry Syrup' (pg. 15)* and a dollop of vanilla Greek yogurt.

Ingredients

1 ½ Cups buckwheat flour
1 Tbsp baking soda
1 Tbsp cinnamon
1 Cup buttermilk
1-2 Tbsp honey
1 Egg
Coconut oil, for frying, optional

Directions

1. Mix dry ingredients and wet ingredients in separate bowl.

2. Pour wet ingredients into dry and beat with a hand mixer

3. Feel free to add fresh fruit, nuts or if you're like me, a small handful dark chocolate chips.

4. Use a non-stick pan or add a small spoonful of coconut oil to a frying pan and heat to medium

5. Pour ¼ cup scoops of batter into a heated frying pan, cook until the pancakes start to have little bubbles on the top, then flip. Enjoy with fresh fruit, maple syrup, honey or Greek yogurt

Fluffy Coconut Flour Pancakes

Serves 2, Total Time: 15 Minutes

This is delicious and fluffy, gluten-free and grain-free pancake recipe. These are the favourite pancake in our house and I usually end up making them a few times a month. The great thing about coconut flour that you may not know is that it is full of fibre. Just 2 Tbsp of coconut flour has 5 grams of fibre! Try mixing it up with one of the flavour options below or serving with my *'Berry Syrup' (pg. 15)*.

Ingredients

4 Eggs
1 Cup milk, or milk substitute
2 Tsp vanilla extract
1 Tbsp honey
½ Cup coconut flour
1 Tsp baking soda
Coconut oil for frying (optional if using non-stick pan or griddle)

Directions

1. In a food processor (or small bowl) beat eggs vigorously until frothy, about 2 minutes.

2. Add the rest of the ingredients and process (or beat) until well combined then allow to sit and thicken. If it's too watery, add coconut flour 1 Tbsp at a time until desired consistency is reached. Only do this after you've allowed it to sit and thicken for at least 5 minutes.

3. While batter is thickening, preheat a griddle over medium to medium-low heat. Add coconut oil, if needed. Ladle about 1/4 cup of batter onto the griddle, spreading the batter out to 2-3-inches in diameter.

4. Cook for a few minutes, until they start to bubble and seem set when shaken gently in the pan. The bottom will be lightly brown, then flip the pancakes over and cook an additional 2-3 minutes. Don't rush this step! If you do it will look more like mashed potatoes than pancakes (but they will still taste great!).

Pancake Variations!

Don't limit yourself to just the basic pancake! Trying adding a variety of spices and flavours like these combinations:

Pumpkin Spice
Add ¼ cup pureed pumpkin
Use maple syrup instead of honey
1 Tsp Pumpkin Pie Spice
2 Tbsp Shredded Coconut

Apple Pie
Add ¼ cup apple sauce
1 Tsp Nutmeg
Use maple syrup instead of honey

Chocolate Chip Cookie
Add ¼ Cup of semi-sweet chocolate chips
½ Tsp coconut extract
½ Tsp vanilla extract
2 Tbsp Shredded Coconut

Peach
Slice a fresh peach
Stir 1 Tbsp chia seeds into batter
Pour batter onto griddle
Put peach slices into wet batter
Cook as usual

19

Chia Seed Jam

Makes 1 Cup, Total Time: 35 Minutes

Most jams in the grocery store are full of added sugars and preservatives that are not good for our health. But on the other hand it takes a lot of time and effort to make your own jam. So here is a delicious alternative! Chia seeds thicken the fruit puree to give it the same texture as traditional jam and a dab of honey give it a bit of added sweetness, making this taste even better than store bought jam! This delicious puree lasts 1-2 weeks in the fridge and makes a great gift! Use any type or combination of berries you want.

Ingredients

2 Cups fresh berries
2 Tbsp chia seeds
2 Tbsp honey

Directions

1. Put all ingredients together in a blender, puree well.

2. Place mixture in a covered mason jar and let sit for at least 30 minutes, or overnight.

Breakfast Cookies

Makes about 12 Large Cookies, Total Time: 30 Minutes

Here is my favourite breakfast cookie recipe! These are full of protein, healthy fats and fibre, and of course chocolate chips. These are made for rushed or very early mornings when getting up and making yourself a good breakfast just isn't going to happen. Enjoy one of these delicious cookies with a cup of coffee and you're on your way!

Ingredients

4 Cups oatmeal cookie mix, bulk food store
¼ Cup ground flax seeds
¼ Cup all natural peanut butter
1/3 Cup semi-sweet chocolate chips
1/3 Cup Raisins
2 Cups of water, or to cookie consistency

Directions

1. Mix all of the above ingredients and let sit for about 10 minutes for the mix to soak up the water. As you are adding the water, make sure the mix is nice and moist without there being any standing water in the bowl.

2. Use the ¼ cup measuring cup to scoop cookie mix on to a baking sheet. Bake for about 15 minutes at 350*F.

Homemade Protein Bars

Makes 10-12, Total Time: 2.5 Hours

These delicious, chocolate and peanut butter protein bars are perfect for mornings on the go or even as a post workout snack. They are chalk full of all natural ingredients, most of which you probably already have in your kitchen. Feel free to experiment with different dried fruits, nut butters and nuts to change the flavour.

Ingredients

1 Mashed banana
1 ½ Cups dry oatmeal
2 Tbsp flax seed, ground
2 Scoops protein powder
¼ Cup peanut butter
¼ Cup shredded coconut
¼ Cup coconut oil, melted
¼ Cup raisins, dates or dried cherries
¼ Cup water
1 large chocolate bar (I used organic dark chocolate) or ¾ cup chocolate chips

Directions

1. Mix all ingredients but chocolate together well (mixture will be somewhat sticky). Line an 8×8-inch pan with foil and spread the mixture evenly in the pan.

2. Melt chocolate on the stove or in the microwave. Drizzle or spread over the mixture in the pan.

3. Place the pan in the freezer for at least 2 hours. Cut into 10 -12 bars and wrap individually in plastic wrap and/or foil and store in the freezer.

4. Thaw slightly before serving.

Homemade Hearty Oat Cereal

Serves 4, Total Time: 10 Minutes

So many of the cereals out there are full of sugar and other ingredients you can't pronounce, so why not try making your own? I'll admit that even I was slightly sceptical, thinking that this might need some added sugar but I really was pleasantly surprised. This simple and natural cereal has a wonderful flavour, texture and sweetness with no unnatural sugars! Enjoy cold or hot!

Ingredients

2 Cups rolled oats
1 ¼ Cups mixed chopped, raw or toasted nuts and seeds
2 Tbsp ground flax seeds
½ Cup raisins or other chopped dried fruit
½ Cup sweetened flaked coconut
1-2 Tsp cinnamon and/or nutmeg, to taste

Directions

1. Mix together in a large storage bowl or jar.

2. When ready to enjoy, scoop it out in to a bowl and let it sit in your choice of milk or milk substitute for a few minutes while the oats soften.

3. Then top it with fresh fruit and enjoy. Or you can enjoy this hot, just throw it in the microwave with milk or water and top with fruit.

BAKING

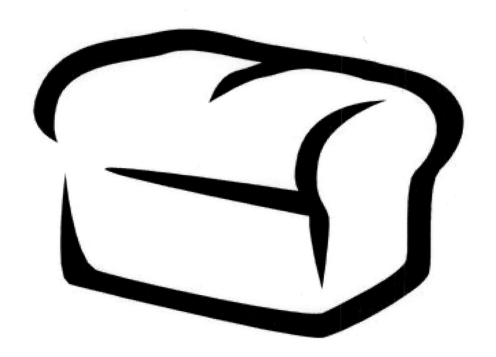

Irish Brown Bread

Makes 1 large round loaf, Total Time: 50 Minutes

This is one of the easiest bread recipes I have ever made. The biscuit-like texture goes perfectly with hearty soups and stews, but it's also perfect for breakfast with a bit of homemade chia seed jam.

Ingredients

4 Cups whole wheat pastry flour
2 to 3 Tbsp organic sugar
1 Tsp salt
1 Tsp baking soda
2 Tsp baking powder
1 ½ Cups buttermilk
2 Tbsp melted butter

Directions

1. In a large bowl, stir together the flour, sugar, salt, baking soda and baking powder.

2. Make a well in the dry ingredients and pour in the buttermilk and the butter. Stir together until blended—some lumps will remain.

3. Turn the dough out onto a floured board and knead about 10 times, or until it all holds together. Form it into a large ball and place it on a lightly greased baking sheet. Cut a deep cross in the top.

4. Bake the bread in a preheated 400°F oven for approximately 40 minutes, or until it a knife inserted into the center comes out clean.

Chocolate Zucchini Muffins
Makes 12, Total Time: 60 Minutes

Chocolate muffins that are healthy definitely seem too good to be true, but it is true! These little gems are moist, chocolaty and best of all hide nutritious zucchini in every bite! Enjoy with a cup of coffee or tea and a piece of fresh fruit for a great start to your day or as an anytime snack. I recommend freezing half of these so they don't get stale.

Ingredients

1 Cup all purpose flour
1 ½ Cup whole wheat flour
½ Cup unsweetened cocoa powder
1 ½ Tsp baking powder
1 Tsp baking soda
1 Tsp cinnamon
½ Cup organic sugar
3 Eggs
1 ½ Cup unsweetened apple sauce
1/3 Cup coconut oil
2 Tsp vanilla
¼ Cup ground flax seed
2 Cups zucchini packed & grated
½ Cup semi-sweet chocolate chips
1 Scoop protein powder *optional

Directions

1. Preheat oven to 350*F. Grease muffin pan with coconut oil or use muffin liners.

2. In a large bowl, combine flours, cocoa, baking powder, baking soda, cinnamon, salt, protein and flax. Set aside.

3. In a medium bowl, whisk together sugar, eggs, applesauce, vegetable oil and vanilla. Stir in zucchini. Add wet ingredients to dry ingredients and mix just until dry ingredients are moistened. Fold in chocolate chips.

4. Pour batter into muffin pans and bake for approximately 50 minutes. Cool for 5 minutes in the pan then remove from pan and cool on wire rack before serving.

Fruity Zucchini Bread

Makes 2 Loaves, Total Time: 90 Minutes

Applesauce and crushed pineapple add a delicious sweetness and moisture to this sweet and fruity bread that overflows with zucchini, nuts and raisins. It doesn't get much better than this! Store in the refrigerator.

Ingredients

3 Eggs
½ Cup organic sugar
1 Large banana mashed
¼ Cup coconut oil
1 Cup unsweetened applesauce
2 Cups zucchini, grated
3 Cups whole wheat flour
2 Tsp vanilla
1 Tsp baking powder
1 Tsp baking soda
1 Cup crushed pineapple, drained
1 Cup chopped nuts
½ Cup raisins

Directions

1. Preheat oven to 325*F.

2. Beat eggs, banana, sugar, coconut oil, vanilla and applesauce until fluffy.

3. Stir in zucchini then add dry ingredients.

4. Stir in pineapple, raisins and nuts.

5. Grease loaf pans with melted coconut oil and dust with flour. Pour in batter and bake for 1 hour or until knife comes out clean.

Dark Chocolate Cherry Buckwheat Muffins

Makes 12 Muffins, Total Time: 40 Minutes

These little guys can also be called black forest muffins since they combine delicious dark chocolate and tart dried cherries. Because these muffins have yogurt in them they must be kept in the refrigerator.

Ingredients

¾ Cup apple sauce
1/3 Cup honey
2 Tbsp coconut oil
2/3 Cup plain non-fat Greek yogurt
1 Egg
1 Cup buttermilk, or milk substitute
2 Tsp vanilla
1 Cup whole wheat flour
¼ Cup milled flax seeds
1 ¼ Cup buckwheat flour
1 Tsp baking soda
2 Tsp baking powder
½ Cup unsweetened cocoa
1 ¼ Cups dried cherries
½ Cup dark (semi-sweet) chocolate chips

Directions:

1. Whisk together apple sauce, honey, oil, Greek yogurt, egg, milk, and vanilla.

2. Stir together dry ingredients and add to oil mixture, stirring just until combined.

3. Add cherries and chocolate, scoop batter into muffin cups.

4. Bake in a 375*F for 15-20 minutes or until tops are browned.

5. Allow to cool in pan for 5 minutes before removing to cooling racks.

Buckwheat Flour Banana Bread

Makes 1 loaf, Total Time: 45 Minutes

Buckwheat flour, which is actually made of ground seeds, is full of fibre and gluten free. It also has a delicious earthy flavour and hearty texture which means this is a fairly dark and dense little loaf that tastes amazing!

Ingredients

1 ½ Cups buckwheat flour
½ Tbsp baking powder
1 Tbsp cinnamon
3 Bananas
2 Tbsp organic honey
1 Egg, beaten
2 Tbsp coconut oil, melted
½ Cup milk, or alternative
1 Tsp vanilla extract
½ Cup walnut pieces
½ Cup dark chocolate chips
½ Cup sweetened coconut flakes

Directions

1. Preheat oven to 375*F. Whisk the egg and add milk, bananas, vanilla extract, honey and coconut oil.

2. Mix dry ingredients in a separate bowl: buckwheat flour, baking powder and cinnamon. Then stir together all ingredients until combined.

3. Add nuts, coconut and walnuts, and put into a greased loaf pan.

4. Bake for about 30 minutes. Stick a fork in the bread to see if it is done (if nothing sticks on the fork= done).

Pear Honey Buckwheat Bread

Makes 1 Loaf, Total Time 90 Minutes

This bread is light and sweet while being full of fresh fruit, fibre and protein. Have a delicious slice of this bread for breakfast or a snack with a hot cup of chai tea. Make sure to keep this bread in the fridge, as it is very moist and will spoil quickly if left out.

Ingredients

1 Cup whole wheat flour
1 ½ Cups buckwheat flour
1 Tsp baking soda
1 Tsp baking powder
½ Cup coconut oil
1 Cup plain yogurt
1 Egg
½ Cup honey
1 Tsp vanilla
1 Pear, cut into a ½ inch pieces
¾ Cup apple sauce
Coconut oil, for greasing the pan

Directions

1. Preheat the oven to 325*F. Grease a 9 inch loaf pan with the coconut oil.

2. Stir the dry ingredients together in a medium bowl. Whisk the wet ingredients together in a large bowl and add the dry ingredient mixture in 2 additions, stirring until just barely combined. Fold in the diced pear

3. Scrape into the prepared loaf pan and bake for 55 minutes, or until a tester comes out clean. Tent with foil if it starts to brown too quickly as honey-sweetened dishes tend to do this.

4. Allow to cool for 10 minutes in the pan, and then finish cooling on a rack.

Carrot Cake Muffins

Makes 12, Total Time: 45 Minutes

These moist little muffins are my new Go-To when craving carrot cake. Not only do they taste just like carrot cake they have less sugar and fat than the original version but with all of the spices and pineapple you won't be able to tell the difference!

Ingredients

1 ¾ Cups whole-wheat flour
2/3 Cup all-purpose flour
2 Tsp baking soda
2 Tsp ground cinnamon
1 Tbsp ground flax seeds
1 Large egg, at room temperature
2 Large egg whites, at room temperature
1 Cup unsweetened applesauce
¼ Cup honey
¼ Cup coconut oil
3 Cups grated carrots
1 Cup crushed pineapple, drained
2/3 Cup buttermilk, or milk substitute
¾ Cup walnuts, roughly chopped
¾ Cup shredded sweetened coconut

Directions

1. Preheat the oven to 350*F. Line muffin tins with paper liners or lightly coat with cooking spray. Set aside.

2. In a medium bowl, stir together the all-purpose flour, whole-wheat flour, baking soda, cinnamon, and salt. Set aside.

3. In a large mixing bowl, beat together the egg, egg whites, brown sugar, and coconut oil. Add the carrots and beat for 1 minute. Add the pineapple and 3/4 shredded coconut and beat until incorporated. Stir in half of the flour mixture, just until incorporated. Stir in buttermilk. Add the remaining flour mixture, continuing to stir in by hand, just until combined. Gently fold in walnuts.

4. Fill prepared tins ¾ of the way with batter. Bake 20-22 minutes, until a toothpick inserted into the center comes out clean. Gently remove cupcakes from tin and let cool on a wire rack.

Cream Cheese Topping

Makes 1 Cup, Total Time: 5 Minutes

For an extra special treat make this cream cheese topping and spread it on top of your carrot cake muffins!

½ Cup light cream cheese, softened
2 Tbsp coconut oil, melted
½ Cup powdered sugar (aka confectioners sugar)
½ Tsp vanilla extract
½ Tsp coconut extract
½ Cup flaked sweetened coconut

1. Mix
2. Spread
3. Enjoy!

Almond Flour Blueberry & Dark Chocolate Chip Muffins

Makes 9 Muffins, Total Time: 30 Minutes

These delicious muffins are gluten free with no refined sugars and burst with fresh blueberries and chocolate chips! This is a recipe that I make quite frequently and they always disappear quickly.

Ingredients:

2 Cups Almond Flour
2 Eggs
2 Egg whites
1/4 Cup honey
1/2 Tsp baking soda
1 Tbsp Apple Cider Vinegar
1 Tsp Vanilla Extract
2 Tbsp Coconut Oil
1 Cup Blueberries
¼ Cup Chocolate Chips *Optional

Directions:

1. Pre-heat oven to 350*F.

2. Place all ingredients excluding blueberries and chocolate chips into your food processor and blend until smooth.

3. Once completely mixed, fold in blueberries and chocolate chips.

4. Grease muffin tin with melted coconut oil.

5. Evenly scoop batter into muffin tin.

6. Bake for 25 minutes.

7. Remove from oven and place on cooling rack.

Chocolate Chip Peanut Butter Banana Bread

Makes 1 Loaf or 12 Muffins, Total Time: 60 Minutes

This is a delicious and nutritious banana bread recipe that is sure to satisfy adults with its whole grains, flax meal, protein and healthy fats, and satisfy kids with its great taste. Great for breakfast or as a snack on the go!

Ingredients

2 Egg whites
3 Mashed bananas
1/3 Cup natural peanut butter
¼ Cup of milk
¼ Cup coconut oil, melted
2 Cups whole wheat flour
2 Tsp baking powder
¼ Cup ground flax seeds
¼ Cup organic sugar
¾ Cup semi-sweet chocolate chips

Directions

1. Preheat oven to 350*F.

2. Mix the wet ingredients in one bowl and mix the dry ingredients in another.

3. Mix the wet and dry ingredients together, pour into a loaf pan and bake for 1 hour or until toothpick inserted in to the middle comes out clean.

Pumpkin Pie Squares

Makes 9 to 16 squares, Total Time: 60 Minutes

This is a delicious, moist and healthy vegan substitute for pumpkin pie. The dates add natural sweetness, the rolled oat flour adds fibre and the pumpkin adds vitamins and minerals. You can't get much more delicious or healthy than this fall-inspired vegan dessert. Serve with *'Macadamia Nut Cream' (pg. 36).*

Ingredients

10 Medjool dates, pitted and diced
$3/4$ Cup water
1 ½ Cups rolled oats, ground into flour
2 Tsp pumpkin pie spice
1 Can pure pumpkin
1 Tsp vanilla extract
½ Cup milk, or milk substitute

Directions

1. Place the 10 pitted and diced dates into a small bowl with the $3/4$ cup of water and soak for at least 15 minutes.

2. Place the flour and Pumpkin Pie spice in a large bowl. In a blender, blend the soaked dates, the date soak water, the vanilla, and the milk until smooth. Pour this into the bowl of flour and spices. Then add the pumpkin, and mix with a wooden spoon until all the dry ingredients are incorporated.

3. Scrape batter into an 8×8-inch baking pan that is lined with parchment paper (or use a non-stick silicone baking pan). Cook for 25-30 minutes at 375*F. (If you see a light browning and some cracks on the top, these are good indications that it's done.)

4. Let cool at least 10-15 minutes before cutting and serving.

Optional: Finish with Macadamia-Vanilla Cream and a drizzle of maple syrup just before serving. Storing in the refrigerator overnight will firm up these squares, then you can pack them in a lunch or as a snack.

Macadamia Nut Cream

Makes about 1 Cup, Total Time: 45 Minutes

This frosting has a nutty flavour to it, for obvious reasons. You can use it right after making it, or put the cream in the refrigerator for 30 minutes first to firm it up. This would taste great on a variety of different cakes and squares!

Ingredients

½ Cup Macadamia nuts
1 Cup of water
6 Medjool dates, pitted and chopped
1 Tsp vanilla extract

Directions

1. Soak nuts and dates in ½ cup of water each for 15-30 minutes

2. Drain the soak water off of the nuts and discard it, leave dates in their soak water. In a blender, blend all of the ingredients; nuts, dates with their soak water, and vanilla until smooth and even in color. Add a little more water as needed to keep the blender moving if it gets too thick.

3. Refrigerate until ready to use.

Orange Glaze

Glazes 24 Muffins or 2 Loaves, Total Time: 5 Minutes

Ingredients
¾ Cup confectioners' sugar
1/8 Tsp tangerine oil or orange oil OR 1 Tbsp orange zest
½ Tbsp water or milk

Directions

1. In a medium-sized bowl, mix together all of the glaze ingredients until smooth, adding additional liquid, a bit at a time, until the glaze has the consistency of molasses or will drizzle from a spoon in a long strand. Drizzle over loaves of muffins, about 1 Tsp per muffin or slice.

Pumpkin Ginger Bread with Orange Glaze

Makes 2 Loaves or 24 Muffins, Total Time: 60 Minutes

This bread tastes like an amazing combination of pumpkin pie and a gingerbread cookie while having a fraction of the sugar of either. The ginger and spices add flavour, the pumpkin adds moistness and the molasses adds sweetness, and all of them together have valuable vitamins and minerals! Finish with *'Orange Glaze' (pg. 36)*.

Ingredients

¼ Cup butter or coconut oil
1 Cup unsweetened applesauce
¼ Cup brown sugar
2 ¾ Cups whole wheat flour
2 Tsp baking powder
2 Tsp cinnamon
1 Tsp nutmeg
2 Tbsp jarred minced ginger
½ Cup pecan pieces
3 Large eggs
2 Tbsp molasses
1 Can pure pumpkin

Directions

1. Preheat your oven to 350°F. Grease two loaf pans for loaves; if you're making muffins, grease 24 muffin cups.

2. In a large bowl, beat together the butter and brown sugar until well blended. Add the flour, baking powder, baking soda, spices and ginger; mix well, the batter will look crumbly. Add the eggs, beating until combined. Beat in both the molasses and the pumpkin until they are evenly distributed. Finally, stir in the pecans. Scoop the batter into the greased loaf pans or the muffin cups, filling the cups about 2/3 full.

3. Bake the muffins in the preheated 350°F oven for 18 to 20 minutes, or until they are lightly browned on the edges and the middle springs back when touched. Bake the loaves at the same temperature for 45 to 50 minutes, or until a knife inserted in the middle comes out clean. Let it cool for 15 minutes before taking it out of the pans.

Layered Pumpkin Loaf

Makes 1 Loaf or 12 Large Muffins, Total Time: 90 Minutes

This is a fantastic recipe and a new favourite of mine. The canned pumpkin gives you a serving of fruit and vitamin C, the milk adds calcium, the protein powder adds extra protein, the flax adds fibre and healthy fats and the pumpkin pie spice makes it taste like pumpkin pie! Serve a slice with a nice hot cup of coffee or a glass of skim milk and a piece of fruit and you've got yourself a delicious and well rounded breakfast or snack to kick start the day! Wrap cooled bread in foil or plastic wrap. Store in refrigerator up to 4 days or freeze.

Ingredients

1 Cup canned pumpkin

½ Cup unsweetened apple sauce

½ Cup plus 2 Tbsp. Organic sugar, divided

½ Cup packed brown sugar

4 Egg whites, divided

½ Cup skim milk

¼ Cup coconut oil, melted

2 Cups whole wheat flour

2 ½ Tsp baking powder

2 Tsp pumpkin pie spice

¼ Cup ground flax seeds

1 Pkg (250 g) light brick cream cheese, softened

Directions

1. Heat oven to 350*F.

2. Mix pumpkin, ½ cup sugar, applesauce, brown sugar, 3 egg whites, milk and oil in large bowl. Add flour, baking powder, spice and salt; stir just until moistened.

3. Beat cream cheese, remaining 2 Tbsp sugar and remaining egg white with whisk until well blended.

4. Spoon half the pumpkin batter into a muffin pan lightly greased with coconut oil; cover with layers of cream cheese mixture and remaining pumpkin batter.

5. Bake for 1 hour to 1 hour 5 min. or until toothpick inserted in centre comes out clean. Loosen bread from sides of pan; cool in pan 10 min. Remove from pan to wire rack; cool completely.

Coconut Cinnamon Coffee Cake

Serves 8, Total Time: 45 Minutes

This simple and easy-to-make little coffee cake is perfect when you have guests over for coffee or, like my Grandmother, for afternoon tea. It's light, fluffy, moist, full of flavour and gluten free!

Ingredients

2 Large eggs, separated
1 Tsp cream of tartar or baking soda
¼ Cup extra virgin coconut oil
3 Tbsp honey
½ Cup coconut flour, sifted
2 Tsp vanilla extract
¼ Tsp baking soda
1/8 Tsp salt

Topping:
¼ Cup organic sugar
¼ Cup extra virgin coconut oil
2 Tbsp coconut flour, sifted
½ Tsp ground cinnamon

Directions

1. Preheat oven to 350°F. Grease the bottom and sides of a 4×8 inch rectangular loaf pan with coconut oil.

2. In a large bowl, combine the egg whites and cream of tartar. Whip until stiff peaks form. In a bowl, cream together honey and coconut oil. Mix in the egg yolks. Add to the mixture: coconut flour, vanilla, baking soda and salt and stir until combined. Mix the batter into the egg whites starting with a little bit at a time. Combine until the batter is completely mixed. Pour the mixture into the loaf pan.

3. In a small bowl, mix together all the ingredients for the topping. Spread the mixture over the batter. Swirl parts of the topping into the batter.

4. Bake for 30 minutes. The cake is done when a toothpick is inserted and comes out clean. Let the cake cool before slicing and serving.

SMOOTHIES

Green Smoothie Cubes

Makes 24 Cubes, Total Time: 2 Hours

This recipe is for a 'Green Cube' that you can put in any fruit smoothie to get an extra serving of vegetables in! It is full of vitamins and nutrients from all of the fruits and vegetables, and it's easy to store and travels well because it is frozen in ice cube trays or muffin pans. Give it a try and see what you think!

Ingredients

¾ Cup fresh parsley, chopped
¼ Cup fresh mint, chopped
1 Naval orange, peeled
1 Tbsp honey
2 Cups frozen mango cubes
2 Cups water
4 Cups Spinach
4 Tbsp Ground flax seeds
½ Tsp Ginger, minced

Directions

1. Place ingredients in a blender in the order listed and blend until smooth. Pour mixture into ice cube trays or a muffin pan and freeze until solid. Then you can pop them out and store them in freezer bags.

2. Add 1 or 2 cubes to any banana or berry smoothie recipe!

Smoothie Recipes Galore!

Each of these smoothies are great for breakfast, as a snack or after your workout! You can add a scoop of protein powder to any of these recipes if you want to but it's not necessary. All you have to do is put all of the ingredients in a blender and enjoy!

Vanilla Peach

Makes 1

½ Cup milk (or substitute)
¼ Cup water
½ Frozen peaches
½ - 1 Scoop vanilla protein powder

Blueberry Citrus

Makes 1

½ Cup water
1/8 Cup orange juice
¼ Cup ice
½ Cup frozen blueberries
1 Tbsp Chia seeds

Strawberry Oatmeal Breakfast

Makes 1

¾ Cup milk, or substitute
¼ Cup rolled oats
1 Small banana
Handful of fresh strawberries
½ Tsp Vanilla

PB & Banana Breakfast

Makes 1

1 Small Banana
1 Tbsp natural peanut butter
¾ Cup milk, or milk substitute
1 Tbsp Honey

Spinach Shake

Makes 2

½ Cup coconut water
1 Small banana
½ Cup grapes
1 6oz Tub vanilla Greek yogurt
½ Cup apple, chopped
1.5 Cups spinach leaves

Pina Colada Recovery Shake

Makes 1

½ Cup coconut water
¼ Cup frozen pineapple
Splash of OJ (a couple of tablespoons)
½ – 1 Scoop vanilla protein
1 Tbsp shredded coconut
½ Tbsp Chia Seeds

Pumpkin Spice

Makes 1

½ Cup ice
½ Cup milk, or milk substitute
1 Heaping Tbsp pure pumpkin puree
1 tablespoon honey
Pinch of pumpkin pie spice
¼ to ½ teaspoon ginger, minced

Iced Mocha

Makes 1

¾ Cup milk, or milk substitute

1 Tbsp Instant Coffee OR

½ Cup Cold Strong Brewed Coffee

1 Small banana

Ice to texture

Mango

Makes 1

½ Cup chopped ripe mango

½ Cup low-fat milk, or milk substitute

½ Cup ice

¼ Cup plain low-fat yogurt

1 Tbsp honey

Pineapple-Carrot

Makes 1

¾ Cup chopped fresh pineapple

½ Cup ice

1/3 Cup fresh orange juice

¼ Cup chopped carrot

½ Banana, frozen

Strawberry Flax

Makes 2

1 Cup frozen strawberries

¾ Cup plain low-fat yogurt

½ Cup fresh orange juice

1 Tsp honey

1 Tbsp flaxseed meal

Ginger Berry

Makes 1

¼ Cup old-fashioned rolled oats

½ Cup frozen blueberries

½ Cup plain low-fat yogurt

½ Cup ice

1 Tsp honey

Berry Breakfast

Makes 1

1 Cup frozen raspberries

¾ Cup milk or substitute

¼ Cup frozen cherries or raspberries

1 ½ Tbsp honey

2 Tsp ginger, grated or minced

1 Tsp ground flaxseed

2 Tsp fresh lemon juice

Green Tea Mint Watermelon

Makes 1

1 Scoop vanilla protein powder

½ Cup frozen watermelon chunks

½ Cup plain Greek yogurt

1/3 Cup strong brewed green tea

2-3 Fresh mint leaves

Green Tea Blueberry

Makes 2

½ Cup water

1 Green tea bag

1 Tsp honey

1 ½ Cup frozen blueberries

½ Medium banana

¾ Cup milk, or milk substitute

MEATS

Marinated Apple Pork Chops

Serves 2, Total Time: 30 Minutes

Pork, 'the other white meat' is a lean meat that often gets over looked for chicken and beef. By marinating these delicious chops in concentrated apple juice and rosemary, they get an amazing flavour. Serve these with *'Sour Cream & Herb Mashed Potatoes' (pg. 69)* and *'Parmesan Asparagus' (pg. 68).*

Ingredients

1 Can concentrated apple juice, thawed
4 Boneless pork chops
¼ Cup fresh rosemary, chopped
Black pepper, to taste

Directions

1. Put pork chops in a baking dish in a single layer.

2. Pour concentrated apple juice over top and sprinkle with fresh rosemary and black pepper.

3. Cover and refrigerate for at least two hours or do it in the morning before you go to work and let it marinate all day.

4. Heat grill or frying pan to medium heat and put pork chops on in a single layer. Grill (fry) flipping occasionally until fully cooked. Approximately 20 Minutes.

Classic Lasagna

Serves 12, Total Time: 40 Minutes

Lasagna was another cold weather staple when my sister and I were growing up. Usually it's a very satisfying and very high calorie meal. But with a few modifications we can keep the comforting taste and lose some of the calories. Instead of using jarred or canned pasta sauce try using home made *'Arrabiata Sauce' (pg. 75)*. Serve with a low-fat Caesar salad and a small piece of garlic bread. And if you don't need a giant lasagne, make two small ones and freeze one for later!

Ingredients

12 Whole wheat lasagna noodles
1Lb Extra lean ground beef
1 Tbsp olive oil
1 Large onion, diced
2 Cups mushrooms, sliced
3 Cloves garlic, minced
1 Jar organic tomato sauce or Arrabiata sauce
1 Tsp dried basil
1 Tbsp dried parsley
1 Tsp dried oregano
1/2 teaspoon black pepper
½ Cup part-skim ricotta cheese
½ Cup fresh parmesan, grated
¾ Cup part-skim mozzarella, grated
1 large egg

Directions

1. Sauté the onions, mushrooms and garlic in the olive oil over medium heat. Add in the ground beef.

2. Season with spices (minus parsley). Add in tomato sauce. Stir and simmer for 5-10 minutes, while breaking up ground beef, cooking until its no longer pink.

3. In a small bowl, mix together the ricotta, Parsley, egg and Parmesan cheese. Set aside.

4. Evenly coat the bottom of a 9-inch by 13-inch baking dish with 1 cup of the sauce (be generous for the bottom layer).

5. To assemble the lasagna: top the sauce in the baking dish with an even layer of noodles, about 4 noodles. Spread ¼ of the cheese mixture over the lasagna noodles. Then layer with 1 cup of sauce mixture. Sprinkle 1/2 cup of mozzarella over this.

6. Repeat step 5 two more times (always starting with the noodles and finishing with mozzarella cheese)

7. Sprinkle the final layer with any reserved mozzarella cheese. Cover with foil.

8. Bake in a 350°F oven for 60 minutes. Uncover and bake for an additional 20 minutes until the cheese is all brown and bubbly! Let stand for 10 minutes before cutting. Enjoy!

Classic Steak Dinner

Serves 2, Total Time: 40 Minutes

Steak is a treat in our house so when we make it, we make it right. We start by marinating it to make it juicy and tender, then add delicious mushrooms sautéed in just a bit of natural butter and serve with a fresh steamed vegetable. It doesn't get much better than this!

Ingredients

2 Steaks
Steak marinade, your choice
1lb Button mushrooms, washed
1 Tbsp Montreal steak spice
2 Tbsp butter
2 Tbsp soft goat cheese
BBQ Sauce, to taste

Directions

1. Marinate steaks according to package directions.

2. Heat grill or indoor grill to medium heat. Grill until desired tenderness and doneness. Meanwhile put mushrooms and butter in a frying pan and sauté at medium heat. Cook until mushrooms begin to soften, add Montreal steak spice and cook for a few more minutes.

3. Plate steak and top with goat cheese and BBQ sauce if desired. Serve with mushrooms and a vegetable such as broccoli or asparagus.

Chicken Divan Casserole

Serves 4-6, Total Time: 60 Minutes

In the cooler months, I love casseroles. They are delicious, hot and you can just pop them in the oven and let them cook without having to fuss over them. This casserole has chicken, tuns of vegetables and a can of soup to make it creamy. This is the perfect dish for cold nights!

Ingredients

4 Cups fresh broccoli, chopped
1 ½ Cups chicken, cooked and chopped
1 Cup carrots, sliced
1 Cup peppers, sliced
1 Cup mushrooms, sliced
1 Can broccoli cheese soup
1/3 Cup milk
1 Tbsp butter, melted
2 Tbsp bread crumbs
¼ Cup parmesan, freshly grated

Directions

1. In a shallow baking dish, arrange the vegetables into a layer. Top with chicken.

2. Combine milk and soup; pour over chicken.

3. Combine butter, bread crumbs and cheese; sprinkle over top.

4. Bake at 450*F for 15-20 minutes until heated through.

Goat Cheese Stuffed Chicken Thighs

Serves 4-6, Total Time: 60 Minutes

This recipe is fast, easy and so healthy! This is one of my favourite meals and one that Zach requests almost weekly, and it is so easy to do! Serve these stuffed chicken thighs with *'Sour cream and Chive Mashed Potatoes' (pg. 69)* and a fresh grilled veggie. Yum!

Ingredients

12 Pack boneless, skinless chicken thighs

1 Pkg peppercorn goat cheese

½ Tsp each rosemary & thyme

½ Tsp red pepper flakes

Salt & pepper to taste

Directions

1. Preheat oven to 350*F.

2. Open up each chicken thigh and put about 1 rounded Tsp of goat inside each, then wrap them back up again.

3. Put them all in a baking dish and then cover them with herbs and spices. In this step you can be creative and use your favourite spices to make this recipe your own!

4. Bake for 35 minutes at 350* and you're done.

* To make this an extra special meal wrap each individual thigh in 1 piece of natural bacon and cook in a roasting pan on a metal rack.

Sweet Coconut Curry Shrimp

This delicious curry has a mild and sweet taste and is full of shrimp, chicken and the veggies you love! Serve over rice or rice noodles. This tastes great as leftovers too and is easy to take for lunches.

Ingredients

1 Bag of frozen, peeled shrimp
2 Chicken breasts chopped
Veggies: Peppers, baby bok choy, mushrooms, onions, frozen Asian stirfry veggies - whatever you want!
½ Jar Patak's mild curry paste
½ Can coconut milk
¼ Cup of sweetened coconut, to taste

Directions

1. Sauté shrimp, chicken and any veggies you are using (except bok choy - add it near the end) until shrimp are cooked and chicken is browned.

2. Add curry paste, coconut milk and bok choy, and simmer for 10-15 minutes. Remove from heat and stir in coconut.

Creamy Chicken Ravioli

Serves 4-6, Total Time: 20 Minutes

This is one of my all-time favourite pasta recipes! I've been making this for years because it is high protein, full of veggies, creamy and satisfying. It tastes like a decadent comfort food but much healthier! Because this pasta dish is fairly high-calorie it's important to keep your portion to about 1 to 1 ½ cups.

Ingredients

1 Pkg fresh chicken & mozzarella ravioli
1 Pkg light spreadable cream cheese
¼ Cup pesto
2 Cups button mushrooms
1 Large red pepper, diced
1 Large cooking onion, diced
2-3 Cloves of garlic, minced

Directions

1. Heat a large frying pan over medium heat and sauté red pepper, mushrooms, onion and garlic.

2. Meanwhile cook fresh pasta according to package directions, about 5 minutes.

3. Add in 1 tub of light cream cheese and about ¼ cup of pesto. Stir it around until it is melted and creamy and then pour it over the pasta and enjoy!

Classic Chili

Serves 6-8, Total Time: 60 Minutes

Ahhhh chili, one of my winter staples! Full of beans, veggies and lean meat it's a full meal in a bowl! This recipe is delicious, not too spicy and freezes great which means you can make a big batch and enjoy it over a few weeks. Serve with a delicious green salad, a bun or a handful of organic tortilla chips and a sprinkle of cheese.

Ingredients:

1lb Ground turkey breast
1lb Extra lean ground beef
2 Cups button mushrooms, sliced
2 Tbsp coconut oil
1 Large onion
4 Cloves garlic, or more to taste
1 Can black beans
1 Can red kidney beans
1 Can maple baked beans
1 Can diced tomatoes
1 Can sweet corn
1 Tbsp chili powder
1 Tbsp red pepper flakes
½ Beer

Directions

1. Heat oil in a large pot or dutch oven sauté the onion and garlic until soft then add turkey and beef and mushrooms and cook until the meat is browned.

2. While meat is browning put all beans, except the maple baked beans and the corn in to a colander and rinse. This step gets rid of a lot of the added sodium.

3. Once meat is browned, add the rest of the ingredients; stir and simmer uncovered for about 1 hour.

 Make it vegetarian: Omit the meat and add ¾ cup of dried red lentils or another can of beans when you mix in the other beans.

Sweet Thai Chili Salmon

Serves 4, Total Time: 30 Minutes

This is a sweet and spicy dish that tastes great served over rice with steamed veggies.

Ingredients
4 Salmon Fillets
¼ Cup Sweet Thai chili sauce
¼ Cup sweetened flaked coconut

Directions

1. Preheat oven to 350*F. Place salmon fillets in a baking dish, drizzle with chilli sauce and sprinkle with coconut.

2. Bake for approximately 20 Minutes. Make sure you cook your fish until it is 145*F to make sure it's cooked thoroughly.

Walnut Crusted Salmon

Serves 4, Total Time: 30 Minutes

This dish is just brimming with healthy fats and flavour! Serve with steamed veggies and *'Herb Roasted Potatoes' (pg. 66)*

Ingredients
4 Salmon fillets
¼ Cup chopped walnuts
2 Tbsp lemon juice
2 Tbsp olive oil
1 Tbsp minced garlic

Directions

1. Dip 4 salmon fillets in a mixture of lemon juice, olive oil and garlic. Then dip them in ground walnuts.

2. Put in a dish, cover with tin foil and bake for about 20 minutes at 350*F. Make sure you cook your fish until it is 145*F to make sure it's cooked thoroughly.

Homemade Pizza

Serves 2-3, Total time: 45 Minutes

Pizza can be a healthy, easy and nutritious meal if it's done right. If you're feeling adventurous, I've got some new flavours for you to try and if you're not the old favourites work great too! The goat cheese in this recipe adds great tangy flavour but if you're not ready to try it then regular pizza mozzarella works just as well. Make this recipe your own with all of your favourite toppings.

Ingredients

1 Large focaccia loaf, or any crusty bread
1 Jar of Pizza Sauce
1 package of Goat Cheddar, grated
1 Large cooking onion, diced
1 Cup mushrooms, sliced
1 Large green pepper, sliced
1 Pkg turkey pepperoni

Directions

1. Caramelize (sauté) the onion, pepper and mushrooms in a frying pan over medium heat. While you're doing that slice the focaccia bread in half and lay both pieces cut side up on a baking sheet. Spread with pizza sauce.

2. Put pepperoni on the pizza followed by the caramelized veggies and then the goat cheese. Bake in the oven at 350*F until the bread is toasted and the cheese is melted - about 20 minutes.

3. Sprinkle with red pepper flakes or hot sauce to taste and enjoy!

 Make it vegetarian: To make this a delicious vegetarian pizza simply add more of your favourite veggies and leave off the pepperoni. Also try topping your bread with a brush of olive oil and Crystal's *'Bruschetta' (pg. 64).*

Meat Loaf Pie

Serves 6-8, Total Time: 90 Minutes

This recipe is an interesting cross between a meatloaf, Sheppard's pie and twice-baked potato that tastes amazing! Serve this with a side salad or steamed veggie and get a delicious nutritious meal that the whole family will love.

Ingredients

1 lb Extra lean ground beef
1 lb Extra lean ground turkey
1 Large cooking onion, chopped
¼ Cup plain bread crumbs
½ Tsp dried sage leaves
1 Egg
1 Lb potatoes
2 Cloves garlic, minced
1 Cup cheddar cheese, grated
¼ Cup chopped fresh tomato, if desired
2 slices precooked bacon, chopped, if desired
2 medium green onions, chopped

Directions

1. Boil potatoes until tender. Drain and mash with salt, pepper and minced garlic.

2. Heat oven to 350°F. In large bowl, mix beef, onion, bread crumbs, sage, salt and egg until well blended. Press in bottom of ungreased 8-inch round glass baking dish or pie plate. Spread mashed potatoes evenly over top. Sprinkle evenly with cheese.

3. Bake uncovered about 50 minutes.

4. Sprinkle with tomato, bacon and green onions.

Classic Beef Stew

Serves 8-10, Total Time: 2 Hours

Beef stew is a wonderful comfort food that combines some many great vegetables and flavours. This good old-fashioned recipe uses all of the classic veggies to make a rich and satisfying meal. Try it with my *'Irish Brown Bread' (pg. 25)*!

Ingredients

2 Lbs stewing beef
1/3 Cup all purpose flour
2 Tbsp olive oil
4 Cups tomato juice
3 Medium onions, quartered
6 Medium carrots, sliced
1 Cup turnips, diced
2 Cups potatoes, diced
1 Pkg frozen peas
1 Tsp parsley
¼ Tsp Thyme
3 Bay leaves

Directions

1. Brown stewing beef in oil. Add seasonings and tomato juice. Stir in flour.

2. Cover and simmer for 10 minutes, stirring occasionally.

3. Add all of the vegetables, except the peas. Cover and simmer for 1 hour, stirring occasionally.

4. Add peas and cook 10 minutes longer. Add salt and pepper to taste.

 Make it vegetarian: To make this a delicious vegetarian stew, simply add more of your favourite veggies and leave out the meat! More potatoes, parsnips, carrots, mushrooms, celery, anything you want!

Actually Delicious Turkey Burgers

Serves 6, Total Time: 30 Minutes

This recipe is called 'Actually Delicious Turkey Burgers' because turkey burgers tend to have a reputation for being bland and lacking flavour. But these are full of flavour thanks to the fresh herbs. My favourite way to serve these guys is to put them on a bed of lettuce or spinach, then top with tomato, red onion and soft goat cheese along side sweet potato fries. You can also use this exact recipe for meatballs or meatloaves too!

Ingredients

2lbs Extra lean ground turkey

¼ Cup plain bread crumbs

¼ Cup onion, finely diced

2 Egg whites, lightly beaten

¼ Cup fresh parsley, chopped

¼ Cup fresh rosemary, chopped

1-2 Tbsp fresh garlic, minced

Black pepper, to taste

Directions

1. Mix all of the ingredients in a bowl and form into 6-8 patties depending on how big you want them to be.

2. Then you can grill them or fry them, I used our indoor grill and grilled them for about 20 minutes until they reached 180*F.

Moroccan Stewed Chicken

Serves 4, Total Time: 45 Minutes

This is very different from your usual chicken stew but it's something I think you will really enjoy. It's a great combination of chicken, chickpeas and vegetables offering tons of protein, fibre and other nutrients. Feeling adventurous? Try this! Serve with a side green salad.

Ingredients

1 lbs chicken, boneless & skinless
1 Large zucchini, cubed
1 Can chick peas, drained and rinsed
1 Can diced tomatoes
½ Tbsp olive oil
1 Cup chicken broth
½ Tsp cayenne pepper
1 Tsp ground cumin
½ Tsp ground cinnamon
¼ Cup raisins

Directions

1. Heat oil in a large skillet.

2. Season chicken with salt and pepper and cook in pan until browned, about 5 minutes per side. Add zucchini and continue cooking, stirring often.

3. When zucchini is lightly browned, add chick peas, tomatoes, stock, raisins and spices.

4. Turn heat to low and simmer until chicken is tender and cooked through, about 20 minutes.

Tex-Mex Chicken Salad

Serves 4, Total Time: 20 Minutes

If you're tired of the same old salads or are looking for something different for lunch, try this Mexican inspired chicken salad. With salsa and guacamole for the 'dressing' this is a calorie wise and filling salad.

Ingredients

2 Medium chicken breasts

1 Can black beans

2 Cups fresh salsa

12 Cups salad greens

8 Tbsp guacamole

½ Cup shredded hot pepper jack cheese

Directions

1. Grill chicken until fully cooked. Chop and set aside to cool.

2. Mix beans, salsa and chicken together.

3. Put all ingredients in a bowl and shake to mix.

Italian Chicken

Serves 6-8, Total Time: 1 Hour 15 Minutes

This is one of my favourite winter recipes but I will tell you right now it is a special treat. It's something my mom used to make when I was a kid and is just too perfect for a cold, dark winter's night not to put in my cookbook for you to enjoy all year long. Serve with a delicious green salad or steamed vegetables to make it a well rounded and satisfying meal.

Ingredients

6-8 Chicken breasts, boneless & skinless
1 Can low-fat mushroom soup
¼ Cup milk
½ Cup Kraft 4 cheese italiano
1 Pkg Stove top stuffing for chicken

Directions

1. Place chicken in a baking dish.

2. Combine soup and milk; pour over chicken.

3. Meanwhile mix stuffing according to package directions

4. Sprinkle cheese over top, then stuffing. Bake for 1 hour at 350*F until chicken is cooked through.

Stuffed Portobello Mushrooms

Serves 2, Total Time 30 Minutes

I absolutely love mushrooms so I was super excited to experiment with stuffing giant Portobello mushroom caps. This recipe tastes like a mushroom stuffed with thanksgiving stuffing and chicken which means it's an instant winner in my books. Serve with a side green salad.

Ingredients

4 Large portabello mushroom caps
1 Cup chicken (or turkey) breast, cooked & diced
¼ Cup dried cranberries
1 Stalk celery, finely chopped
1 Small onion, finely chopped
1 Garlic clove, minced
2 Slices bread, cubed
¼ Tsp each oregano, basil and rosemary
1 Tbsp butter
½ Cup mozzarella, grated

Directions

1. Pre heat oven to 350*F. Meanwhile sauté butter, celery, onion and garlic in a frying pan. Add cubed bread and spices, toss to combine. Combine cooked chicken and cranberries.

2. Wash and de-gill mushrooms and place top down on a baking sheet so they make little bowl shapes.

3. Spoon chicken mixture on top of mushroom, then top with bread mixture followed by the cheese.

4. Bake at 350*F for 30 minutes or until mushrooms become tender.

Make it vegetarian: Omit the chicken!

VEGETARIAN

Bruschetta

Serves 6, Total Time: 15 Minutes

This recipe is courtesy of my best friend Crystal, who is also a healthy food lover like me and a ZUMBA instructor. I think I request this every time she asks what she can bring over for dinner because this is one of my favourite appetizers and hers is the best. It's simple, tangy and tastes so delicious with its fresh tomatoes and fresh basil. Serve this on a lightly toasted baguette or with crackers.

Ingredients

6-8 Medium tomatoes
1/3 Cup olive oil
¼ Cup balsamic vinegar
1 Tbsp salt
1 Medium onion
2 Tbsp garlic, minced
5 Leaves fresh basil, chopped
½ Cup fresh feta, crumbled
1 Fresh baguettes

Directions

1. Pre-heat over to 350*F.

2. Dice and seed tomatoes, let drain in a strainer for 30 minutes.

3. Mix all ingredients except feta and baguette in a large bowl.

4. Slice baguette, place in a single layer on a baking sheet. Bake until lightly toasted, flip and toast the other side.

5. Put tomato mixture in a serving dish, top with feta cheese and serve with fresh toasted baguette.

Grilled Veggie Stack

Serves 2, Total Time: 30 Minutes

Here is a super easy recipe that is full of delicious vegetables. This almost tastes like a lasagne with out the noodles! The creamy goat cheese and tangy tomato sauce make this rich and flavourful. Why not use homemade *'Arrabiata Sauce' (pg. 75)* and serve with a gorgeous green salad and/or side of *'Herb Roasted Potatoes' (pg. 66).*

Ingredients

1 Eggplant, sliced into 1" rounds
1 Zucchini, sliced lengthwise into 1" pieces
1-2 Bell peppers, sliced
4 Portobello mushrooms, de-gilled & sliced
1 Large sweet onion, sliced
1 Cup tomato sauce, or Arrabiata Sauce

Directions

1. Heat the grill, brush with oil and throw all of the veggies on. If you're using a BBQ use a grill pan or tin foil so you don't lose any. Grill the veggies just until tender.

2. Meanwhile heat about 1 cup of tomato sauce.

3. Once the veggies are done stack ¼ of them on each of two plates, top with a slice of soft goat cheese.

4. Next divide the rest of the veggies and stack them on top of the first layer, top with the tomato sauce then sprinkle goat cheese on top and finish with fresh basil.

Herb Roasted Potatoes

Serves 4-6, Total Time: 45 Minutes

The mixture of white potatoes and yams in this recipe gives you a great mix of flavour and texture as well as a variety of vitamins and nutrients. And the pairing of fresh rosemary with the thyme and black pepper makes this a wonderfully scented and flavoured dish. Serve as a side dish to a wide variety of dishes.

Ingredients

2 Large sweet potatoes, washed & cubed

2 Large baking potatoes, washed & cubed

3 Cloves garlic, minced

2-3 Tbsp olive oil, to coat potatoes

½ Tsp Oregano

½ Tsp Thyme

¼ Cup fresh rosemary, chopped

Salt & Pepper, to taste

Directions

1. Heat oven to 350*F. Meanwhile put all ingredients in a large bowl, toss to coat.

2. Spread potatoes in a single layer in a baking dish or roasting pan. Bake uncovered for approximately 30 minutes or until potatoes are tender yet crisp on the outside.

3 Layer Lunch Dip with Organic Tortilla Chips

Serves 1, Total Time: 10 Minutes

It can be really hard to come up with new and fresh lunch ideas day after day. This recipe is a quick, nutritious and of course delicious lunch option. This easy dish is full of protein from the beans, cheese and yogurt and you get a serving of vegetables from the salsa. Try this next time you're stuck on what to have for lunch!

Ingredients

¼ Cup Re-fried Beans

¼ Cup Plain non-fat Greek yogurt

¼ Cup natural salsa

1 Serving Organic tortilla chips

¼ Cup grated cheese

Directions

1. Warm up re-fried beans and put in the bottom of a dish. Layer Greek yogurt over top, followed by the salsa.

2. Spread grated cheese over tortilla chips and warm in the oven or microwave until the cheese is melted or serve with plain tortilla chips.

3. Dip chips in 3-layer dip and enjoy!

Parmesan Asparagus

Serves 4, Total Time: 30 Minutes

Fresh asparagus is one of my favourite veggies, as you can probably tell because it's in so many of my food pictures! To dress it up and add a bit of extra flavour, I use this parmesan recipe. Serve this delicious veggie with any meat dish or with a side salad and baked potato if you're vegetarian.

Ingredients

1 Bunch fresh asparagus
1 Tbsp butter
Sea salt or Mrs. Dash No Salt, a sprinkle
3 Tbsp fresh parmesan, grated

Directions

1. Snap woody end of off asparagus and rinse. Meanwhile heat oven to 350*F.

2. Place asparagus in a single layer on a baking sheet and brush with melted butter. Cook in the oven until asparagus becomes tender. Sprinkle with fresh parmesan and bake for a few minutes more until cheese is melted.

3. Remove to a serving plate, sprinkle with sea salt to taste and enjoy!

'Sour Cream' and Chive Mashed Potatoes

Serves 4-6, Total Time: 30 Minutes

Oh mashed potatoes, is there a dish or an occasion that doesn't call for them? Not in my family! This delicious recipe replaces the butter and whole milk with plain Greek yogurt, fresh chives and black pepper. Even a mashed potato connoisseur won't be able to tell the difference between these and the original!

Ingredients

1 Lb potatoes
1/3 Cup 0% fat Greek yogurt
¼ Cup fresh chives, chopped
Salt & pepper to taste
Milk* If needed

Directions

1. Wash, cube and boil up your potatoes leaving the skins on to add fibre.

2. Drain potatoes and add freshly chopped chives and a 1/3 cup of plain 0% fat Greek yogurt.

3. Mash. Add milk 1 Tbsp at a time to get the creamy texture desired.

4. Sprinkle with sea salt and fresh black pepper to taste. Serve hot

Sweet Potato Fries

Serves 4-6, Total Time: 30 Minutes

Sweet potato fries are surprisingly easy to make at home and taste great! Change up the seasonings to change up the flavour and serve with a huge variety of dishes.

Ingredients

2 large sweet potatoes
1 Clove garlic, minced
½ Tsp brown sugar
½ Tsp red pepper flakes
2 Tbsp coconut oil

Directions

1. Cut sweet potatoes into French fry-like sticks. Meanwhile pre-heat frying pan to medium heat.

2. Add coconut oil. Add sweet potato.

3. Cook until fries begin to soften. Add garlic, brown sugar and red pepper flakes. Continue to cook for another 5-10 minutes. The longer you cook them, the crisper they will be.

Salad Rolls

Makes 12, Total Time: 60 Minutes

I love food, as you can probably tell by now, and Asian cuisine is no exception. Spring rolls are my favourite but being deep fried they are an occasional (very occasional) treat. Salad rolls on the other hand are stuffed full of veggies and wrapped in rice paper meaning they are low calorie and full of nutrients. Then to make them even more delicious, they can be dipped in whatever delicious sauce you want to use. I recommend Teriyaki sauce, Sweet chili sauce, peanut sauce or sweet and sour sauce!

Ingredients

½ Pound firm tofu
12 Spring roll wrappers
1 Carrot, julienned
½ Cucumber, julienned
1 Cup sprouts
1½ Cup lettuce, chopped
Dipping sauce, to taste

Directions

1. Press tofu, then cut block into 4 slabs. Cut each slab into 3 pieces for a total of 12 sticks and set aside.

2. Use a dish or pan that's big enough to easily lay your spring roll wrapper in and fill with about ¼ inch water (I used a large pie pan) – enough water to cover 1 wrapper when completely submerged.

3. Place 1 spring roll wrapper in cold water for 30-40 seconds until it softens enough to easily roll.

4. Place the wrapper on a flat surface, like a clean cutting board. Place 1 stick of tofu and a few pieces of rice, carrot, cucumber, sprouts and a little lettuce in the center. Pick up the bottom of wrapper and fold over the fillings.

5. Next fold in each side then continue to roll wrapper all the way to the top. Set spring roll aside and repeat the process with remaining ingredients.

 Make it meat-atarian: For those meat lovers or for extra protein try adding cooked shrimp, chicken or pork.

Lettuce Fajita Wraps

Serves 2, Total Time: 30 Minutes

This is just your basic fajita recipe with the difference being you don't put lettuce in the tortilla with the fillings; the lettuce takes the place of the tortilla! This cuts down on overall calories of the meal and cuts out unnecessary carbohydrates. And trust me you won't miss them!

Ingredients

Romaine lettuce
1 Large onion, chopped
1 Large red pepper, chopped
1 Cup mushrooms, sliced
½ Cup black beans, drained and rinsed
½ Cup cheese, grated
1 Tbsp chili powder
Salsa
Plain, non-fat Greek yogurt

Directions

1. Sauté all veggies and beans in a frying pan until tender.

2. Add chili powder and 1 Tbsp water, stir until veggies and beans are coated.

3. Put a few whole romaine leaves on each plate so they look like little boats. Top with a few spoonfuls of the sautéed veggies.

4. Top fajita boats with cheese, salsa and plain Greek yogurt, fold up like a fajita or taco and enjoy!

Kale Chips

Serves 2, Total Time: 10 Minutes

Who knew you could make a potato chip substitute out of a vegetable? These easy and quick to make Kale chips are full of vitamins including Vitamin K and can take care of that pesky craving for a salty and crunchy snack. Give them a try, I think you will be pleasantly surprised.

Ingredients

1 Bunch kale
Olive oil
Sea salt, or Mrs. Dash No Salt Seasoning

Directions

1. Preheat oven to 200*F. Meanwhile wash kale and pat dry.

2. Place parchment paper on a baking tray; arrange kale in a single layer.

3. Brush kale with olive oil. Sprinkle with sea salt.

4. Bake just until kale feels crisp to the touch or until just starting to brown around the edges < 10 minutes.

Veggie & Pasta Soup

Makes 8 Cups, Total Time: 90 Minutes

This is a soup that I remember my mom making when I was a kid and is the first soup that I ever made by myself. It is hearty and more like a meal than most soups. Its so easy to make and is great on its own or paired with a grilled cheese sandwich on cool days.

Ingredients

1 Large can tomato juice
3 Cups water
3 Cups of veggie broth
1 Cup celery, diced
1 Cup carrot, grated
1 Large onion, diced
2 garlic cloves, minced
2 Cups mushrooms, sliced
1 Bunch kale, chopped
1 Cup macaroni
1 Pkg Lipton soup mix

Directions

1. Add first 8 ingredients to a large pot (or Dutch oven) and bring to a boil.

2. Simmer for 30 minutes

3. Add macaroni, soup mix, and kale. Cook about 10 more minutes or until noodles are al dente.

4. Serve with a small piece of bread and a sprinkle of your favourite cheese for a perfect cold weather lunch.

Arrabiata Tomato Sauce

Makes 10 Cups, Total Time: 90 Minutes

I stole this recipe from my dad and then modified it a bit. I also usually steal all of the necessary tomatoes and onions out of his garden in August in order to make this. Taking the time to peel the tomatoes is a labour of love but it's well worth it. The recipe here is for the base sauce; when you are ready to eat it, serve over delicious pasta and add what ever additions you like - meats, more vegetables or cheeses. It cans well, freezes great and I promise after you make this once you will never be able to eat store bought pasta sauce again.

Ingredients

8 Garlic cloves, minced
2 Large onions, diced
¼ Cup olive oil
12 Regular tomatoes, peeled, seeded and diced
1 Can tomato paste
2 Tbsp each dried oregano & basil
1/3 Cup chopped fresh basil
1 Tsp red pepper flakes

Fast way to peel tomatoes:
Bring a pot of water to a boil. Slice an X in the bottom of the tomatoes and using a slotted spoon, drop the tomatoes a few at a time in to the boiling water for 30 seconds. Remove tomatoes from boiling water, put in ice water and the skins slide right off!

Directions

1. Peel and coarsely chop tomatoes. Set aside.

2. Heat oil in a large sauce pan over medium-low heat. Add onions and garlic and stir until onions start to soften, about 15 minutes.

3. Add tomatoes, juice and seeds to the pot. Stir in tomato paste. Add herbs and spices.

4. Increase heat to high and bring to a boil, then reduce heat to low. Simmer, partially covered and stirring occasionally to thicken sauce, about 1 hour. Remove from heat and stir in fresh basil.

 Make it meat-atarian: Add 2 lbs extra lean ground beef by sautéing it with the garlic and onions. When meat is browned continue on as normal.

Broccoli & Wild Rice Casserole

Serves 6-8, Total Time: 1 Hour 15 Minutes

This broccoli and wild rice casserole is perfect to take to potlucks. Its full of delicious nutrient rich broccoli and fibre filled wild rice, and it's easy to make, travels well and reheats well!

Ingredients

2 Bunches broccoli
2 Cans low-fat mushroom soup
1 ¾ Cups wild rice
½ Cup medium cheddar cheese, grated

Directions

1. Soak wild rice in cold water overnight.

2. Cook broccoli just until tender. Mix the soup and cheese together.

3. Layer casserole: Broccoli, rice, soup mix, then repeat.

4. Cook at 350*F for 1 hour.

Chipotle Rice & Beans

Serves 6-8, Total Time: 45 Minutes

Combining rice and beans creates a complete protein that we humans need to build and repair our body tissues. This recipe does just that in a delicious way, packing in as many veggies as possible on top of the rice and beans.

Ingredients

1 Large cooking onion, chopped
1 Large green pepper, chopped
1 Large red pepper, chopped
3 Celery stalks, chopped
2 Cloves garlic, minced
1 Can diced tomatoes & juice
1 ¼ Cups Veggie broth
1 Cup basmati rice, uncooked
2 Tbsp Tomato paste
1 Tsp each chili powder, chipotle powder & dried oregano
1 Can black beans
Black pepper & red pepper flakes to taste
1 Tbsp coconut oil

Directions

1. Sauté onion, peppers, celery and garlic in coconut oil, until they begin to soften.

2. Stir in all remaining ingredients except beans and bring to a boil. Reduce heat and simmer for 25 minutes until rice is cooked.

3. Add beans and cook for 5 more minutes.

 Make it meat-atarian: Add 2 lbs extra lean ground beef by sautéing it with the garlic and onions. When meat is browned continue on as normal.

Creamy Cauliflower Alfredo

Makes 8 Cups, Total Time: 20 Minutes

Who would ever have thought that pureed cauliflower would make a good Alfredo sauce substitute? Whoever originally came up with this idea is a genius. This recipe is low calorie, low fat and still full of creaminess and flavour. The recipe here is just the base, Wwhen you are ready to enjoy, feel free to add whatever you like! Some of my personal favourites are sautéed mushrooms, diced red pepper and fresh grated parmesan cheese.

Ingredients

3 Large cloves garlic, minced
1 Large cooking onion, minced
2 Tbsp butter
5-6 Cups cauliflower florets (1 Large Cauliflower)
6-7 cups vegetable broth or water
1 Tsp salt
½ Tsp pepper
½ Cup milk, or substitute

Directions

1. Sauté the minced garlic with the butter in a large non-stick skillet over low heat. Cook for several minutes or until the garlic is soft and fragrant but not browned. Remove from heat and set aside.

2. Bring the water or vegetable broth to a boil in a large pot. Add the cauliflower and cook, covered, for 7-10 minutes or until cauliflower is fork tender. Drain liquid from pot but reserve it! You will need it later.

3. Add 1 cup of liquid back to the cooked cauliflower and using an immersion blender, puree the cauliflower, cup of liquid, garlic, pepper and milk. Blend or puree for several minutes until the sauce is very smooth, adding more broth or milk depending on how thick you want the sauce. Add more of the reserved liquid if needed to get the consistency you want.

Spaghetti Squash Alfredo

Serves 2, Total Time: 60 Minutes

This dish is amazing. It's made up of nothing but vegetables and a bit of cheese and yet it tastes as rich and decadent as anything I've ever made before. Try this once and it will become part of your regular rotation and no one will notice there isn't actually any pasta! And instead of a fat laden regular Alfredo sauce use the *'Creamy Cauliflower Alfredo' (pg. 78)*.

Ingredients

1 Spaghetti Squash
1 ½ Cups 'Creamy Cauliflower Alfredo Sauce'
2 Cups sliced mushrooms
¼ Cup mozzarella, grated
¼ Cup fresh parmesan, grated
Chopped fresh basil, to taste
Black Pepper, to taste
Red Pepper Flakes, to taste
Water

Directions

1. Cut spaghetti squash in half and scoop out all seeds. Place it cut side down in a baking dish and add 1 inch of water. Cover and bake at 375*F for 30 minutes or until the flesh of the squash is easily pierced with a fork.

2. Meanwhile sauté the mushrooms until tender, set aside. Add the alfredo sauce to the pan and warm through.

3. When squash is cooked, transfer cut side up to a dry baking dish. Using a fork scrape the squash until it looks like a bowl full of little noodle like fibres.

4. Put sautéed mushrooms on to the squash, add the warmed sauce. Then top with the mozzarella, fresh grated parmesan, fresh basil and the pepper and pepper flakes if desrired.

5. Broil the squash until cheese is melted and bubbly.

6. Transfer squash halves to a plate and enjoy right out of the squash!

Roasted Vegetables with Olive Oil & Parmesan

Serves 6-8, Total Time: 1 Hour

Such a simple recipe yet so flavourful and nutritious. Roasting vegetables seems to really bring out the amazing flavours of each and every bite and by adding the chickpeas you get a satisfying meal complete with protein.

Ingredients

1 Large eggplant, peeled & chopped
2 Large zucchinis, chopped
1 Large red pepper, sliced
1 Large orange pepper, sliced
3 Cup mushrooms, sliced
1 Bunch asparagus, cut in to 2" pieces
1 Can chickpeas, drained and rinsed
½ Cup parmesan, freshly grated
¼ Cup olive oil
1 Tsp Italian seasoning

Directions

1. Put all cut vegetable and chickpeas into a large bowl. Toss to coat with olive oil and seasoning.

2. Put into a large baking dish and sprinkle with fresh parmesan. Bake at 350*F until veggies are tender about 20 minutes.

Make it meat-atarian: Start by putting one chicken breast per person in a baking dish, sprinkle with salt and pepper, and put in the preheated over. Once the chicken is in, start prepping the veggies, the chicken will take much longer to cook. Then roast the veggies as directed and serve with the chicken.

Grilled Portobello Mushrooms

Serves 2, Total Time 15 Minutes

Who needs a steak when you can grill a Portobello mushroom to taste almost the same? Serve with *'Herb Roasted Potatoes' (pg. 66)* and a grilled veggie on the side.

Ingredients

4 Large portabello mushroom caps
1 Tbsp Montreal steak spice
Olive oil

Directions

1. Heat indoor grill to medium-high heat, lightly brush with olive oil.

2. Wash and de-gill mushrooms. Rub with Montreal steak spice.

3. Place on grill and cook for about 5 minutes each side or until mushrooms become tender.

Frittatas

Serves 4, Total Time: 30 Minutes

Frittatas are a super easy and quick meal, and you can stuff them full of so many different vegetables, herbs and cheeses that you never get bored! Below is the base frittata recipe and a few different options, but the sky is the limit!

Base Ingredients

2 Large egg
1 Cup egg whites
½ Cup milk, or milk substitute
Black pepper to taste
½ Cup mozzarella, grated
1 Cup fillings, spinach, mushrooms, ham, onions, tomato, cooked potato, peppers, etc.

Directions

1. Whisk first 4 ingredients together as you heat a non-stick pan over medium heat.

2. Add any veggies that need to be sautéed and cook until softened.

3. Add egg mixture and top with cheese. Cover tightly and cook over medium heat until set in the middle.

Western

¼ Cup diced ham
¼ Cup diced onion
¼ Cup diced peppers
½ Cup Hot pepper jack cheese, grated

Margarita

¼ Cup fresh basil, chopped
1 Medium tomato diced
1 Medium onion, diced
½ Cup fresh mozzarella, grated

Quesadillas

Serves 2, Total Time: 30 Minutes

Quesadillas are another very quick and easy recipe perfect for quick lunches or busy nights. and just like frittatas you can make this different every time!

Ingredients

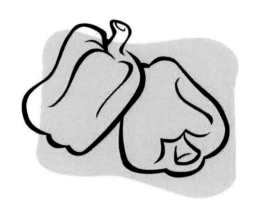

2 Whole grain tortillas
½ Cup black beans
1 Medium green pepper, sliced
1 Small onion, finely diced
1/3 Cup cheese, grated
½ Cup fresh salsa
¼ Cup plain, non-fat Greek yogurt

Directions

1. Place all ingredients onto half of each tortilla, fold over.

2. Heat oven to 350*F. Place filled tortillas in the oven and cook until top begins to brown. Flip and continue cooking until cheese is melted.

3. Cut each into thirds with a pizza cutter and serve with yogurt and salsa.

Ratatouille

Serves 8, Total Time: 60 Minutes

Ratatouille is basically a fancy word for a delicious Italian style vegetable stew. It's packed full of colourful vegetables and herbs and is as comforting and warm as any other stew I've had. This makes a great meal when paired with a crusty bun.

Ingredients

1 Medium onion, diced
1 Eggplant, peeled and diced
2 Medium zucchini, diced
1 Red bell pepper
1 Green bell pepper
1 Can tomatoes, diced
1 Can chick peas, drained and rinsed
5 garlic cloves, minced
½ Tsp each thyme, parsley & oregano
A pinch of basil
Salt and pepper to taste
Extra virgin olive oil

Directions

1. In a large sauté pan or Dutch oven set over medium sauté the onion and garlic in a bit of olive oil until translucent. Add the diced eggplant and sauté until it becomes golden in color.

2. Add a dash more olive oil and add the zucchini, then the peppers, tomatoes and canned tomatoes. Add the spices, salt and pepper, stir.

3. Turn the heat down to medium low and simmer for at least 30 to 40 minutes.

Yam Stew

Serve 6-8, Total Time: 45 Minutes

I don't think I've ever seen such a colourful stew before, or one with so many health benefits from the delicious array of vegetables. Fibre and protein from the beans, beta carotene from the yams, Vitamin K from the kale, lycopene from the tomatoes, capsaicin from the chili pepper and healthy fats from the peanut butter, just to name a few! Not to mention the satisfying feeling of eating a hearty, piping hot stew that is nourishing your body. Serve this with *'Irish Brown Bread' (pg. 25).*

Ingredients

1 Large cooking onion
1 Tbsp fresh ginger, ginger
1 Tbsp garlic, minced
2 Tsp chipotle chili powder
1 Tsp red chili flakes
10 Medjole dates, pitted and roughly chopped
(or ¼ cup raisins)
6 Sweet potatoes, chopped in to 1" Cubes
2 Cups organic low-salt veggie broth
1 Can diced tomatoes
1 Can black-eyed peas
1 Can chickpeas
½ Cup natural peanut butter
1 ½ Cups corn
1 Bunch Kale roughly chopped

Directions

1. Sauté onion in 1 Tbsp of water until translucent. Add ginger, garlic, chili powder and chili flakes and cook for 1 more minute.

2. Mix in yams, veggie broth, tomatoes, dates, beans and peanut butter. Bring to a boil, reduce heat and simmer for 20 minutes.

3. Add corn and kale simmer for 10 more minutes until yams and kale are tender.

4. Enjoy over rice or, my favourite, with Biscuit bread!

Classic Butternut Squash Soup

Serves 6-8, Total Time: 60 Minutes

After you make this soup, you may never be able to eat store bought butternut squash soup again! It's got a delicious earthy flavour and a lovely fall spicy-ness. Give it a try and I promise you will love it! You can serve it as an appetizer before dinner or as a meal or snack with whole grain crackers or a crusty bun.

Ingredients

1 Large butternut squash
1 Medium onion, diced
2 Stalks celery, diced
3 Medium carrots, diced
3 Cloves of garlic, minced
6 Cups low sodium vegetable broth
1 Tsp nutmeg
2 Tsp cinnamon
Pinch of pepper flakes to taste
Salt and pepper to taste

Directions

1. Split the squash and remove the seeds, put in a casserole pan with about an inch of water. Roast in the oven about 45 minutes at 350*F.

2. Sauté the onion, celery, carrots and garlic for 5-10 minutes until veggies are semi-soft, adding garlic only for the last couple minutes.

3. Add the veggie broth and spices, and simmer for about 15 minutes while the squash is finishing up roasting.

4. Scoop out the cooked squash, add it to the soup and let it cook for another 10 minutes or so. Blend in a blender or with the immersion blender, and then I add half a brick of light cream cheese. The cream cheese will melt as you stir it in; you can cube it up to make it easier. That's it! Soup!

Veggie Lentil Soup

Serves 6-8, Total Time: 60 Minutes

Veggies and lentils get pureed all together in this thick and creamy soup. It's full of vegetables - as you can see from the ingredient list - protein filled lentils and just enough cream cheese to make it creamy. Serve this with a little dollop of plain Greek yogurt and a sprinkle of red pepper flakes.

Ingredients

¼ Cup olive oil
1 Large clove garlic, minced
1 Large cooking onion, sliced
2 Tbsp red curry powder
¼ Tsp cinnamon
3 Stalks celery, roughly chopped
3 Cups carrots, roughly chopped
2 Cups butternut squash, peeled and chopped
1 Medium sweet potato, roughly chopped
6-8 Cups water or vegetable stock
1/3 Cup light cream cheese
¼ Cup fresh basil, chopped
1 Tbsp nutmeg
¾ Cup green lentils, rinsed and drained
Salt and freshly cracked pepper to taste

Directions

1. Add olive oil, garlic, onion, curry, cumin and cinnamon to a large saucepan or Dutch oven. Sauté for a few minutes, then add celery, carrots, squash and sweet potato, and sauté for a few minutes more.

2. Add enough water or chicken stock to cover vegetables, add lentils and bring to a boil, then lower to simmer at medium-low, stirring every so often until lentils are cooked, approximately 30 minutes.

3. Once vegetables are soft, stir in cream cheese and fresh basil. Purée everything in the pot with a hand blender or carefully transfer to a blender. Season with salt and pepper to taste.

Vegetarian Lasagna

Serves 6-8, Total Time: 2 Hours

Vegetables, pasta and cheese, what could be better? This rich vegetarian lasagne uses sweet potato instead of cheese to create the creamy texture and just the right combination of fresh cheeses to make it taste delicious.

Ingredients:

1 Package whole wheat lasagna noodles
1 Large sweet potato
3 Cloves garlic, minced
1 Can crushed tomatoes
2 Cups mushrooms, sliced
1 Zucchini, cut in to thin slices
1 Medium orange pepper, sliced
1 Jar pasta sauce, or *2 Cups Arrabiata Sauce (pg. 75)*
¾ Cup quality mozzarella cheese, grated
¼ Cup fresh grated parmesan

Directions

1. Soak the lasagna noodles in cold water, meanwhile sauté mushrooms and microwave a large sweet potato, peel and mash. Add salt, pepper, and minced garlic to the sweet potato and stir in ¾ of a can of crushed tomatoes.

2. In a large baking dish, pour in the remaining crushed tomatoes. Put in a layer of noodles. Add a few scoops of the sweet potato mix. Add half of the mushrooms, half a yellow zucchini sliced and some sliced green pepper. Layer of noodles.

3. Add another layer of noodles, sweet potato mix, mushrooms, yellow zucchini, and ½ of the grated cheese mozzarella. Cover in noodles. Cover the noodles with the remaining sauce. Cover with organic mozzarella.

4. Bake at 375*F for 1 hr 15 min. Let rest for 15 minutes before serving.

Made Over Mac & Cheese

Serves 6, Total Time: 45 Minutes

Don't be scared to try this recipe because it has pumpkin in it! I promise you'll never know it's in there and neither will anyone else. The pumpkin takes the place of tons of cream and cheese to make this dish creamy and comforting while decreasing the calorie count significantly.

Ingredients

1lb whole wheat macaroni
2 Cups canned pumpkin
2 Cups low-sodium vegetable broth
½ Cup mozzarella cheese, grated
2 Tbsp fresh parmesan, grated
2 Cups of kale, chopped (Optional)
Olive oil

Directions

1. Preheat oven to 375*F and coat a 9×13 (I used a 9×9) baking dish brushed with olive oil.

2. Drain noodles.

3. Put pumpkin and broth in a sauce pan over low heat; stir occasionally until well combined. Bring it to a simmer.

4. Remove the pan from heat and stir in the grated cheese until it's melted.

5. Mix squash mixture and noodles. Stir to combine and pour into the baking dish. Sprinkle with parmesan.

6. Bake for 20 minutes and serve!

Baked Butternut Squash Casserole

Serves 8, Total Time: 2 hours

By this point in the cookbook you can probably see that I'm quite fond of casseroles. This one is full of veggies and quiona and makes a great side dish. Toasted pecans add to the nutty flavour of the dish and the parmesan makes it taste like its bad for you. Serve along side a portion of meat with a side salad if you want it to be the main course.

Ingredients

2 Regular butternut squash
⅔ Cup uncooked quinoa
⅔ Cup pecan halves, roughly chopped
2 Tsp olive oil
½ Tsp cinnamon
1 Tbsp brown sugar
¼ Cup breadcrumbs
½ Cup fresh grated parmesan cheese, divided
Salt & pepper to taste

Directions

1. Preheat the oven to 450*F. Wash the outside of the squash. Cut the squash in half lengthwise and scoop out the seeds. Place the squash halves cut-side up in a large baking dish. Sprinkle the surface of the squash with salt and pepper. Pour ¼ inch of water in the bottom of the pan and cover the pan tightly with foil. Bake the squash until it is tender when pierced with a fork, 50 minutes depending on the size. Remove from the oven, discard foil, and allow the squash to cool. Reduce oven temperature to 400 degrees F.

2. Meanwhile, cook the quinoa by bringing 1 and ⅓ cup water to boil in a small pot. Add the quinoa, reduce to a simmer and put a lid on the pot. Simmer for 15 minutes.

3. Heat a skillet over low-medium heat. Toast the pecans until fragrant, about 5 minutes. Set aside.

4. Using a spoon or an ice cream scoop, gently scrape the flesh out of the roasted squash halves. In a large bowl combine the squash, cooked quinoa, pecans, shallot, oregano, and salt. In another small bowl, whisk together the breadcrumbs and butter.

5. Finely grate the parmesan cheese. Add 2 Tbsp. of the cheese to the breadcrumbs. Add the remaining parmesan to the squash mixture and stir to combine all of the ingredients.

6. Gently spoon the squash mixture into the squash shells. Sprinkle the bread crumbs and parmesan over the top. Return squash to the oven and bake, uncovered, until the tops are golden brown, 20-25 minutes.

Red Lentil Chili

Serves 6-8, Total Time: 8.5 Hours

The dates in the recipe add a delicious natural sweetness which is balanced out by the tex-mex flavour of the chipotle powder creating a really delicious and unique flavour that tastes deceptively like a 'normal' chili. And the best part? It is just chocked full of fresh delicious vegetables and the lentils add protein and fibre! And you can always experiment, why not try adding beans, corn, squash, carrots or anything else you imagination can think of!

Ingredients

~ 9 Medjool dates, pitted and chopped
1 Lb red lentils
~ 7 cups water (don't overflow your slow cooker)
2 Cups sweet potatoes, peeled and cubed
2 Cans diced tomatoes
1 Can tomato paste
1 Large cooking onion, diced
8 Cloves garlic, finely minced
4 Tbsp apple cider vinegar
1½ Tbsp chili powder
2 Tsp paprika
½ Tsp chipotle powder, or more to taste
¼ Tsp crushed red pepper flakes, or more to taste

Directions

1. Place all ingredients in a slow cooker and cook on low for 8 hours. Serve with baked organic tortilla chips.

HOT BEVERAGES

Matcha Green Tea Latte

Makes 1, Total Time 15 Minutes

Ingredients

1 Cup milk, or milk substitute
1 Tsp matcha green tea powder
¼ Tsp Vanilla Extract
1 Tsp organic sugar

1. Heat all ingredients in a sauce pan while whisking. Continue whisking until the mixture is steaming but not boiling, pour into a cup and enjoy!

Pumpkin Spice Latte

Makes 1, Total Time 15 Minutes

Ingredients

1 Cup milk, or milk substitute

1 Tbsp instant coffee

1 Tsp heaping pure pumpkin puree

¼ Tsp Pumpkin Pie Spice

½ Tsp Vanilla Extract

1-2 Tsp Pure Maple Syrup

1. Heat all ingredients in a sauce pan while whisking. Continue whisking until the mixture is steaming but not boiling, pour into a cup, sprinkle with cinnamon and/or nutmeg and enjoy!

Peppermint Mocha Latte

Makes 1, Total Time 15 Minutes

Ingredients

1 Cup milk, or milk substitute

1 Tbsp instant coffee

1 Tbsp cocoa powder

½ Tsp mint extract

1 Tsp organic sugar

1 Candy cane

1. Heat all ingredients in a sauce pan while whisking. Continue whisking until the mixture is steaming but not boiling, pour into a cup, stir with a candy cane and enjoy!

White Mocha

Makes 1, Total Time 15 Minutes

Ingredients

¾ Cup milk, or substitute
½ Cup water
1 Tbsp instant coffee
2 Tbsp white chocolate chips
1 Tsp organic sugar

Directions

1. Heat all ingredients in a sauce pan while whisking. Continue whisking until the mixture is steaming but not boiling, pour into a cup, stir and enjoy!

Hot Chocolates

Serves 1, Total Time 10 Minutes

Taking the time to make your own hot chocolate is so much healthier than the cheap pre-made mixes at the store. If you look at the ingredients on the label, how many of them can you pronounce? Also by making your own you can customize it based on your mood, the season or for a special occasion!

Base Ingredients

¾ Cup milk, or milk substitute
½ Cup water
1 Heaping Tbsp cocoa powder
1 Tsp organic sugar

Directions

1. Heat milk in a sauce pan over medium heat (or in the microwave) until steaming, but not boiling.

2. Whisk in cocoa powder and sugar until well combined.

3. Pour in mug and serve!

If you love hot chocolate in the winter like me, you need some variety! Give these interesting new flavours a try. These recipes are also great for parties when you want to serve something a little fancier.

Spicy:

Cinnamon: Add ¼ Tsp of cinnamon to the mix, and then add a cinnamon stick to each mug

Gingerbread: Add ¼ Tsp each of ground ginger, all spice and cinnamon.

Mexican: Add 1 Tsp chili powder or cayenne powder for a spicy twist

Mint: Add ¼ Tsp peppermint extract or stir with a candy cane

Flavourful:

White Chocolate: Leave out cocoa powder from base, melt 2 Tbsp of white chocolate chips and ¼ Tsp vanilla extract

White Chocolate Mint: Leave out cocoa powder from base, melt 2 Tbsp of white chocolate chips, ¼ Tsp mint extract, a few drops of green food colouring and a few marshmallows

Dark Chocolate: Melt 2 Tbsp chopped dark chocolate in to the mix

Hazelnut: Melt 2 Tbsp Nutella

Pumpkin: Add 1 Tbsp canned pumpkin and 1 Tsp brown sugar

Caramel: Melt 2 Tbsp caramel chips

Butterscotch: Melt 2 Tbsp butterscotch chips

Fruity:

Raspberry: Add 1 Tbsp raspberry jam or preserves

Orange: Add ½ Tsp orange extract and ¼ Tsp vanilla extract

Coconut: Add ½ Tsp coconut extract and 1 Tsp coconut oil

Banana: Add ¼ Tsp cinnamon, mash 1 banana. Add banana & hot chocolate to blender and combine quickly. This recipe turns out velvety smooth and rich!

DESSERTS

Greek Yogurt Cheesecake

Serves 12, Total Time: 60 Minutes

Cheesecake is a great dessert that just about everyone loves and this recipe is perfect for a crowd or special occasion. It tastes just like the creamy original recipe but with fewer calories and fat. Serve this with delicious fresh fruit on top!

Ingredients

1 ½ Cups vanilla Greek yogurt
½ Cup light cream cheese
2 Eggs
1 Tbsp corn starch
1 Cup graham crumbs
1 Cup oatmeal, not instant
3-4 Tbsp butter
3-4 Tbsp milk, or substitute
¼ Cup brown sugar

Directions:

1. Preheat over to 350*F.

2. Mix all creamy ingredients in a medium bowl then process all of the crust ingredients in a food processor.

3. Press the crust in to a spring form pan, then pour the creamy part on top.

4. Bake for approximately 45 mins or until almost set in the middle

5. Cool the cheesecake, then cover with fresh fruit and a drizzle of honey or if you're a choco-holic like me a drizzle of chocolate sauce.

Berry Pudding

Serves 4-6, Total Time: 45 Minutes

Berry pudding is quite possibly one of my all-time favourite desserts. It's sweet, warm, full of berries and goes great with a cup of coffee and a small scoop of vanilla frozen yogurt.

Ingredients

2 Cups berries
¾ Cup organic sugar, divided
½ Tsp cinnamon
¼ Cup butter
¾ Cup unsweetened apple sauce
1 ½ Cups whole wheat flour
1 ½ Tsp baking powder
1 Cup milk
1 Tsp vanilla

Directions

1. Lightly butter bottom and sides of pan. Put berries in pan with ¼ cup of sugar and cinnamon over top of them.

2. Cream together butter, ½ cup sugar and applesauce. Add eggs, milk and vanilla, beat well.

3. Stir in dry ingredients. Then pour the batter over top of berries.

4. Bake at 375*F for 35 minutes or until set and lightly browned.

Apple Crisp

Serves 6-8, Total Time: 45 Minutes

A classic fall dessert that, if done right, is quite a healthy one. By modifying classic apple crisp recipes to have slightly less sugar, add oats and make the focus apples, you make an already fairly good dessert that much better without losing any of the delicious taste and sweetness. Serve with a ¼ cup of low-fat vanilla frozen yogurt or natural vanilla ice cream.

Ingredients

9 Macintosh apples, peeled and sliced
¼ Cup butter, melted
½ Cup flour
½ Cup old fashioned oats
¼ Cup organic sugar
¼ Cup brown sugar
Nutmeg to taste

Directions

1. Mix nutmeg and apples.

2. Mix all other ingredients together.

3. Lightly grease a 9"x13" baking dish. Pour in apples, then topping.

4. Bake for 30 minutes at 350*F

Chocolate Hazelnut Mousse

Serves 12, Total Time: 20 Minutes

This high protein dessert is great for a crowd. Its creamy, sweet (but not too sweet) and tastes amazing with a bit of fresh fruit on top, especially strawberries. Below is also the recipe for a single portion for when you're craving something sweet.

Ingredients

3 Cups non-fat plain Greek yogurt
1 Cup non-fat vanilla Greek yogurt
12 Tbsp cocoa powder
2-3 Tbsp organic honey
5 Tbsp Nutella

Directions

1. Mix all ingredients, put in a trifle bowl or in 8 individual cups then refrigerate – and that's all there is to it!

Make a Single Serving:

Sometimes I need a little something sweet at the end of the day but I do not need 12 servings of this! Also by making one serving at a time I have to really want it to measure out and mix all of these ingredients.

½ Cup non-fat plain Greek yogurt
2 Tbsp non-fat vanilla Greek yogurt
2 Tbsp cocoa powder
½ Tbsp organic honey
1 Tsp Nutella

Peanut Butter Banana Ice Cream

Makes 2 servings, Total Time: 5 Minutes

Who knew you could make a delicious frozen treat out of frozen bananas! This super quick and easy recipe is perfect for those hot summer nights. And this is another recipe that you can change up all the time! Try adding frozen raspberries, nutella, chocolate chips or peanuts! If you're a choco-holic like me you can add a Tbsp of nutella on top and it becomes the most decadent peanut butter chocolate ice cream ever made!... well maybe not ever made but for the calorie count and little fat it can't be beat! If there are leftovers store it in the freezer and make sure you get it out 10-15 minutes before you want to eat it because it gets very hard.

Ingredients
2 Medium bananas, sliced & frozen
2 Heaping Tbsp natural peanut butter
1 Tbsp chia seeds
1-2 Tbsp milk, or substitute

Directions

1. Put bananas, peanut butter and chia seeds in a food processor and blend.

2. Add Soy milk 1 Tbsp at a time until it gets nice and creamy like ice cream and there you have it!

Not Old Fashioned Chocolate Chip Cookies

Makes 15 Small Cookies, Total Time 20 Minutes

This is another one of my 'who knew?' recipes because who knew that you could make delicious cookies out of pureed chickpeas! These high-protein little gems are perfect for dessert or for a snack. This recipe is also vegan and gluten free!

Base Ingredients

1 Can of chick peas, rinsed and drained

½ Cup all natural peanut butter

¼ Cup honey

1 Tsp baking powder

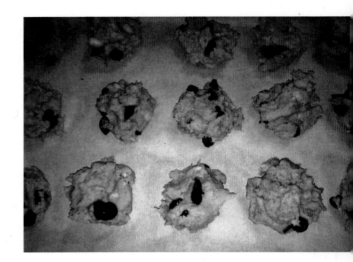

Optional Ingredients (½ Cup)

Chocolate chips, chopped nuts, raisins, crasins, chopped dates... really ½ of a cup of any healthy items or combination of items you can think of.

Directions

1. Put all base ingredients in a sturdy food processor and blend until its smooth. You will probably need to scrape the sides down – it is unbelievably sticky.

2. Pre-heat oven to 350*F. Stir ½ cup of chocolate chips and with wet hands, shape in to 1" balls and place on a parchment lined cookie sheet. Then press them down a little bit to look more like a classic cookie, otherwise they stay in a ball shape. Cook them for about 10 minutes or until just starting to brown. Then remove from the oven, cool and enjoy!

Fudgey Chocolate Brownies

Makes: 12, Total time: 30 mins

These fudgey and dense brownies get their fudgey-ness from pumpkin! But again trust me that they don't taste anything like pumpkin. They taste more like a cross between fudge and a brownie. I've taken these guys to a lot of events and, unfortunately, I never have any leftovers.

Ingredients

2 Ounces Baker's Special Dark
¼ Cup coconut milk *(I used soy milk)*
3 Tbsp coconut oil
½ Cup – ¾ Cup maple syrup or honey, to taste
½ Cup pumpkin puree
¼ Tsp sea salt
¼ Tsp baking soda
¼ Cup unsweetened cocoa powder
¼ Cup coconut flour
¼ Cup tapioca or arrowroot flour

Directions

1. In a microwave safe bowl or double boiler, melt the unsweetened chocolate, coconut milk, and coconut oil over medium heat. Heat just enough to melt the chocolate, and remove the heat.

2. Mix in the honey, pumpkin, salt, and baking soda.

3. Mix in sifted cocoa powder, sifted coconut flour, and tapioca flour. Stir in a handful of dark chocolate chips for added chocolaty goodness

4. Line pans with tinfoil. Pour into a prepared 8 x 8 pan.

5. Bake in a preheated 350*F oven for 20-25 minutes when a knife inserted in the middle comes out clean.

6. Cool completely and cut. These bad boys don't even need icing.

Dark Chocolate Peanut Butter Cups

Makes 12, Total Time: 30 Minutes

Peanut butter cups are delicious but the ones in the store have way too many preservatives and ingredients that I can't pronounce. So, why not make your own? There really super simple and taste amazing!

Ingredients

1 Large bar good quality dark chocolate
2-3 Tbsp milk, or substitute
¾ Cup natural peanut butter

Directions

1. Put muffin liners into a standard muffin pan

2. Melt ½ chocolate using the microwave or double boiler to melt ½ of the chocolate bar and add 1 to 1 ½ Tbsp milk. You want the chocolate to be slightly softer but NOT runny. Stir to combine well.

3. Put 1 Tbsp of chocolate in the bottom of each muffin cup. Refrigerate for 5 minutes to set it. Meanwhile melt the rest of the chocolate and 1 to 1 ½ Tbsp milk.

4. Put 1 heaping Tsp of peanut butter on top of the chocolate in the muffin pan. Cover with 1 Tbsp of chocolate.

5. Refrigerate to set and enjoy!

TRAVEL CAREER DEVELOPMENT
Instructor's Resource Manual

Institute of Certified Travel Agents

Patricia J. Gagnon, CTC
and
Karen Silva, M.A.

Irwin
Mirror Press
Homewood, IL 60430
Boston, MA 02116

Fifth Edition

Table of Contents

Chapter

1.	The Travel Industry, Past, Present, and Future	7
2.	Destination Geography	33
3.	Air Travel	65
4.	International Travel	93
5.	Ground Transportation	113
6.	Cruising	129
7.	Accommodations	151
8.	Tours	173
9.	Sales Techniques	193
10.	Customized Sales	225
11.	Follow-up	249
12.	Marketing	275
13.	Automation	297
14.	Industry Communications	321
15.	Money Management	339
16.	Career Development	361

Introduction

The *Instructor's Resource Manual* is designed to help you direct your classes along with the *Travel Career Development* text and *Student Workbook*. Use this manual as your own personal guide — underline passages, take notes, and write in other ideas. Adapt the material to your particular level of students.

Chapter Contents

Chapter contents may vary, but all sections contain:

■ A review of chapter objectives

■ A list of vocabulary

■ Transparency masters, including an outline of each chapter

■ Answers to textbook review and discussion questions

■ Answers to *Student Workbook* exercises

■ Suggestions for classroom activities

■ A selection of articles from travel industry sources to serve as a basis for lectures or discussions

■ An end-of-chapter review

Semester Project

The following activity is an optional semester-long project. It combines elements of many chapters in the text.

Activity — Have students plan and execute a one-day familiarization tour of your area. Students should be selected to work on operations, market-ing, and sightseeing. Choose one or two project directors who will oversee the excercise and pre-pare the final report and evaluation. You may have to adapt the project to your students, time restrictions, and area. Use the following as a guideline for responsibilities.

Operations — Design the itinerary. Identify area attractions, sights, hotels, or other points of interest to visit or see. Contact the appropriate representatives of these sites and make arrangements for the visit. Investigate transportation alternatives (motorcoach, van, limo) and make appropriate arrangements. Students also may choose to do the fam as a walking tour. Send out written confirmations and produce a final itinerary.

Marketing — Promote the tour. Students may want to invite guests. A fee can be charged to cover the cost of any admissions or transportation. This team may want to organize a fund raising activity to cover expenses (car wash, flea market, bake sale, raffle). Consider different forms of publicity to advertise the tour.

Sightseeing — Research the sights to be visited and select tour guides to provide commentary during the trip. This should include historical and cultural information. If motorcoach transportation is being used, this team may also want to consider games for entertainment between stops.

Final review — Have students consider the following questions at the end of the project: Was it a success? What did they learn? What would they have done differently?

An Exclusive Career Opportunity

The Travel Career Development Test Certificate

Students who complete a course of study using *Travel Career Development* have a unique opportunity for career advancement. It's the Travel Career Development Test Certificate.

When students pass the Travel Career Development Test, they receive ICTA's Travel Career Development Test Certificate — a nationally recognized travel industry credential. ICTA circulates the names of certificate recipients among travel professionals nationwide. Here's how the process works:

Step One

Students complete a course that is based chiefly on *Travel Career Development*.

Step Two

Students who want to participate in the testing program fill out an Application for Testing (see next page) and pay a $25 administrative fee. The instructor then submits the applications along with a Test Request Form to ICTA's headquarters located at 148 Linden Street, PO Box 812059, Wellesley, MA 02181-0012.

Step Three

Instructors receive and administer copies of the Travel Career Development Test. The test consists of 100 multiple-choice questions, and students have up to two hours to complete it.

Instructors return completed tests to ICTA for scoring. ICTA awards a passing grade to students who earn a score of 70 percent or better.

Step Four

Students who earn a passing grade receive the Travel Career Development Test Certificate from their instructor. The certificate is recognized by travel industry employers nationwide. ICTA also publicizes the names of certificate recipients among industry professionals. The certificate gives beginning travel professionals a competitive edge in the marketplace.

Test Request Form

Please fill out the following information. Tests will be sent out approximately two weeks prior to your test date. To ensure delivery by the date required, the following items should be received by ICTA's testing department 30 days prior to the test date:

■ Test Request Form
■ An Application For Testing Form completed by each student
■ A single school check or money order for the total amount

_____
Instructor

_____
School

_____
Address

_____
City   State   Zip

_____
Telephone

Test Information
Number of tests requested _____   Test date _____

Amount enclosed _____
Please mail to:

 Institute of Certified Travel Agents
Testing Department
148 Linden Street, P. O. Box 812059, Wellesley, MA 02181-0012

Travel Career Development

Application For Testing

I understand that:

1. I must submit $25 to my instructor to be eligible to take the Travel Career Development Test.

2. I will be allowed up to two (2) hours to complete the exam that consists of 100 multiple-choice questions.

3. To earn a passing grade I must score 70 percent or better.

4. I will receive the Travel Career Development Test Certificate when I earn a passing grade.

5. If I miss my assigned test date for any reason, I will be charged $25 to reschedule. If I fail the test, I may retest for $15. All application fees are nonrefundable.

When I earn a passing grade, my score will be mailed to my instructor along with the Travel Career Development Test Completion Certificate.

_____   _____
Signature   Date

_____
Name   (Please print your name as you want it on your certificate.)

_____
Address

_____
City   State   Zip

_____
School

_____
City   State

 Institute of Certified Travel Agents
148 Linden Street, P. O. Box 812059, Wellesley, MA 02181-0012

The Travel Industry -
Past, Present, and Future
Chapter 1

Review Chapter Objectives
- Identify the contributions of three pioneers in the travel industry
- Describe Maslow's theory of human motivation
- Compare today's travel market with the past's
- Differentiate man-made attractions from natural ones
- Describe a typical familiarization trip
- List five sources of information for travel professionals
- Explain why destinations go in and out of fashion
- Discuss the features of a good travel video

Review Vocabulary
- Accessibility
- Fam trip
- Infrastructure
- Intangible need
- Man-made attraction
- Natural attraction
- NTO
- Personal bias

Destination Careers
- Cartographer
- Tour Host
- Tourist Board Representative
- Travel Researcher
- Travel Video Producer
- Travel Writer

Transparencies
- Chapter outline
- Plog's psychographic position of destinations
- Travel agent influence
- Ways to use videos successfully

The Travel Industry -
Past, Present, and Future
Chapter 1 Outline

I. Origins of Travel

   A. Travel Pioneers

II. The Travel Market Today

   A. Maslow's Hierarchy of Needs

   B. Plog's Psychographic Position of Destinations

III. How Destinations Go In and Out of Fashion

   A. Attractions

   B. Cost and Standards of Living

   C. Accessibility

IV. Sources of Information

   A. Familiarization Trips

   B. Associations and Tourist Offices

   C. Written References

   D. Travel Videos

V. The Future of the Industry

Plog's Psychographic Position of Destinations

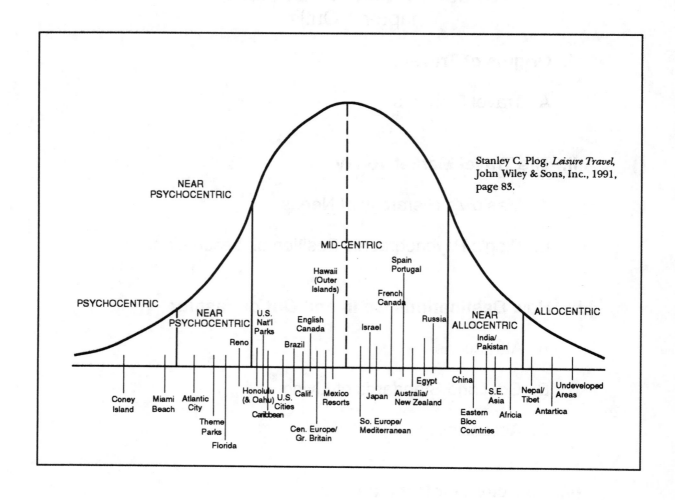

Stanley C. Plog, *Leisure Travel*, John Wiley & Sons, Inc., 1991, page 83.

PSYCHOCENTRIC

NEAR PSYCHOCENTRIC

NEAR PSYCHOCENTRIC

MID-CENTRIC

NEAR ALLOCENTRIC

ALLOCENTRIC

U.S. Nat'l Parks

Reno

Brazil

English Canada

Hawaii (Outer Islands)

Israel

French Canada

Spain Portugal

Russia

India/ Pakistan

Coney Island

Miami Beach

Atlantic City

Theme Parks

Florida

Honolulu (& Oahu)

Caribbean

U.S. Cities

Calif.

Cen. Europe/ Gr. Britain

Mexico Resorts

Japan

So. Europe/ Mediterranean

Australia/ New Zealand

Egypt

China

Eastern Bloc Countries

S.E. Asia

Africia

Nepal/ Tibet

Antartica

Undeveloped Areas

Travel Agent Influence

Average Percentage of Time Travel Agent Performs Specific Job Functions

Job Function	% of Time
Conferring with Clients	36
Actual Booking Process for all Types of Reservations	20
Referring to Reference Materials and Doing Research for Client Trips	18
Following Up on Trips in the Process of Being Booked or Making Changes to Existing Trips	10
Office Administration Such As Visiting with Reps or Familiarization Trips	10
Handling Refunds or Exchanges	6

(Information based on the 1991 Louis Harris Survey of
U.S. Travel Agents conducted by the Louis Harris Organization
for *Hotel &Travel Index*)

Ways to Use Videos Successfully

- Training Sessions for Staff

- Group Presentations

- In-house Viewing

- Gifts to Clients

- Revenue Production through Sales or Rentals

Answers to Textbook Review Questions

1. **Since the Roman Empire, what have been some of the most significant advances in travel?**
   Many new forms of transportation have developed, such as the stage coach, rail systems, steamships, airlines, and so on. In addition, hotels have emerged as an industry in their own right. Refer to the Historical Perspective for a complete list of answers.

2. **Can you name destinations where any of the following contribute significantly to their popularity or unpopularity: ease of access, cost of living, religious beliefs, history?**
   Examples may include: ease of access (most United States, Canadian, and European destinations); cost of living (expensive — Japan, Bermuda); value (the United States and Canada); religious beliefs (Iran, Vatican City, Mecca); history (Egypt and Europe)

3. **Choose one pioneer in travel and tourism and discuss his or her impact on the industry.**
   Answers may vary.

4. **Relate Maslow's theory to the reason(s) your family most frequently travels.**
   This will vary from family to family. Most will probably mention self-fulfillment, relaxation, reduction of stress, and so on. This is a good time to mention Plog's theory and discuss where students think their family is on that continuum.

5. **How would you set about improving your local area as a destination if you had unlimited funds?**
   Answers may vary. Remind students that most of their responses will relate to the infrastructure of the area.

6. **List four ways travel counselors can gain additional information about destinations.**
   Fam trips, brochures, videos, guidebooks, publications, associations, and tourist offices are all ways to obtain additional information about areas.

Answers to Discussion Topics

Papua New Guinea
Plog's theory suggests that Papua would appeal to the allocentric traveler, one who is characterized by a considerable degree of adventure, self-confidence and willingness to experiment.

Disasters
Answers will vary.

Plog's Theory
Answers will vary.

Answers to Workbook Exercises

Worksheet 1-1

Accessibility	The ease of getting to a destination
Fam trip	Trips designed for travel agents to acquaint them with a destination and its facilities or with a particular travel product
Infrastructure	The network of highways, utilities, airports, entertainment, stores, and so on that make tourism possible
Intangible need	The reasons why people travel
Man-made attraction	Attractions that are not natural, but constructed by human beings, such as Walt Disney World.
Natural attraction	An attraction determined by nature
NTO	National Tourist Office — an agency sponsored by the government of its country, dedicated to promoting tourism and shaping tourism policy
Personal bias	Individual judgments

Worksheet 1-2

1. A man-made attraction is constructed; a natural attraction is created by nature. Examples will vary.

2. A fam trip is designed to acquaint travel agents with destinations.
   Agent benefits — no substitute for a personal visit, can experience the local culture, build confidence for successful selling, agents can network with their peers.
   Supplier benefits — allow agents to experience a destination, hotel, or attraction first hand.

3. Answers may vary.

4. Choose from: ease of access, attractions, entertainment, reasonable living costs, culture, intangibles, high health standards, climate, desirable accommodations.

5. NTOs and state tourist offices actively promote travel to their countries. Services include: marketing assistance, seminars and workshops, brochures and maps, help in developing group travel.

6. Choosing a video: It should be professional in production, presentation, editing, and sound quality. It should be short in length and feature practical information. Images of people and places should sell the destination. It shouldn't get outdated too quickly.
   Ways to use a video: for training staff, group presentations, in-house viewing, gifts to clients, revenue production by sales or rentals.

Worksheet 1-3
Answers will vary.

Classroom Activities

1. Bring in various travel industry publications. Pass them out and ask the students to analyze the different styles, markets, and so on. For contrast, use both industry and retail publications. This will help familiarize students with current writers and journals. After reviewing the publications, ask students to choose a particular sector of the industry and research a topic using two or more publications. Ask them to review, critique, and discuss their new-found knowledge in a well-developed essay.

2. Choose a particular destination, then select two or three different videos showcasing that destination. What are the students' perceptions of the area? Are these good videos? Why or why not? Would they be more useful to clients or to agents? Discuss.

3. Bring in a sample of industry guidebooks. Choose a specific destination and ask students what information the guidebooks provide. Which guidebooks did they find most useful? Why? This activity could be related to the video exercise, if you choose to use the same destination. In this way students can compare the type of information obtained from two different sources.

Articles

Chapter 1 — Article One
"How to Track Down a Travel Agent Who Gets You Great Deals"
Ask students to consider the importance of a travel agent when planning a trip. How frequently does their family use the services of an agency? How did they choose the agent? What characteristics/skills/traits are important for an agent's continued success? What makes one agent better than another?

Chapter 1 — Article Two
"Diary of a First Year Agent"
This article describes how travel agents typically spend their days. Overall, agents spend only 20 percent of their time actually making bookings. The vast majority of their time is spent on issues related to the process: tasks that require research analysis and decision making. First, ask students for their perceptions of a travel agent's daily routine. After reading the article, discuss their revised impressions. What is the most interesting part of the diary? Choose one of the situations listed and discuss how students might have handled that day differently. Three possible related activities:

1. Ask students to keep a similar diary concerning what they learn as travel students. Suggest that they clip articles from local newspapers as part of their diaries. At the end of the course, ask them to review the material and see what they have learned.

2. Ask students to interview a local travel agent. Ask for his or her perceptions of the job. Compile a list of standard interview questions. Discuss those skills deemed most important for success in the position. This is a good networking opportunity for students and may provide leads for future guest speakers.

3. Invite a local agent to visit the class and share his or her impressions of the position. Ask students to prepare a list of questions and be willing to share their concerns.

Chapter 1 — Article One

How To Track Down a Travel Agent
Who Gets You Great Deals

By Beth Kobliner

    Confused and confounded by today's fast-changing travel packages and prices? Here's a solution: Team up with a dedicated travel agent who can save you hundreds of dollars — and steer you around travel nightmares. Most travelers have gotten part of the message: They use agents. Currently, more than 80% of all airline tickets are booked by agencies, up from 38% in 1978. In addition, fully 90% of all packaged tours and 95% of cruises are booked by agents, according to the American Society of Travel Agents in Alexandria, Virginia.

    Consumers still tend to think, however, that all travel agents are created equal. They're not. Different agents' suggestions for the same trip range widely in price, perks and comfort (for example, see our quiz, "How You Can Test Fly a Travel Agent," at the end of this article). Another indication: when the New York City Department of Consumer Affairs called 49 travel agents last year requesting the lowest round-trip fares for flights from New York to several other U.S. cities, the rates varied by as much as 115%. "The main reason for the fare differential is simple," says the report. "Some travel agents are lazy, negligent or poorly trained."

    So the key to special deals and memorable vacations is learning how to separate good agents from bad ones. The following guide to choosing a travel agent was compiled from dozens of interviews with industry insiders and critics. Here's what you need to know:

Is the agency reputable?

    The country's roughly 40,000 travel services, up from 27,000 in 1985, now run the gamut from computerized mom-and-pop shops to local branches of high-volume chains; from bargain wholesalers to velvet-glove packagers; and from airline tour desks to "niche" agencies that specialize in one activity or destination, such as cruises or Africa.

    The problem is that virtually anyone can call himself a travel professional. Only nine states require any type of agent regulation or certification: California, Florida, Hawaii, Illinois, Iowa, Ohio, Oregon, Rhode Island and Washington. Faced with the clutter of choices, remember that it's the experienced and knowledgeable individual agent who counts - not just the agency. One credential worth noting: the certified travel counselor (CTC) designation. To get it, the person has to have been in the business for at least five years and to have completed travel courses. Of the more than 200,000 travel agents in the U.S., only 14,000 have earned CTC degrees. For names in your area, call the Institute of Certified Travel Agents (800 542-4282 or 617 237-0280). Other industry affiliations, such as an agency's membership in the American Society of Travel Agents (ASTA), should not be your only measure because the qualifications are hardly rigorous.

    At the very least, seek out an agency that has been around for five years or more. Also, check with your Better Business Bureau to learn whether any complaints have ben registered against the company.

Is the agent working for you?

    On average, a travel agent earns only $16,000 annually. "You have to remember," says Chicago travel industry attorney Beverly Susler Parkhurst, "this is one of the few businesses that have never charged for professional advice, though some are starting to institute service fees."

    Most agencies collect commissions on sales, typically 7% to 15% of an airline ticket, hotel rate or tour package price. On top of that, suppliers often pay as much as 30% more, known as "commission overrides," to high-volume producers.

    To pump up the volume and make more money — particularly in these tough times — agencies tend to channel their business to as few suppliers as practical. In other words, they may put their own financial interests ahead of your needs. A recent poll in *Travel Weekly*, a leading trade publication, revealed that more than a third of travel agents admit that commission level is a major reason they recommend one tour to clients over another.

Most travel pros will not answer questions about commission overrides. To check whether an agent is biased toward a supplier, ask why he or she recommended a specific tour operator or airline, and judge whether the answer makes sense. Then shop around at other agencies to compare prices and choices. Once you come to trust an agent, you can skip the homework.

What type of computer reservation system (CRS) does the agent use?

In the late 1970s, airlines introduced computerized pricing systems, called yield management, which have revolutionized airline reservations and sales. These proprietary programs allow carriers to match unsold seats to demand, hour by hour. When a fare war is raging, airlines may make as many as 200,000 fare changes in a single day.

Travel agents use four major computer reservation systems: American Airlines-owned Sabre System; United's Apollo; Continental's System One; and Worldspan, owned jointly by Delta, TWA and Northwest. As a result, your best fare on major airlines will come from a diligent agent, not from calling airlines directly. But be alert for agents who always punch up the same airline.

The U.S. Department of Transportation is currently reworking the rules to prevent the CRS from favoring an owner-airline. What's more, the states are on the case. Attorneys general in 27 states announced that they are monitoring the development of a new version of Worldspan, due on-line in 1993, to make sure the system is not biased toward its three owner-airlines.

Also, some no-frills airlines, like Southwest, do not list fares on any CRS. To consider those fares, ask your agent to call the airlines directly.

Will the agent take time for a creative computer search?

To find the lowest fare, an agent must log a lot of time on the CRS. Make sure he or she uses direct access, which taps into the airline's main computer system to get the most up-to-the-minute information. A hard-working agent will also explain that you can nab a better deal by shifting your departure by a day or a few hours, or by flying into a different airport. For example, it recently cost $420 to fly round trip from New York's La Guardia to Los Angeles' LAX airport. If you booked from JFK to Orange County airport (a 45-minute drive from L.A.), however, the price dropped to $298.

Most agents will also negotiate with consolidators — the wholesale brokers that purchase discounted airline tickets in bulk.

Business fliers and last-minute travelers can benefit from an agent who specializes in "back to back" or "hidden city" fares, in which you get off the plane at the connecting city rather than at the last leg of a flight. Hidden-city deals are not illegal per se, but airlines say that those tricks break their rules. As a result, airlines have begun to monitor some routes — such as New York to San Antonio via Dallas — to discourage such ploys. If caught, you'll end up paying full fare. On back-to-back tickets, which don't break any rules, you save money by purchasing two round-trip tickets, which include a Saturday night stay, rather than one round-trip, full-fare coach ticket at midweek peak prices.

If the fare drops after you purchase your ticket, will the agent re-issue a nonrefundable ticket for the better price?

In most cases, agents can reissue such a ticket if, say, a fare war breaks out. They may resist, though, because they must then refund part of their commission to the airline.

Does the agent have an automatic fare-checker program?

Designed to beat the yield management system, these are new computer programs that can constantly search for the lowest price. Last May, for instance, American Airlines tried to put a damper on this technology by charging travel agents for extensive searches, but computer whizzes simply sidestepped the problem by reducing the number of computer checks.

You probably get the best fare by buying a ticket at least two weeks in advance. But if you need a last-minute flight, a fare-checker system can be a real boon. Most agencies reserve the technology for corporate clients.

What happens if the agency goes bust or if the airline or tour operator goes belly up?

Only seven states require travel agencies to provide any kind of consumer protection against their going out of business, such as a bond or an escrow account: California, Hawaii, Illinois, Iowa, Oregon, Rhode Island and Washington. This protection is very limited, however. For instance, when Apollo Travel in San Pedro, California, went bankrupt last July, among its creditors were an estimated 300 clients claiming losses of approximately $900,000.

The same is true for suppliers. The agency is not liable if an airline or tour operator folds before you depart, as long as the agent has correctly forwarded the funds and can prove it checked out the operator somewhat.

One way to protect yourself is to use a credit card to pay for travel expenses. Federal law allows you to dispute an item charged on your card for which you didn't receive the service or product. Usually you must submit a written claim to the issuing bank within 60 days of receiving your statement, though some banks are more flexible. If you're paying in advance for a trip, try to pay only the deposit, then deliver full payment 45 days before your scheduled departure.

Most of the time, a savvy agent will be your best source for travel deals. It may take some work to find one, but it's an investment that can pay off for years.

How You Can Test-Fly a Travel Agent

To learn what you can expect from a travel pro, we asked a dozen agents to plan two vacations for a family of four (kids aged eight and 12). When shopping for an agent, you can try a similar, scaled-down audition. To test value, six were asked to find the best price for a four-night trip to Florida's Disney World. To rate creative ability, we asked the other six to plan a seven-night ski package anywhere in Colorado. The trips were to originate from New York City during the first week of February 1992.

In this test of a cross section of small firms, national chains and tour packagers, we found that enthusiasm and knowledge differed sharply, even within the same company. Most agents scored well on package price but fumbled the all-important details, such as the cost of ski lessons or the exact location of the hotel. Our Disney request brought quotes ranging from $1,821 to $2,398. For Colorado, all but one agent came in on budget. Here's what else we found:

Disney World

We asked for a real bargain, including air fare, passes to area theme parks, rental car or transfers, and a moderately priced hotel as close to Disney World as possible.

- **The hotel.** Despite the Orlando area's 77,500 hotel rooms, four of our six agents checked us into Disney's 2,112-room, budget Caribbean Beach Resort. "It's a good choice, but only one of several in the same category," says Mary Mitchell, Travel Weekly's Disney World correspondent, who reviewed the agents' picks for us. In fact, two newer Disney properties, Port Orleans and Dixie Landing, offer identical rates. The lack of options suggests that the agents "haven't kept current," says Mitchell.

- **Location.** For Disney devotees, staying close to the Magic Kingdom is heaven. But when we asked agents about hotel proximity to the park gates, they fed us a few fantasies: one, for instance, described the Holiday Inn Lake Buena Vista as the hotel "closest to the park." It's actually three miles away.

- **Getting around.** Only one agency, Thomas Cook, wisely advised against a rental car if we stayed at a Disney hotel. Mitchell notes: "Disney's transport system is a master at moving people." The others, she says, should have at least warned us about Disney's parking charges ($4 a day) and distant lots.

- **Activities.** Although we asked about water theme parks, Carlson Travel Network was the only agency to point out that early February's 65°F to 70°F might be a little chilly for getting wet and wild.

Rocky Mountain Ski Vacation

For our winter getaway, besides specifying a budget of $3,500, including air fare, we asked for a

Colorado resort suited to downhill novices. We wanted all the features that agents could include — such as lift tickets lessons, rental car or transfers.

- **The resort.** Claire Walter, author of four ski guidebooks, approved of the five agents who suggested Steamboat, Crested Butte or Silver Creek. "Each had a good idea for a family of beginners," notes Walter, who considered the terrain, ski schools and lift prices. The exception was Snowmass, near Aspen, which not only came in $137 over budget but also crammed the family into a one-room condo. Responds the agency: "The condo is quite spacious, and we thought Aspen would be fun even if the family didn't like to ski."

- **Lifts and lessons.** Only one agent managed to cover both lift tickets and lessons. And one agency that sells ski packages to consumers and to other agents, failed to include lift tickets at all. Explains the agency, "Normally we don't include those extras because they don't provide commissions for the retail agents we service."

- **Package perks.** Three agents who recommended Steamboat touted the resort's "Kids Ski Free" program. But two of them didn't mention that only the lifts, not the lessons, are free. Since our kids were novices, reminds Walter, we could still have had to enroll them in ski school at a cost of $45 each a day.

Chapter 1 — Article Two
Diary of a First-Year Agent
Fun! Glamour! Foreign Intrigue!
(Stress! Crazy Clients! "Help!")

By Shelia McKinnie-Teel

How far have you come since your first day on the job? Compare your progress to that of novice agent Shelia McKinnie-Teel, whom we asked to keep a yearlong diary of her entry into the travel life. Before she enrolled in the Central Florida Academy of Travel in Orlando (where she graduated at the head of her class), Shelia had only the typical outsider's impression of the travel profession, "Gee, that looks like fun. Little did she know …

December 13, 1989

Here I am, a college graduate with degrees in nursing and elementary education, looking for a new career. After years of unsatisfying shift-work and no weekends off, I have reached a point in life where I can choose a job that really interests me. Being a travel agent seems both challenging and exciting — like having a different job every day of the week.

So, today is the big day: travel-school graduation. Goodbye to three months of intense work, computer training, memorizing world maps and those darn city codes, and worrying about the ever-dreaded FIT project (creating a 14-day itinerary without overlooking a detail). I bet we came up with enough memory tricks to fill a book. Now it's time to go out into the real world.

January 8, 1990

I've had four interviews. Everyone wants either an outside-sales person (which I've turned down because I don't relish the idea of pounding the pavement) or a gofer to deliver tickets and open mail (which is not what I went to school for). Today I go to a small family-owned agency that's looking for a full-time agent recently out of school. As the owner reads my resume I wait for him to ask, "Why are you changing careers again?" But he doesn't. He says he'll get in touch with me.

January 12

The family agency calls, "Can you come to work Monday?" I guess I'm on my way.

January 15

Today I start a new job and a new career. The first thing my boss asks me is, "Do you know how to quote military fares?" I look at him, look at the computer, and respond, "No." He explains that since we are located near a Navy base, we receive a lot of calls from recruits going home on leave, most of whom travel on military discounts the same day they call. So I need to learn to give fare quotes over the phone quickly. I feel as though I'm back in school.

As my co-worker gives out quote after quote over the phone, I practice pulling up schedules, hoping I won't have to answer the phone, not today. I thought that being first in my travel-school class would mean that I'd be able to keep pace with other agents — wrong! After just one day, I see that this is a business you can only learn hands on. No matter how smart you are, you soon discover that you aren't as smart as you think!

January 16

Tell me again, how do I sign in? How do I pull up my queues? My phone rings. An anxious customer wants the fare for a flight this afternoon. I write down the information and ask if I can call her back in a few minutes. She says no, she'll wait. Panic! After five minutes of pulling up schedules, I find the fare she wants. I can tell by her voice that she is tired of waiting. I apologize for the delay using that old trade secret: *Boy, these computers are slow today.* After I hang up, I realize that I just made my first sell!

I practice using the computer and make a cheat sheet of the basic commands to keep at my desk.

January 17

I get my first call from a corporate account. The secretary is so nice when she learns that I am new — she boosts my ego by telling me that I am doing a great job and that I should call her when I have all the information. The perfect client.

Now … how do I do a first-class upgrade using frequent-flier miles? How do I insert hotel and car rental info into a flight itinerary? My cheat sheet looks more like a cheat *book*. My co-worker, however, comes to my rescue. He ought to have his salary doubled — since he's doing the work of two agents.

January 19

I feel as though I've been thrown into a den with a ferocious lion — a.k.a. my computer — that's waiting to devour me if I make one mistake. First thing this morning, a client asks if she can speak to someone who can get the job done faster. There goes my confidence. I now know I won't become America's number-one travel agent overnight.

January 22

Week two. I'm more relaxed. I am trying to organize a group cruise to the Bahamas for a friend and his co-workers. I call the cruise company to get all the info for booking and hold 15 cabins, then I make a presentation to the group and everyone seems interested. I feel optimistic about this sale. I have no problem dealing with the public — it's just the office machinery that I can't master.

January 23

When I call to get a booking number for my group cruise, the rate has changed. So I have to shift the date of the trip to keep the same price. No one told me to get a booking number on the first call. Since the office is busy today, there's no chance to get help from anyone. I feel really incompetent.

January 24

I wish we'd spent more time in school developing selling techniques and dealing with the public. My boss tells me that it will take about a year to feel comfortable at that. This is going to be the longest year of my life.

January 30

I've been designated brochure filer. This prestigious job entails filing hundreds of brochures that come in daily. As the new agent you get all of the great office duties that no one else wants.

January 31

My first big sell! A $1,200 airline ticket. I wanted to get everything just right, so when the client asked me to double-book his flight on the same airline, just different times of the day, I did. *Mistake* — especially when you call the airline to ask about the booking. After a stern lecture from the airline agent, I learned my lesson about double-booking.

February 7

I'm getting better at military tickets. The only bad part is that the people are always calling from pay phones, so it's important to get all of the information correct — you don't get a second chance with these sales.

February 15

A lady calls for a round-trip ticket for Boston. She also wants the cheapest fare on the market, which happens to be for nonstops only, but they are sold out. I can get her on a connection flight, however, for just $5 more than the cheapest fare. No good, she tells me. She needs to transport the cremated remains of a loved one, and she doesn't want to change planes and risk dropping them in an airport. What can I say? She takes the train.

I start my second month with great anticipation! As a new agent I'm probably looking at the business through rose-colored glasses, yet for the first time in my working life I wake up looking forward to the day ahead. Everyone tells me that after the newness wears off and the stress sets in, I will change my mind.

February 20

I'm cleaning out files and re-ordering brochures. I try to read everything that comes in, but I'm beginning to realize that's impossible. A client wants to go to a country that I can't even pronounce. After an hour of searching, I find the cheapest fare available — $1,800. The caller informs me that the fare is too high and we are making too much commission, so she'll call the airline herself for a cheaper price. (Be my guest!)

February 23

I've gone to so many trade shows this week that I can't remember the last time I watched the evening news. I'm usually at work by 8:30 a.m. and not home again until 9 p.m. Maybe this is too much of a good thing.

My co-worker always seems so busy. He's in charge of queues. He checks all the records each day and looks for changes in flight schedules and prices. And I thought I was getting the hang of things merely by pulling up a schedule to sell a ticket.

There are so many things I see in my data manual that I haven't learned, and there's little extra time to practice. So I learn things when I need them — which provides plenty of opportunity for mistakes.

March 5

For the first time I regret my career choice. A client calls to say that a friend found a much cheaper fare to St. Thomas than I had given her yesterday. I agree that yesterday's price did seem rather high and tell her that I'd like to research other dates to try to find a better one. She agrees and seems satisfied. But a co-worker overhears our conversation and asks me if I've ever been taught never to tell a client that a price is too high. Hmmm. Service the people or the pocketbook? I want my customers to know that I will give them the best price I can and don't mind telling them so. I know that the bigger the sale, the more profit for the agency, but how many clients will give us repeat sales if they think they can get a better deal somewhere else. I give clients what they ask for.

March 6

There are so many things I still don't know. As in any busy office, there just isn't time for the boss to show me the ropes. I tip my hat to all agency managers who hire new agents. We can be more of a hindrance than a help at times.

I still keep my cheat sheet close by and use it daily. I wonder when this job will start to click.

March 7

Lonely hearts club. A gentleman comes in, and seeing an old England poster on the wall, proceeds to tell me about his experiences during World War II. He spends an hour at my desk talking about the war, his family, his car repairs, and the recent death of his wife of 30 years. I know he's not looking to buy — just to talk. I'm not so busy so I listen. He says he has plenty of time on his hands and would like to travel, so I give him some brochures. Who knows, maybe he'll take a trip someday.

March 13

Mr. and Mrs. Seasoned Traveler walk in. He's been around the world, and he wants to go again. Everything I come up with look greats to him but is of no interest to his wife. After an hour, he finally says, "This is what I want, and this is what we are going to take." I was patient, professional, and helpful — and this time it paid off! A fantastic sale! As they leave, he mentions that he's traveled with the chosen tour company before and was dissatisfied with the service, so he hoped this trip would be better. Now I will have to worry about this couple for three months until they get back from Europe.

March 20

I'm beginning to feel comfortable with walk-in clients. Today a lady comes in looking for a Las Vegas package. After checking with several tour companies, I find three prices for the same trip. She chooses the most expensive one. I feel good because I not only made a good sale, but I also gave my customer options. I could never be a high-pressure salesperson. I look at the individual and try to sum up his buying ability. I know I will be wrong sometimes, but at least I won't be known as a rip-off agent.

March 23

I've been told about house accounts and outside-salesperson accounts, but where does helping another agent fit in? I'm working on an emergency sale when I receive a long-distance call from another client. My co-worker isn't busy, so he completes my sale — and takes the credit. I admit, I was irritated for a moment, until I remembered how much he's helped me.

It strikes me that in all job situations, especially sales, the competitive spirit comes out. Everyone wants to be number one or look good to the boss. I've heard several envious comments about the unusual number of international sales I've made this week. But I'm here to do my best, because the more sales I make, the more the entire company will profit.

March 30

Shoppers, shoppers! I feel like Bob Barker on *The Price Is Right*. Everyone is looking for a bargain, and nobody is ready to buy.

April 3

A perfect transaction. A repeat customer wants reservations for a family trip to Europe next month. No questions about air fares. Just book it. And she says she'll take whatever kind of rental car is available. This is my kind of client.

April 11

It's common knowledge that when agents leave an agency, their clients follow them — the *good* clients, that is. The others keep coming back. Today an irritated man stormed into the office and walked directly to my desk (which used to belong to someone else), demanding satisfaction regarding a previous transaction. He did not stop to see if I was the same person that he had dealt with before. I, of course, had no idea what was going on. My boss came to the rescue as I sat in shock. Once satisfied, the man left without even acknowledging that I was in the room, much less that he had yelled at the wrong person. And to think that I was told this would be a prestigious job!

April 12

Here's the difference between pleasure travel and business travel. If the client's paying for it, it has to be cheap, cheap, cheap. If the company's paying, it must be first class all the way.

April 17

Mr. Seasoned Traveler, the man who booked my first big sale, returns threatening to cancel. His wife (who didn't want to go in the first place) has been talking to friends who are also going to Europe — for a much lower price. It doesn't matter that they are staying in roach motels while my clients will sleep in five-star hotels or that the friends are not traveling by air-conditioned motor coach. I explain all the differences between the tours and remind him that he is accustomed to traveling in style. He appears satisfied. Their departure is still a month away. I just hope his wife doesn't talk to many more friends.

April 19

I receive several calls from people who have been referred by previous clients. Maybe I am starting to build a clientele.

April 23

A secretary calls to inform me that she knows that I am "supposed to be a travel agent" but that she would like to straighten me out on a few things. Apparently, a gentleman who sat next to her boss on a plane last night purchased his ticket for $100 less than her boss had paid, and he is quite upset! It was my duty to see that her boss had the lowest price available, she continues, oblivious to the facts that he had booked the trip eight days before departure and had requested a specific routing and specific travel times. I explain that I do not control the air fares and that I can only sell available seats. This doesn't satisfy her, so I decide to write a letter to her boss to explain the situation. I hope I haven't lost the account.

May 22

A woman wants to send her two children, ages 6 and 8, on a trip alone. I explain that most airlines will not let small children change planes without an adult. She doesn't seem to be listening — she just wants her kids on the plane. I then tell her that for an extra fee, some carriers will escort her children from one connection to the other, but she doesn't want to spend any extra money. Finally I tell her that I do not want to be responsible for her children getting lost in an airport. She decides to call another agency. Maybe I didn't handle this very well.

June 13

Find that city! A client wants to bring her brother to the U.S. from Europe. I ask for the city of departure. I've never heard of it, so I ask her what city it's near. She doesn't know but promises to call her brother to find out. He doesn't know either — he's only lived there for two months. I tell her I will find out and call her back with the price. First resource, *OAG*. Second, *World Atlas*. Third, the airline. Nobody could find the town. I felt dumb in the beginning, but even when the airlines couldn't locate it, I felt better. Decided to brush up on my world geography.

June 18

Two clients bound for Europe on a shoestring come in for hotel reservations. Their choices do not have American booking services, so I have to call overseas to reserve rooms. After two hours, they leave happy. But the phone calls cost more than the commissions we will get, so our company won't make any money. Maybe I'm carrying this customer satisfaction thing too far.

June 22

I'm on the line with an airline-reservation agent, trying to request a children's meal. After five minutes, the agent locates the record, and I request a hot dog — dead silence! I can hear papers being shuffled and am told to "Hold, please." So I sit listening to Mozart while the phone receiver makes a permanent indentation in my ear. Finally, the agent comes back on the line, "Hamburger, hot dog, or PBJ?" I select a hot dog for the second time, then listen to more Mozart. She finally returns to let me know that the meals are confirmed. Do I dare ask for advance seat assignments?

June 25 to 29

I cruise to the Bahamas with six friends who have never cruised before.

Everything starts off great. The ship is popular for short cruises and usually booked to capacity. On an agent's tour I took last week, I saw that the lounges were beautiful, but the staterooms needed some improvements. No matter, said my friends, we wouldn't be spending much time in them anyway. Their main concern was that this was the best cruise for the money.

As usual, you get what you pay for.

Having been served prime rib on my tour, I raved about the food — *wrong*. Our first dinner was below fast-food standards. The air conditioning didn't work in one of the cabins. It rained all day at the first port of call, and we didn't get off the ship. The public toilets backed up. The crew's entertainment was a repeat performance every night. Topping things off, on the last night the cabin steward told one of the guests that the cruise line did not pay him a salary and that the only money he made was from tips, and that he had a wife and three children to support in another country.

I doubt that I'll have any repeat business from this group. How can I recommend trips to people when I've never been there? I would hate for this to happen again.

July 2

My desk is a mound of unopened mail, refunds, and paperwork.

July 23

As a service to our clients, we offer free delivery. My boss usually delivers all the military tickets for clients at the Navy base. Today he told a young seaman when and where to meet him. After the fellow paid for his ticket, he picked up his bags and began to walk toward my boss's car. When asked where he was going, he replied, "Well, you are going to take me to the airport, aren't you?" My boss explained that the ticket delivery was free but that we were not a shuttle service. The seaman persisted, "Aren't you a full-service agency?"

August 1

Sometimes I want to scream! Eight months ago I thought everything was always going to be rosy — what a joke! A very demanding business client calls three times today to change his reservations. I had to rebook them over and over. Are some sales worth the effort? I know that attitude won't make the company any money. This has proven to be a profession with quite a few frustrating moments.

Pet peeve? People who call you for visa information for a vacation they are taking next week that was booked through another agency.

August 14

I spend most of the day writing down phone numbers and addresses of local businesses that might be potential customers. I've been here eight months and don't have an account of my own. It's hard to go out and look for business when you have to be in the office all day.

August 17

Mr. and Mrs. Seasoned Traveler, my first big sale, call to say they had a wonderful time in Europe. Though they went two months ago, they had put off calling because of the problems we went through booking the trip, when they almost canceled twice under the influence of their friends. But it turned out well. Maybe I shouldn't be so hesitant in doing follow-up calls. After all, if someone had a bad time, I'd surely hear from them immediately.

August 20

Things are still unusually slow. Air fares go up one day and down the next. I spend most of the day writing cash refunds for previously purchased tickets. I decide to go through my files and see if there are any other customers who are entitled to a refund. This is a lot of extra work and an owner's nightmare, but my boss thinks that the customers' interests should always come first. I think he is right.

August 21

A client wants to go to India, but not via Europe due to the Mid-East crisis. This means routing her through Malaysia, which entails several stops and plane changes. Our customers are very concerned about traveling outside the U.S. I think that's part of the reason business is so slow.

August 29

Today is the worst day of my career. I know it is going to be busy, since all air fares are going up at midnight. The phones ring nonstop, I get several walk-ins, and then the computers go down. Technology fails us. In school, manual bookings seemed simple — "use the *OAG* and your travel planner and you can do anything." What a giant misconception! When will 5 o'clock come?

September 14 to 29

Vacation? Seven-night cruise to Alaska, one week in Washington State.

I'm Jane Q. Public on this trip — but looking at things through a travel agent's eyes. Upon arriving in Vancouver, exhausted after the long trip from Orlando through Denver and Spokane, my companion and I go through customs and decide to share a limo with two women going to the same hotel. After the driver drops us off and is paid, he comes running back after us holding out his business card. We accept it and thank him again. While we're laughing and wondering whether all cabbies in Canada are this friendly, it dawns on me that this novice travel agent has just tipped him $25 for a 10-minute ride. He would probably like to have a carload of us every day!

The ship is above all expectations — magnificent crew, food, cabins, and scenery. You do get what you pay for. But just because we're travel agents doesn't mean our trips are postcard-perfect. Yes, I lost my luggage. (Luckily, on the return home!)

October 5

Today a client wants to know what seat she sat in on a flight that she took two months ago. She lost a piece of jewelry and needs the exact seat number before the airline will give it to her. Luckily we keep records of everything, including copies of itineraries. It takes me about an hour, but I find the information. She calls the airline and gets her jewelry back. Another satisfied customer.

October 8

Back from my first weekend fam trip. It was really a hotel inspection, and the hotel was nice enough to allow us to bring a guest. My companion and I were given a lovely oceanview room. The following morning, I went to the required agents-only breakfast alone and noticed that several other agents had brought their husbands. Then after our seminar and hotel tour, one agency manager in our group asked for a room upgrade so she could get a balcony. It really disturbs me that when agents are given the opportunity to travel and stay at nice properties, they abuse the privilege or take advantage of the hotel's generosity by requesting changes. Some industry employees need a refresher course in professionalism.

October 17

A lot of bookings for Christmas travel today. Especially around the holidays, it seems, reading the rules in order to obtain a certain air fare is like unscrambling a puzzle. One morning you — or worse, your client — open the paper to find rock-bottom prices around the world. Needless to say, you need a magnifying glass to read all of the restrictions printed at the bottom of the page. I think restrictions should be printed before the prices.

October 19

Today's client wants to buy tickets for a convention six months from now. "Will the air fares go down?" he asks. It still amazes me that the general public expects the travel agent to know everything about anything related to travel.

October 23

A client calls to say that she and her husband had a wonderful time in Europe. It really brightens my day when I hear positive feedback.

October 30

Today I get my commission for a $1,500 car rental: $3.50. When I call the company to ask why I did not receive my full commission, the response is that my client only kept the vehicle for one day. After pondering the situation, I decide to call my client to find out how the trip was. She had a wonderful time, she says; the only problem was that their minivan wasn't big enough, so they had to drive to another town to pick up a larger one — but at no extra charge and without having to sign any papers. My next step? Inform the rental agency and try to get my due commission. After several calls they agree to remit it. I know we lose a lot of commission by these foul-ups.

November 15

A lot of military calls. It seems like everyone is being shipped out for duty in the Middle East.

December 13

A client wants to take a Christmas cruise. Why do people wait until the last minute?

December 14

Everything has been falling into place lately, though some days are so hectic I feel like screaming. I've learned a lot, yet I still have far to go. Everything changes constantly: computer techniques, rates, rules, and most frustrating, people changing their minds.

The whole world is looking for a bargain, and they don't understand if you can't find them one. I've come to realize that you must go the extra mile to make a sale, and then catch your breath and *keep* giving your all in order to maintain the client. There's always another agent to grab your customers away.

The biggest pitfall, though, has been stress. You either learn to cope with it or you get out of the business. Luckily, I've been able to handle it well — thanks to my great team of co-workers who, despite a few ups and downs, have always been there to teach me.

Next year? I plan to enroll in a CTC program to bolster my abilities. I'm also looking into teaching at a travel school. And I think I'll continue to be satisfied at this small full-service agency. Job status and pay scale may not be great, but what other job would let you travel around the world in eight hours?

I think I've finally found the career for me!

Reprinted with permission from *Travel Life* magazine, March/April, 1991, a publication of Whittle Communications

The Travel Industry -
Past, Present, and Future
Chapter 1

End of Chapter Review

Name _____ Date _____

Directions: Fill in the blanks.

1. What place does Thomas Cook hold in the history of the travel industry?

    _____

    _____

    _____

2. Describe the beginning of modern commercial aviation.

    _____

    _____

    _____

3. Explain the relationship of the hotel porter to the early development of the travel industry.

    _____

    _____

    _____

4. How can agents get the most value out of a fam trip?

    _____

    _____

5. List two guidebook series and discuss their specialties.

    _____

    _____

    _____

Answers to End of Chapter Review Questions

1. Thomas Cook is often credited as the first travel agent. He organized group tours and established the principle of agent commission. He introduced the voucher system.

2. In the United States commercial aviation got its start after World War I. The post office awarded contracts to fly the mail. Manufacturers turned attention to developing aircraft for commercial use. Passengers were soon hitching rides on the mail planes. The federal government began regulating aviation in 1926.

3. Porters would purchase tickets for hotel guests in return for compensation from the railroads and tips from the customers — providing a service.

4. Fam trips can best be enjoyed by careful planning and setting objectives.

5. Answers will vary. Guidebooks mentioned in the chapter are Frommer, Baedeker, Insight, Fodor, Michelin, Birnbaum, and Best Places to Stay.

Destination Geography
Chapter 2

Review Chapter Objectives
- Discuss three types of geography
- Identify map terminology
- Relate the differences between weather and climate
- Discuss some important regional sightseeing attractions in the United States
- Identify popular worldwide tourist destinations

Review Vocabulary
- Continent
- Cultural geography
- Gulf
- Index
- Island
- Latitude
- Legend
- Locational geography
- Longitude
- Physical geography
- Relief
- Scale

Destination Careers
- Cartographer
- Climatologist
- Convention and Visitors Bureau Representative
- Tourist Bureau Representative
- Travel Photographer
- Travel Writer

Transparencies
- Chapter outline
- Types of geography
- Map terminology

Destination Geography
Chapter 2 Outline

I. Types of Geography

    A. Locational

    B. Physical

    C. Cultural

II. Destinations

    A. The United States

    B. Canada

    C. Mexico

    D. The Caribbean

    E. Central and South America

    F. Europe

    G. Asia and the Pacific

    H. Africa

Types of Geography

- **Locational**

  "Where Is It?"

  "How Do You Get There?"

- **Physical**

  "What Is the Weather Like?"

  "When Is the Best Time to Go?"

- **Cultural**

  "What Is There to See and Do at the Destination?"

  "What Is the Food Like?"

Map Terminology

- **Title**

  What the Map Is Going to Be About

- **Scale**

  How Much Detail Will the Map Cover

- **Relief**

  The Altitude of the Area

- **Legend**

  An Explanation of the Symbols

- **Index**

  A Guide to Where Information
  Can Be Located

- **Compass points**

  North, South, East, and West

Answers to Textbook Review Questions

1. **Using the three themes of geography — physical, cultural, locational — how would you describe your hometown to a potential visitor?**
   Answers will vary.

2. **What features distinguish these national parks: Yellowstone, The Everglades, and Acadia?**
   Yellowstone - the first and largest national park, it is best known for the geyser "Old Faithful."
   The Everglades - a subtropical Florida wilderness, home to many rare and endangered species of birds, plants, reptiles, and mammals.
   Acadia - New England's only national park, it offers spectacular scenic drives that pass jagged cliffs and coves coupled with inland mountains and forests.

3. **Name some areas in the United States and Europe that are popular for their wineries.**
   California (Napa and Sonoma)
   New York (The Finger Lakes region)
   Washington and Oregon
   Europe (France, Italy, Spain, Germany, Portugal)

4. **How would you distinguish between Cancun and Guadalajara as tourist destinations?**
   Cancun - Mexico's premier luxury resort in the Caribbean; it has golf, great beaches, watersports, and shopping.
   Guadalajara - Often used as a base for exploring the country's colonial past. It blends the modern with the traditional. It's rich in handicrafts.

5. **Do all the Caribbean islands offer the same experience? Explain.**
   Answers may vary. Although most people think of the Caribbean as all sun, sand, and sea, the area offers an endless variety of cultures, languages, cuisines, and history.

Answers to Discussion Topics

Climate
A. Areas of the world with Mediterranean-type climates
   1. West Coast of California
   2. West Coast of Chile
   3. West Coast of South Africa
   4. Around the Mediterranean Sea
   5. West Coast of Australia - Perth

B. **Vegetation** needing little water. Such flora as cactus, evergreen trees, evergreen oaks, flowering scrubs, and brush-covered landscape. The shrubby growth is called maqui in Europe and chaparral in California.
   Fauna - Man has eliminated much. Snakes and insects remain.
   Mountainous - A typical scene in many Mediterranean lands shows orange trees and palms on the coastal plain with snow-covered mountains in the background. An exception is Western Australia where mountains are lacking.
   Rainfall - A temperate climate with dry, hot summers, wet winters.
   Temperature - Range is small. Summer temperatures on the coast are mild, inland hot. Winter temperatures on the coast are mild, inland cooler. Frost is rare.
   Winds - Westerly, can be strong, especially off the sea.

C. This combination of mild winters and much sun makes these Mediterranean climates excellent resort areas.

Cultural Geography
Answers will vary.

The South Pacific
The South Pacific islands are comprised of islands from low coral atolls to high volcanic formations. Polynesia is known for sun, sand, and surf. Melanesia is good for adventurous travelers because of their remoteness. Micronesia are for those seeking an out of the way destination.

Itinerary
Answers will vary.

Answers to Workbook Exercises

Worksheet 2-1

Continent	A large land mass of the earth
Cultural geography	The study of the division of the world into groups and contrasting societies
Gulf	A large body of salt water that is bordered by a curved shoreline
Index	A guide to where information can be located
Island	A body of land surrounded by water
Latitude	Parallel lines that measure distances north and south of the equator
Legend	An explanation of what symbols the map will use
Locational geography	The study of where countries, regions, attractions, etc., are located
Longitude	Lines that measure distances east and west of the prime meridian.
Physical geography	The study of climate and the description of terrain.
Relief	The altitude of the area
Scale	How much area and how much detail a map will cover

Worksheet 2-2

1. Legend
2. Relief
3. Index
4. Longitude
5. Cartography
6. Scale
7. Atlas
8. Latitudes

Worksheet 2-3

1. New York
2. Virginia
3. Kansas
4. Oregon
5. Salt Lake City
6. New Mexico
7. Ohio
8. Choose from: Valley Forge State Park, Pennsylvania Dutch Country, and the Poconos.
9. The Midwest
10. South Dakota
11. Oahu
12. San Francisco
13. Boston
14. Michigan
15. Yellowstone
16. California
17. Montana
18. Alaska
19. Louisville
20. Idaho

Worksheet 2-4

1. Newfoundland, Nova Scotia, Prince Edward Island, and New Brunswick
2. Toronto
3. Choose from: Shopping, Underground Montreal, Notre Dame Basilica, Place des arts, Man and His World
4. Quebec City
5. Prince Edward Island
6. Choose from: The world's largest mall and indoor amusement center, Space and Science Center, Klondike Days Carnival.
7. Halifax

Worksheet 2-5

1. The northern section has a dry desert-like climate, and the south has a wet tropical climate.

2. Oaxaca

3. Negril, Montego Bay, Ocho Rios

4. Bermuda

5. St. Thomas, St. Croix, St. John

6. Aruba, Bonaire, Curacao

7. Sint Maarten, St. Martin

Worksheet 2-6

1. Guatemala, Belize, Honduras, El Salvador, Nicaragua, Costa Rica, Panama

2. Quito — sights include colonial buildings, religious art, Spanish architecture

3. La Paz, Bolivia

4. It's the only remaining habitat of substantial size where man has conserved huge quantities of wildlife.

5. Rio de Janeiro

6. Bogota

Worksheet 2-7

1. Finland

2. Vienna

3. Belgium, the Netherlands, and Luxembourg

4. Choose from: Buckingham Palace, Parliament, Westminster Abbey, Piccadilly, the Thames, and the Tower of London.

5. Answers will vary.

6. France, Italy, Spain

7. Spain and Portugal

Worksheet 2-8

1. Australia

2. Sydney. Choose from: the Sydney Opera House, harbour bridge, the Rocks.

3. Christchurch

4. Polynesia — French Polynesia, The Samoas, Tonga, and the Cook islands
   Melanesia — Fiji, New Caledonia, Vanuatu, Solomon islands, Papua New Guinea
   Micronesia — the Carolines, the Marianas, the Marshalls, the Republic of KiriBati, the Republic of Nauru

5. Rotorua

Worksheet 2-9

1. Bangkok

2. Delhi and New Delhi

3. Mt. Fuji

4. It was erected to protect China from northern Nomads. It can be distinguished from space.

5. Choose from: the Ginza, Asakusa, the Imperial Palace, and Ueno Park

Worksheet 2-10

1. D

2. A

3. A

4. D

5. A

6. A

7. C

8. B

9. D

10. C

11. B

12. B

13. C

14. A

15. A

16. D

17. B

18. D

19. A

20. D

Classroom Activities

1. Ask students to find a mystery location on their atlas by providing geographic clues. For example, consider providing: latitude and longitude, bodies of water, mountains or deserts, local customs, climate, time zones, language, and so on. After providing one or two examples, ask students to design their own mystery destination. This type of activity could be used as homework, an in-class review session, or quiz. As an in-class activity this works well if students are divided into teams so that the team requiring the fewest clues is declared the "winner."

2. Ask students to design a geographic trivia game for use in class. Divide the class into groups according to various areas of the world. As you cover different continents or countries, use the students' games as review activities. Consideration should be given to originality, depth of information, interest level, and so on. Again, teams can be used.

3. Bring in copies of *National Geographic* or *Traveler* and other local magazines such as *New York*, *Boston*, or *Rhode Island Monthly*. Ask students to compare these to typical travel sales magazines. How are they alike? How do they differ? What types of clients would be most interested in these magazines? How can agents capitalize on their offerings?

Articles

Chapter 2 — Article One
"Drawing the Line in Yosemite"
Ask students to provide a brief history of Yosemite. Ask students to research other national parks listed in the text, then compare Yosemite to these other examples. What makes each unique? What facilities are available in national parks? How are national parks protected?

Chapter 2 — Article Two
"Geographic Pursuits"
Provide copies of these articles. Why is geographic information so vital to travel agents? What type of geography is most important for the leisure client? For the business client? Why?

Chapter 2 — Article One

Drawing the Line in Yosemite
Tourism vs. Resource Preservation

By Susan Nolte Reid

Introduction

My husband and I had been looking forward to our trip to Yosemite for weeks. Six days long, it would only be a mini-vacation, but it represented a major respite from the stress and clamor that comes with living in the L.A. Basin. I didn't know very much about the park; I knew that it was less than one day's drive from California's and Nevada's major cities, so I expected it to be popular. I knew that some famous monuments were there: Half Dome, El Capitan, Bridalveil, and Yosemite Falls. And I knew that it would have mountains and streams, clear air and real trees — things that I wanted my eighteen-month-old son to become better acquainted with. So on a mild Saturday morning in June, we packed up our camping gear, diapers, and blankets and started what should have been an eight-hour drive.

Traveling with a baby made the drive longer than we expected, and we were disappointed that we would have to wait until the next morning to see the park's scenery. The sun was setting as we climbed the road that would lead over the mountains and into Yosemite Valley. No other headlights flashed past; we were alone on the road, wondering what sights were passing us by. There was no moon, but the stars were bright. Suddenly, looming out of the night, the three-thousand foot Sentinal Rock proved with awe-inspiring impact that Yosemite is too big to be hidden — even by darkness. My spine tingled as we drove past lacy, ethereal waterfalls and under enormous masses of stone. I suddenly felt the weight of rock and time, of the ancient and titanic forces that shaped this place. I could imagine what the first person must have felt who wandered into this magic land, and I felt a special kinship with every soul who was ever moved by this, one of Nature's grandest crescendos. I fell in love with Yosemite.

And then we drove into the campground.

There were lights and people and music and cars parked everywhere. The office was part of a large complex containing a store, laundromat, and showers. I stepped out of the car and felt like I was walking into a small town; the feeling of primeval wilderness had evaporated. The air was thick with woodsmoke and a migraine headache was starting to beat out a very urban rhythm inside my skull. We had made reservations to stay in a "housekeeping unit": a concrete and canvas lean-to with a small sleeping area containing cots, and a covered porch with a picnic table and electrical outlet to serve as kitchen and dining area. A partial stockade-type fence provided some privacy, something that was hard to come by in a compound containing nearly three hundred units. A heavy pall of smoke from over a hundred campfires obscured the stars, but did nothing to hide the numbers of people. As we drove several times around the complex looking for parking, I started to wonder: how does the Park absorb this kind of impact? I knew there were several other campgrounds, cabins, and lodges in the valley; how did the ecosystem withstand the numbers of visitors they represented? The infrastructure supporting the operation had to be enormous; what was the cost of all this development? And how did Yosemite come to be so heavily developed in the first place?

The History of Yosemite

Horace Greeley praised it as "the most unique and majestic of nature's marvels," unsurpassed by any other wonder like it "on earth." John Muir, naturalist writer and one of the founders of the environmental movement, wrote of its "noble walls ... all a-tremble with the thunder tones of the falling water," a place where "every rock in its walls seems to glow with life ... as into this one mountain mansion Nature had gathered her choicest treasures." Yosemite became an American icon, a symbol of national pride and spirit, almost immediately after its discovery.

Hunting down a band of "renegade" Indians, the Mariposa Battalion (a volunteer "militia" made up primarily of miners and traders) stumbled into the Yosemite Valley on March 27, 1851. Although a few explorers had seen it previously, none had circulated written descriptions of its astounding scenery.

Dr. Lafayette Bunnell, the battalion's physician and diarist, wrote of the "grandeur of the scene" and " ... the awe with which I beheld it ... . I found my eyes in tears with emotion."

The Yosemite Valley, seven miles long and about a mile wide, is the setting for some of the most spectacular scenery in the world, one amazing feature following after another. According to the Yosemite Natural History Association, there are just two other glacial valleys like it on earth, but only Yosemite is under government protection. Edged with sheer granite cliffs, the valley floor is four thousand feet above sea level, nestled in the High Sierras. Standing beside the Merced River, one can view familiar landmarks like the massive El Capitan to one side or the sheer, lacy drop of Bridalveil falls on the other. Round another bend in the river and you are rendered breathless by the spectacular, knife-edged grandeur of Half Dome rising forty-seven hundred feet above the trees, while Yosemite Falls' triple cascade plunges twenty four hundred thundering feet behind you. The Sentinel, North Dome, Vernal Falls, Royal Arches — at every turn there is something remarkable. Five of the world's highest waterfalls tumble from the park's granite cliffs. And geology is not its only treasure; Yosemite is home to over fifty rare or endangered plant and animal species. It contains three groves of giant sequoia — including the Mariposa Grove — with specimens up to twenty feet in diameter and over 2,700 years in age. This outstanding collection of features in one area makes Yosemite truly "one of the great wonders of the world."

Word of the spectacular valley and its accompanying grove of giant sequoias spread quickly. By the end of 1855, just four years after its initial exposure, 42 tourists had endured the dangerous and grueling 12-hour ride into the valley. By 1864, spurred by magazine articles, paintings, and photographs, the number of tourists had swelled to about seven hundred. To accommodate this influx, trails had been cut, meadows fenced for livestock, orchards planted and buildings erected. Concern over this private exploitation of a great natural resource spurred a few far-sighted conservationists to appeal to Congress.

Senator George H. Williams of Oregon, in support of the valley's preservation, wrote, "It stands unrivaled in its majesty, grandeur, and beauty ... . It is one of those magnificent developments of natural scenery in which all of the people of the country feel a pride and an interest, and to which their equal rights of access and enjoyment ought to be protected." And on July 30, 1864, Abraham Lincoln signed the Yosemite Land Grant deeding in trust to the state of California the incomparable valley for "public use, resort and recreation."

The 1864 grant was "the first recorded action by a government to set aside land for preservation in its natural state" and "is considered to be the foundation upon which all national and state parks were later established." Although Yellowstone, established eight years later, is considered the first National Park, Yosemite was the birthplace of the National Park concept and the world's first nature preserve.

In October 1890, Congress officially founded Yosemite National Park with the creation of a giant reserve around the valley to save the beautiful but fragile "fountain region above Yosemite, with its peaks, canyons, snow fields, glaciers, forests, and streams." In 1906, Congress consolidated the state preserve and national acreage into what are, basically the park boundaries we find today.

The Organic Act was passed in 1916, establishing the National Park Service, "To conserve the scenery and the natural and historic objects and the wildlife therein and to provide for the enjoyment of the same in such manner and by such means as will leave them unimpaired for the enjoyment of future generations." With this inherently contradictory mandate, the National Park Service attempts to provide for both the needs of visitors and the fragile ecosystem that that very visitation threatens. At the start of this century, however, most park supporters did not see any conflict between serving the public and preserving the resource.

Men like John Muir and the first Director of the Park Service, Stephen T. Mather, believed that popular support for the fledgling service needed to be cultivated. They believed that the future preservation of the national parks rested on the goodwill of those tourists who would come to experience what nature had to offer ... and then enjoy their stay. From the beginning, the Park Service emphasized visitor service, and development in the name of visitor use was encouraged as a means of creating a loyal constituency. Facilities were upgraded. Bridges, roads, and buildings were constructed to blend in with the natural surroundings. Often, in an attempt to create visual harmony and provide tourists with easy access, rustic stone and log edifices would be built virtually on top of major scenic features. As J. Horace McFarland, leader of the "City Beautiful" movement, put it, parks were "playgrounds" which should be "made comfortable" for the American public.

Parks were managed and marketed with the comfort and enjoyment of the public as their primary objective. According to a National Park Service brochure, "The American public in the late 1800s and early 1900s, viewed this nation as teeming with natural resources; conservation seemed unnecessary. No wonder that the people who campaigned and fought for the establishment of the first National Parks thought of them only as scenic recreational areas! Americans made a business of scenery. Some early park proponents wanted our national parks developed … in sufficient abundance to meet all demands. Lodges and chalets commanding all the best scenic viewpoints. The best and cheapest accommodations for hikers and motorists … . A strong philosophy of commercial development was a stimulus for creating a National Park Service."

In Yosemite, tourism and commercial development were established early and, to the consternation of present day planners, inextricably linked together. Use and preservation, concessionaires and government — the controversy over "drawing the line" stretches back to the very establishment of the park.

Use vs. Resource

According to Alfred Runte, environmental historian and authority on national park management, when the Yosemite Park Act was passed in 1864 it allowed "private individuals to apply for the privilege of building and operating tourist accommodations in the park. Leases to this effect were to be granted for ten-year intervals … . The irony was that Congress, having disallowed private ownership in the park, nonetheless openly promoted private investment in its facilities.. a major foundation of the park experiment had been grounded in contradiction. Individuals could still profit by promoting development; they simply could not acquire the attractions themselves … . With barely a pause for reflection, the nation had allowed business a legal means for exploiting the preserve."

Development proceeded at an ever accelerated pace. Between 1864 and 1870, almost five thousand tourists visited Yosemite. That was more than seven times the number accommodated between the valley's discovery in 1855 and the end of 1863. Ten years later, nearly twenty thousand tourists had descended into the awesome but fragile valley, and their effect was highly visible. Open meadows had been fenced to provide pasture for cattle and horses. Fields were plowed and sown with non-native varieties of hay, grain and other crops. Several hotels and businesses had been built, including a multitude of studios for both artists and photographers. A sawmill provided lumber for building and a blacksmith serviced the transportation sector (stagecoaches, horses, and mules). The ever-expanding infrastructure needed to support the valley's growth was causing permanent changes in the resource on which it relied.

As early as 1865 Fredrick Law Olmstead, landscape architect and designer of New York's Central Park, warned in a report to the Yosemite Park Commission that the primary responsibility of the valley's stewards was "preservation and maintenance as exactly as is possible of the natural scenery." Allowances for structures should be made only "within the narrowest limits consistent with the necessary accommodation of visitors" excluding "all constructions markedly inharmonious with the scenery or which would unnecessarily obscure, distort, or detract from the dignity of the scenery." He was nearly prescient in foreseeing the consequences of unguarded compromise between preservation and use. Laws were necessary to "prevent the unjust use by individuals , of that which is … public property," or managers would find themselves yielding "to the convenience, bad taste, playfulness, carelessness, or wanton destructiveness of present visitors." He foresaw that "in a century the whole number of visitors will be counted in the millions," and that the duty of the commission was to protect the "rights of posterity as well as of contemporary visitors." Now considered a classic, his report was ignored and suppressed. The commission asked William Hammond Hall, the state engineer, for a second report and received, in 1882, one more to their liking. Alfred Runte, in his environmental history of Yosemite, summarizes it this way: "Development of the valley had been forced by the commissioners; they were blameless for succumbing to 'necessary evils.' Yosemite Valley, as public land, must accommodate the public, including by adding those facilities that appeased popular social tastes."

New influxes of tourists required more accommodations and services, which encouraged more tourists, which required more development. Add to this equation the natural tendency of business to maximize profits, and the resulting promotion of the attraction multiplied the number of visitors and further increased pressures for expansion. Park managers did little to control this spiraling growth, and in many cases contributed to the problem. A popular park would bring prosperity to neighboring communities, and for the government, satisfied constituents meant continuing voter support. Park popularity was quantified by the number of visitors to the park, a barometer of accomplishment that was easy to comprehend. In the conflict between recreation, which was popular, and preservation, which required visitor restrictions, the government frequently sided with the visitor. To both concessionaires and management alike, increased visitation spelled success.

From the beginning, park officials and concessionaires shared two of the same goals: providing services for tourists and increasing visitation. Conflicts arose because both groups had additional priorities: preserving the resource and making a profit. The resource frequently lost because park managers had an inherent contradiction in their set of goals; increased visitation and tourist services negatively impact the resource. The concessionaires had a unified approach — happy tourists, plus more tourists, equals bigger profits — that put them in a stronger bargaining position. And bargain they did.

In theory, the government made strict rules which the concessionaires were required to follow, but the government never firmly established just what visitor services were necessary and appropriate and which were merely luxuries and not to be provided within the park. To the concessionaire, profits were made by providing as many services as possible. By delegating the operation of visitor services without establishing clear limits, the government was forever negotiating with persistent and motivated concessionaires. "Squeaky wheels" eventually were oiled and the "never take no for an answer" approach was responsible for much of the Curry Company's success.

The Curry Company

The most successful of Yosemite's concessions, Camp Curry was originally established in 1899 by David A. Curry and his wife Jennie, using a handful of tents on the valley floor directly under Glacier Point. The very first summer, Curry accommodated over three hundred guests and, by the end of the season, the number of tents in his campground had doubled. In subsequent years, with an emphasis on "family atmosphere," dogged persistence in pursuit of his goals, and a shrewd understanding of marketing and public relations, Curry's enterprise continued its phenomenal growth. An example of his showmanship and business acumen was the appropriation of the celebrated valley firefall. On summer evenings a bonfire would be lit on top of Glacier Point, and on a signal from below, the burning embers would cascade straight down the cliff wall, over fifteen hundred feet. Originally only a periodic and unorganized event, Curry established it as a regular tourist attraction and included it in his promotional material. The nightly spectacle became a park tradition, one of the high points of many visitors' stays, forever linked in their minds with Camp Curry.

As the business grew, Curry pressed park management for expansion of both the camp and the range of services provided. If turned down, Curry would go over the superintendent's head and petition the Interior Department, Congress, or the public directly, and would continue to persist with his requests until they were eventually granted. A successful businessman identifies what the public needs and fulfills that need; Curry was able to determine what the public wanted and convince management that it was a need. For example, in 1911 Curry asked for permission to sell fruit, photographic supplies, bread and pastries — all available from other vendors in the village a mile from camp — because it "requires too much exertion for 3,800 guests, staying an average of six or seven days each, to walk more than two miles every time they wish some little thing ... . " He repeated his request, adding additional services to the list until eventually the government relented. In 1915, Camp Curry was given permission for a bowling alley; billiard and pool tables; the operation of a motion-picture projector and stereopticon; the sale of fruit, bread, pastry, and tobacco; charging admission for dancing; and the sale of music and records published by the company.

According to Runte, "each 'need,' when introduced, took on a life of its own. The guest who found candy and swimming pools one year expected similar luxuries on the next visit. The possibility that one or more might undermine the purposes for which the park supposedly had been established seemed to elude even government officials. The issue of park control still begged for resolution, not only to strike a working balance for accommodations and services but also to ensure that increased development would not overwhelm the natural scene."

Soon golf courses and California's first ski resort expanded the tourist season in Yosemite, approved and endorsed in the name of increased visitation. Growing numbers of tourists required a greater number and broader range of accommodations. Under pressure from the Secretary of the Interior, the two largest concessions, Yosemite National Park Company and Curry Camping Company, were required to merge in 1925. The Park Service believed that by awarding a virtual monopoly on all accommodations and sales, regulation of the new organization, called the Yosemite Park and Curry Company, would be "easier and more direct." And by pooling their resources, more capital would be available for investment in major construction projects that the park seemed to need so badly. One result of the merger was the opening in 1927 of the sumptuous Ahwahnee Hotel, providing more "civilized" accommodations for the well-to-do. Yosemite was taking on more and more of the appearance of a resort, rather than a natural preserve.

Additional attractions sponsored by the concessionaires, became over time, an established part of the visitor experience, accepted as park traditions. The "bear shows" were a good example of how concessionaires, with the tacit approval of the park service, could subvert a natural resource to provide a tourist attraction. "Sanitary" garbage was placed at night on a platform lit to illuminate the antics of the feeding bears for the amusements of tourists on viewing stands. A small admission fee was charged and the show was a huge success: nearly two thousand visitors turned out for the demonstration on July 16, 1929.

Unfortunately, the resource was consistently paying for each of these promotional stunts. Obvious damage could be seen in the Wawona Tree, a sequoia whose base was hollowed out in 1881 to permit the passage of stagecoaches through its trunk, and in the scarring on the face of Glacier Point from years of firefalls. Not so obvious were the hundreds of bears killed for damaging property or wounding visitors. Throughout the park's history, no human visitor has ever been killed by a bear in Yosemite, but the bear, a natural resident of the park, was made to pay the price for years of mismanagement. Preservationists pointed to the nightly "bear shows" as an indication of the government's lack of scientific perspective and overall lack of commitment to resource protection over visitor recreation.

Voices for Change

By 1928, criticism of park management led to the creation of the Yosemite Advisory Board, headed by Fredrick Law Olmstead, Jr., who also espoused the environmental views his father put forth back in 1865. Recommendations from the board did lead to a few victories for the natural resource. Some attractions that were "artificial," without historical or natural basis, were discontinued; like the Indian Field Days (a rodeo-like affair) and the Tule Elk herd (which, while native to California, had never existed in Yosemite Valley). Also, cars were prevented from driving across the meadows by the placement of ditches on either side of the roadbed. But expansion continued. The inauguration of the Sierra Winter Sports Carnival in 1931, and the installation of a nine-hole miniature golf course on the grounds of the Ahwahnee Hotel, proved that visitor attraction was still emphasized.

At times, suggestions to advance the cause of conservation and preservation over commercial development were raised from within the government. In 1945, the director of the National Park Service, Newton B. Drury, proposed "moving as much as possible of the government facilities out of the Valley … eliminating Yosemite Lodge, broadening the range of service at the Ahwahnee, and eliminating the resort-type entertainment featured at Camp Curry, thereby reducing the tourist impact on the Valley Floor." He suggested that facilities be moved to the borders of the park, such as Wawona, a better place to locate "the entertainment and other resort features that … are based on desires other than those of seeing and enjoying the natural features of the Park." His proposals were not adopted, but similar suggestions made through the years can be found today in the controversial 1980 Yosemite General Master Plan.

During the post-war years, tourism nationwide began to increase dramatically. In Yosemite, a milestone was reached by the end of 1954 when annual visitation figures reached the one million mark predicted by Olmstead in 1865. The Park Service eventually answered the pressure on aging and outdated facilities by launching "Mission 66" in 1956, a ten-year plan to upgrade and expand the infrastructure in all national parks. One of the important effects on Yosemite was the paving and widening of the Tioga Road, an old mining route which bisected the park roughly east-to-west, improving access to Yosemite from neighboring areas. Preservationists were concerned. They viewed the Tioga Road as another example of the emphasis the Park Service was placing on expansion and development. "A highway down the center aisle of a cathedral would enable more people to go through it, but it would not enable more people to come there for peace and spiritual inspiration," wrote Alex Hildebrand, president of the Sierra Club.

The numbers of tourists continued to increase, and of course, the infrastructure was expanded to accommodate them. In 1967, annual visitation figures topped two million and continued to climb rapidly. On long summer weekends traffic jams on valley roads echoed the urban congestion that many visitors had sought to leave behind. Campgrounds were unregulated and overflowing; drunken or rowdy groups wandered the area all night disturbing other guests; smog, drugs and crime pervaded the park. On July 4, 1970, Vietnam war protests escalated into a riot. Changes were necessary and work began on an overall management plan.

Introduced in 1980, the Yosemite General Management Plan (GMP) outlined bold new measures to "de-develop" the Yosemite Valley. The planners ruefully admitted, "Fifty years ago we were busy building roads and parking areas to 'open up' Yosemite and make it more accessible ... . Today we look with irony on the acres of pavement, the traffic congestion, the noise we have created." The plan called for limiting the number of cars accessing the valley and reducing the number of parking spaces. A study would be undertaken to determine how to eventually eliminate all automobiles from the valley floor and provide shuttle buses from satellite parking areas. Resort-like facilities (skating rinks, golf courses, tennis courts and swimming pools) and non-relevant programs (like square dancing and the study of non-indigenous Indian cultures) would be removed. The headquarters, administration and maintenance facilities for both the Park Service and Curry Company would be moved to El Portal, just outside the park. Overnight visitor accommodations and employee housing would be reduced to a specified amount. The Plan provided a unique and exciting opportunity to turn back the clock and remove a century's accumulation of commercialism and development.

Writing in *Audubon* magazine, John G., Mitchell considers the GMP "a plan that would seek neither the even 'balance' between protection and use that now seems to dominate the policies of George Bush's National Park Service, nor a flat-out regurgitation of public preferences, which would simply substitute popular referendum for professional planning, but rather a document to honor obligations — the obligations inherent in the Service's mandate from Congress." As the Service itself would explain it in the text of the final plan, the first and foremost of these obligations is to protect and preserve the resource. And the second is to make the resource available for public enjoyment, education, and recreation. There is, of course, a third obligation, though no one in either Congress or the Park Service felt obliged at the time to spell it out in so many words. This is the obligation to know where and when to draw the line, lest too much enjoyment and recreation overwhelm not only the stability of the resource but the visitor's experience as well. The 1980 Yosemite General Management Plan attempted to honor all three of these obligations.

In the ten years since the GMP debuted, there has been little progress in implementing any of their goals. A golf course has been removed from the valley floor, a few park service administrative offices have moved outside the valley, and the Curry Company has moved its reservation facilities to Fresno. However, the buildings that housed those functions have stayed in the valley and are being used for other purposes. During the Reagan era of deregulation, many of the GMP's goals were put on hold, and the Curry Company was given permission to expand its operations. Since 1980, overnight accommodations increased a net amount of twenty-one units, and additional attractions like a video outlet and river raft rentals were added to the valley's commercial establishments. The Park Service's apparent lack of commitment to implementing the goals of the GMP is partly due to the limited availability of federal funding to finance these changes, and partly due to understandable resistance on the part of the Curry Company. Any decommercialism of the valley will directly affect its bottom line, and since the government has little real control over the concessionaire, the company is able to exert all of its considerable muscle to influence policy in this area.

Legislative control of concessionaires was attempted with the passage of the Concessions Policy Act of 1965 which specified that "public accommodations, facilities, and services ... should be provided only under carefully controlled safeguards against unregulated and indiscriminate use ... . It is the policy of the Congress that such developments shall be limited to those that are necessary and appropriate for public use and enjoyment of the national park area in which they are located and that are consistent to the highest practical degree with the preservation and conservation of the areas." Such high-minded rhetoric was also coupled with regulations that limited competition and gave incumbent concessionaires enormous advantages in contract negotiations with park managers. The Yosemite Park and Curry Company, which in 1973 became a wholly-owned subsidiary of the entertainment conglomerate MCA, has the most advantageous contract of any park concessionaire — one that has sparked a raging national controversy.

Mitchell's article for *Audubon*, "Uncluttering Yosemite," points out that the Curry Company's gross receipts are greater "than the combined revenues of the nation's second and third most lucrative concessionaires (at Grand Canyon National Park and Statue of Liberty National Monument)." And yet their franchise fee, only three quarters of one percent, is the lowest in the entire park system. In 1989, MCA's gross yearly revenues from operations within Yosemite National Park exceeded $84 million and of that, the government received a little more than $635,000. It is interesting to note that Curry spends more money each year on advertising than it pays into the U.S. Treasury in franchise fees.

The concessionaire's presence in the park is pervasive. Within the Yosemite Valley, the Curry Company provides 1,764 overnight accommodation units; thirteen retail stores and gift shops; nine hamburger-pizza-snack counters, one deli, four restaurants, four bars, two cafeterias and two ice cream parlors. In addition they offer ski packages, video rentals, photo-finishing, guided tours, saddle trips, bicycle and raft rentals, and more. Several of these services have been added since the 1980 GMP, with government approval. It is so large and so popular, it is not surprising that Curry's lobbying efforts on behalf of its own special interests are so effective. Paul Pritchard, president of the National Parks and Conservation Association, observed, "[The concessionaires] are to parks what the defense industry is to the military." An example of Curry's influence was the congressional appropriation in 1989 of $1.5 million for a new employee dormitory. Yosemite's entire federal budget for that year was only $13.8 million — not enough to provide funding for maintenance of the park's 800-mile network of trails.

But Curry's popularity should not be underestimated. The company is acknowledged, even by its critics, to be very effective in pleasing its customers. Mitchell admits that it is considered "a topnotch provider of goods and services ... [perhaps] the best in its field." And it has an enviable corporate image as an environmentally active organization. For example, it was a recipient of the "Take Pride in America Award" at a White House ceremony in 1989 and was labeled by Interior Secretary Manual Lujan as one of President Bush's "thousand points of light."

David Brower, former executive director of the Sierra Club which has battled long and hard against the commercialism of the park, exemplifies the ambivalent attitudes held by many conservationists. In a recent editorial in the L.A. Times he wrote, "Let the Yosemite master plan phase private automobiles out and phase rail and more shuttle service in. A few further accommodations as superbly planned as those at Yosemite Lodge can be fitted in nearby ... . Be grateful for the company that manages the wonderful shuttle system, that has driven Styrofoam out of the valley ... . It is a company run by people who care about Yosemite and stay there long enough to learn how to protect it well." However, George Frampton, president of the Wilderness Society, sees things differently. "Yosemite deserves better than to be treated as an MCA profit center. In the management of this extraordinary park, nature should come first — not the shareholders of MCA."

In 1993 the thirty-three year contract which gives Curry a monopoly on concession services in Yosemite is up for renegotiation. Japan's Matsushita Electric Industrial Co., which acquired MCA in January 1991, will transfer title of Curry's holdings (hotels, restaurants, stores, etc.) to the American people for $49.5 million dollars — a deal they agreed to only after a national furor arose over the specter of enormous profits earned from an American national park potentially going directly into Japanese coffers. The Park Service will then lease the concession operations out to the winner of a new contract. Several for-profit institutions like Disney, Marriott, and MCA/Curry will be bidding, as will the non-profit Yosemite Restoration Trust. The Trust, whose board includes leaders of the Sierra Club and the Wilderness Society, promises to reinvest any concession "profits" directly back into the park, to support implementation of the goals of the General Management Plan.

That the Park Service should delegate the operation of such visitor services to a single business may make some sense, but historically the Curry company's operations have presented a problem. "There is a rationale behind giving a monopoly concession," says Jan Van Wagtendonk, chief scientist for Yosemite National Park. "It is a sizeable investment, a limited season, and there are many restrictions, including rate regulation. But the Company likes to look on itself as a *partner* in managing the Park, and that isn't really right. The concessionaire is a *contractor*, working under the policies of the Park Service. We have to set those policies in the interest of the people, for the protection of the Park, not to make money for the concessionaire."

Conclusion

Perhaps the root of the problem lies in the profit motivation driving all businesses. Curry spent close to three quarters of a million dollars marketing Yosemite in order to increase visitation, thereby increasing revenue. It is unrealistic to expect that any for-profit organization will voluntarily forgo efforts to improve those profits. But according to Ira J. Winn, in his article "Yosemite's Fall," the impact of increased visitation on the Park's resources is inescapable: "Should the visitation season expand in response to the advertising promotions, there will be less and less time for the delicate meadows and woodlands to recover from the summer onslaught of tourists. As things stand in peak season, the valley of the Yosemite ... exhibits the pall of a tawdry city carnival."

On a summer weekend day in Yosemite, an average of 20,000 visitors enter the Park; yearly visitation is equivalent to the population of Los Angeles. In 1991 the Park service had 755 total staff available to serve the public, including full- and part-time interpretive, law-enforcement, and back-country rangers; administration; maintenance; science; and other support functions. The Yosemite Park and Curry Company's staffing for the summer of 1991 was 1,800 people, all of whom were housed within the Park. The infrastructure supporting tourism in Yosemite is enormous; as an example, twenty-five tons of disposable garbage is hauled out of Yosemite every summer day.

Some of the interim solutions to the problems caused by such vast numbers have already been put into place. Quotas on the maximum number of vehicles allowed in the valley have been set since 1985, when a warm Memorial Day weekend brought so many cars to the Park that gridlock occured on the valley roads — no traffic could move for several hours. A reservation system has been set up to regulate both the number of visitors using the Park's campground and hikers backpacking in the Yosemite's wilderness areas. Long-term solutions await the implementation of the 1980 General Management Plan.

Education is the prime tool for effecting a lasting change. The public's attitude must reflect a greater understanding of what is appropriate to experiencing a national park: that enjoyment of a sublime natural resource does not include all the comforts and entertainments of civilization. Commercial attractions are actually visitor distractions; they only interfere and even destroy the unique experience a wilderness has to offer. People's expectations of what to see and do in a national park like Yosemite need to be put more in line with what this magnificent resort has to offer. Resort-like amenities are available elsewhere; only in Yosemite can the thunder of falling water and the high, sweeping reaches of rock touch the quiet places in the soul.

As for myself, we enjoyed our visit to Yosemite despite the hordes. Yosemite can't be hidden by the crowds any more than it can be shrouded by the night. I even shopped at the concessions, buying little pieces of Yosemite to take home with me. But I will write to the Park Service in support of the removal of those convenience stores. I will insist that the government that acts for me as a steward of our natural heritage move to draw the line on tourism: to put the resource first as it should have always done. As a member of the tourist industry, I will do my part where I can, to educate the public on how to protect and value our special places. And as a parent, through example and experience, I hope to pass on my love of Yosemite and all other special sanctuaries to my children ... and theirs.

Reprinted with permission of the Institute of Certified Travel Agents

Chapter 2 — Article Two
Geographic Pursuits

Should Agents Invest the Time and Expense to Enhance Intangibles Such As Geographic Knowledge, or Is It All an Exercise in Trivia?

Jessie Ardolino, a senior ASTA member with 43 years experience in the industry, says a person has to be really good to bluff. "One thing I impress on my staff is to never bluff," she says. "I tell them if they don't know something, then say so."

But more and more Ardolino is finding that agents, when asked questions of a geographic nature, must either bluff or admit they don't know. She finds the current status of geographic knowledge in agency offices "appalling."

"Today's agents aren't even travel agents any more," she says. "They sell the package that somebody else planned anyway, and they don't know what's in it. They're simply interested in making money, the mechanisms of it, the electronics of it. The day of creating excitement because you're planning a trip to, say, Paris is over. It's cut-and-dried now."

Agent's don't sell dreams anymore, she continues. "It was such a thrilling time when I first came into the business in 1947, and it's still thrilling — I read one of the travel magazines and I get excited. "But how many people feel that way now?"

Perhaps the dream sales have been taken over by the marketing departments of cruise lines, tourist boards and others. Nevertheless, some owners/managers still believe that agents should be able to envision the far-off places they recommend to their clients and have taken measures to enhance world awareness among the sales staff.

One outspoken advocate of such study is ASTA President and CEO Voit Gilmore. "One of the most-uttered phrases is, 'I don't use a travel agent because I know more about it than they do.' I'm tired of hearing that," he says.

"Knowledge of geography is one of the most important selling tools that we've got," he adds. "If you teach somebody how to write a ticket, if you teach somebody how to keep books, if you teach somebody how to handle any part of the weekly processing, then why aren't you also teaching them something that helps them enhance their selling? It's like having one arm tied behind your back if you don't have that knowledge."

Gilmore's administration has functioned on the premise that if public schools aren't going to teach geography, then "let's start picking geography out and enhancing the education of our own people as well as that of the general public," says Gilmore, who has a doctorate in geography.

An example of what he wants to eliminate took place in his own office in Pinehurst, North Carolina, when a client mentioned having just returned from Barbados. Another client booking a cruise overheard and remarked, "By the way, I've always wanted to go to Barbados, Where is it?"

"I don't know," replied the other. "We landed at night."

Geographic Goals

With geographic knowledge high on his administration's agenda, Gilmore approached the National Geographic Society and ultimately joined with *National Geographic TRAVELER Magazine* and other sponsors to develop the World Explorer Context for ASTA agents. And gradually he found that agents were showing more interest in geography.

"We found more of our seminars on geography were selling when we signed up people for the regionals," Gilmore says. "It all cumulatively began to build, and many travel agency managers that I have known have said, 'Thank goodness, because our own students are coming out of school without any geography knowledge and we need that enhancement of knowledge.'"

Sure, critics argue, geography is important, but how can agents justify the time and expense of enhancing intangibles such as geographic knowledge when there is so much more they could be doing in agency automation, increasing sales or just taking care of business at hand?

Gilmore says he knows that all too well. "I'm a travel agent, too," he says. "I'm busy. I'm swamped. I've got more stuff than I can handle. Six o'clock comes so fast every evening that I don't know what to do with it. But I also know it's a tremendous drawback if I've got agents out there talking to people and they don't know what destination somebody's talking about. Professionalism and profitability — I say one can't get along without the other."

He argues that being a geographically well-informed travel agent doesn't cost anything. Rather than taking time away from sales, it enhances them, which is one reason why ASTA has developed more geography seminars in recent years. One of the seminar instructors is Lynne Sorenson, CTC, founder of the Canada College Tourism Program in Redwood City, California.

Sorenson's seminar, "Geography: Become the Instant Destination Expert," proposes to achieve that goal with pencils and maps of the world's seven continents. The maps are blank save for numbers which denote various countries and bodies of water, and agents are expected to replace those numbers with names.

Early in the process, she distributes a map of Europe with 49 numbers. "The average agent gets about 10 percent of those correct," Sorenson says, adding that those agents have about 10 years' experience each in the industry.

But that percentage will increase during the course of the day, as Sorenson drills agents with more blank maps and teaches them to use atlases, globes and other references. "People don't realize what a difference knowledge of geography can make for them professionally," she says, admitting that attendance at her geography seminars is less than it might be for a seminar on, say, automation. "It [geographic knowledge] will greatly improve the profit picture of their agency. Front-line sales staff shouldn't have to waste time hunting for information that they should already have in their heads."

Asked whether agents couldn't simply rely on automation to get clients to and from distant lands, she replies with an emphatic no. "Once they start looking for the cheapest airfare from some gateway in the United States to, say, Jakarta, they'd better know through which international gateway they're going to be flying," she says.

True, Sorenson concedes, if it is a simple round trip the agent might be able to get away with it, but if it is a multi-leg itinerary and they don't put the cities in the proper geographic sequence, a client may wind up paying a mileage surcharge that he wouldn't have paid otherwise. "It's foolish for a travel agent to rely on airline rate desks to straighten them out on airline routings that have been caused by a lack of knowledge of place-name geography in the first place," she says.

Just how severe is that lack of knowledge? Consider that in a Gallup survey of adult geographic knowledge conducted in 1988 and 1989, one in seven Americans could not identify the United States on an unmarked map. That the lack of awareness extends to the travel industry is also clear.

Even World Explorer Contest finalist Phil Bennet, vice president of Carefree Tours and Travel in Honolulu, admits that agents who work in his office know very little about geography. "They know their travel and know how to book, but you ask them certain questions like, 'What's south of Hawaii?' and you'd be surprised how few of them know."

Bennet adds that clients often do not know how much distance lies between destinations, nor do they realize how long it takes to get from point A to point B. "We have people trying to do things where they would spend all of their time on a plane instead of enjoying the vacation," he says. "They'll tell you they want to go to Paris and Hong Kong on the same trip. Essentially, you've got to know what's possible given a time span and point them in the right direction."

To ensure that this happens in his own agency, Bennet gives weekly quizzes to his employees during staff meetings, and quizzes his agents after their clients come back from tours. When one of his agents returned from Scandinavia recently with flags from the different countries, he says, "We had our agents name the countries and match the flags."

Places and Cultures

The difference between knowing the flags and knowing where the countries are located brings up an important point: There are two types of geography, place-name or destination geography and cultural geography. While place-name geography is simply what the name implies — a knowledge of destinations and their locations on the world map — cultural geography includes those elements that make a destination unique, such as language, ethnicity, cuisine, religion, politics, and social mores.

Agents differ on the relative value of the two categories. According to Dan Morris, CTC, president and owner of Lansing Travel Bureau Inc. in Albany, New York, cultural geography is not important to agents. "That's not what clients are going there for," he says. "A businessman who has to conduct business in a foreign country doesn't care what the political setup is or the religion. If anything he needs to know social procedures so he won't be embarrassed."

But Gilmore insists that a well-rounded knowledge is most important. "You have people coming in who literally just want to go see butterflies in the Amazon forest," he says. "You've got to know where that part of the world is and a little bit about it, and how you get there and what you do when you get there. And when you do you've sold a far better ticket than if you're just sitting there talking about the shuttle from Washington to Boston."

Abstract principles, personal preferences and experience may figure in an agent's decision to focus on location, delve into the cultural aspects of destinations or simply sell the package that some-one else constructed. Given those choices, Ardolino cautions, "Agents shouldn't recommend the same thing to everybody. 'You've got a good deal, sell that good deal whether it fits that person or not' — I never operated that way. I'd rather lose money and sell something that fits that person. You've made a customer then."

Reprinted with permission from *ASTA Agency Management* magazine, October, 1990

Destination Geography
Chapter 2

End of Chapter Review

Name _____ Date _____

Directions: Using your atlas and text, circle the appropriate letter.

1. Which Mexican city located 45 miles SW of the capital is renowned as a silver center?

   A. Acapulco   C. Chichen Itza

   B. Guadalajara   D. Taxco

2. A tour of what city would include the Freedom Trail, *U.S.S. Constitution,* Faneuil Hall, and Beacon Hill?

   A. Philadelphia   C. New Haven

   B. Boston   D. Providence

3. In what windy city can one see the Loop, Hyde Park, Michigan Avenue, North Side, South Side, the Lakefront, and Gold Coast?

   A. Miami Beach   C. Chicago

   B. Fort Lauderdale   D. Detroit

4. From what city can one most easily visit Pennsylvania Dutch Country and see the Amish?

   A. Lancaster   C. Pittsburgh

   B. Philadelphia   D. Allentown

5. Which of the following city pairs are also known as the Twin Cities?

   A. Minneapolis-St. Paul   C. Miami-Ft. Lauderdale

   B. Kansas City, MO & KS   D. San Francisco-Oakland

6. Where can you see Independence National Historical Park, the Liberty Bell, Betsy Ross House, Christ Church Burial Ground, Society Hill, and the Franklin Institute?

   A. Providence   C. Boston

   B. Philadelphia   D. New York City

Directions: Using your atlas and text, circle the appropriate letter.

7. On what Caribbean Island will you find El Morro fortress and El Yunque rain forest?

   A. Haiti   C. Grenada

   B. Puerto Rico   D. Jamaica

8. Where is Mt. McKinley?

   A. Washington   C. Canada

   B. Alaska   D. Maine

9. Your client wants to vacation in Cancun. Where is it?

   A. Azores   C. Mexico

   B. Spain   D. South Pacific

10. Which Pacific island is closest to Australia?

    A. Tahiti   C. North Island, New Zealand

    B. Papua, New Guinea   D. Fiji

11. Your client will be attending a convention in the Canary Islands? Where are they?

    A. South Pacific   C. Atlantic Ocean off North Africa

    B. Mediterranean Sea   D. Atlantic Ocean off Portugal
       near Spain

12. The Galapagos are off the coast of Ecuador and the Great Barrier Reef is off the coast of

    A. South Africa   C. California

    B. Australia   D. Brazil

13. Which country is not part of the same land mass as England?

    A. Scotland   C. All occupy the same land mass

    B. Wales   D. Ireland

14. Mykonos is located in the _____ Sea.

    A. Adriatic   C. Ionian

    B. Aegean   D. Mediterranean

End of Chapter Review (continued)

_____

Name   Date

Directions: Using your atlas and text, circle the appropriate letter.

15. Which of these islands is closest to Puerto Rico?

    A. Trinidad   C. Barbados

    B. Martinique   D. Antigua

16. The Grand Canyon is located in

    A. Arizona   C. California

    B. Colorado   D. Utah

17. Which of the following Florida cities is not on the Gulf of Mexico?

    A. St. Petersburg   C. Orlando

    B. Sarasota   D. Fort Myers

18. Which Caribbean island is part French and part Dutch?

    A. Martinique   C. St. Martin

    B. Guadeloupe   D. Aruba

19. Which Caribbean island is divided into two separate countries?

    A. Curaçao   C. Hispaniola

    B. Seychelles   D. Sicily

20. What point of land in the United States is nearest to Bermuda?

    A. Cape Cod, MA   C. Cape Hatteras, NC

    B. Cape Kennedy, FL   D. Cape Henlopen, DL

21. Biloxi, Mississippi, is located on the Gulf of

    A. Bothnia   C. Mexico

    B. Oman   D. Carpentaria

22. Which Australian city is known for its spectacular harbor and Opera House?

    A. Perth   C. Brisbane

    B. Darwin   D. Sydney

23. The Acropolis is in Athens and the Colosseum is in

    A. Pompei   C. Rome

    B. Capri   D. Naples

24. Where is The Hague?

    A. England   C. Netherlands

    B. Belgium   D. Luxembourg

25. Match the island with its country.

    A. Eleuthera   _____ 1. England

    B. Ibiza   _____ 2. Mexico

    C. Cozumel   _____ 3. Bahamas

    D. Sark   _____ 4. Spain

26. What city lies directly south of Detroit, Michigan?

    A. Toledo, Ohio   C. Milwaukee, Wisconsin

    B. Lansing, Michigan   D. Windsor, Ontario

27. Casablanca is in

    A. Algeria   C. Morocco

    B. Tunisia   D. Libya

28. Sardinia is part of

    A. Spain   C. France

    B. Italy   D. Greece

60

End of Chapter Review (continued)

Name _____   Date _____

Directions: Using your atlas and text, circle the appropriate letter.

29. Match each country with one of its major cities.

A. France   _____   1. Rome

B. Germany   _____   2. Paris

C. Spain   _____   3. Oslo

D. Italy   _____   4. Zurich

E. Norway   _____   5. Amsterdam

F. Switzerland   _____   6. Frankfurt

G. Netherlands   _____   7. Madrid

Answers to End of Chapter Review Questions

1. D
2. B
3. C
4. A
5. A
6. B
7. B
8. B
9. C
10. B
11. C
12. B
13. D
14. B
15. D
16. A
17. C
18. C
19. C
20. C
21. C
22. D
23. C
24. C
25. A-3, B-4, C-2, D-1
26. A
27. C
28. B
29. A-2, B-6, C-7, D-1, E-3, F-4, G-5

Air Travel
Chapter 3

Review Chapter Objectives
- Explain interline agreements and provide two examples of them
- Discuss the relationship between fares and classes of service
- Define promotional fares and relate three reasons for their use by an airline
- Describe the difference between a non-stop and direct/through flight
- Trace the history of the hub and spoke concept
- Explain the effect of deregulation on airline default

Review Vocabulary
- Bumping
- Circle trip
- Commuter airline
- Configuration
- Connection
- FAA
- Hub and spoke
- Open jaw
- Planned capacity
- Waitlist

Airline Careers
- Co-pilot
- Flight Attendant
- Flight Engineer
- Gate Agent
- Ground Crew
- Pilot
- Reservations Agent
- Sales Agent
- Traffic Supervisor

Transparencies
- Chapter outline
- Hub and spoke system
- Kinds of journeys
- Kinds of flights
- Airplane configuration
- Top ten reasons for choosing an airline

Air Travel
Chapter 3 Outline

I. Regulation

II. Deregulation

III. Types of Airlines

    A. Hub and Spoke System

    B. Charters/Commuters

IV. Interline Agreements

    A. The Airline Ticket

    B. Baggage/Pets/Special Requests

    C. Planned Capacity/Denied
       Boarding Compensation

V. Fare Structures

    A. Promotional Fares/Discount Fares

VI. Frequent Flyer Programs

    A. Inflight Services

VII. Airports

    A. Check-in Procedures/Security

    B. Kinds of Journeys/Kinds of Flights

VIII. Liability of Airlines

Hub and Spoke System

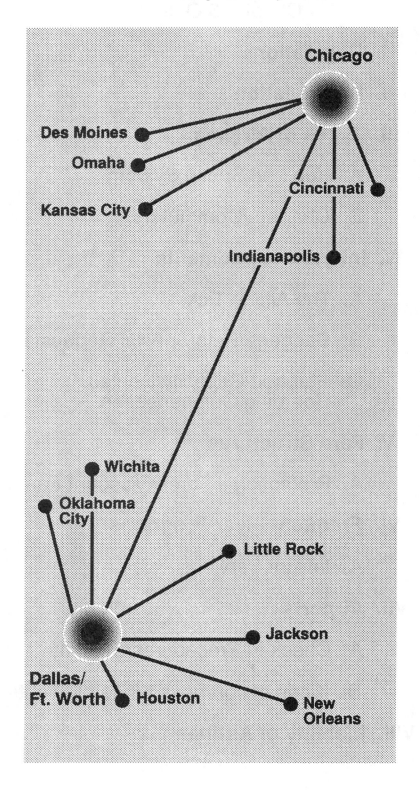

Kinds of Journeys

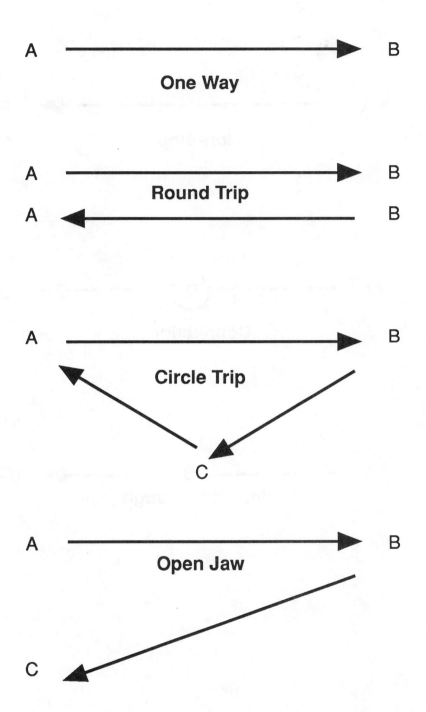

Kinds of Flights

A      B

Non-Stop

A   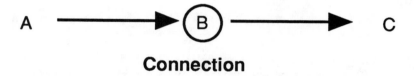   C

Connection

A ——————— B ——————▶ C

Direct or Through

Airplane Configuration

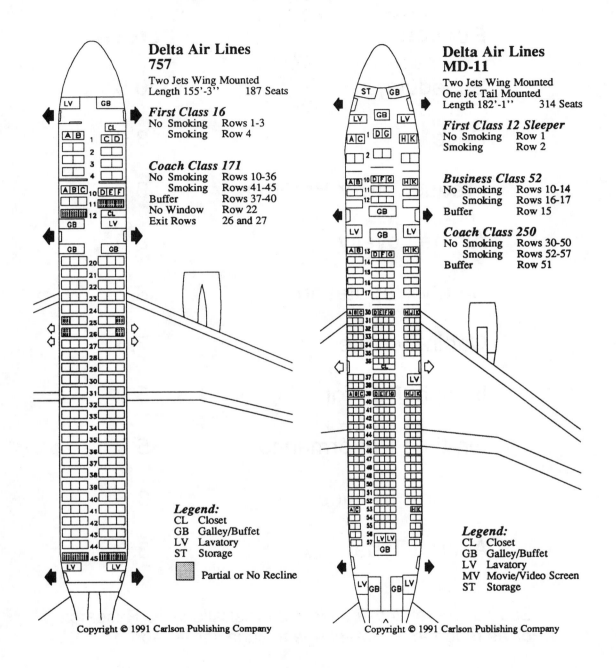

**Delta Air Lines
757**

Two Jets Wing Mounted
Length 155'-3''   187 Seats

First Class 16
No Smoking   Rows 1-3
    Smoking   Row 4

Coach Class 171
No Smoking   Rows 10-36
    Smoking   Rows 41-45
Buffer   Rows 37-40
No Window   Row 22
Exit Rows   26 and 27

Legend:
CL   Closet
GB   Galley/Buffet
LV   Lavatory
ST   Storage

░░ Partial or No Recline

Copyright © 1991 Carlson Publishing Company

**Delta Air Lines
MD-11**

Two Jets Wing Mounted
One Jet Tail Mounted
Length 182'-1''   314 Seats

First Class 12 Sleeper
No Smoking   Row 1
Smoking   Row 2

Business Class 52
No Smoking   Rows 10-14
    Smoking   Rows 16-17
Buffer   Row 15

Coach Class 250
No Smoking   Rows 30-50
    Smoking   Rows 52-57
Buffer   Row 51

Legend:
CL   Closet
GB   Galley/Buffet
LV   Lavatory
MV   Movie/Video Screen
ST   Storage

Copyright © 1991 Carlson Publishing Company

Reprinted by permission of Carlson Publishing Company, Los Alamitos, CA

Top Ten Reasons for Choosing an Airline

Reason	Percent
Schedule	20.5
Price	13.0
Frequent-flyer Program	9.5
Airline Loyalty	8.9
Safety Reputation	8.7
Cabin Service	7.6
In-flight Comfort	5.9
On-time Performance	5.9
Airport Facilities	3.5
Aircraft Type	3.0

Source: Travel and Tourism Administration/CIC Research
Poll as reported by *Travel Agent* Magazine — April 13, 1992

Answers to Textbook Review Questions

1. **How has the hub and spoke system affected air travel in your area?**
   Answers will vary.

2. **How much do you think people are influenced by the kind of plane they fly on? Why?**
   Answers will vary. Small planes and small airport runways can be frightening. People with claustrophobia like the space provided by a jumbo jet.

3. **Which in-flight services might be most important to passengers?**
   Answers will vary. Discuss meals and dietary needs, seat space for large people, unaccompanied children, space for carry-on bags, no-smoking policies, and so on.

4. **Which current promotional fares advertised in the newspapers seem to achieve their aims best? Which do not ? Why?**
   If local papers do not carry any airfare promotions, buy a copy of a large city paper for examples.

5. **How important is it to be aware of the limits of airline liability?**
   Depending on the severity of the problem, very.

6. **What are the principal features of the nearest major airport? How would you advise people to get there?**
   If possible, take a field trip to the local airport. Consider: accessibility from major population areas, parking, ground transportation services, spaciousness of terminals, airport hotels, and so on.

Answers to Discussion Topics

Lost Luggage
On domestic flights the liability of most airlines is limited to $1,250 per fare-paying passenger. Travel agents may be held liable by the client for the actions of a supplier if they do not clearly disclose that they are agents. Travel agents often inform clients of their status as agents with a printed statement on each invoice, ticket jacket, or similar document. Agents should listen sympathetically to problems and help clients channel questions to appropriate sources. The sale of luggage insurance would have been a good idea, but it is too late for that now. Is the complaint justified? Yes. Most lost baggage is found within a few days. Counsel patience. Clients should be treated with respect and sympathy.

Bankruptcy
Airline bankruptcies have become common occurrences. Travel agencies who have forwarded client monies to a carrier that subsequently declares bankruptcy are in a difficult position. Payments by credit card might protect individuals as credit card payments delay cash flow to the carrier. The agent's first step should be to find an airline with space available willing to handle the group. Deposits and guarantees for the land portion would be lost if the group does not go.

Bumping and Advanced Seating
Depending on circumstances, the gate agent can solicit volunteers to give up seats on the oversold flight, but Mr. and Mrs. Collins cannot expect that the agent will bump someone so that they can have their originally-scheduled seats. Passengers should be advised to check in at least 30 minutes before a domestic flight so that baggage can be loaded. Advise longer — depending on local circumstances. According to the ARC *Handbook*, even passengers holding advance-issued boarding passes and traveling without baggage should be in the boarding area not less than 20 minutes prior to scheduled flight departure. The travel agent must advise clients of this responsibility.

Frequent Flyer

At this point, nothing. Frequent Flyer upgrade rules are strict and differ from airline to airline. Upgrades are not automatic. Most airlines require passengers to call in to list themselves for upgrades a certain number of hours before check-in.

Answers to Workbook Exercises

Worksheet 3-1

Bumping	Another term for being denied boarding on an aircraft
Circle trip	A round trip journey in which the outbound routing, class of service, and/or airline are not the same as on the return
Commuter airline	Airlines that operate short flights from small airfields
Configuration	The arrangement of seats, bathrooms, galleys, and other areas inside a plane or motorcoach
Connection	A flight from origin to destination with an intermediate stop
FAA	The agency of the United States Department of Transportation responsible for civil aviation
Hub and Spoke	The airline practice of using certain cities as connecting centers for feeder flights
Planned capacity	The practice when an airline takes reservations for more seats than are on the airplane

Worksheet 3-2

1. The hub and spoke system uses an airport as the center, or hub, at which as many flights as possible arrive from outlying cities at the same time. Passengers can then make convenient connections and proceed to many different destinations in planes that depart a short time later.
Benefits — The airlines can provide convenient on-line service between a much greater number of cities. Airlines are able to maximize passenger loads from smaller cities and save fuel.

2. Among the benefits are: The major airline provides advertising, promotion, and accounting support; it was a sophisticated computer reservations system; and it shares its name and image with the smaller commuter carrier.

3. Charter airlines operate under different rules from those that govern regularly scheduled flights. Their popularity dimmed with the advent of deregulation. Answers may vary as to the future of charters. The future is dependent on the direction that regular airfares take.

Worksheet 3-3

1. Round trip

2. Circle

3. Circle

4. One way

Worksheet 3-3 (continued)

5. Open jaw

6. Nonstop — A flight with no intermediate stops — example will vary.

7. Connection — A flight from origin to destination with an intermediate stop — example will vary.

8. Direct or through — A flight from origin to destination with one or more intermediate — example will vary.

Worksheet 3-4

1. To stimulate bookings on a new route, to promote travel between particular destinations during the off-season

2. Answers may vary.

Worksheet 3-5

1. Airlines overbook to compensate for the high no-show factors.

2. If an airline delivers a bumped passenger to a destination within an hour of the originally scheduled time, no compensation is required. If the arrival time is more than an hour later, but less than two hours (four hours on international flights originating in the United States), the passenger must be paid the face value of the ticket up to the maximum of $200. After more than two hours, the compensation doubles, to a maximum of $400.

3. Passengers who voluntarily relinquish their seats are compensated with a cash payment or a voucher for a free future trip. They are then placed on the first available flight to their destination.

4. The best protection is early check-in.

Worksheet 3-6

1. Seat pitch — The front-to-rear spacing of seat rows

   Seat width — The side-to-side space available at seat cushion or chest level

   Configuration — The arrangement of seats, bathrooms, and galleys

2. Choose from: Seats are wider, more heavily padded, and spaced for more leg room. There is more personalized service from flight attendants. Meals are more elaborate, have more choices, and are often served on china with cloth napkins. First class passengers receive free alcoholic beverages, and free headsets.

3. Bulkheads are the partitions that separate the compartments of the plane. Bulkhead seats offer more legroom, but they have no space to stow carry-on luggage and offer no fold-down tables. These seats are best suited for families with young children or people who could use the extra leg space.

4. Business or executive class seats are generally located halfway between first class and coach.

5. Smoking is banned on all domestic flights lasting less than six hours. Smoking is still allowed on international flights.

Worksheet 3-7

1. The boarding pass permits a passenger to get on the plane.

2. Boarding passes can be obtained from travel agencies and airline city ticket offices, airline check-in counters, airline club lounges, and airline departure gate agents.

3. Airlines request domestic passengers to check in at least one hour before a flight. Passengers traveling on an international flight should check in at least two hours before a flight.

4. Choose from: An area with a quiet relaxed atmosphere; a place to obtain newspapers and magazines; a place to store coats and baggage; television; a bar; telephone and fax machines; check-in facilities; meeting rooms.

5. Cameras do not have to go through the X-Ray device. They can be handed to security people — thus avoiding the X-Ray.

Worksheet 3-8

1. CO
2. DL
3. UA
4. SR
5. NW
6. QF
7. AC
8. AA
9. BA
10. US
11. YUL
12. MCO
13. MSY
14. BDA
15. LAX
16. DFW
17. BOS
18. ATL
19. MIA
20. PHL

Worksheet 3-9

1. The Delta MD-11 has more seats (314); the Delta 757 has 187 seats.

2. On the Delta 757, rows 23-31 are over the wings. On the MD-11, rows 30-45 are over the wings. One advantage of seats over the wings is that they provide a smoother ride. One disadvantage is that the view can be obscured.

3. Seats near emergency exits often have more legroom, and seats in the row immediately in front of the emergency exit usually do not recline.

4. Row 20 would probably be noisier because it's located right next to the Galley/Buffet.

5. Answers will vary.

Worksheet 3-10

1. D
2. D
3. A
4. B
5. A

Classroom Activities

1. These questions and statements make good class starters. They offer a light-hearted look at client statements or misconceptions.

    A. Do I have to fly on one of those little airplanes?

    B. Will I have a problem connecting?

    C. When I asked the airline agent to change my ticket, she said I wasn't allowed to open-jaw?

    D. Can I take my skis?

    E. How come my friend is paying only $135 and she's on the exact same flight?

    F. How come my friend can fly at the cheap rate on Thursday and I can't on Friday? You said that there were plenty of seats available on my flight.

    G. I hope this flight is on time because I have a very important business meeting within an hour of arrival. If it's not, you will hear from me!

    H. How come you've booked me on this airline when the newspapers say it is going to go broke?

2. Arrange a field trip to tour the local airport. Airline representatives or the authority in charge of the airport will be happy to arrange guided tours. Ask students to consider and evaluate the following:

accessibility

parking

ground transportation services (include car rentals)

security

food service

baggage areas

shopping opportunities (including duty-free)

airline club lounges

customs and immigration facilities

currency conversion facilities

airport hotels

meeting space and waiting areas

restroom facilities

handicapped facilities

information booths

overall service

Articles

Chapter 3 — Article One
"Flight Patterns"
and Chapter 3 — Article Two
"Why Hubs?"
These articles deal with the issue of deregulation. Divide the class into two teams with three to four representative panel members. Have both sides research the question: "Deregulation: Is it working?" Each group should be prepared to support their ideas in a formal or informal debate. Those individuals not chosen to be official panel members should be prepared to ask questions and add their opinions.

Chapter 3 — Article Three
"Pan American World Airways: 1927-1991 and
and Chapter 3 — Article Four
"With Pan Am's Passing, Industry Loses Symbol of its Golden Age"
Present these articles as case studies of an airline from beginning to end. How has the passing of Pan Am marked the end of an era in airline travel? How could this have been averted? What is the future of this industry?

Flight Patterns
In vogue again, deregulation bashing has revived both sides of the regulation issue

By Barbara S. Peterson

In the heady years after 1978, attacking airline deregulation was akin to taking on Mom and apple pie. The landmark law had something for everyone: It was a boon for consumers and freed businesses from government control, appealing to both sides of the political spectrum.

The witty and ever-quotable Alfred Kahn was a media darling as he presided over Jimmy Carter's Civil Aeronautics Board. Unsurprisingly, critics usually were dismissed as oddballs, and travel agents voicing disapproval were largely ignored.

But what seems to be the newest sport among airline watchers? You guessed it — deregulation bashing.

Barely a week passes without another blast. Numerous newspaper columnists have taken an anti-deregulation slant, sometimes to avenge a particularly awful trip. Politicians have also found that the "blame it on dereg" tack works well when explaining to aggrieved constituents why their air service has deteriorated. Re-regulation bills in Congress have garnered support from some prominent travel industry figures as well.

The perception that deregulation is the chief cause of air service problems, whether or not it's accurate, may indeed be the strongest argument by those supporting re-regulation.

Are Airlines Different?

Another contention has been that airlines are different from other businesses, a position advanced by opponents when airline deregulation was first being debated and more or less discredited then. But it's making a comeback, even though utilities such as telephone services have since been deregulated.

Former ASTA President Joseph Stone is one who uses the utility argument in calling for more government intervention in the airline business. He points out that the government is already regulating slots at airports and has a role in other matters that affect airline operations. "I'm not saying we should go back to the way it was — but I don't want anyone telling me deregulation is a fabulous success," he says.

"I don't think you can call something good that gets rid of almost 22 airlines. You are down to eight major carriers, and at least three are ailing — is that good for the consumer?"

On pricing, Stone raises one of the re-regulationists' favorite arguments — that fares are inherently discriminatory: "You can go to Hawaii for $400, but it costs $600 to fly to Idaho. The on-line cities are being subsidized by the off-line cities. In the old days the government could have blown the whistle."

This view also rests on the assumption that the fare structure discriminates by charging higher fares to those with the least flexibility. "The business traveler is being ripped off — and an agency such as ours hears a lot of complaints," says Stone.

But unfair or not, deregulation was intended to give greater freedom to airlines to adjust their prices to demand. It makes sense that someone willing to submit to more restrictions and to purchase a fare well in advance should get a price break — at least that is the way it works in most other industries.

Providing further fodder for the debate are the occasional scholarly studies that seem to emerge from some academic institution just when they're needed to advance a particular cause. One such report comes from a University of Denver law professor and ex-CAB official, Paul Dempsey, who makes a case that deregulation was a colossal mistake.

With the ominous title of "Flying Blind — the Failure of Airline Deregulation," the Dempsey report, issued by the Economic Policy Institute in Washington, D.C., has become a sort of manifesto for the re-regulation side. Dempsey rehashes the familiar complaints that airline service and competition have declined since 1978 — points that even many dereg partisans concede these days. But his report also seeks to puncture what has been one of the most compelling arguments in favor of deregulation — that consumers have saved billions in airfares.

Fuel for Thought

Dempsey argues that if airline ticket prices are adjusted for the impact of changes in inflation and fuel prices, fares are at least 2.6 percent above the level that they would have been if the industry had not been deregulated. Although there have been short-term benefits — right after deregulation fare wars brought about a sharp drop in average prices — the wave of bankruptcies and mergers that followed has threatened the competition that fosters the low fares, says Dempsey.

Dempsey makes his calculation by holding fuel prices constant (since 1978) and taking the real yield or revenue per passenger mile as a way of measuring the average fare in each year through 1988. Venturing into more subjective territory, Dempsey asserts that since service has declined, consumers are really paying more.

But arguing over whether airfares have risen or declined in "actual terms" is an exercise that would amuse the author of *How to Lie With Statistics*. Dereg stalwarts have, naturally, marshaled plenty of data to support their view that airline passengers have benefited despite the general consensus that service is not what it used to be.

Take the case of Kahn, now back at his old teaching post at Cornell, who has conceded that the wave of mergers and bankruptcies has created an airline industry that is hardly what he envisioned. For him, however, deregulation is not to blame, but the government's lack of antitrust law enforcement is. Kahn also continues to claim that inflation-adjusted airfares have dropped 30 percent since 1976. Other sources have supported his view, albeit more conservatively; the Air Transport Association has calculated that real yields have fallen 22 percent since 1978 and 28 percent since 1977, when Kahn's CAB began to allow more fare flexibility.

Of course, the re-regulation advocates pounce on those conclusions by arguing they lack a comparison with the trends operating before deregulation. When the formula is revised to reflect fluctuations in the price of jet fuel — a major expense item for airlines — then, Dempsey concludes, the real price of air travel fell more rapidly in the years before deregulation.

Dempsey also focuses on the enormous increase in price discounting in the past decade, arguing that accompanying lower fares with steep restrictions dilutes product quality. He attacks a pro-dereg review by a respected Washington think tank, the Brookings Institution, which estimates that lower fares saved consumers $6 billion thanks to deregulation.

The Brookings report also said that consumers benefited because the number of flights had increased as a result of the hub-and-spoke system created by airlines following deregulation. But Dempsey counters that argument by saying that "the time [consumers] lose stranded at airports, imprisoned in aircraft or routed through circuitous hub connections seems to have increased significantly under deregulation."

It takes more than mind-numbing figures to sway people, however, and the Dempsey side cagily capitalizes on growing consumer dissatisfaction. The report states that its statistical analyses "show dramatically what the person on the street senses about deregulation ... the consensus of most of what is written about airlines in this environment is that service has declined significantly."

Dempsey may have a point on that score; in recent years numerous magazines and newspapers have reported on the growing consumer revolt against flight delays, crowded aircraft and the like. Yet Dempsey also might have noted that few detractors have actually gone so far as to call for re-regulation, since the problems plaguing airline service stem from a number of causes, such as inadequate air-traffic control or lack of airport capacity to handle a surge in flights.

Avoiding Extremes

In a way, the current vogue for deregulation bashing may be just one part of the natural evolution that occurs when an industry as tightly regulated as the airlines were is suddenly opened up.

Dr. Frank Spencer of Northwestern University's Transportation Center has followed the Dempsey-

Kahn debate and remarks that while Dempsey "does have some good points, it is way overblown. He can't find a good thing to say about deregulation."

Spencer's view falls somewhere in between; he argues that while things may have gotten bad, they could be a lot worse since the airlines are engaging in "internal" regulation to avoid the return of external regulation.

This self-policing mechanism is the main factor keeping re-regulation at bay, says Spencer. "If they [the airlines] raised rates like a monopoly, Congress would jump in, so they tread pretty carefully in areas that are likely to provoke public ire."

The spate of discount fare coupons and buy now-fly later promotions should be proof enough that low fares are still available, and that regulating pricing would provoke more outrage than any problems that exist now. And while the average businessperson finds service less pleasant than it used to be, it's difficult to see how resurrecting a federal bureaucracy — as called for in Dempsey's report — would satisfy disgruntled consumers.

Reprinted with permission from *ASTA Agency Management* magazine, August, 1990

Chapter 3 — Article Two
Why Hubs?

By Robert L. Crandall, American Airlines Chairman

Long before deregulation was even a glint in the Congressional eye, there were a few airline hubs. The largest was in Atlanta, and Southerners often joked that when their time came, whether they headed for heaven or for Hell, they'd have to change planes in Atlanta.

Today there are 24 hubs on the United States mainland and about two-thirds of all airline passengers pass through a hub to get to their destination. Since most people prefer nonstop service, our customers often ask why so many trips must be made by way of hubs. The answer lies partly in the preferences of our customers and partly in the economics of the airline business.

As much as customers like nonstop service, they like frequent service and time-of-day choices even more. Thus, when there are many flights from a city to one or more hubs, few people are willing to wait several hours for infrequent nonstop service. As a result, most nonstop service from small and medium-size cities to destinations other than hubs has become uneconomical. Of course, in large markets, there is nonstop service aplenty. For instance, three carriers operated 17 flights a day between New York/Newark and Los Angeles in 1978. Today, nine carriers offer 22 nonstops.

When a market lacks nonstop service, it is not — as some suggest — because of an absence of competition. In fact, intense competition, between multiple carriers offering frequent service to multiple hubs, tends to drive out nonstop service because it does a better job of providing what customers want most — which airlines are able to provide because hubs are an efficient way to use airplanes, people, and airport facilities.

American's service from Albuquerque to Dallas/Fort Worth offers a good example of how a hub works. On an average day, the typical flight from Albuquerque to DFW carries 123 passengers. Of those, only 43 are bound for DFW. Two are bound for Atlanta, three for Boston, two for London, and 71 for 28 other destinations. In all, 65 percent of the people on our flights from Albuquerque — and approximately 65 percent of the people on all our flights to DFW — are bound for destinations beyond the hub. The important point is that all those people ride between Albuquerque and DFW on the same airplane.

After the plane from Albuquerque and lots of others land at DFW, all within a half hour, and the folks not staying in Dallas/Fort Worth change planes, our outbound trips begin. A typical flight from DFW to Boston, to cite just one example, carries 158 passengers — 61 from DFW, two from Austin, two from Burbank, the three from Albuquerque, and 90 from 27 other points of origin.

The citizens of Albuquerque, although they do most of their traveling via hubs, have a wider choice of services than they had pre-deregulation. In those days, seven airlines offered 88 daily non-stops to 26 destinations; today, nine carriers offer 121 flights — including 74 to 12 airline hubs, where passengers can make connections to virtually anywhere in the world. Competition has given the citizens of Albuquerque lots more air-travel choices than they had when regulators drew the airline map.

People who live in hub cities are particularly fortunate. Raleigh/Durham's experience is a good example. In 1978, six airlines offered 61 daily flights to 23 destinations. In 1987, American launched its Raleigh/Durham hub and today, the airport boasts 251 flights by five airlines to 67 destinations.

Across the country, American has six mainland hubs, as well as one in Puerto Rico — all offering frequent, convenient service to many destinations.

To sum up: Airline hubs provide enormous benefits for the cities they serve, allow airlines to use their assets more efficiently, facilitate competition, and allow us to offer our customers the many departure and arrival options they want. For all these reasons, we think hubs make a lot of sense.

We hope you agree.

Reprinted with permission from *American Way*

Chapter 3 — Article Three
Pan American World Airways: 1927-1991
A national institution prepares for a last landing

By John Schwartz

This is not a story about planes. It's about romance. The death knell for Pan American World Airways was imminent last week. Pan Am agreed to sell its major European routes, its East Coast shuttle and 45 planes to Delta Airlines, America's third largest carrier, for $260 million. The latest sale leaves it with a few domestic routes and its profitable Latin American lines, which United Airlines was negotiating to buy over the weekend for perhaps as much as $300 million. The carrier had been under bankruptcy protection since January, and its obituaries have been written for well over a decade. "Its pretty clear that a year from now, Pan Am will only be a legal entity," says Thomas Longman, an analyst for Bear, Stearns. "It will no longer be an operating airline."

It may be hard for today's all-too-frequent fliers to remember that once, air travel was an adventure; that airlines once had a soul. Pan Am certainly did. It ushered in cross-Pacific air travel in the mid-'30s with its China Clipper and commercial-jet travel with its Boeing 707 — the first jet was christened in grand manner by First Lady Mamie Eisenhower. The carrier came to stand for a questing American spirit — and sound business sense. The entrepreneur who built Pan Am, Juan Trippe, was perfect for the role: part swashbuckler, part tyrant, he made the airline his toy and his obsession. Trippe saw the competitive advantages in going global, often negotiating personally with foreign officials for landing rights. His consultant on new routes was aviator Charles A. Lindbergh. The airline was also a point of civic pride in New York, where the unabashedly ugly headquarters building had almost the star status of Chrysler's nearby skyscraper.

Through it all, the company — and an eager press — built on air travel's aura of glamour and luxury. For long flights in the 1940s, passengers could reserve sleeping berths; New York-to-London passengers were served breakfast in bed. A 1940 Saturday Evening Post article marveled at Annabella Power, wife of movie idol Tyrone, who made three transatlantic crossings in less than two weeks. Trippe had cannily named his sea-route planes "clippers," evoking the tall seagoing vessels of the past. But he was also pushing the future with aggressive aircraft orders; he was often first in line to snap up new planes like Boeing's gorgeous Stratocruiser, or the massive 747 jumbo jet. And while Pan Am never explicitly got the "chosen instrument" status on government business that Trippe coveted, his airline served Washington often; during World War II, Clippers quietly — and profitably — shuttled important passengers, mail and war materials throughout the Pacific, their shiny hulls painted gray to avoid detection. Later, in Vietnam, the airline flew soldiers on furlough "freedom flights" to distant Asian vacation spots virtually free of charge.

Trippe's solo management style eventually caught up with his company. When he stepped down as chairman in 1968, he had groomed no strong successor. The airline began its long descent. Competition had grown as domestic carriers crowded Pan Am's routes, and many foreign airlines used their government subsidies to undercut Pan Am's prices and at least match its service. Airline-industry deregulation in 1978 removed the last protection old-line carriers like Pan Am had enjoyed. Without a strong domestic-route system to support it, Pan Am's losses mounted. The company spun off assets for cash, from the headquarters building to the Inter-Continental hotels, as well as its pioneering Pacific and London routes. Yet around the world, Pan Am's planes were still a symbol of America's global reach — a point tragically driven home by the terrorist bombing of Flight 103 over Lockerbie, Scotland, in 1988.

Pan Am hasn't been the only airline in pain, of course. Through the 1980s, airlines became pretty much like other businesses, except perhaps more poorly run. Green-eye-shade boys and corporate raiders turned CEOs flew by their bottom lines — and profits still plummeted. The past two years have seen Eastern and Braniff grounded, and such airlines as Continental and America West seek bankruptcy protection. The Gulf War's chill on travel and the recession's squeeze has been especially cruel to the major carriers, which lost $2 billion in the three months before Pan Am filed for Chapter 11. Industry analysts will tell you that there is a bright side to the airline consolidation. Delta, the conservatively run Atlanta-based carrier, is likely to be a good home for the transferred routes. Pan Am's workers won't be so lucky; Delta has pledged to hire 6,000 of them, leaving some 16,000 to add to the unemployment rolls. More has been lost than memories.

So long, Pan Am. You were a victim of so many things. The history books will probably say the chief cause of your demise was deregulation. Your managers, raised in Juan Trippe's government-protected fiefdom, never learned how to scrap in a fiestier world. Moses had to wander through the desert for 40 years — no doubt to weed out those Israelites who couldn't adjust to the deregulated environment of the Promised Land. You didn't get that much time.

Reprinted with permission from *Newsweek*, July 22, 1991

Chapter 3 — Article Four
With Pan Am's Passing, Industry Loses Symbol of Its Golden Age

By Martin B. Deutsch

When Pan American World Airways went down for the final count on December 4, 1991, it went down with a whimper, not the bang that would have befitted the airline that once carried the sobriquet of this country's "chosen instrument."

That Pan Am passed away so quietly is hard to believe, but then so is just about everything that's happening to the U.S. airline industry, an industry that was once the model and envy of air-transportation systems everywhere. (Boy, am I tired of writing these airline eulogies!)

Why did Pan Am slip away so unobtrusively, without much same-day fanfare in the print or broadcast media?

For one thing, Pan Am was the third U.S. airline to bite the dust in 1991. Eastern died in January and Midway folded just a month before Pan Am.

For another, the demise of U.S. airlines has reached epidemic proportions since the advent of deregulation in 1978. What's one more airline obituary? Only America West — flying in bankruptcy — survives from the pathetic ranks of the 104 air carriers spawned after deregulation. As Agatha Christie's murder mystery would have it: "And then there were none."

Pan Am also chose a bad week to shut down. On the day Pan Am closed, the media were preoccupied with the William Kennedy Smith trial, Robert Maxwell's imploding media empire, the Israel-Arab negotiations in Washington, the Balkanization of the Soviet Union, the Sununu-Skinner spectacular at the White House, New York Gov. Mario Cuomo's ongoing performance as Hamlet and the Charles Keating trial in the Lincoln Savings & Loan scandal. Whew!

Beyond that, I don't think the media recognized the magnitude of the Pan Am Loss. One long-time aviation observer got it about right when he said: "It would be like Ford Motor Company rolling the last cars off the assembly line."

It took the media a few days to realize that Pan Am wasn't just another defunct airline, but an airborne symbol of what we once naively called "The American Century."

What happened at Pan Am? Why is the blue Pan Am ball now history? What forces and personalities conspired to ensure its ultimate downfall?

Apart from the broad impact of deregulation, I think the watershed year was 1980. That was the year Pan Am "won" a long and bitter fight with Eastern and Texas International, run by then-unknown Frank Lorenzo, to acquire National Airlines. The $400 million deal was an unmitigated disaster.

Signed that January, the merger was not actually consummated until October. In the intervening months, National took a strike; National's chairman resigned two hours after the first press conference; and the east-west routes of Pan Am never really meshed with National's north-south orientation — nor did their respective unions.

In fact, the marriage of Pan Am and National was a clash or irreconcilable cultures. And it marked the beginning of Pan Am's decline in earnest, even if no one recognized it at the time.

To keep flying, Pan Am sold the Pan Am building in New York in 1980; the Inter-Continental Hotels subsidiary in 1981; the sprawling Pacific Division, to United, in 1985; the Internal German Service in 1990; the London routes in April of 1991; the shuttle last September; the Frankfort hub in November; and Pan Am Express in December.

Delta's decision to withdraw from a deal to save Pan Am as a smaller, Miami-based carrier to Latin America was the final straw, but I believe it only hastened the inevitable end. The handwriting had been on the wall for more than a decade.

It wasn't always that way. Pan American Airways was founded in 1927 by Juan Trippe, a wealthy Yale graduate, originally to fly charters and mail.

Its first scheduled passenger service, Key West-Havana, began in 1928.

One of the early names affiliated with Pan Am was Charles Lindberg. But the marriage was short-lived and by mid-1932 Lindberg was with TWA.

Pan Am's initial transpacific service began in 1935; transatlantic flights started four years later.

Pan Am was in the forefront of the Jet Age. Trippe's Pan Am was the launch customer for the Boeing 707, America's first commercial jet. Trippe ordered 20 Boeing 707s when most of the U.S. aviation industry wasn't convinced jets would be needed.

And even though it didn't have a domestic route network, Pan Am was also involved in the very first domestic jet service on December 10, 1958.

National, which flew a 707 from New York to Miami, had leased the jet from Pan Am. I was on that flight. So was Gypsy Rose Lee, the stripper, who had been booked as the celebrity guest passenger.

Trippe himself was generally considered to be autocratic, aristocratic, and aloof. I met him only once, at a kick-off luncheon in New York for the never-quite-successful Panamac Reservation System, developed with IBM. I have no particular recollection of Trippe, only that his entourage acted as if it were in the presence of royalty.

Trippe was nonetheless a visionary. The 747 is generally considered to be his concept: a 400-seat plane that could carry mass traffic at lower fares.

Boeing President William Allen was on the same wavelength, but he couldn't proceed without a financial partner, so Trippe obliged by making an advance payment on an order of 25 747s. Pan Am would buy 20 more of the jumbo jets in the next 12 years.

The first Boeing delivery flight, Pan Am 004, was from Seattle to New York's Kennedy airport on December 13, 1969. (I was aboard.) Pan Am launched the 747 into scheduled service on January 21, 1970, but would never again be the launch customer for an aircraft.

The 747 was, and is, a magnificent airplane: It thrust the industry and the passenger experience into a new dimension. Among my many warm memories of Pan Am's 747 fleet were several candlelight dinners in the lounge on transpacific flights. Nice!

After 41 years at the helm, Trippe retired in the spring of 1968, four months before the 747's epic rollout. Despite their pedigree, none of his successors had Trippe's drive or vision. But one, Ed Acker, who came from Air Florida, made a big splash when he took over the reins in August 1981. Explaining why he left Air Florida, then a high-flying newcomer, for the troubled Pan Am, Acker said he had always wanted to be captain of the *Titanic.* He got his wish.

When Pan Am closed down, as many as 9,000 employees lost their jobs. This ill-fated work force — where do you find airline jobs today? — compares with about 50,000 in Pan Am's peak years.

Just when was that heyday? Hard to pinpoint, but when Trippe stepped down in 1968, the route structure spanned 81,430 miles. In fact, our current so-called U.S. megacarriers are dwarfs compared to Pan Am's global reach in its prime.

Even now, Pan Am remains the only U.S.-flag airline ever to offer scheduled passenger service to all of the continents.

Pan Am had a glorious run of 64 years, and I for one will miss it. *Sic transit gloria mundi … .*

Reprinted with permission from *TravelAge MidAmerica*

Air Travel
Chapter 3

End of Chapter Review

Name _____   Date _____

Directions: Fill in the blanks with the letter of the correct answer.

_____
1. A circle trip is a journey in which the same routing is used for the return trip from the turnaround point as was used in the outbound journey.
   A. True   B. False

_____
2. On a roundtrip, the same routing is followed in both directions and the final destination is the same as the point of origin.
   A. True   B. False

_____
3. Air transportation from a point of origin to a destination with a return to a point other than the point of origin is known as
   A. Roundtrip   B. Circle trip   C. Open jaw   D. None of these

_____
4. Air transportation from a point of origin to a destination with a return from a point other than the destination back to the point of origin is known as
   A. Roundtrip   B. Circle trip   C. Open jaw   D. None of these

_____
5. A destination is defined as the point farthest from
   A. The point of origin
   B. The point of departure
   C. The originating city
   D. All of the above

Directions: Decode each of the following abbreviations.

6. ATB _____

7. ARC _____

8. CRS _____

9. CRT _____

10. DOT _____

11. PNR _____

Directions: Identify each journey as either: OW   RT   Open Jaw   Circle Trip

12. JFK - ORD AA   _____

ORD - LAX AA

LAX - ORD AA

ORD - JFK AA

13. MIA - DFW DL   _____

DFW - SAT surface

SAT - MIA EA

14. LAX - LAS AA   _____

LAS - SFO UA

15. Encode each of the following cities:

Atlanta, GA   _____

Boston, MA

Denver, CO

Dallas/Ft. Worth, TX

90

Answers to End of Chapter Review Questions

1. B

2. A

3. C

4. C

5. D

6. ATB = Automated ticket/boarding pass

7. ARC = Airlines Reporting Corporation

8. CRS = Computer reservation system

9. CRT = Cathode ray tube

10. DOT = Department of Transportation

11. PNR = Passenger name record

12. RT

13. Open jaw

14. Open jaw

15. ATL
    BOS
    DEN
    DFW

International Travel
Chapter 4

Review Chapter Objectives
- Describe IATAN's primary functions
- Summarize the principles of international airfare construction
- Calculate time differences between two points
- Recommend ways to avoid jet lag
- Name three forms of proof of citizenship
- Identify three common health problems when traveling abroad
- Discuss the role of consolidators

Review Vocabulary
- Consolidator
- Duty-free
- Dysynchronosis
- GSP
- IATA/IATAN
- International dateline
- NUC
- Passport
- Proof of citizenship
- Tourist card
- VAT
- Visa

International Travel Careers
- Air Courier
- Attraction Employee
- Foreign Service Officer
- Film/Videomaker
- Ground Operator
- Interpreter
- Tour Escort
- Travel Writer

Transparencies
- Chapter outline
- 24-Hour clock
- Time zones

International Travel
Chapter 4 Outline

I. International Air

    A. IATA/IATAN

    B. Bilateral Pacts/Six Freedoms of the Air

II. International Airfares

    A. Airline Rate Desks

III. Regulation of International Travel

    A. Passports/Visas/Tourist Cards

    B. Proof of Citizenship

    C. 24-Hour Clock/Time Zones

IV. Customs Regulations

    A. Duty-free Items

    B. Forbidden and Restricted Items

    C. VAT/GSP

V. Health Issues

    A. Medical Assistance Abroad

    B. Jet Lag

VI. Terrorism

    A. State Department Warnings

VII. Foreign Currencies

    A. When and Where to Exchange Money

24-Hour Clock

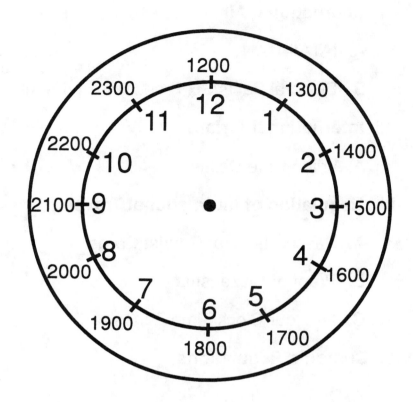

Time Zones

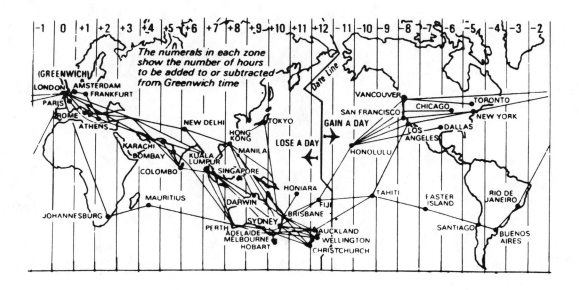

Answers to Textbook Review Questions

1. **How has the United States government's international aviation policy affected service from your nearest international gateway?**
Answers will vary.

2. **Explain briefly what a duty-free port or a duty-free store is.**
Answers will differ. Main concept is that duty-free at point of purchase does not mean duty-free on return to the United States.

3. **How can jet lag affect business travelers?**
Long flights disrupt normal eating and sleeping patterns. Business travelers must be mentally alert.

4. **Are there benefits to purchasing United States dollar travelers cheques rather than foreign currency travelers cheques?**
It is easier and quicker to obtain United States travelers cheques.

5. **How would fluctuations in currency rates affect supplier prices?**
Once suppliers have published rates, they must honor them with their retailers unless specifically noted in their promotional material. Sometimes this is to the benefit of the supplier, while at other times it results in a loss of revenue.

Answers to Discussion Topics

Machu Picchu
Acts of God, as most of the events related in this scenario can be called, do happen. A seasoned traveler anticipates them and rolls with the punches. Good weather and the absence of strikes can never be assured. Travelers should rest and take the first day easy when visiting high altitude destinations such as Cuzco. Agents can warn clients what to expect if they travel to the same or similar areas.

Visa Requirements
The Koalas should contact the nearest office of the Australian government. The Qantas representative can tell them where the office is and its office hours. SFO might have an Australian consulate. Australian visas are issued speedily. Perhaps the Koalas can make tomorrow's plane. The travel agent who neglected to tell the Koalas is responsible. Counseling travelers about documentation is part of a travel or airline reservation agent's job.

Proof of Citizenship
Items packed away do not have to be produced unless the United States customs agent asks to see them. Then the bus driver will have to unpack the bus and inconvenience the other passengers. Returning citizens must declare any items purchased in Canada that exceed their duty-free limits when they cross the border to return to the United States. Items declared "duty-free" at a store in Canada are not necessarily duty-free on entry to the United States. Incidentally, the point of entry may be at a border point or at a Canadian airport equipped with facilities to pre-clear people going to the United States. The Guide should remind passengers, in writing, the night before departure that they should have documents with them and easily available for the next day's border crossing. In this case the tour escort should call back to the coffee shop to try to locate the missing documents. It is possible that someone could deliver them to the border. Consider the convenience of the majority.

Missing Documents
Each lost item must be taken care of separately. A first step is to report the robbery to the hotel management and to the Rio police. Then notify the United States Embassy of stolen passports, credit card companies of credit cards, the theft of travelers cheques to the appropriate company, call the airline, etc. The problem is serious. The language of Brazil is Portuguese. Travelers should not expect everyone to speak their language. On Sundays offices might be closed.

Answers to Workbook Exercises

Worksheet 4-1

Consolidator	Companies that offer deeply discounted airfares to international destinations
Duty-free	A term that describes purchases that are not subject to taxes
Dysynchronosis	Jet lag
GSP	Generalized System of Preferences — a system exempting many goods from duty in an effort to stimulate that country's economy
IATA/IATAN	IATA is an association of international airlines whose aim is to create order and stability in the international aviation community. IATAN is the organization that appoints United States travel agencies to sell tickets for international airlines serving the United States.
International dateline	The international dateline is the point at which one day is separated from another.
NUC	Neutral Units of Construction — a worldwide currency conversion system that establishes an equitable method of calculating airfares
Passport	The official document issued by a person's own country, necessary for travel to most foreign countries.
Proof of Citizenship	A document that establishes nationality to the satisfaction of a foreign government
Tourist Card	A type of visa issued to travelers before they enter certain countries.
VAT	Value-Added Tax — a government-imposed tax
Visa	A permit to enter a foreign country, issued by the government of that country

Worksheet 4-2

1. IATA's aim is to create order and stability in the international aviation community.

2. IATAN replaced IATA as the organization that appoints United States travel agents to sell tickets for international airlines serving the United States. The primary difference between IATA and IATAN is that the latter is a service organization.

3. The IATAN travel agent ID card is meant to be a standard recognizable identification form for travel agents. Answers will vary if it serves a useful purpose.

4. Countries that have one official airline refer to that airline as their flag carrier. The United States does not have a flag carrier.

5. Mileage, maximum permitted miles, higher intermediate points, add-ons, neutral units of construction

6. The agents at an airline rate desk calculate fares for itineraries if the passenger is originating with the carrier or taking the first substantial international flight with it. One drawback might be that they are very busy, and it may take the rate desk agents some time to come up with an answer. Plus, the airline rate desks will not quote a fare for an unconfirmed itinerary.

Worksheet 4-2 (continued)

7. Consolidators offer deeply discounted airfares for international flights. Some of the drawbacks include: Severe penalties apply for any changes; no travel advice or counseling is available; routings may be unusual and/or time consuming; travelers may be required to use an airline with which they are not familiar.

8. Attend a training course in international air tariff and ticketing; read carefully through the IATA Ticketing Handbook; practice international fare calculation as time and opportunity permit.

Worksheet 4-3

1. 24

2. Greenwich, England

3. The international date line is on the opposite side of the world from the prime meridian.

4. a. 0913 b. 1525 c. 1150 d. 2058 e. 2205 f. 1359 g. 2100 h. 1230 i. 0500 j. 1902

5. 5:00 p.m. or 1700

Worksheet 4-4

1. Proof of Citizenship, two recent photographs, proof of identity, the fee.

2. Most Post Offices, and state and federal court buildings.

3. Ten years from the date of issuance.

4. $55 (first-time applicants pay an additional processing fee of $10)

5. A visa is an endorsement or stamp placed in a passport by officials of a foreign government.

6. The tour operator, a visa service, the consulate or embassy of the foreign country.

Worksheet 4-5

1. Choose from: a valid passport, an expired passport, a birth certificate with a raised seal, a naturalization certificate.

2. A duty-free port is one located in a country or territory where goods may be less expensive because no duty or taxes are levied on them either entering or leaving the country.

3. Choose from: narcotics, dangerous drugs, fireworks, switchblade knives, dangerous toys, and automobiles that don't conform to standards. Other items include articles made from whale teeth, African ivory, tortoise shell, alligator skin, and furs.

4. The purpose of the GSP is to help developing countries stimulate their economy.

5. A Value Added Tax is a surcharge or additional sales tax placed over and above the cost of an item.

Worksheet 4-6

1. Choose from: adjusting eating and sleeping schedules, scheduling arrivals close to the passengers' normal bedtime, not rushing around on the day of departure. While on the flight — don't drink alcohol or overeat. Try to sleep, and walk around the plane. Finally after arrival at the destination, don't rush into a hectic schedule.

2. F

3. F

4. T

5. C

6. A

Worksheet 4-7

1. **Advantage** — When first arriving at a destination, travelers do not have to spend time looking for places to exchange money.

   Disadvantage — Choose from:
   a. The exchange rate may not be favorable.
   b. Many countries limit the amount of banknotes that a visitor can bring.
   c. Some countries forbid the export of their currency.
   d. Not all banks stock supplies of foreign currency.

2. **Advantage** — Travelers cheques are safer than cash. Travelers do not have to spend time looking for places to exchange money.

   Disadvantage — There is usually a loss on the exchange rate. In addition to paying a service charge or commission to the seller, the traveler also pays a charge each time he cashes a cheque.

3. **Advantage** — Some banks or companies will waive the charge for U.S. travelers cheques. They are worth full value on the client's return to the U.S. They may not be subject to the import restrictions of foreign countries.

   Disadvantage — There is usually a small service charge for obtaining travelers cheques.

4. **Advantage** — They are widely accepted around the world. They provide a useful record of all purchases. Use of a credit card helps to spread vacation payments over time, because billing may not appear for several months after the purchase.

   Disadvantage — The rate of exchange when the billing occurs may be less favorable from the rate of exchange when the charge was made.

Worksheet 4-8

1. Yes

2. Chicago and New York

3. Dublin

4. Shannon; 9 miles southeast

5. Yes

6. Yes

7. 6 miles north of the city

8. Short term — £ .70 one hour; Long term — £ 2.50 per day

9. April

Classroom Activities

1. This is a good opportunity to introduce the *OAG Worldwide Edition*. Design exercises relating to destinations commonly serviced from your area.

2. Ask students to bring in passports, visas, or other formal government documents. Compare those issued to American citizens with those issued to international citizens studying in the U.S. Ask international students to discuss the restrictions placed on them when traveling throughout the U.S. What restrictions are placed on Americans traveling through the international students' countries? What are some common cultural differences that were most interesting to international students in the U.S.? What were some common problems or cultural differences Americans experienced when traveling abroad?

3. Multiculturalism is a vital topic in today's global economy. Have students organize an international bazaar complete with food, videos, slides, and posters from various countries. Currency from the host countries can be used to barter for items. Local costumes should be worn, local languages spoken, and cultural differences and customs discussed. If only one or two students are international, ask them to discuss their country's cultures and customs.

Articles

Chapter 4 — Article One
"The Anatomy of a Travel Advisory"
Copy this article for students. Ask them to discuss the effect of the Persian Gulf War on travel to the Mideast. What are the duties and responsibilities of travel agents to their clients during these times of crisis? Where can agents obtain additional information? What are other areas of the world that require special consideration before making recommendations to clients?

Chapter 4 — Article One
The Anatomy of a Travel Advisory

By Barbara Cook

During the tense months leading up to the Persian Gulf war, Americans became accustomed to listening for travel advisories from the U.S. State Department as a barometer of the world situation.

Non-travelers as well as potential travelers and their travel counselors gauged the U.S. government's concern for international terrorist activity by the number of countries added to the travel warning list. And as the list grew, international travel plummeted, despite the absence of actual terrorist activity.

The U.S. State Department, through its Citizens Emergency Center (CEC), issues travel advisories to warn Americans considering going abroad about adverse conditions they might find in specific countries. An advisory is not issued every time an American is hurt overseas; there has to be a significant risk to travelers as a whole.

Travel advisories are not travel bans. They gibe specific information about problem areas within a country and note the rest of the country may be safe for travel. The advisories concern civil unrest, natural disasters and outbreaks of serious disease.

The State Department's process for issuing a travel advisory is not an exact science. The birth of a travel advisory typically begins "at post," a State Department term which refers to the U.S. Embassy in a foreign country. The U.S. consular affairs officers in a foreign country read local newspapers, make personal visits throughout the country and have excellent local police sources. Based on information gathered from these resources, they determine whether or not an advisory is needed at any given time.

Another option is for the regional security officer (RSO) of the embassy to become aware of potential trouble and begin the groundwork toward eventual issuance of an advisory. Normally an advisory is not issued until further research and deliberation is conducted in Washington.

In the case of the Persian Gulf crisis, a decision was made at the highest State Department levels to issue an advisory as soon as Iraq invaded Kuwait on August 2, 1990. The statement was brief, simply alerting Americans to postpone all travel to Kuwait.

All travel advisories carry an expiration date: The Kuwait warning noted the duration of the advisory was "indefinite." Michael Brennan, director of public affairs for the Consular Affairs Bureau at the State Department, explained the three types of travel advisories: cautions, warnings and notices.

- **A notice**, the lowest level of travel advisory, is defined by the State Department as an alert when conditions exist in a country that can cause a traveler "inconvenience." This refers to such conditions as potential hotel overcrowding due to festivals or holidays. These alerts have a short shelf life and more limited distribution.

- **A caution** is the next level of intensity in advisories. This refers to unusual situations that have the potential for "unexpected detention or serious health problems" for American travelers.

- **The warning** is the highest level of advisory, It was used for the Persian Gulf war. A warning means conditions exist "that have the potential for actual physical danger such as terrorism, civil disorder or natural disaster."

The CEC published more than 100 travel advisories during the Persian Gulf conflict, Brennan said. However, the one travel advisory issued during the conflict that probably proved to be the most devastating to the travel industry wasn't technically an advisory at all. It was the "announcement" by the State Department's press officer on September 7, notifying Americans that "Iraq offers support, assistance and encouragement to terrorist groups capable of undertaking attacks at almost any time throughout Western Europe and the Middle East. Among the potential targets for such attacks are Americans and American interests."

The "announcement," while not actually an advisory, began as a new form of travel communication from the State Department in 1989. Originating from the department's Office of Security and Counter-Terrorism, these statements are read by the press officer to the media and describe situations in an area regarding terrorism. The statements often include hints for travelers on how to make themselves less visible as terrorist targets.

The department distributes its travel advisories on computer reservations systems, on CompuServe, which may be accessed on personal computers, and through country-by-country recordings on a special CEC telephone number (202-647-5225).

The CEC recorded list of advisories gives first a recitation of affected countries by region of the world. Callers may then select up to three advisories to hear before the recording disconnects. Each advisory begins with a brief summary followed by the entire content of the message. Through use of touch-tone phones, callers can hear just the summary or the entire advisory; the process takes almost five minutes to get one complete advisory.

The CEC formerly issued a one-page, written listing of advisories, noting only the country affected, the date the advisory was issued and the level of the advisory (caution or warning). That list is no longer made public, Brennan said, because feedback from the travel industry indicated people weren't reading the substance of the advisories and were simply avoiding travel to the countries listed. "It scared too many people who then didn't read the actual advisory," Brennan explained.

Philip Davidoff, CTC, president of Belair Travel in Bowie, Md., and president of the American Society of Travel Agents, criticized the scope of the advisories issued during the Persian Gulf conflict. "Especially early on the advisories were exceedingly broad and maybe covered areas they shouldn't have," he said. Davidoff specifically referred to the Western Europe announcement that depressed international travel. "These advisories affect the lives and businesses of a lot of people," he noted.

There has been some criticism of travel agents recently for not adequately informing their clients of existing travel advisories even though the information is readily available in CRS systems, Davidoff said.

To make it easier for the travel counselor to inform clients of existing travel advisories, ASTA is lobbying CRS vendors to flag flights to areas that have travel advisories. A simple notice to "check State Department advisory" would remind agents to access the advisory menu, Davidoff said.

"This is technically possible," he said. So far, however, vendors are resisting adding the flaging procedure to CRS systems, saying it is too expensive to implement, Davidoff said.

Case Study

At the height of the Persian Gulf crisis, the State Department's Citizens Emergency Center (CEC) — normally staffed with 25 personnel — grew into an around-the-clock operation with 150 staff members.

Georgia Rogers, deputy director of the CEC, explained the normal function of the office is to assist Americans who have run into problems while traveling or living abroad.

"People may have had accidents or have medical problems or even die overseas," Rogers said. "Or there may be a family emergency here, and the person abroad needs to be contacted. We are a facilitator to help the family."

When a major crisis develops abroad, however, the CEC immediately pulls together an expanded staff from other offices in the Bureau of Consular Affairs and forms a task force. The potential members of the task force have been identified in advance and trained for emergency work. In their normal jobs, these staff members are consular officers who may process passports or handle similar functions. "It only takes us 15 minutes to set up an emergency task force," Rogers said, since the personnel have been selected in advance. The task force does not work out of the CEC office — which becomes too small at this point — but sets up a special area of the State Department. The Persian Gulf task force was established in five separate rooms, utilizing 50 staff members on each eight-hour shift , 24 hours a day.

Separate phone numbers are set up for the task force to use to free up the regular CEC number (202-647-5225) for its routine work.

"The initial week of the crisis in August, we were getting hundreds of calls each hour — probably 4,000 a day," Rogers said. "August was the worst. By January, most Americans had departed the affected area, and our call volume fell off to 200 calls per shift."

In addition to receiving calls from Americans seeking travel advice or information about family and friends, the CEC telephone bank was making calls, attempting to keep in touch with Americans caught up in the war.

One phenomenon that developed during the Gulf conflict was "CNN-itis" — loosely described as Americans' addiction to television news.

"Any time the media has a story affecting Americans, our phone banks light up," Rogers said. "Just be patient and call later if you can't get through." The first 15 minutes after a story breaks on CNN is the worst possible time to try to reach the center.

The Persian Gulf emergency gave the CEC an opportunity to refine its operation, Rogers said. "We learned an awful lot and we will continue to work in cooperation with some outside groups again." For example, Rogers said the CEC worked with groups such as the National Organization of Victims Assistance, a counseling group, in its efforts to assist American travelers. These outside organizations supplemented the CEC's own resources.

The CEC advises American travelers to routinely get into the habit of checking in with the U.S. Embassy when traveling in remote areas. This way, in the event of a natural disaster or civil unrest, the embassy will be able to check up on the group or individual to determine if assistance is needed.

The CEC also advises travelers to make a photocopy of their passport information page and carry it separately from the passport. In the event that the passport is stolen, the embassy is able to replace the document sooner.

Case Study
Anatomy of a Crisis

August 2, 1990 - Kuwait - Warning
The Department of State advises that due to the Iraqi Military invasion of Kuwait, American citizens should postpone all travel to Kuwait. Expiration: Indefinite.

September 7, 1990 - Announcement
Iraq has expanded its support for numerous international terrorist groups, particularly radical Palestinian elements, within the last several months. As a consequence, on September 1, Iraq was placed on the U.S. government list of state sponsors for terrorism.

October 5, 1990 - Middle East, Africa, and South Asia - Warning
The Department of State advises all U.S. citizen residents of, and travelers to, the countries of the Middle East, South Asia and North Africa that increased tensions due to the Iraqi military invasion of Kuwait may lead to demonstrations or other actions that may be directed against the United States. Expiration: Indefinite.

January 11, 1991 - Middle East, Africa and South Asia - Warning
The Department of State advises all U.S. citizen residents of, and travelers to, the countries of the Middle East, South Asia and North Africa that increased tensions due to Iraq's failure to comply with the United Nations Security Council resolutions may lead to demonstrations, terrorist attacks and other hostile actions against the U.S. government and U.S. citizens in the area. Should hostilities occur in the Persian Gulf, this threat will be heightened. Expiration: Indefinite.

January 16, 1991 - Persian Gulf - Warning
With the outbreak of hostilities in the Persian Gulf region, U.S. citizens are advised to avoid travel near the scene of military operations. Travelers should also be aware of the threat of terrorist actions against U.S. citizens or property in other locations worldwide and adjust their travel plans accordingly. Information on affected locations and specific travel advisories can be obtained from the Department of State at 202-647-5225 or 202-647-0900. Expiration: Indefinite.

January 25, 1991 - Middle East, Africa and South Asia - Warning

With the outbreak of hostilities in the Persian Gulf region, U.S. citizens are advised to avoid travel near the scene of military operations. As stated in our advisory issued January 16, travelers should also be aware of the threat of terrorist actions against U.S. citizens or property in other locations worldwide. In particular, the outbreak of hostilities in the Persian Gulf may lead to demonstrations, terrorist attacks and other hostile actions against the U.S. citizens in the Middle East, Africa and South Asia.

March 10, 1991 - Worldwide - Persian Gulf Cancellation

With the cessation of hostilities in the Persian Gulf, the Worldwide-Persian Gulf advisory of January 16, 1991, has been cancelled.

March 10, 1991 - Middle East, Africa, South Asia - Caution

With the cessation of hostilities in the Gulf area, the Department of State is reassessing the security situation in the Middle East, Africa and South Asia and will be updating country-specific travel advisories. Although a ceasefire is in place, tensions still remain in many parts of the area.

While demonstrations, terrorist attacks and other hostile actions against the United States and its allies have slackened, Americans traveling throughout the region should continue to exercise caution … . While the precise health risk caused by the oil fires in Kuwait has yet to be determined, travelers to the northern Gulf area should be aware of the potential danger. Expiration date: Indefinite.

Reprinted with permission from *Travel Counselor* magazine, a CMP publication

International Travel
Chapter 4

End of Chapter Review

Name _____ Date _____

Directions: Answer the questions in the space provided.

1. A passport is issued by

    _____.

2. A visa is issued by

    _____.

3. To obtain a passport a United States citizen must present a proof of citizenship. Name three documents that are acceptable as proof:

    A. _____

    B. _____

    C. _____

4. Name two countries that would accept proof of citizenship only instead of a passport.

    A. _____

    B. _____

5. What is the duty free exemption for United States travelers returning from

    A. Paris _____   B. St. Thomas _____

6. How much liquor is allowed duty free for a U.S. citizen returning from Barbados?

    _____

7. What should a travel counselor tell a client who must carry prescription drugs on an international trip?

    _____

8. How many years is an adult passport valid for?

    A. 2   B. 5   C. 7   D. 10

9. Gifts purchased abroad and mailed to the United States are not subject to duty provided they do not exceed $ _____.

A. $50   B. $100   C. $150   D. $200

10. No documents are necessary to obtain a tourist card.

A. True   B. False

Answers to End of Chapter Review Questions

1. A government to its own citizens

2. Officials of a foreign government

3. Birth certificate, Certificate of Naturalization, old passport

4. Canada, Bermuda, Bahamas, Mexico, many islands of the Caribbean. Passport preferred by all.

5. a. $400
    b. $800

6. 1 litre

7. Carry a copy of the prescription; carry prescription drugs in clearly-marked, original containers.

8. D — 10 years

9. $50

10. F

Ground Transportation
Chapter 5

Review Chapter Objectives
- Describe four types of Amtrak accommodations
- Summarize three differences between domestic and international rail service
- Explain the restrictions that apply to a Eurailpass
- List the requirements for car rental
- Note the factors that determine car rental rates
- Identify four possible problems when renting cars abroad

Review Vocabulary
- AAA
- Amtrak
- BritRail
- CDW
- Eurailpass
- Liter
- LRC
- Roomette
- Slumbercoach
- VIA

Ground Transportation Careers
- Car-rental Agent
- Chauffeur
- Dispatcher
- Lead Service Attendant
- Motorcoach Driver
- Reservationist
- Sales Representative
- Ticket Agent

Transparencies
- Chapter outline
- Amtrak map
- Car rental qualifiers
- Choosing a car rental company

Ground Transportation
Chapter 5 Outline

I. Rail Transportation

   A. Amtrak

   B. International Rail

       1. Rail Europe/VIA Rail Canada

   C. Rail Passes

       1. Eurailpass/BritRail Pass

II. Rental Cars

   A. Qualifications

   B. Domestic

   C. International

Amtrak Map

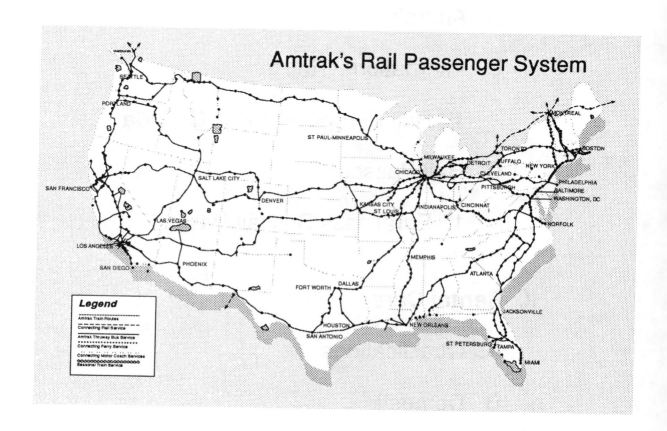

Car Rental Qualifiers

1. When and where will
   the client pick up the car?

2. When and where will
   the client drop off the car?

3. What kind of car does
   the client wish to rent?

4. When and for how long
   will the client want to rent?

5. What additional charges
   might be added?

6. Is the client eligible for discounts?

7. Will the client need insurance?

Choosing a Car Rental Company

Factor	% of Respondents
Ease of Getting Car	65
Return-location Options	49
Express Return	47
Airport Location	47
Directions to and from Places	43
Special Discounts	43
Mileage Plan	42
Reputation of Company	39
Additional Charges	38
Models Offered	34
Insurance	30
Price of Gas	29
Part of Package	28
Frequent-flyer Tie-ins	17

Answers to Textbook Review Questions

1. **For what reasons might clients prefer to travel by train in Europe?**
   It is less expensive than flying within Europe.
   Train travel is very popular in Europe and can be a good way to meet locals.
   A traveler can enjoy the local countryside without having to concentrate on driving.
   European trains are fast, modern, clean, and reliable.

2. **What rail service exists in your area?**
   Answers may vary.

3. **How would you compare seeing the Canadian Rockies by train and by motorcoach?**
   Trains can travel to out-of-the-way scenic areas where there are no roads.

4. **What clients might appreciate a Eurailpass?**
   Clients who want flexibility and freedom or clients who are planning a lot of rail travel

5. **What are the benefits of traveling by car?**
   Freedom — Cars provide the freedom and flexibility to deviate from an itinerary.
   Versatility — Travelers can visit areas inaccessible by other means of transportation.
   Room for baggage — Travelers can bring extra items on their trip.
   Economy — A car rental is economical when a large group of people travel together.

6. **In what situations might a car rental be necessary?**
   A business traveler requiring a speedy means of transportation
   A business traveler needing to visit a client in an area not serviced by air
   A traveler touring an area not serviced by public transportation
   A traveler who wants independence

7. **For what reasons might a client accept or refuse Collision Damage Waiver and Personal Accident Insurance?**

   Accept   Clients will not be liable for damages if they are in an accident.
                Clients will avoid having to leave a large cash deposit.
                Clients will have peace of mind.
   Refuse   Clients gamble that they won't be in an accident.
                Clients have individual policies that cover them in the event of accident.
                Clients have coverage provided by their credit card company when they use the card for the rental payment.

8. **What is the difference between renting and leasing a car?**
   Leasing a car is a good option for clients who need a car for a month or longer. They come new from the factory and usually cost less over an extended period than rental cars.

Answers to Discussion Topics

Advertised Rates

A. The counter agent should review the advertisement with the customers and explain why the car choice is inappropriate for their situation. The agent should then assist them in selecting a car better suited to their needs.

B. a full sized car or a station wagon; unlimited mileage

Train Travel

The Atrics could take the train back to Spokane and then proceed to Portland. They should also consider renting a car, flying or taking a motorcoach. At this stage of the journey, the Atrics may want to compare cost versus time.The travel agent could investigate the above options and present all the information for the clients to choose. Amtrak is not responsible for the Atrics having wandered to the wrong section of the train. However, an Amtrak agent can assist should the clients want to continue their trip by train.

Transfers

On arrival at the airport, clients could look for a bank to exchange their money to pay the driver. If time does not permit, the cab driver would probably accept American money. They will make their flight if they left enough time for an emergency. They should contact their travel agent to obtain a refund for their unused transfer.

Answers to Workbook Exercises

Worksheet 5-1

AAA	The American Automobile Association — an organization offering travel and motoring services
Amtrak	The National Railroad Passenger Corporation — a government-subsidized corporation that operates almost all passenger train service in the United States
BritRail	The North American division of British Rail. BritRail Travel issues the BritRail Pass, a pass used for travel in Great Britain.
CDW	Collision Damage Waiver — the waiver of the rental company's right to charge the renter for damages if the rental car is involved in an accident
Eurailpass	A train pass good for unlimited train travel in 17 countries of Europe.
Liter	A metric measurement — a liter equals 0.908 percent of a dry quart or 1.057 percent of a liquid quart.
LRC	A type of Via Rail coach — it stands for Light, Rapid, and Comfortable.
Roomette	On an Amtrak train, a slightly larger single room with toilet facilities
Slumbercoach	On Amtrak, a sleeping room with toilet and washroom facilities
VIA	Canada's passenger train network linking Canadian cities from the Atlantic to the Pacific Coasts

Worksheet 5-2

1. National routes are principally for leisure travel whereas corridor routes are commercially oriented.

2. The LRCs (Light, Rapid, and Comfortable), VIAs (First Class Affordable), Transcontinentals

3. Eurailpass — Austria, Belgium, Denmark, Finland, France, Germany, Greece, Holland, Hungary, Italy, Luxembourg, Norway, Portugal, the Republic of Ireland, Spain, Sweden, and Switzerland

   BritRail — England, Scotland, and Wales

4. Plot an itinerary following a continuous loop or the hub-and-spoke approach

5. Answers will vary.

6. The *Thomas Cook European Timetable* and the *Thomas Cook Overseas Timetable*

7. F

8. F

9. F

10. T

Worksheet 5-3

1. Be of a certain age, have a valid driver's license, be credit worthy, be personally responsible

2. Freedom, versatility, room for baggage, economy

3. Choose from: Familiar cars appear under strange names; automatic transmissions must be specifically requested in advance; gasoline prices may be substantially higher than in the United States; distances are expressed in kilometers; international currencies fluctuate; quoted rates may not include VAT; some countries require local travel permits.

4. CDW — Collision Damage Waiver — the waiver of the rental company's right to charge the renter for damages if the rental car is involved in an accident

   LDW — The waiver of responsibility for damages resulting from theft or vandalism as well as collision.

   PAI — Personal Accident Insurance — Provides coverage in the event of bodily injury to the renter.

Worksheet 5-4

Answers will vary.

Worksheet 5-5

1. 8:07 a.m.

2. sandwiches, snack, and beverage service

3. Boston, MA — South Station

4. 10:40 a.m.

5. Yes — No

Classroom Activities

1. Ask students to provide directions from your school to a popular local tourist attraction. Remind them to use standard street names, route numbers, landmarks, mileage, and so on. Some may draw maps, while others will write out everything. Then, break them into groups and ask them to decide on a universally acceptable set of directions. Share their ideas with the class. How would these directions differ if driving after dark? Ask if this was difficult.

2. Ask students to compare prices for a trip to Washington, DC, from Boston, MA, via train, rental car, limousine, and local motorcoach. Use substitute cities, if necessary. What is the best value in terms of time? What is the best value in terms of money? Consider out-of-pocket expenses such as parking, drop off charges, and so on.

3. Contact Amtrak for a copy of their promotional material including video. Show video and ask students for their perceptions. How many of them have ever traveled via Amtrak? What tour packages would seem to be the most appealing? Why? Using the Amtrak timetable, cost out a tour for one of these tourist trips using a family or senior citizen group. What special instructions would be necessary when counseling these clients?

4. Use the *Thomas Cook Timetables* or others obtained from rail companies. Choose city pairs to have students learn how to read a timetable. To increase difficulty, use city pairs that require one or more connections.

Articles

Chapter 5 — Article One
"Grand Canyon Railway"
Copy the following article about the Grand Canyon Railway. Possible topics of discussion for students include:

1. What compelling influence motivates the investors of the Grand Canyon Railway to undertake the construction of a project of such magnitude? Why?

2. Discuss how to position this new product in the consumer's mind through nationwide advertising.

3. What are some external influences that might affect promotion of the Grand Canyon Railway? Describe their positive or negative effects.

Chapter 5 — Article One
The Grand Canyon Railway

By John P. Butters, CTC

The Grand Canyon is once again served by a steam train after many years. To make this possible the Grand Canyon Railway, a privately founded enterprise, is spending over $80 million on a tourist project that will cover more than a thousand acres. The once popular train ceased operating over twenty years ago due to a steady decline in ridership attributed to the automobile. Now with a bit of irony, the National Park Service praises the project's potential for providing much-needed relief from auto congestion in the area. The historic steam train not only links the Grand Canyon National Park to new lodging, dining, and shopping facilities, but plays a vital role in both restoring much of the lost environmental quality of this great American heritage site and bringing back a bit of nostalgia to America's western frontier. This case study details the revival of this service.

Rail Travel

Tourism literature often refers to the Grand Canyon as the most awe-inspiring and spectacular natural phenomenon on earth. Listed as one of the Seven Natural Wonders of the World, the Grand Canyon became a national park in 1919. In 1979 it was named a World Heritage Site, a place which has superlative natural and cultural features and is considered to have universal value to all mankind.

The volume of tourists visiting the Grand Canyon increases each year. The shift of the U.S. population to the sunbelt states of the South and the Southwest is a contributing factor to the growth in number of park visitors. In addition, 35-40% of all the visitors to the Grand Canyon are from outside the United States, with the greatest number arriving from Western Europe and Japan. With the Grand Canyon National Park hosting more tourists than any other major western national park, it is often referred to as America's number one natural tourist attraction.

The new railway company acquired the track and rights-of-way from the Atchison, Topeka, and Santa Fe Company. The train follows the original run of the old Santa Fe from Williams, Arizona, to the Grand Canyon depot just steps from South Rim. Four 1910 steam-fired engines pull Harriman coaches, all restored to museum quality at a cost of over $15 million. The 64-mile route across Northern Arizona's plains and forest lands gives the passengers the feeling of going back in time.

Both depots, the original buildings dating from 1908, have been renovated and are listed on the National Register of Historic Places. The Williams Depot houses the Grand Canyon Railway Museum. The story of early railroading and the development of the Grand Canyon region are depicted through displays of railroad equipment, uniforms, signs, and tools together with mining, logging, and ranching paraphernalia.

The steam train pulls out of Williams every morning for the two-hour ride to the South Rim. The railway ticket booth dispenses information pertinent to the day's activities. A complimentary newspaper distributed on board details the history of the canyon. Snack and beverage service is available. During the three-hour layover, motorcoach tours, at an additional cost, show the visitors the spectacular scenery. After an eventful day the steam train puffs its way back to Williams in the early evening.

The return of the Grand Canyon Railway involves a major team effort with private enterprise and agencies of the federal, state, county, and local governments working together to solve a critical environmental problem within one of our nation's most important national parks. The Grand Canyon National Park is plagued by traffic congestion, resulting in poor air quality and gridlock. The return of rail service from I-40 at Williams to the Grand Canyon offers the potential for decreasing motor traffic in the National Park by a significant percentage.

In addition, the new railway company should have a strong economic impact upon the entire Northern Arizona area, acting as a catalyst in changing the status of the magnificent Grand Canyon from an international tourist attraction to an international tourist destination. Presently, the majority of visitors stay less than a day. The full spectrum of family entertainment and recreational activities, plus the attraction and convenience of a nostalgic steam train ride, will certainly help to extend vacations in the area. This project intends to generate several hundred million dollars in annual tourism revenues.

The City of Williams, which will once again reign as the "Gateway to the Grand Canyon," has been selected as the site for an American West amusement and recreational project of theme park magnitude. A new high-quality, full-service hotel; extensive RV facilities; a major Old West theme town with authentic street fronts, shops, and restaurants; a rodeo arena; a Native American Cultural center; and an entertainment complex remain on the drawing board. The long-shuttered landmark, Fray Marcos Hotel, now contains restaurants, retail shops, and other passenger services. It also serves as the business headquarters for the Grand Canyon Railway.

A new branch line track to link the main line to the Grand Canyon Airport is under study. This link would provide domestic and international passengers with mass transportation direct to the Canyon's South Rim. The airport area is also under consideration for hotel development and initial parking facilities for over 2,000 automobiles, motorcoaches, and recreational vehicles.

Reprinted with permission from *Travel Industry Management*, a publication of the Institute of Certified Travel Agents

Ground Transportation
Chapter 5

End of Chapter Review

Name _____ Date _____

Directions: Fill in the blanks.

1. The _____ offers high-speed service between major cities.

2. A _____ is an economy single room with washroom facilities, designed for day and night use.

3. What publication gives detailed information about Amtrak's and VIA Rail Canada's timetables, fares, and services?

_____

4. On European trains, what are second class sleepers normally called and how are they composed?

_____

_____

5. Name the time periods for which Eurailpasses are valid.

_____

_____

6. How old must you be to qualify for a Eurail Youthpass and for what time periods are they valid?

_____

_____

7. The bullet trains, sometimes reaching speeds of 256 miles per hour are in

_____

8. Who issues international driver's permits and what is required to obtain one?

_____

_____

_____

9. On what basis are car rental rates calculated? When are the rates computed for the customer?

_____

_____

10. What five features must car rental firms include in their print ads?

   1. _____

   2. _____

   3. _____

   4. _____

   5. _____

Answers to End of Chapter Review Questions

1. Metroliner

2. slumbercoach

3. the *Official Railway Guide*

4. couchettes — composed of compartments with six bunk beds

5. 15 or 21 days — one, two, or three months

6. They are available to anyone under 26 years of age and are valid for one or two months.

7. Japan

8. AAA - a valid license, a fee, and two passport-sized photos

9. They are calculated on a 24-hour basis. The rates are computed when the car is returned.

10. Airport access fees, mileage fees, geographical limits, blackout dates, and optional fees for additional drivers or early/late returns.

Cruising
Chapter 6

Review Chapter Objectives
- Discuss four benefits of cruising
- Explain what is included in the cost of a cruise
- Name two possible cruising disadvantages
- Generalize about cruise line clientele
- Name the four factors that determine the cost of a cruise
- Differentiate among cruise ships, yachts, freighters, and ferries

Review Vocabulary
- Bareboat charter
- Berth
- Bow
- Bridge
- CLIA
- Forward
- Leeward
- Shore excursion
- Starboard
- Stern
- Tender
- Windjammer

Cruise Line Careers
- Bridge Officer
- Captain
- Chief Purser
- Deck Officer
- Navigation Officer
- Radio Officer
- Staff Captain
- Cabin Steward
- Dining-Room Steward
- Engineer
- Sailor
- Cruise Director
- Entertainer
- Host/Hostess
- Purser
- Shore-Excursion Manager
- Casino Croupier
- Photographer

Transparencies
- Chapter outline
- CLIA brochure analysis (handout)
- Deck plan
- Cruising areas
- Price of a cruise

Cruising
Chapter 6 Outline

I. The Cruise Market

    A. What is a Cruise Like?

    B. Amenities

II. The Benefits of Cruising

III. Possible Disadvantages

IV. What is Included and Not Included

V. Cruising Areas

VI. Non-Traditional Cruises

VII. The Price of a Cruise

    A. The length, the season,
       the ship, the cabin

VIII. Selling Cruises

    A. Cruise-only Agencies

    B. Cruise Directories

IX. New Ships and Technology

LINE: _____ SHIP: _____

P.O.E. _____ SAILING DATE: _____ VOYAGE LENGTH:_____

EMBARKATION TIME: _____ SAILING TIME: _____

G.R.T. _____ CRUISE CAPACITY: _____ SPACE RATIO: _____

USUAL DINING HOURS: _____ _____ _____

                             (FIRST)   (SECOND)   (ONE)

FORM(S) OF PAYMENT: _____

SIGNIFICANT "SELLING FEATURES": _____

_____

_____

_____

SIGNIFICANT "SELLING FEATURES" OF CATEGORY: _____ CABIN NO: _____

_____

_____

APPROXIMATE SIZE OF CABIN NO: _____ _____ FEET _____ FEET

RATE PER PERSON (BASIS TWO) FOR CATEGORY: _____$ _____

AIR FARE (CREDIT) $_____

PORT TAXES $ _____

CANCELLATION INS $ _____

TRANSFERS $ _____

TOTAL $ _____

DEPOSIT REQUIREMENT: WHEN _____AMOUNT $ _____

BALANCE DUE: WHEN _____AMOUNT $ _____

COMMISSION: $ _____AMOUNT NET $ _____

3RD, 4TH PERSON & CHILDREN'S FARES: _____

_____

PER DIEMS PER PERSON (BASIS TWO) INCLUDING AIR FROM: _____

TOP: _____ AVERAGE: _____MINIMUM:_____

Deck Plan

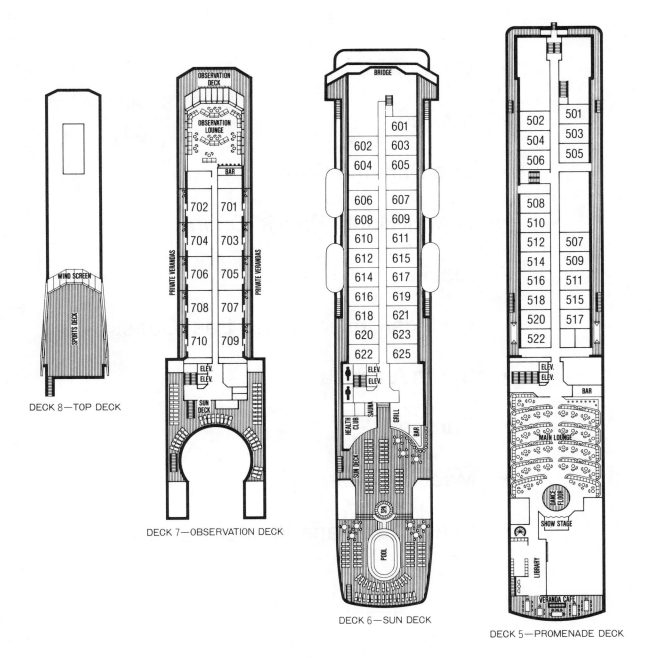

DECK 8—TOP DECK

DECK 7—OBSERVATION DECK

DECK 6—SUN DECK

DECK 5—PROMENADE DECK

Seven Seas Cruise Line
Song of Flower
Total Capacity: 216 Passengers

Cruising Areas

- The Caribbean

- Bermuda

- Mexico

- The Panama Canal

- Hawaii/South Pacific/Orient

- Alaska

- Canada/United States East Coast

- South America

- Europe

- Mediterranean

- Scandinavia and Western Europe

The Price of a Cruise

- The Length

- The Season

- The Ship

- The Cabin

Answers to Textbook Review Questions

1. **Why might clients prefer one ship over another?**
    Answers may include history, reputation, service, design, and price.

2. **If you could take a cruise, where would you like to go and why?**
    Answers will vary.

3. **How does river or canal cruising differ from ocean cruising?**
    Passengers remain close to shore, there are frequent stops, the ships are much smaller.

4. **What makes cruises desirable?**
    Answers may include: all-inclusive, relaxing, include a wide range of activities, service, prepaid

5. **Why might you purchase shore excursions in advance?**
    To better predict how much money you need
    To pre-reserve the most popular ones
    On some cruises, you can purchase all shore excursions as a package. The package price represents a savings for people planning to take most or all of the shore excursions.

6. **Which cruises attract older clients? Younger? Richer? Why?**
    Older clients may take longer cruises.
    Younger clients may be attracted to the party cruises.
    Richer clients may be attracted to the cruises that emphasize luxury and pampering.

7. **For what reasons might clients prefer an inside cabin?**
    Clients who plan to use the cabin only for sleeping
    Clients looking for a bargain

Answers to Discussion Topics

Group Sales
Ensure that the cruise line is aware of any special needs the group may have.
Check with the cruise line to ensure that it has facilities for the handicapped.
The Queen Elizabeth 2 would provide the luxury and romanticism that would particularly appeal to a group of senior citizens.

Repeat Clientele
The agency should explain the cruise line's policy to the Travelalots. It may be best to avoid mentioning the possibility of an upgrade in case it doesn't happen.

Honeymoon Present
Your fiance has been given incorrect information by his friends. There are endless activities on a cruise. Also, it will not be expensive because the only additional expenses will be for shore excursions, alcohol, tips, and souvenirs.

Bargain Rate
You must explain to the callers that lead rates are available only in limited quantity. The next step is either to sell a higher category of the advertised cruise or sell a different cruise of similar value.

Answers to Workbook Exercises

Worksheet 6-1

Bareboat charter	The chartering of a boat without a crew or provisions
Berth	A bed on a ship or a place for a ship to dock
Bow	The front or forward portion of a ship
Bridge	The navigational and command control center of the ship
CLIA	Cruise Lines International Association — an organization offering promotional materials, training guides, reference books, and seminars on behalf of member cruise lines
Forward	At or near the front part of the ship
Leeward	The direction away from the wind
Shore Excursion	Land tours of ports of call
Starboard	The right side of the ship
Stern	The very rear of the ship
Tender	A boat used when docking is not possible to transport passengers from ship to shore and back
Windjammer	A sailboat with multiple sails

Worksheet 6-2

1. N
2. N
3. I
4. I
5. N
6. N
7. N
8. I
9. I
10. I
11. T
12. T
13. F
14. F
15. T

Worksheet 6-3

1. Choose from: relaxation, entertainment, service, the ship, value, prepayment

2. Choose from: A cruise provides only a fleeting glance of destinations visited; some people feel confined on a cruise, and weather can reduce the pleasure of a cruise.

3. The length, the season, the ship, the cabin

4. Choose from: the Ohio River, the Mississippi River, the Rhine, the Amazon, the Thames, the Loire, the Nile, the Danube, the Yangtze

5. Tips are usually given to the dining room steward, the busboy, and the cabin steward. The usual amount of the tips is from $3 to $5 a day per person. Bar personnel, wine stewards, or cocktail waiters are tipped the normal 15% whenever a tab is paid.

6. A cruise that transfers a ship from one cruising area to another between seasons. They are good opportunities for veteran cruisers to try an unusual itinerary with their favorite ship. They can also offer substantial discounts.

Worksheet 6-4

1. B

2. B

3. C

4. C

5. C

6. C

7. A

8. A

Worksheet 6-5

Answers will vary.

Worksheet 6-6

1. Tuesday, September 8 — or Friday, September 18

2. Vancouver, Juneau, Sitka, and Victoria

3. Lido, Aloha, Baja, Caribe, Dolphin

4. $88

5. Choose from: jogging track, paddle tennis court, three pools, and whirlpool spa

6. A deposit is required within seven days of booking. The per person deposit is $450 per person.

7. Children under two years are not permitted to travel. They also reserve the right to restrict the number of those under three years of age. Any passenger under the age of 21 must be accompanied by a parent or legal guardian over the age of 21.

8. Depart San Francisco at 5:00 p.m. They will return Monday September 28th at 8:00 a.m.

9. Five hours — from 8:00 a.m. to 1:00 p.m.

10. $2,299 per person

11. Yes — three pools.

12. Yes.

Worksheet 6-7

Answers will vary.

Classroom Activities

1. Use the four-part CLIA sales video series, *Selling the Ultimate*, and related workbook exercises to discuss how to sell cruises. The workbook exercises could be used as group activities or quiz grades. This is a good way to introduce students to the resources that CLIA provides to the industry. The CLIA manual could also be introduced as part of this activity. If so, assign students cruise lines and/or ships and have them fill in the information using the brochure analysis form. Have them compare ships and discuss suitability for various client types.

2. Show three different cruise videos and bring in the corresponding brochures. Ask students to compare the ships themselves, their markets, and the overall marketing efforts. Ask them to choose one of the ships and develop a sales letter for an appropriate client. References should be made to the brochure in terms of amenities, itinerary, season, cost, payment schedule, optional sightseeing, flights, etc. The letter should demonstrate why this ship is a good match for the chosen client.

3. If possible, organize a field trip for a site inspection on a ship. This could be a local ferry, freighter, charter, riverboat, lake cruise, or international cruise line. Another alternative could be a visit to a local dock or marina to interview the port authority. Use the CLIA checklist found in the CLIA manual.

4. Divide students into teams and ask them to consider the benefits of the cruising for these clients:
   A. A couple celebrating their twenty-fifth anniversary. They have never traveled more than 50 miles from home and are on a limited budget.
   B. A retired couple who have never cruised before but have saved their entire lives for this event.
   C. A young professional couple with no children who travel frequently and love nightlife.
   D. Two young women on their first cruise. One lives on the East Coast and one lives on the West Coast.

Articles

Chapter 6 — Article One
"Steamboatin' — Come Live a Legend"
Bring in brochures from the Delta Queen Steamboat Company to supplement this article. Ask students to research this area of the cruise industry. To what markets does this type of cruising appeal? Why? What other parts of the country lend themselves to steamboats? If you have a local sales representative from Delta Queen, ask them to lead a guest lecture on this topic.

Chapter 6 — Article Two
"Specialty Shops — The Pros and Cons of Cruise-only Agencies"
Copy the following article. Discuss the benefits of cruise-only agencies to the consumer. To the agency? Are there any disadvantages? Are there any cruise-only agencies in your area?

Steamboatin' — Come Live A Legend!

By John P. Butters, CTC

The Delta Queen Steamboat Company is a "niche" cruise line, offering a quintessentially American vacation experience that highlights river heritage, national history, and lovely river towns, many of which might have come from the pages of a Mark Twain novel. The company is also the sole survivor among scores of steamboat lines that once plied the Mississippi River and its tributaries. Steamboatin' then, remains the "real" thing — not a theme park recreation.

For many years, America's vast network of rivers carried goods and people who discovered, explored, and then settled the continent's heartland. From the earliest explorers' dugout canoes to today's diesel-powered tow boats, the multi-branched Mississippi River system has pulsed with activity. For a hundred years, from 1811 to the opening decade of this century, paddle wheel *steamboats* dominated the rivers. They carried settlers to a new life, hauled farm and other products to market, and supplied small towns with manufactured goods and consumer luxuries. Steamboats spread the news of the day — from politics and world affairs to the latest happenings in fashion and society.

Steamboats were the primary mode of transportation, taking Southern planters to New Orleans for the social season and farmers to Pittsburgh or Cincinnati on business. The packet steamers served regular trade routes; short town-to-town runs were reserved for smaller boats while the longer distances — between Memphis and New Orleans, for example — were covered by famous fast boats. These paddle wheelers, such as the legendary *J. M. White* with its mirrored and gilded Main Cabin, Reed and Barton silver water coolers and monogrammed linen, offered deluxe passenger accommodations that rivaled hotels anywhere. Mark Twain lived and worked aboard these vessels and brought to life for generations of readers the adventure of the river, the romance of the paddle wheelers, the personality of the towns, and the character of the people.

In 1890 a 28-year-old river pilot purchased his first steamboat in Nashville, Tennessee, founding the company that was to become known as the Delta Queen Steamboat Company. Like many little boys growing up along America's rivers in the 19th century, Gordon C. Greene dreamed of becoming a steamboat pilot. At the age of 16, he crewed on a flatboat from the Ohio River to New Orleans and, eventually, he saved the $250 needed to pay for his pilot's apprenticeship—a three-year process whereby the student paid for the right to learn through working.

By the time Captain Greene purchased his first steamboat, river packets were fast losing ground to their archrival, the railroad. Unlike riverboats, trains were not dependent on water levels to transport goods and passengers, and they couldn't be snagged by shifting riverbeds. But as changing times sent more and more boats to the bank forever, the reduced competition meant that a canny captain could take a larger share of what business did remain on the river.

The young Captain Greene put his steamboat, *H. K. Bedford*, in trade between Pittsburgh and Wheeling, West Virginia, and shortly afterwards married Mary Becker from nearby Marietta, Ohio. He brought his bride to live aboard the *Bedford*, and it became a regular practice for the young couple to stand watch together in the pilot house. By 1895, Mary B. Greene had learned enough at her husband's side to pass the examination for her own pilot's license and thus joined a handful of women licensed to pilot on inland Western rivers. Although she told a newspaper reporter that she didn't share many of the "new woman ideas," it wasn't long before she had applied for and was granted a master's credential, thus becoming a riverboat captain in her own right. Within a year, she was in command of their second steamboat, the *Argand*.

As the Greenes' fleet of steamboats grew, so did Mary Greene's renown. By 1903, she was the only woman to hold papers for both master and pilot on the Ohio River and, as captain of the *Greenland*, she beat her husband by an hour in a steamboat race from Pittsburgh to Cincinnati. The novelty of a woman steamboat captain coupled with family life on the river meant that the Greenes were able to garner a good deal of publicity. Not only were the sailing schedules and events aboard the Greene steamers covered in newspapers in river towns, but several national magazines featured stories on Mary

Greene and her unusual occupation.

When hurricane force winds blew the *Greenland* into a showboat on the Kanawha River, Captain Mary Greene stopped the panic among passengers on both boats, thus becoming a heroine. One newspaper account of the incident read: "With an infant in her arms, Captain Greene stood at her post and gave orders and commands to her crew and passengers. Through her coolness, she succeeded in landing all safely." The four trips they made to the 1904 World's Fair in St. Louis marked the first service of Greene Line steamboats on the Mississippi River.

With the construction of the *Greenland,* the Greenes had consciously targeted the passenger trade rather than freight or a combination of the two. This led a St. Louis newspaper to banner, "Only Woman Pilot … bids defiance of the railroads and for the first time in twenty years revives the passenger traffic from Pittsburgh to St. Louis … ."

But in 1907, the successful life the Greenes had carved out for themselves on the river was changed abruptly. Their oldest child was taken ill and died within four days. At that point, Mary Greene retired to Cincinnati to live and educate her two remaining sons. The move to town didn't sever the boys' or their mother's ties to the river. The children worked on the boats at every opportunity and Mary Greene kept her license active, ready to pilot and play hostess to passengers.

In addition to a changing fleet of steamboats, Captain Gordon Greene purchased wharfboats at strategic spots on the river. This gave his steamers priority over other packets when landing and enabled him to diminish or eliminate competition. He succeeded in establishing a virtual monopoly on the inland waterways.

Working with her sons, Mary Becker Greene helped keep the steamboat company afloat during the harsh years of the Depression. The Greenes removed staterooms on the *Tom Greene* and the *Chris Greene* to create room to carry automobiles. They purchased another boat in 1935, renamed the Gordon C. Greene, specifically to carry passengers. In the late thirties, the *Gordon C.* made pleasure trips along the inland rivers, including a cruise to New Orleans for Mardi Gras.

During World War II, the passenger steamboat secured the survival of the company. With Mary Greene living aboard, the *Gordon C.* carried war-weary travelers up and down the Ohio and Mississippi with occasional trips on the Cumberland and the Tennessee. Of these war years, Captain Fred Way has written, "The *Gordon C. Greene* was a floating summer hotel … . She disconnected herself from civilization every time her gangplanks were hauled in and went away into a dream river world of her own making."

In 1943, Chris Greene died of a heart attack and Tom stepped in to run the company. Mary Greene lived to see Tom's million-dollar "dream" boat, the *Delta Queen,* make the hazardous trip from California to the Mississippi and Ohio Rivers in 1947. When Mary Becker Greene died in the captain's cabin aboard the Delta Queen in 1949, she had been a river boat captain for 55 years. In an editorial called "Lady of the River," the Cleveland Plain Dealer eulogized her as a "unique figure: The only woman pilot and captain … in the last years of the packet's glory, and the person who kept passenger traffic on the Ohio and Mississippi alive after the stern-wheel steamboat had all but vanished."

The *Delta Queen* steamboat's early roots were on the West Coast with the California Transportation Company. To capture the luxury travel trade on the Sacramento River, the entrepreneurial company began building a boat that would be used as a shuttle between Sacramento and San Francisco. They contracted for an iron hull and machinery to be fabricated at the Isherwood Shipyard in Glasgow, Scotland. From there, the hull was broken down and shipped by cargo to a small shipyard in Stockton, California, where in 1926, it was reassembled along with its twin paddle wheeler — the *Delta King.*

The *Delta Queen* worked her shuttle route on the Sacramento River from 1927 to 1940. Prices were reasonable, and the boats ran at capacity in the summer months. During World War II, the Navy took over the *Delta Queen,* and made her conform to the standards of other ships of the line by painting her gleaming white exterior a dark grey. Rechristened as Yard Ferry Boat 56, she carried contingents of military personnel to and from ocean vessels in San Francisco Bay. At the war's end, the U.S. Maritime Commission took over the *Delta Queen* and put her up for auction. It was Tom Greene, president of the Greene Line Steamers, who longing for a "bigger and better steamboat," purchased the *Delta Queen* for a bid of $46,250, considerably lower than her original cost of $875,000.

Although he might have made a deal on his future "dream boat," Tom was faced with the expense and obstacles of moving the shallow draft riverboat from California to her new home on the Ohio River. With the help of Captain Frederick Way — an experienced riverman — and other experts, watertight crating was constructed to protect the *Delta Queen* from the ocean and arrangements were made for her perilous journey. The *Delta Queen* was towed 5,260 miles along the Pacific Coast, through the Panama Canal and up the Gulf of Mexico to New Orleans, where she was uncrated and inspected from bow to stern. From New Orleans, she made her way under her own steam to Cincinnati, where thousands of well-wishers celebrated her arrival. The boat was then sent to the Dravo Shipyards in Pittsburgh for the $750,000 transformation from her dull grey "Navy" look to that of the sparkling white floating palace she is today.

The Greene family continued operating the *Delta Queen* as a pleasure steamboat on the Ohio River until they sold the company in 1958. She is a survivor, a legend, and every bit the "dream boat" her former owner Tom Greene imagined. Listed on the National Register of Historic Places since 1970 and designated a National Historic Landmark by the federal government in 1989, the *Delta Queen* is the only authentic, fully restored, overnight steamboat in the world.

On board modern conveniences combine with the "feel" of a nineteenth century paddle wheeler. She is furnished with antiques and reproductions that enhance the original fixtures: the only Siamese bark floor aboard a steamboat, rich hardwood paneling, gleaming brass, stained and diamond-cut windows, and the dramatic grand staircase—crowned by an elegant Tiffany crystal chandelier.

To meet the growing demand of river travel, the Delta Queen Steamboat Company commissioned the building of another steamboat. The *Mississippi Queen*, launched in 1976, mixes the Victorian elegance of the steamboat era with modern day comfort and convenience. The vessel — deliberately designed to be larger than the grandest boats of a century ago — carries over 400 passengers who can pamper themselves with a dip in the Sun Deck pool, or a visit to the redwood sauna or beauty salon. Amenities include a gym, movie theater, a library full of river lore, gift shop, and even two-passenger elevators. Staterooms feature individual climate control and room-to-room telephones. A state-of-the-art microwave telephone system is available for necessary calls to the twentieth century only a riverbank away.

The *Mississippi Queen's* graceful design reflects the talent of skilled craftsmen. The boat was designed by London's James Gardner, the renowned naval architect responsible for Cunard's *QE II*, and constructed by Jeffboats, Inc. in Jeffersonville, Indiana, builder of more than 4,800 steamboats in the 19th century. Towering more than seven stories above the river, the *Mississippi Queen* is crowned by three twin fluted stacks that proclaim her a true Mississippi River steamboat. Inside, the feeling of stepping back in time to a slower, more romantic time is equally pronounced with Victorian gingerbread, embossed ceilings, and crystal chandeliers.

1990 marked the 100th year anniversary for the steamboat company founded by Gordon C. and Mary B. Greene. Two paddle wheel steamboats, the *Mississippi Queen* and the *Delta Queen*, still uphold that century-old tradition of carrying passengers on the river. And the Mississippi is still Mark Twain's river: majestic, mighty, marvelously poetic in both fable and fact. The best way to get acquainted with his river is the way he learned it — by paddle wheel steamboat. River cruise vacations combine traditional luxury with entertaining and educational on-board activities and interesting stops along the river, thus making steamboatin' a destination in itself. The scenery ranges from farmland dotted with barns and cows to soaring cliffs and Southern levees protecting picturesque river towns. Mark Twain's Hannibal, the antebellum mansions of Natchez, and Vicksburg's Civil War sites are only three of the dozens of stops where visitors can trace the course of the nation's history. Delta Queen Steamboat Company definitely owns a slice of American history.

Delta Queen Steamboat Company, now in its second century of steamboatin', has kept alive Twain's "wonderful adventure" of steamboat travel on the river system that drains, divides, and defines the American continent. As the nation's oldest flag line, the company offers nostalgic, romantic, and leisurely vacation cruises on its "floating white wedding cakes"—the only two overnight steamboats left in America. The legendary *Delta Queen* and the luxurious *Mississippi Queen*, like the fabled riverboats of Twain's era, continue to provide luxurious river passage in grand Victorian style. They take pride in introducing passengers to the "exultant sense" that Mark Twain felt on his first steamboat journey: "I was a traveler! A word never had tasted so good in my mouth before."

The Delta Queen Steamboat Company, based in New Orleans, presently offers 3- to 12-night vacation cruises on the Mississippi, Ohio, Cumberland, and Tennessee Rivers.

Reprinted with permission from *Business Management*, a publication of the Institute of Certified Travel Agents

Chapter 6 — Article Two
Specialty Shops

The Pros and Cons of Cruise-only Agencies

By Dan and Carol Thalimer

Many retail agencies have gone full-circle. Originally a specialized business, the agencies evolved into one-stop shops as people began to travel. The last five years, however, have seen a return to specialization. Let's look at why this is happening and if it makes sense for you to consider narrowing your agency's focus.

The most successful and best-known specialty operation is the cruise-only agency. We've also seen tour-only agencies and destination specialists do well. Each works a little differently, but all share the advantage of not having to meet the significant capital outlay of a full-service agency.

Consider the following numbers.

The largest outlays for a new full-service agency are the capital tied up in its bond and leasing an airline reservation system. They account for $20,000 to $30,000 of upfront capital and at least $6,000 in annual lease payments. Add to that the cost of employing a qualifier at $20,000 to $30,000 per year and all the fun of applying for ARC and IATAN approval.

Overrides are another matter. Few agencies are in a position to receive airline overrides until their air revenues reach $2,000,000; even then it's subject to the market. Cruise lines and tour operators, by contrast, regularly offer override commissions almost from the outset.

Then look at the size of each sale, the size of the overrides offered and the level of training needed — salary requirements that must be met — for an agent selling such a limited product.

A small specialty agency, well-situated and selling the right product mix, can be significantly more profitable than the small full-service agency.

Let's consider these qualifiers.

While growth in a full-service agency produces economies of scale and the opportunity to take advantage of the extensive automation offered as a part of the reservations system, this isn't the case in specialty agencies. There is little automation in most of the specialty agency areas to add efficiency to the booking and tracking process. This make the process very labor intensive. What's easy to handle for half a million or even a million dollars of revenue becomes prohibitive when dealing with five or ten million dollars of sales.

Even at a relatively small size, a careful check-in and check-out system must be maintained for all documents. The agency must keep close track of due dates for all deposits and final payments, get checks out to suppliers on time and make sure that documents arrive on time and are correct.

The importance of location of a retail travel agency cannot be overemphasized. Most of the successful specialty agencies we've seen have been located in high-volume retail centers, where the client base has a significant amount of discretionary income. The offices are easily seen by people passing by and have plenty of easily accessible parking.

The Match Game

The third qualifier, matching the product to the client base in your area, is a bit more complicated than saying, "There are a number of young people in this area; I guess we'll sell cruises."

You must decide which cruise lines you will specialize in, or if you will specialize at all. If you don't, some lines won't give you an override. Also, make sure that the cruise lines you're selling fit your client base. Selling a top-of-the-line cruise line in a moderate income neighborhood just doesn't work.

In addition to matching the products you sell to clients, you must also select those suppliers who will work with you to provide competitive prices, co-op funds for advertising, space on hard-to-get sailings or tours and a good commission rate with a favorable override structure.

Another consideration is your sales staff. While it's not necessary to have a staff with years of airline ticketing and computer expertise, you do need a knowledgeable sales force. Part of what the client expects when he walks into a specialty shop of any kind is a sales force that knows its product intimately. If you are presenting yourself as a specialist in your area, you had better be able to deliver or you'll lose your clients to the full-service agencies.

Because the traveling public has become much more sophisticated concerning price, this is an area that demands careful attention. Travelers expect to receive a discount, especially from a specialty agency.

In these days of high costs and low returns, any agency owner takes risks and faces new challenges. All of the elements must be taken into consideration so the owner/manager can make an informed, thoughtful decision on what type of agency would work best for him or her. As always, ingredients are careful analysis and planning.

Cruising
Chapter 6

End of Chapter Review

Name _____ Date _____

Directions: Use your atlas to identify which countries contain the following ports.

1. Bergen _____

2. Ocho Rios _____

3. Cozumel _____

4. Cape Town _____

5. Hamilton _____

6. Sydney _____

7. San Juan _____

8. Mykonos _____

9. Lisbon _____

10. Skagway _____

Directions: Fill in the blanks.

11. The front of the ship is called the _____.

12. If you face the front of the ship, the right side is called the _____, and the left

    side is called the _____.

13. What are the popular seasons for cruising in

    a. Bermuda? _____

    b. Alaska? _____

    c. Caribbean? _____

    d. Mexico? _____

14. For what reasons might a client prefer an inside cabin?

    _____

Answers to End of Chapter Review Questions

1. Norway

2. Jamaica

3. Mexico

4. South Africa

5. Bermuda

6. Australia

7. Puerto Rico

8. Greece

9. Portugal

10. Alaska

11. bow

12. port — starboard

13. a) April to October
    b) Mid May to late September
    c) Mid December to Mid April
    d) Winter and Spring

14. Less expensive — don't plan to spend time in cabin

Accommodations
Chapter 7

Review Chapter Objectives
- Distinguish among the types of properties
- List the factors that affect the price of a room
- Describe meal plans
- Discuss hotel reference guides
- Inspect a property
- Explain the importance of yield management

Review Vocabulary
- Adjoining rooms
- All-suites
- Club Med
- Corporate rates
- Family plans
- Meal plan
- Overbooking
- Rack rate
- Run-of-the-house
- Spa
- Yield management

Hotel Careers
- Accounting and Financial Management
- Food and Beverage Service
- Front Office
- Housekeeping
- Meetings and Conventions
- Reservations
- Sales and Marketing
- Human Resources
- Security
- Engineering and Facility Maintenance

Transparencies
- Chapter outline
- Types of segmentation
- Typical lodging customer in 1991
- Top ten corporate hotel chains in the world
- Factors that affect the price of a hotel room

Accommodations
Chapter 7 Outline

I. History of Accommodations

II. Organization of Accommodations

A. Hotel Affiliations/Independent Properties

III. Market Segmentation

A. Motels

B. Budget Properties/Economy Properties

C. Full-Service and Mid-Priced Properties/
   Full Service Upscale

D. Luxury Properties/Resort Hotels

E. All-Suites

F. Airport Hotels/Commercial Hotels

G. Spas

Accommodations
Chapter 7 Outline
(continued)

IV. What Affects the Price of a Hotel Room

    A. Yield Management

    B. Property Location

    C. Currency Fluctuations

    D. Room Location/Room Size/
       Amenities/Occupancy

    E. Length of Stay and Season

    F. Special Rates/Special Features/Meal Plans

V. Making a Hotel Reservation

    A. Representatives

    B. Computers/Telephone/FAX

    C. Hotel Reference Guides

    D. Overbooking

Types of Segmentation

- Motels

- Budget Properties

- Economy Properties

- Full-Service and Mid-Priced Properties

- Full-Service Upscale Properties

- Luxury Properties

- Resort Hotels

- All-Suites

- Airport Hotels

- Commercial Hotels

- Spas

Typical Lodging Customer in 1991

Vacationers	31%
Transient Business Travelers	25%
Conference Attendees	24%
Travelers with Personal or Family Plans	19%
Other	1%

Top Ten Corporate Hotel Chains in the World

Rank	Organization	Hotels
1.	Holiday Inn Worldwide	1,606
2.	Best Western International	3,348
3.	Choice Hotels International	2,102
4.	Accor	1,421
5.	Hospitality Franchise System	944
6.	Marriott Corporation	476
7.	ITT Sheraton Corporation	429
8.	Days Inn of America	1,112
9.	Hilton Hotels Corporation	263
10.	Hyatt Hotels	161

Rankings are based on total rooms open
as of December 31, 1990.

Factors That Affect the Price of a Hotel Room

- Yield Management

- Property Location

- Currency Fluctuations

- Room Location

- Room Size and Amenities

- Occupancy

- Length of Stay and Season

- Special rates

- Special Features and Marketing Efforts

Answers to Textbook Review Questions

1. **Why is the choice of accommodations sometimes more complicated than the choice of transportation?**
   Many more variables. The choice of hotel is dependent on subjective judgments.

2. **What hotel features would the following clients prefer?**
   a. Business traveler — location, corporate rate b. City vacationer — location, promotional rates, special features (concierge) c. A vacationer touring by car — ease of access, room location, property-to-property reservations systems

3. **Which factors most affect the cost of a hotel room?**
   Answers may vary but should include location of the hotel and location of the room.

4. **Are there times of the year or days of the week when hotels in your area offer special rates?**
   Answers may vary.

5. **At which destinations might MAP be a preferable option?**
   A resort.

Answers to Discussion Topics

Overbooking

A. G. Whiz could rant and rave; it sometimes works, but he probably is stuck with the problem with few options. Depending on the hotel the group is walked to (assuming it is an equivalent of the original property), G. Whiz can make or break the situation by personal upbeat style — the responsibility of a tour manager.

B. G. Whiz should call back to the office. Perhaps someone there has the clout to unlock 22 rooms or at least give the authority for a partial refund if the substitute hotel is not up to standard.

C. Tell the waiting group the truth.

D. Yes, by reconfirming before departure or along the way.

Neighbors

A. Prices are affected by the season. Mr. Solitaire might have hit high season. Prices are always subject to change, unless guaranteed.

B. Resort room rates are usually based on double occupancy.

World Travelers

This is a complicated question and would best be worked out as a research project.

Lost Reservation

A. Unfortunately, "lost reservations" are a frequent occurrence. The reservation process offers many possibilities for human error.

B. Responsibility is not easily determined. Travel counselors must keep records, record names, dates, reservations numbers. In time responsibility can be assigned.

C. Meanwhile, Mr. and Mrs. Dive need a room. The hotel clerk can be of help. Clerks can often "find" a room.

Answers to Workbook Exercises

Worksheet 7-1

Adjoining rooms	Rooms that share a common wall but not necessarily connected by a common door
All-suites	A type of hotel that offers units that include a living room, kitchen, and bedroom
Club Med	One of the largest resort hotel chains in the world. Club Med caters to all market segments.
Corporate rates	Rates negotiated between a supplier and employees of large companies
Family plan	A hotel rate that allows children to stay in a room with their parents at no additional charge
Meal plan	Meals are included in some room rates. Meal plan options include EP, CP, BP, MAP, and AP.
Overbooking	The practice of accepting more reservations than there are hotel rooms available
Rack rate	The official posted rate for each hotel room
Run-of-the-house	The flat rate for which a hotel offers any of its available rooms to a group
Spa	A resort with mineral springs, also health resorts that specialize in diet and fitness
Yield management	The practice of using frequent price changes to keep hotel rooms filled

Worksheet 7-2

1. Chains can represent an easily accessible inventory of rooms with predictable standards. The chain properties also provide a sense of security — the agent knows what is being sold, and the client knows what is being bought. Reservations can be easily confirmed, and prices are competitive with other hotels of equal rating.

2. Choose from: Ryokans are Japanese-style inns with floor-level sleeping accommodations; Paradores are government-run inns and hotels, often located in historical buildings or on interesting sites; Posadas are government-run inns and hotels in Portugal; Bed and Breakfasts are prevalent in the United Kingdom and Ireland. They are lodgings in a guest house or private home that include sleeping accommodations and full breakfast; The Gasthaus is a small hotel or inn in Germany.

3. Membership organization — Consists of individually owned and operated hotels that have united to centralize reservations and to pool advertising costs.

   Franchise hotel — A hotel permitted to use a well-known name in accordance with a legal agreement from the parent group.
   Management contract — The operator has the right to manage the property without the owner's interference; the owner is responsible for all operating and financing costs, and the operator is not liable for operating results except in the case of fraud.

Worksheet 7-3
Answers will vary.

Worksheet 7-4

1. The location of the property

2. Adjoining rooms have separate entrances but no means of getting directly from one room to another. Connecting rooms, on the other hand, are linked by a common door inside the rooms.

3. The *Official Hotel Guide* (OHG), the *Hotel and Travel Index,* and the *Star Service*

4. D

Worksheet 7-5

1. European Plan — No meals

2. Continental plan — A rate that includes continental breakfast

3. Bermuda Plan — A rate that includes full breakfast

4. American Plan — A rate that includes breakfast, lunch, and dinner

5. Modified American Plan — A rate that includes breakfast and one other meal

6. MAP — If the resort is secluded, there are probably no other restaurants available in which to eat.

Worksheet 7-6

1. Business travelers — Answers will vary but may include: hotels with meeting facilities; fax machines; in downtown locations or close to corporate areas; and easy check-out.
   Flight attendants — Answers will vary but may include: close to the airport; easy check-out.
   Honeymoon couples — Answers will vary but may include: romantic spots; room service; ambience; personalized treatment.

2. Answers will vary.

Worksheet 7-7

Answers may vary.

Worksheet 7-8

1. How many rooms in the hotel? — Biras Creek-33; Little Dix-102

2. How many miles from the airport? — Biras Creek-8; Little Dix-1

3. What credit cards are accepted? — Biras Creek-American Express, Discover, MasterCard, Visa; Little Dix-American Express, Discover Card, MasterCard, Visa

4. What is the hotel's classification? — Biras Creek-Superior First Class; Little Dix-Moderate Deluxe

5. How old is the property? — Biras Creek-1973; Little Dix-1964

6. Does it have a beach? — Biras Creek-Yes; Little Dix-Yes

7. Answers will vary.

8. Answers will vary — subjective opinion.

9. Answers will vary — subjective opinion.

Classroom Activities

1. Ask students to use hotel reference guides to find some or all of the following:

    A.   Three hotels near Chicago's O'Hare Airport

    B.   Two hotels with tennis courts in Acapulco

    C.   The nearest hotel to the World Trade Center in New York City

    D.   A hotel in Tokyo in the Ginza district

    E.   Unique qualities about the Budapest Hilton

    F.   Three hotels in the French Quarter of New Orleans

    G.   A hotel on the beach in Palm Beach

    H.   A deluxe resort in the Canadian Rockies

    I.   A hotel with efficiency units and a pool near Disneyworld

    J.   Two corporate hotels in Washington, DC, and a similar hotel in nearby Arlington, VA

Articles

Chapter 7 — Article One
"Brochure Double Talk"
Make copies of the following article. Discuss what makes a good brochure — clear color photos, logo, trademark, directions, maps, toll-free numbers, clear copy, etc. Pass out sample hotel brochures to students, and ask them to critique their brochure. If students are familiar with the property in their brochure, ask them how accurately the brochure describes the property. Then pass out the article, and ask how many of these descriptions are used in the students' brochures. Can the students offer their own translations for any of the phrases in their brochures?

Chapter 7 — Article Two
"Yield Mismanagement?"
Ask students to comment on the various rates used by a single property. What does the term perishable commodity mean? What would be the repercussions if other travel vendors followed these policies? Do hotels in your area subscribe to similar philosophies?

Chapter 7 — Article One
Brochure Double Talk
For the Skeptical Travel Planner, an Insider's Guide to Reading Between the Lines

Description	Translation
Charming ambience	Not newly renovated
Old-world charm	Never renovated
Lovingly restored	Cheaply renovated
Historic	Dilapidated
Distinguished facade	Old and crumbling
Understated elegance	Spartanly furnished
Evokes another era	Shared bath
Cosmopolitan	Little English spoken
Unspoiled setting	Trees
Spectacular setting	Grass and trees
Natural setting	Weeds
In the heart of the Old City	Near slums
Private	An hour from where you want to be
Desirable address	Police station nearby
Under new ownership	Japanese-acquired
Service charge included	Tips expected
Concierge desk	Empty desk bearing that name
Evening turndown	A lost reservation
Warm hospitality	No air conditioning
Cozy atmosphere	No lobby
Intimate atmosphere	Crowded lobby
Chic	Robin Leach slept there
First class	Second class
Luxurious	Formerly first class
Standard room	A bed and a chair
Superior room	A standard room, plus $25
Deluxe room	A superior room, plus $50
Junior suite	A former deluxe, now $100 more
Oceanview room	A room with trick mirrors
Oceanfront room	A real oceanview room
Gardenview room	The root cellar or worse
Overlooks ocean	Long walk down to beach
Climate-controlled room	The window opens
Victorian bath	Claw-foot tub, no shower
Elegant bath	A bidet
Complimentary breakfast	A roll and coffee
Gourmet cuisine	A meal at twice the price
Championship golf course	No tee times
Executive golf course	A large putting green

Reprinted with permission from *Andrew Harper's Hideaway Report*, a publication of Harper Associates, Sun Valley, Idaho

Yield Mismanagement?
In the Hotel Industry the Concept Has Reached a Seemingly Ridiculous Level, with the Proliferation of Rates Causing Confusion for Agents and Clients Alike

By Howard Feiertag

The Atlanta Travelodge Hotel overlooks one of that city's more heavily traveled highways, and so does the electronic sign on which it advertises its room rates. The dollar amount on the sign can be changed at will, rising or falling in response to how much business the hotel is doing. As general manager Dean Taylor reports, the rates can, and often do, change in the course of a single day.

The ever-changing Travelodge sign is a visible example of how hotel yield management practices, with their up-to-the-second inventory control, have inspired a breathtaking pace in rate adjustment.

No matter what the destination, hotels now list a variety of rates based on season, day, location (high up, low down, overlooking pool, ocean view, inside, outside), type of room (king, queen, twin, executive, parlor, suite) and other factors. In addition, it seems there are always "special" or discounted rates depending on who the guest may be or how the guest is affiliated. Sometimes the price even depends on who is taking the reservation.

Rates vary greatly. There are rack rates (the published rate for those who don't know better): corporate rates (which vary tremendously based on volume); AARP, AAA and various club discounts; and hospitality industry discounts granted to members of such organizations as AARP, AAA, AHMA, HMSAI and ASTA.

There is also the group rate, usually available to meetings and tours filling 10 or more rooms. Not quite as well-known, but equally important, is the annual contract rate hotels have for airline crews and truck drivers whose companies guarantee volume on a daily basis.

No wonder there is profusion confusion. And according to some hoteliers, frequent travelers and agents interviewed by *ASTA Agency Management*, it's likely to get worse before it gets better.

Why So Many Rates?

Hotels generally measure how well they are doing by establishing budgets or goals for average rates, computed by dividing daily rates by rooms sold. A lodging property's objective is to maximize both rates and occupancy in order to come up with a high daily average.

Teresa Goldsmith, guest services manager at Holiday Inn in Research Triangle Park, North Carolina, says: "Obviously, like any business, we want to get the maximum amount of revenue available on any given day. It's like any money-making business in that we need revenue to produce profit."

To produce revenue and profits, the Holiday Inn needs to provide a variety of rates to accommodate a variety of needs. Room selections range from wheelchair rooms with a minimal amount of furniture to executive suites with deluxe amenities, concierge service, a better location in the hotel and continental breakfast.

Overall, the hotel promotes over a hundred different rates. Says Goldsmith: "We change our rates daily. For instance, weekend rates are about 30 percent less than weekday rates. The idea on the weekend is that's the low demand period for us. We reduce our rates so that anyone that's coming through won't say, 'No, that's too high. I'm not going to stay there.'"

The growing oversupply of rooms across North America and in leading resort destinations has industry veterans convinced that such rate variation will continue, and possibly even mushroom. William Cooper, CTC, of Adventure Travels in Pompano Beach Florida, says, "Corporations are always looking for better rates to keep their travel dollars down, and they'll go back and forth from hotel to hotel until they get the rock-bottom rates."

This creates a problem for hoteliers. In Goldsmith's words, "A full-service hotel simply cannot survive a $40 room rate." To combat $40 room rates, hotels employ a yield management philosophy dictating that a room night is a perishable product — if a room is not sold tonight that night is gone forever — so the rate should drop when supply exceeds demand (and go up when demand is higher).

Then and Now

It's oversimplifying matters to assume that the multiplicity of special rates is a recent development inspired by high-tech yield management practices.

Thad Riddle, a retired 40-year veteran of the hotel industry, recalls that in the 1950s decent rooms could be found for as little as $3 per night at places practicing an early, individualistic form of yield management. "If someone we knew reserved a room at rack rate, we knocked off a couple of dollars when they arrived at the front desk," he says.

Almost 40 years later the practice of knocking off a couple of dollars (or even more) for travelers arriving at the front desk continues, although it's usually a more impersonal action. And now, as back then, some people lining up at the desk complain because the person in front got essentially the same room for a little less.

Much else, however, is different. Rate profusion throughout the marketplace has led to more changes, more types of rooms and more types of lodging operations. And in 1990 agents are far more affected by this practice than was the case 40 years ago, in part because agents are booking so many more hotel rooms.

So it comes as little surprise that many ASTA members are complaining when the front-desk clerk quotes a lower rate than was available to the agent who sought a "good" rate by going through the CRS or CRO, or even by contacting the hotel directly. Not only is the agent's reputation injured when the client thinks he or she did not obtain the best available rate, but insult is promptly added to injury when the hotel cancels commission due to the so-called "negotiated rate."

Bernice Rosmarin, CTC, of VTS Travel Enterprise in Edison, New Jersey, also ASTA's Hotel Committee chairman, reports that the committee has been fighting for payment of commission by hotels when a client receives a lower rate than the one quoted. At the very minimum, hotels should pay commission on the lower rate, maintains Rosmarin. To date, however, progress has been painfully slow in this arena.

Rate Relations

Generally, Rosmarin's attitude toward special rates is the fewer the better. A smaller number of rates reduces the likelihood of error — and of a client's receiving a lower rate upon arrival. She does add, however, that the profusion of rates could be a useful sales tool for retailers if more chains would design programs for agents seeking reduced rates for clients. Hilton International already makes special U.S. dollar rates available in Europe to agents' clients, but most chains do not have this policy.

What hurts the most, says Adventure Travels' Cooper, is when he books a corporate rate for one of his clients and that client, upon check-in, sees someone else get the same room for less.

Cooper understands how this can happen, but his client doesn't. The agent cites a recent situation in which he booked a group at $400 per couple on a package program and then found out that the hotel was marketing the same package through AAA at $260 per couple. He was advised by the hotel, when he complained about it, that if each member of his group was a member of AAA he would then be able to get the same rate.

There is no real answer to the question of rate profusion. Cooper says, even though it doesn't make for good working relationships with hotels. Agents just have to do the best they can to negotiate and continue asking for the best rate possible.

Rosmarin's advice: "You need to be a good travel agent," she says. "Do your homework." She advises sitting down on a quiet day and making a list of the hotel chains you normally use. Then call the central 800 reservations number and ask if they have any special rates.

The central reservations office of a chain operation is somewhat effective, if only because more rates are available and agents can sometimes negotiate with the other end. But Rosmarin and Cooper both agree that calling a hotel directly (with an 800 number) is a more effective way to seek the best rate for a client, mainly because rate quotes and availability are more current at the source than in central reservation offices or computers. But Rosmarin cautions that it is important to ask the right questions.

"Hopefully ASTA will develop a seminar that will help agents to know the right answers and to ask the right questions," says Rosmarin, who finishes her term as chairman of ASTA's Hotel Committee this year.

"Agents have to know to ask for the best rate," she adds. "It's a question of whether the corporate rate is always the best rate. It isn't, and you may not be doing the corporation you're dealing with a favor by taking the corporate rate and not explaining to them there are some specials. If you've been in the business, you know that certain chains are going to have special rates during the summer, for instance. Those are in many cases lower than some of the corporate rates."

Cooper and Rosmarin give airline CRSs for hotel chain reservations the lowest rating as a potentially successful option, since they most often list only the highest available rates.

"Depending on how agents are going to be making reservations for their clients, agents would probably be least secure in getting the best rate with the CRS right now, simply because it's an airline reservation system which has been adapted for hotel rates, Rosmarin says.

She adds that the systems have to adapt so when special rates come up they will be in the computer. "People are becoming more and more dependent [on automation], and it does seem rather foolish when you're paying all that money for computerized services, and you can't get the information that you needs out of it."

Varied Viewpoints

Some hotel operators actually join agents in condemning the multiplicity of rates in the marketplace. It would be easier for them to operate, after all, with fewer rates to choose from — especially if they were able to sell more rooms at rack rate. With the current oversupply of rooms in lodging operations, however, it's unlikely the variety of rates will be reduced.

While the existing rate variances can be a headache for both agents and hoteliers alike, Michael Littler, general manager of the new Hotel Macklowe in New York City, thinks the development may turn out to be a good one for the consumer. "As they become more knowledgeable about hotel rates and learn how to use resources for information, they can take advantage of lower rates, just as they do for airlines," says Littler.

For this to happen, Littler says, both agents and hotel operators need to help educate the consumer and make the system more user-friendly.

Already, though, many frequent travelers are beginning to understand the situation and are playing the game accordingly — generally not to the benefit of travel agents.

ASTA Agency Management recently interviewed one such traveler from upstate New York who travels two to three times per month on corporate business. His company, which uses a travel agent, obtains a corporate rate from all the major hotel chain operations. He has found, however, that for the most part the corporate rate his company gets is not the best rate, so he always asks upon checking into a hotel if there is a lower rate. Generally, he obtains one with no trouble.

The frequent traveler never complains to the travel agent about this since he understands the business and why there are different rates at different times. Thus he ignores the advice of hotel management at several locations and at different chains where he has been told to call the hotel directly next time instead of using a travel agent.

Harvey Davidson, a certified meeting professional and manager of special events for *Newsweek* magazine says, "It's like buying a car. You never know what price you'll pay." Davidson's experience suggests that you can get one rate from a travel agent and another directly from a hotel almost every time. There are plenty of rates out there, according to Davidson, but he understands that hotels have to adjust rates depending on the business and those rates can change as often as daily.,

Other such examples abound. Jack Kahn, president of Hotel and Resorts Consultants of America in Sarasota, Florida, tells of a meeting he booked at a West Coast hotel at a "very special, lowest possible rate." One member of his group called directly and got a room for $10 less. In this economy, Kahn says, it is a buyer's market. "You've got to keep fighting for the best rate."

And as long as that situation exists, relations between agents and hoteliers are going to be strained.

Reprinted with permission from *ASTA Agency Management* magazine, September, 1990

Accommodations
Chapter 7

End of Chapter Review

Name   Date

Directions: Which feature(s) on the following checklist might appeal most to each client?

a.   airport location

b.   downtown location

c.   close to beach

d.   courtesy van

e.   close to public transportation

f.   convenient parking

g.   close to restaurants and stores

h.   on a highway that bypasses city center

i.   MAP available

j.   choice of restaurants and bars in hotel

1.   The business client

_____

_____

2.   The vacation traveler visiting a city for three days

_____

_____

3.   The vacation traveler interested in sports and relaxation

_____

_____

4.   The vacation traveler touring by car

_____

_____

5.   List three types of accommodations and explain their differences.

_____

_____

_____

6. Discuss the importance of marketing segmentation in the hotel industry.

   _____

   _____

7. Define the following types of meal plans:

   a. AP   _____

   b. BP   _____

   c. MAP   _____

   d. CP   _____

Answers to End of Chapter Review Questions

1. a, b, d, e, f, g, h, j

2. b, d, e, f, g

3. c, f, g, i, j

4. c, f, g, h

5. Answers may vary. Budget, economy, mid-scale, resort, and so on are some of the possibilities.

6. Marketing segmentation allows hoteliers to focus on a particular target to better service that sector and remain more profitable.

7. a. AP - (American Plan) — Three meals daily
   b. BP - (Bermuda Plan) — Breakfast only
   c. MAP - (Modified American Plan) — Two meals daily
   d. CP - (Continental Plan) — Continental Breakfast

Tours
Chapter 8

Review Chapter Objectives
- Differentiate the various components of a typical tour package
- Identify three types of tours
- Review five benefits of tours to passengers
- Describe two benefits of tours to travel agents
- Explain the responsibility and liability of a tour operator

Review Vocabulary
- Escorted tour
- FIT
- Hosted tour
- Incentive tour
- Independent tour
- Room block
- Shell
- Special interest
- Step-on guide
- Tour operator
- Transfers
- Wholesalers

Tour-related Careers
- Convention and Visitors Bureau Representative
- Host/Hostess
- Marketing Representative
- Negotiator
- Operations Manager
- Reservationist
- Tour Guide
- Tour Manager/Escort
- Negotiator

Transparencies
- Chapter outline
- Stages of tour development
- Types of tours
- Benefits of tours

Tours
Chapter 8 Outline

I. Components of a Tour

    A. Tour Operators

II. Stages of Tour Development

III. Kinds of Tours

    A. Package Tours

        1. Independent

        2. Hosted

        3. Escorted

    B. Prearranged Tours

        1. Incentive

        2. Convention/Special Interest

        3. Weekend

        4. Custom-Made

IV. Benefits of Tours

    A. Benefits to the Client/Benefits to the Travel Agent

V. How to Choose a Tour

VI. How to Read a Brochure

Stages of Tour Development

- Planning

- Negotiation with Suppliers

- Costing

- Promotion

- Documentation

- Operations

- Maintaining Good Relationships with Suppliers

Types of Tours

Package Tours

- Independent Tour

- Hosted Tour

- Escorted Tour

Special Prearranged Tours

- Incentive Tours

- Convention Tours

- Special Interest Tours

- Weekend Tours

- Custom-Made Tours

Benefits of Tours

Benefits to Clients

- Prepayment

- Peace of Mind

- Volume Discounts

- Assured Entrances

- Reliable Sightseeing/Features

Benefits to Travel Agents

- Speed

- Maximum Earnings

- Objective Advice

Answers to Textbook Review Questions

1. **Describe briefly the differences between an independent tour and a hosted tour.**
   Independent Tour — prepackaged but characterized by a minimum of structure and scheduled activities.
   Hosted Tour — A host is available at each major tour destination to assist clients in planning their activities and to arrange sightseeing.

2. **Under what circumstances would clients need FIT arrangements?**
   Clients who want arrangements custom-made to their individual requirements

3. **How do tour operators build a relationship with a particular travel agency?**
   Experience, financial responsibility, reputation, service

4. **What features can be used to provide direct comparisons among various tour programs?**
   Accommodations, sightseeing, meals, forms of transportation

5. **What does the price of a tour usually exclude?**
   Tips, some transfers from an individual's home to embarkation point, optional sightseeing, meals not included in the tour itinerary, and so on.

6. **For some participants on escorted tours, enjoyment of the tour depends on the tour escort. Why?**
   Good tour escorts can make a substantial difference in the enjoyment of a package because these individuals are responsible for: establishing a friendly environment, providing important factual information, entertaining passengers during long stretches of time, and many other responsibilities.

7. **What weekend getaway tours are available from your area?**
   Answers may vary.

Answers to Discussion Topics

Closed Attractions
It was not the tour operator's fault that the gardens were closed. The group leader did act responsibly by providing alternate plans. If the alternate arrangements were of equal value, there is no obligation for monetary compensation. To appease the group, the tour operator could offer a discount on a future booking or send a small goodwill refund. If the group is serviced properly, it could represent future business for the tour operator.

Brochure Advertisement
The travel agent can sympathize with the clients' unhappiness but can do little else. The brochure is accurate.

Seat Rotation
The tour guide should try to accommodate everyone's wishes as much as possible. As stated in the contract, the tour guide decides where everyone sits. The tour guide should sit down with both parties to see if a reasonable compromise can be worked out. The side that doesn't get the front seat may later complain to the tour operator.

Answers to Workbook Exercises

Worksheet 8-1

Escorted tour
A tour characterized by a structured program of sightseeing, meals, transportation, and accommodation

FIT
A custom-designed, prepaid tour with many individual components

Hosted tour
A tour in which a host is available at each major tour destination to assist participants in planning their activities and to arrange excursions or sightseeing for them

Incentive tour
A tour for individuals offered as a prize or bonus for superior performance

Independent tour
A tour that is prepackaged but characterized by a minimum of structure and scheduled activities

Room block
Group space reserved by travel agencies, wholesalers, or tour operators that they hope to resell

Shell
A brochure provided by a supplier complete with artwork and graphics, but with space for a travel agency or tour operator to imprint an itinerary, price, and booking information

Special interest
A special interest tour would include people who have joined together in clubs, societies, teams, or informal groups for the purpose of pursuing or discussing a particular interest or hobby.

Step-on guide
The guide who steps on a motorcoach at a destination to give the local sightseeing tour

Tour operator
The company that organizes the travel components into prepackaged, inclusive arrangements and then sells the tour through travel agencies

Transfers
Transportation between airports, docks, railroad stations, and hotels

Wholesaler
A company that packages components of a tour. Typically, they work exclusively with travel agents, acting as an intermediary, and paying a commission or offering a net rate to the retailer.

Worksheet 8-2

1. Choose from: transportation (air, rail, motorcoach, ship), accommodation, meals, transfers or sightseeing.

2. Air transportation on the flights of one or more IATA members; Accommodations for the duration of the tour; At least one other feature, such as transfers, a sightseeing tour, or a car rental.

3. The terms are sometimes used interchangeably to refer to the company that contracts the suppliers of accommodations, transportation, and sightseeing and then packages the tour for sale through travel agencies. Tour operators may sell directly to the public and in some cases own retail travel agencies. Typically, a tour wholesaler works exclusively with travel agents.

4. Meal costs, hotel quality, length of stay in principal cities, and sightseeing.

5. Planning, negotiation with suppliers, costing, promotions, documentation, operations, and maintaining good relationships with suppliers.

180

Worksheet 8-3

1. Incentive
2. Escorted
3. Convention
4. Independent
5. Hosted

Worksheet 8-4

1. Prepayment, peace of mind, volume discounts, assured entrances, reliable sightseeing/features
2. Answers could vary but students probably should mention assured entrances.
3. Speed, maximum earnings, objective advice
4. Answers will vary.

Worksheet 8-5

1. Meet the People — Ireland
2. Grand Tour of Ireland
3. Irish Extra Value
4. Answers will vary.
5. Choose from: Powerscourt Gardens, Newgrange, Carrigglas Manor, Galway Cathedral, Connemara Marble Factory, Rathbaun Farm, Cliffs of Moher, Bunratty Folk Park, Ring of Kerry, Blarney Castle, Blarney Woolen Mills, Waterford Crystal Showrooms, Walking tour of Wexford, St. Patrick's Cathedral, Trinity College
6. September 10 or September 11
7. Yes
8. Mainly first class
9. No
10. Yes
11. A non-refundable deposit of $100 per person per tour is required.
12. No — it is non-refundable
13. Yes — $20 per transaction

Worksheet 8-6

Answers will vary.

Classroom Activities

1. Often clients will ask their travel agent what and how to pack for a vacation. Many times tours restrict the number of pieces of luggage that passengers can bring. Ask students if they have any general advice or tips that they would offer. What items would students recommend clients pack in a carry-on bag? What additional items are necessary to pack when traveling through Europe (currency converters, money belts, electrical converters)?

2. Have students participate in role-playing exercises. Bring in a representative selection of tour brochures. In each role play, the counselor chooses from this selection to meet the client's needs. The students not involved in the role play should take notes and be prepared to answer the following questions.

- Did the counselor select a tour appropriate for the client's expressed needs?
- Did the counselor present all the benefits of the tour?
- What other tours might have better suited the client?
- Did the counselor use the brochure to answer the client's questions?

Consider the following scenarios or have students create their own.

Role Play 1
You are Mr. and Mrs. Ben Brown. Your last child has just gotten married and now you are free to travel. You want to go to Hawaii or maybe to a national park where you have never been before. For 25 years your traveling has been mainly by automobile with the family during holidays. You both now want to spend time together. You are both active and healthy and are able to spend to get what you want.

Role Play 2
You are Susan Jacobs, a 25-year-old living in Milwaukee who wants to visit Eastern Canada with two friends. You have a two-week vacation but not much money. Luckily, one of your friends has relatives in Montreal with whom you can stay for a few days. You are more interested in seeing the coast of Nova Scotia, but your friends like big cities and nightlife.

Articles

Chapter 8 — Article One
"The National Audubon Society Travel Ethic for Environmentally Responsible Travel"
Using their atlases, ask students to choose an area of the world which lends itself to environmental tourism. Have them plan a one-week trip within the area. What types of clients (allocentric, psychocentric, or midcentric) would be most interested in this area of the world? How can we as travel agents further the public's knowledge about environmental impacts?

Chapter 8 — Article Two
"What Escorted Tour Clients Really Want"
Make copies of the following article. Ask students if they have ever been on an escorted tour. Do they know anyone who has? This is a good chapter for "war stories." How accurate do they perceive this article to be? Which tour destinations seem to be most popular from your area?

The National Audubon Society Travel Ethic for Environmentally Responsible Travel

Tourism is one of the fastest growing industries in the world today. In some countries, so far little-known to travelers, where there are huge problems of unemployment and weak national economies, tourism is being regarded as a new primary industry. It creates employment and often brings in foreign currency to economically marginal areas. Sightseers from more affluent nations are ever searching for new places to explore. The trend seems to be growing away from sun, sea and sand holidays toward adventure, the outdoors, wildlife watching, and cultural interests.

Close encounters with the animal kingdom are at very high interest levels. This coincides with a rapidly developing public awareness of environmental matters. Such a combination of conditions could lead to an influx of excursionists into environmentally sensitive areas which, if not carefully managed, could exert pressure on and do possibly irrevocable damage to the natural resources it seeks.

The National Audubon Society realizes that the maintenance of these sensitive resources will ensure the continuation of tourism in such areas. The resource in question is the entire natural world, from coastal Alaska and the high Arctic and Greenland, to the wilderness of Antarctica and all that lies between.

The National Audubon Society has become increasingly aware of both the potential and actual conflict between tourism development and the natural environment. We are completely convinced that more can be done to create a positive balance between the two and to create an atmosphere where commercial operators and environmentalists can interact positively. We recognize the tourism can be a powerful tool favoring environmental conservation—particularly through enhancement of public awareness of environmentally sensitive areas and their resources and the stimulation of action and mobilization of support to prevent the erosion of such environments.

Toward these goals, the National Audubon Society urges all tour operators promoting exploration in wilderness areas to adopt the guidelines here stated.

1. Wildlife and their habitats must not be disturbed.

Fragile habitats must not be stressed. Trails will be followed. Plants will be left to grow.

In delicate habitats, vegetation destruction and rock slides can easily be caused by the trampling of too many people. Mosses, lichens, and certain wildflowers and grasses, may take as much as 100 years or more to regenerate, and must not be walked upon. It is the obligation of the tour company and the naturalist leaders to promote a "stay on the trail" policy. No responsible tour operator or naturalist should allow the removal or picking of plant specimens or other ground cover. Introduction of exotic plant species must be avoided.

Coral reefs take anywhere from several years to several decades to regenerate. Therefore the National Audubon Society insists that all of its tour operators provide the broadest protection possible for this underwater life form. Destruction of any part of any coral reef calls for the greatest censure.

Animal behavior will not be inhibited. Because many of the most well-subscribed tours are operated during various animals' breeding seasons, tour operators and leaders should establish and always maintain at least minimum distance from these animals.

Scientific studies predict that a specific animal behavioral function, such as courtship, nesting, or feeding young, demands a specific amount of energy on the part of the breeding animal. Approaching animals too closely causes them to expend energy needlessly in a fury on defensive territorial display. This can cause an energy deficit that reduces the animals' productivity in the same way as does a food shortage. If disturbances are caused by visitors early enough in the breeding cycle, the parents may abandon the breeding site. Additionally, while the adults are warning off intruders, eggs and young are vulnerable to chilling and unguarded young are more susceptible to predation.

Animals will not be harassed or approached too closely. Our recommendation is that all tour participants keep a minimum distance of 20 to 30 feet from seals, walruses, otters, giant tortoises, lava lizards, sea turtles, koalas, all marsupials, and unwary plains herd animals.

We recommend that all visitors stay on the periphery of animal assemblages (e.g., penguin colonies, seabird colonies, albatrosses on nest, courting groups). This means:

- Visitors should never be allowed to surround an animal or group of animals.

- Visitors must remain alert never to get between animal parents and their young.

- Visitors must never be allowed to get between marine animals and the waters' edge.

- Nesting raptors should be viewed only through binoculars or telescopes at considerable distances from the nest.

- Crowd control ethics should keep the decibel level as low as possible, thereby minimizing the potential threat to animals.

- The advent of sophisticated photograph technology means that even amateur photographers can get professional looking photographs while keeping a respectable distance from the subject. Photography of birds and animals should never include the removal of nestlings or young from the nest or removal of foliage or camouflage from close to the breeding sight. Removal of animals from burrows, dens, caves, or tree cavities must be prohibited at all times.

- Relentlessly following or harassing birds or animals for the sake of a photograph should never be allowed. Lingering obtrusively in close proximity to a nesting site, preventing the animal from returning to the sight, should never be allowed.

- Touching animals must never be allowed.

Every effort will be made to minimize a visit's impact, and if that effort is inadequate, the visit will be curtailed.

2. Audubon tourism to natural areas will be sustainable.

Audubon will encourage local guides, landowners, and conservation representatives to develop and implement long-term visitor plans to ensure the sustainable use of their wildlife habitats. Audubon also encourages patronage of locally benign concessionaires.

3. Waste disposal must have neither environmental nor aesthetic impacts.

All tour operators must take into account the fragility of the areas visited with regard to proper waste disposal. All cruise ships, whether operating in the Arctic or sub-Arctic, the Great Barrier Reef of Australia, the islands of the Southern Ocean, along the Antarctic Peninsula, the Pacific shores of South American and Galapagos, or along the reaches of the Orinoco and Amazon rivers must commit to a shipboard anti-dumping/anti-garbage policy. This policy ensures that the shipboard crew and staff will not foul any waters, particularly with regard to non-biodegradable (plastic) materials.

If necessary, all trash must be contained and carried back to port where proper disposal is available. Any tour operator offering the opportunity for visiting land wilderness areas overnight or for several days must make provision for carrying out all trash generated while there.

The tour operator and naturalists should promote an attitude of keeping every specific site as clean as possible. No littering of any kind should be tolerated.

The National Audubon Society will neither patronize nor approve any vendor that does not *strictly* adhere to this guideline.

4. The experience a tourist gains in traveling with Audubon must enrich his or her appreciation of nature, conservation, and the environment.

Every trip to a wilderness area must be led by experienced, well-trained, responsible naturalists and guides. These naturalists should have a solid background in the various habitats to be visited, the flora and fauna contained there, and the sensitive nature of those habitats. These naturalists and guides must be able to provide proper supervision of the visitors, prevent disturbances to the area, answer questions of the visitors regarding the flora and fauna of the area, and present the conservation issues relevant to the area.

All tour operators should provide adequate space for these naturalists so that the leader-to-group size ratio never exceeds one to 25. The maximum size of a visiting group will depend upon the fragility of the surroundings, in which case the ratio could drop to as little as one to ten.

These naturalist/guides serve as the environmental conscience of the group and as such should be an integral part of every tour.

5. Audubon tours must strengthen the conservation effort and enhance the natural integrity of places visited.

One constant theme in Audubon tours will be the problems facing wildlife and their habitat, and the solutions that may be achieved. On tours, particularly to other countries, contacts will be sought and established with conservation organizations working in the areas visited. Their representatives will be encouraged to speak to our tours and sought, when appropriate, to serve as local naturalist leaders and lecturers to accompany Audubon enroute.

6. Traffic in products that threaten wildlife and plant populations must not occur.

The National Audubon Society cannot condone a laissez-faire attitude with regard to purchase of certain types of souvenirs or mementos. Habitat loss remains the single largest threat to animal species; however, commerce and poaching have depleted countless animal and plant populations. All our vendors must conscientiously educate their travelers against buying the following items:

- All sea turtle products, including jewelry, sea turtle eggs, and skin cream made from turtle meat;

- Most reptile skins and leathers, particularly those from Latin America, the Caribbean, China, and Egypt (including all Crocodilian products);

- Snakeskin products from Latin America and Asian countries, including India;

- Lizardskin products from Brazil, Paraguay, India, Nepal, and Pakistan;

- Leather products made from pangolin (anteater) from Thailand, Malaysia, and Indonesia;

- Ivory from any source, especially worked ivory from elephants, and from marine animals, such as whales, walruses, and narwhals;

- Birds, including large parrots from Australia, Brazil, Ecuador, Paraguay, Venezuela, and the Caribbean islands;

- Wild birds and their feathers and skins, used in or as artwork (including mounted birds);

- Coral from the Caribbean and Southeast Asia, Australia;

- Furs of spotted cats (e. g., snow leopard, jaguar, ocelot, etc.);

- Furs and fur products of seals and other marine mammals and polar bears;

- Any orchids and cacti.

7. The sensibilities of other cultures must be respected.

Audubon tours travel in areas of widely varying ethics and practices. On our trips we are the guests of these cultures and our opportunities are to learn and enrich our own understanding of human nature, not to intrude and criticize. In the long run, our abilities to advance conservation will be strengthened by the bridges that understanding will establish.

The effectiveness of the the preceding guidelines rests on the performances and cooperation of the tour operator, the naturalist leaders, and the expedition travelers. Each of these parties must possess and promote a sense of propriety if the collective effort is to succeed. Harmless viewing of wildlife and habitats in which wildlife abounds can proliferate while preserving both the activity and the resource.

Chapter 8 — Article Two
What Escorted Tour Clients Really Want

By Melinda Stovall

One might have called it the escorted tour from hell. Forty-two people travelled by motorcoach from Pennsylvania to Washington, D.C., for the annual springtime Cherry Blossom Festival, and just about everything went wrong once they arrived.

The rains came and temperatures hovered near freezing, leaving the tour group wet and cold at the parade. The group's hotel, marginal at best, botched their breakfast service, so nobody got to eat. And to top it off, the cherry blossoms weren't there because high winds had knocked them off the week before.

After returning home, the tour participants were asked what they thought about the trip. "It was great," they said. On a scale of one to 10, with one being the worst, the participants gave the tour an eight.

The response naturally surprised Margaret Persia, who surveyed the group while a master's degree candidate at Pennsylvania State University in State College, Pennsylvania. "The destination was what got them interested in the tour, but the community of people is what made them satisfied," she says now.

Building on that experience, Persia, now a tourism doctoral candidate at Clemson University in Clemson, South Carolina, and a former travel agency owner, has further examined escorted tours. The result is her recently released "National Escorted Tour Survey" — still in a preliminary stage, but a substantial beginning in determining why people choose escorted tours, what they expect from the experience, how satisfied they are after the tour, and whether there is any connection between their expectations and their level of satisfaction.

Developing Relationships

"I've been on a few escorted tours myself," says Persia, who likens agent fam trips to a "rigid form" of the escorted tour. "You go on one of these things, especially one with a long itinerary, and a community develops among the members on that tour. It's interesting to sit back and view what goes on, how people develop relationships among themselves and with the tour conductor and the driver, if it's a motorcoach tour, and as a group with the destination.

"If you go on a vacation with your family, you don't have to interact with anyone else," she adds. "But on a tour, with the combination of people, there is a special relationship that develops that can enhance or detract from the experience."

Persia intends to explore these social aspects later; early results in the "National Escorted Tour Survey" focus on clients' purchase characteristics. This data is being gathered via a self-administered "pre-experience" questionnaire, whose respondents will also answer a post-experience questionnaire after returning from their tours.

To find her participants, Persia contacted a random sample of agency owner/managers and tour operator executives and asked if they would each forward pre-experience questionnaire packets to five qualified clients—those who had already booked an escorted tour or who had recently inquired about doing so.

Persia is conducting the survey with the cooperation and endorsement of ASTA and the National Tour Foundation, the educational arm of the National Tourism Association. She is funding the study with a cash prize she was awarded by the ASTA Scholarship Foundation for her master's thesis.

Preferred by Elderly Women

So far 136 people have responded to the pre-experience questionnaire— 64 were clients of tour operators and 72 of travel agencies—and the respondents come from 29 states. The respondents are predominantly female (83 of the participants), older (113 are ages 51 through 80) and educated (75 respondents have some college or more). This dominance by the senior market corresponds with NTA data showing that three out of four escorted travelers in 1989 fell in the 50-plus group.

Escorted tours — long associated with the stereotypical "blue-haired wonders" by those in the travel industry — appeal to older people for particular reasons, notes Janet Hammond, CTC, a member of ASTA's Tour Protection Board of Trustees

"Older ones like to be with the group," says Hammond, president of Travel Planners/Carlson Travel Network in Miami Lake, Florida. Chances are the women in the survey are widows; they don't have husbands to make decisions. They can have a circle of people to socialize with, a nice group of people, and they don't have to worry about comfort and safety.

"Younger people, on the other hand, don't want to be pinned down today; they are more adventurous," she adds. "They may have a set itinerary, but not down to the hours of the day."

Reputaton and Destination

In Persia's pre-experience questionnaire, respondents were asked to rate the importance of 12 features of the escorted tour purchase. A breakdown of the ratings between agency clients and tour operator clients showed only one significant difference — tour operator clients rated "reputation of the tour company" highest while agency clients cited "destination" as most important.

"A tour operator typically has developed a loyal following," Persia says. "A major reason why someone goes with a tour operator is because of the experience, if it was a good and happy time in the past.

Now, a travel agency client is not asking for a particular tour operator; their primary interest is in the destination," she continues. "They want to see what it is they want to see. The tour operator is unknown to them, but they have expectations that they will do what they say they want to do."

Hammond believes that more agents have become educated about tour operators and are offering tour protection but suspects that not all clients share their concern. "Experienced travelers more likely know the reputation of the tour operator or have been taught that by their travel agent, but the average person taking a vacation is thinking of where he wants to go, the cool breezes … . He's not thinking about someone's reputation."

Even so, when combining figures for both groups, the most important factors in the tour-purchase decision were reputation of the tour company and then destination — the number one choice probably reflecting that many of the respondents were experienced travelers. Ninety-six of the survey participants indicated they had been on four or more escorted tours, while 32 had been on three such tours. Another seven had never been on an escorted tour.

Inclusion of a tour guide ranked third, followed by scheduled time of tour, previous experience with the tour company, element of safety in the group setting, ease of booking through a travel agent, and brochures and other advertising matter. These features could be stressed by agents in promotional materials and methods, notes Persia.

Contrary to popular theory, the recommendation of friends or relatives was not rated as particularly important by either tour operator or travel agency clients in this sample. Hammond and Persia speculate that one reason the travel agent's recommendation also rates low for both groups of clients is that these respondents are more knowledgeable, more traveled; they know what they want to do and don't need recommendations.

The idea of looking at expectations versus reactions has been around awhile, notes Dr. Charles Duke, a professor of marketing at Clemson and Persia's co-worker on the study, but this comprehensive look at tours and tourism is new. When complete, the data should help tour operators and travel agencies devise the most appropriate and ethical ways of marketing their services so that ultimately they have satisfied escorted-tour clients.

Before this research, "their have been assumptions of what people expect, but no hard research data," Persia says. "We've looked at expectations through a scientific approach, and I chose escorted tours because they have a specific goal in mind." But her interest is also inspired by a trait shared by many travel agents — "I'm just very curious about people."

Reprinted with permission from *ASTA Agency Management* magazine, January, 1992

Tours
Chapter 8

End of Chapter Review

Name _____ Date _____

Directions: Answer the following.

1. What is a step-on guide?

   _____

   _____

2. What is an incentive tour?

   _____

   _____

3. What are the three major types of prearranged package tours?

   1. _____   2. _____

   3. _____

4. What are some special benefits to clients of escorted tours?

   _____

   _____

5. An FIT is an abbreviation for any escorted tour.   True   False

6. As a rule, tour operators try to avoid any day involving more
   than ten hours of travel or more than 350 miles.   True   False

7. On a hosted tour, sightseeing admissions are always included
   in the cost.   True   False

8. Most tour operators reserve the right to substitute features on
   a tour with or without notice.   True   False

9. Any wholesaler who operates an escorted tour can qualify for
   a special group airfare.   True   False

10. What four areas can tour operators economize in?

   _____

   _____

Answers to End of Chapter Review Questions

1. A guide who joins a tour for a day or half-day to conduct sightseeing of a particular city or destination.

2. A tour usually offered as a prize or reward to employees of a company based on their productivity or sales performance.

3. Independent, hosted, escorted

4. Answers may vary but should include: relaxation, efficiency, companionship

5. False

6. True

7. False

8. True

9. False

10. Accommodations, meals, sightseeing, length of stay

Sales Techniques
Chapter 9

Review Chapter Objectives
- Recall two principles of selling travel
- Review five basic questions involved in qualifying the client
- Describe four tips for effective listening
- Translate four features into benefits
- Explain the major parts of any successful sale
- Identify three steps in closing a sale

Review Vocabulary
- Benefit
- Close-ended question
- Discretionary travel
- Elasticity of demand
- Feature
- Feedback question
- Non-verbal signals
- Objection
- Open-ended question
- Qualify
- Recap
- Recommendation

Transparencies
- Chapter outline
- Tips for listening effectively
- Types of questions
- Elements of a successful sale
- Role play observer checklist

Sales Techniques
Chapter 9 Outline

I. The Sales Personality

   A. Interpersonal Skills and Customer Service

II. The Importance of Travel

   A. Why People Travel/Desire to Travel

III. Elements of a Successful Sale

   A. Introduction

      1. Qualifying the Client

      2. Listening Effectively

   B. Presenting Features and Benefits

   C. Closing the Sale

      1. Making Recommendations

      2. Recapping

      3. Overcoming Objections

      4. Offering to Book

Tips For Listening Effectively

- Limit Your Own Talking

- Listen for Ideas

- Shut Out Distractions

- Try Not to Interrupt

- Take Notes

- Use Client's Language in the Conversation

- Don't Let Clients Irritate You

- Don't Jump to Conclusions

- Use Verbal and Non-verbal Signals

- Watch Client's Body Language

- Be Aware of Client's Attitudes and Biases

Types of Questions

Open-Ended Question

- Discover More about a Client's General Tastes and Preferences

- Encourage Clients to Open Up

Closed-Ended Question

- Narrow Down Possibilities

- Force Clients to Supply Precise Information

Feedback Question

- Confirm Details from Conversation

Elements of a Successful Sale

- **Introduction**

  Qualifying the Client

  Listening Effectively

- **Presenting Features and Benefits**

- **Closing the Sale**

  Making Recommendations

  Recapping

  Overcoming Objections

  Offering to Book

Role Play Observer Checklist

		Yes	No
1.	Was there potential for a sale?	_____	_____
2.	Was a reservation made?	_____	_____
3.	Did the agent determine:		
	Where? (give city or destination)	_____	_____
	When? (specific date/time)	_____	_____
	How long?	_____	_____
	What kind/class?	_____	_____
	Who?	_____	_____
	Name/Address/Phone?	_____	_____
4.	Did the agent listen effectively?	_____	_____
5.	Did the agent establish rapport?	_____	_____
6.	Did the agent offer to book?	_____	_____

Suggestions or comments to help the participants.

_____
_____
_____
_____
_____
_____

Answers to Textbook Review Questions

1. **Why is it advisable to postpone presenting recommendations until you are ready to close the sale?**
Making recommendations too early could make clients feel pressured.

2. **How should agents present recommendations to clients? What should they avoid?**
Agents should: emphasize the benefits, incorporate the client's own statements, refer directly to brochures, itineraries, or maps.
Agents should avoid: exaggerating or lying, guaranteeing enjoyment by referring to other clients, guaranteeing anything beyond their control.

3. **What are the major benefits of recapping?**
Enables agent to pull together details from the conversation; provides the client an opportunity to comment on, upgrade or add to arrangements; uncovers possible disagreements or objections; reduces the possibility that a disappointed client may later accuse the agent of not having explained things clearly; starts the client saying "yes" and can lead easily into the agent's offer to book.

4. **What are the advantages and disadvantages of offering conditional reservations?**
Advantages: Ensures the client against disappointment, saves the agent the bother of scrambling to get space at the last moment.
Disadvantages: Certain promotional fares have immediate payment demands and stringent cancellation penalties that would prohibit the use of a conditional reservation; should never be a substitute for a careful qualification of a client.

5. **There are many reasons why clients resist or object to the agent's offer to book. Which do you think are the most common: psychological resistance, social obligations, prejudiced objections, informational resistance, guilty objections, guarantee objections?**
Answers will vary.

6. **How could you find out how much clients want to spend on a particular trip?**
Ask them if they have a total budget in mind. However, clients could spend more than they originally budget for if an agent can offer good value for the money.

7. **The travel agent typically performs a number of services for clients. How would you rate the following services in order of importance: informing, recommending, persuading, convincing?**
Answers will vary.

Answers to Discussion Topics

Qualifying

A. All questions are close-ended.

B. The counselor needs to know the exact dates in April the client intends to travel.

C. The counselor may want to incorporate an open-ended question to determine if the clients have any other travel needs.

Budgeting

A. The advertisement with the features is more meaningful.

B. To compare value you have to compare features. The ad for $499 and up does not list features.

Answers to Workbook Exercises

Worksheet 9-1

Benefit	A benefit implies what a feature means to a client and what it can do for them.
Close-ended question	A question designed to narrow down possibilities. They expect precise answers like "yes" or "no."
Discretionary travel	Travel undertaken voluntarily
Elasticity of demand	Travel will increase during periods of prosperity and decrease during inflationary times.
Feature	A product or service offered or any fact about that product or service that is always true
Feedback question	A question designed to confirm details that have emerged in the conversation
Non-verbal signals	Using body language to convey feelings and opinions
Objection	Resistance to an idea or a suggestion
Open-ended question	A question designed to enable someone to discover more about a person's general tastes and needs
Qualify	Asking a series of questions to determine the person's wants and needs
Recap	Pulling together details from conversations
Recommendation	The relating of personal experiences or likes and dislikes

Worksheet 9-2

1. Assistance, logic, control, commitment

2. When are you going? Where are you going? Who/How many are going? How long are you staying? What kind/class of service or arrangements do you require?

3. Counselors must learn to listen to understand the client's needs and to empathize with them.

4. Presenting recommendations and setting priorities; recapping; and overcoming resistance or objections

5. Choose from: allows clients an opportunity to comment on, upgrade, or add to arrangements; reduces the possibility that a disappointed clients may later accuse the agent of not having explained things clearly; starts the client saying "yes."

6. Psychological — Clients may feel pressured. Most people prefer to delay decisions, especially those that cost money. As the moment of decision draws nearer, they forget all the benefits of purchasing and how much they need something.

   Social — Clients often feel they must consult their traveling companion before committing to final arrangements.

   Prejudice — This type of resistance arises from a client's ignorance and bias.

   Guilt — When the final moment arrives when clients have to commit to spending money, they often wonder if they should be spending the money on themselves.

7. Answers will vary.

Worksheet 9-3

1. Open-ended — This type of question enables the agent to discover more about a person's general tastes and needs. Examples will vary.

2. Close-ended — This type of question narrows down possibilities. The agent forces the client to supply precise information. Examples will vary.

3. Feedback — This type of question is useful to confirm details that have emerged in the conversation. Examples will vary.

Worksheet 9-4

Answers will vary but may include:

1. Unnecessary to call several airlines — one call to us can check them all — this will save time.

2. We have first hand knowledge to help you choose the destination to best suit your travel needs.

3. This will save you time and the inconvenience of having to come into our office.

4. You can better calculate your vacation costs; you won't have to bring as much money with you.

5. At each stop you will have local, knowledgeable guides.

6. This will save you time and costly phone calls; we have information about all car rentals and all hotels and can help you select the best ones.

7. You will be taken from the airport to your hotel and back again — no need to spend time looking for local transportation.

8. While you are in London, if you have any questions or need any assistance you can visit our office.

Worksheet 9-5

1. I
2. A
3. I
4. A
5. I
6. A
7. I
8. B
9. N
10. B
11. B
12. B

Classroom Activities

1. To make students aware of the importance of selling, solicit their sales encounter experiences and have them describe their reactions either favorably or unfavorably. Guide class discussion from the following questions:
   A. When was the last time you ran into a salesperson who seemed indifferent, rude, or negative?
   B. What effect did it have on you?
   C. What effect would these attitudes have if they existed within a travel agency?

2. A sales blitz is a unique sales opportunity for students. Check with local hotels, restaurants, and travel agencies to see if they could use students to help promote their property. In most cases, sales blitzes should be one day in length and should concentrate on a small area. When negotiating this activity, request that the property provide a briefing session including question-and-answer time, and site inspection prior to the sales blitz. In this way students feel more comfortable in their product knowledge. Usually, properties will also provide a food function, and sometimes gas money if students use their own cars. A final debriefing is usually included in the day's activities.

3. There is probably more opportunity for role playing in this chapter than any other. Have students set up situations for their classmates. Students should be encouraged to evaluate their own performance before the comments of others are expressed. They should know that this is not an evaluation of the individual — only an evaluation of the handling of the sales situation. Present role-play scenarios for students to play out. A role play should last five to eight minutes unless it is naturally concluded in less time. Each student is given a fact sheet describing his/her roles. Those not involved in the role play should be given a Role Play Observer Checklist (see reproducible master). Observers should be encouraged to take notes and be prepared to evaluate the session after it is over. Observers should also be given copies of the client fact sheet.

Each student is given a fact sheet describing his/her role.

1. Client/student gets information with instructions to release the information in parenthesis only if asked.
2. Agent/student needs to get enough information to book the trip. By proper questioning they should be able to obtain the important information contained in the parenthesis.

Sample Role Play 1

Who	Joan Wiley from Acme Industries.
How Many	Just you.
Where	Have to visit companies in or near San Francisco, Billings, and Tempe. (Specifically, you must visit these in reverse order. Make sure agent asks you for the correct order. The California office is in Berkeley.)
When	Leave tomorrow.
How Long	Need to allow a full working day at each plant.
Class/Kind	Company does not allow first class. (Hotels needed at each location.)
Suggested Opening Statement	"Can you get me some arrangements real fast?"

Sample Role Play 2

Who	Mr. or Mrs. MacGregor
How Many	You will be traveling with your spouse. (You are celebrating retirement.)
Where	Europe. (You've never been.)
When	When would the agent recommend? (You're flexible.)
How Long	That depends on the cost. (You'd like to see everything but you're thrifty.)
Class/Kind	You like to be independent. (You've traveled with your spouse before but never outside the United States. You don't like to be regimented.)
Budget	You've been saving for this trip for a long time. (You'd like to know what you're getting before committing to a figure.)
Suggested Opening Statement	"What do you offer in the way to trips to Europe?"

Articles

Chapter 9 — Article One
"Building Repeat Business"
Ask students why repeat business is so important in the travel industry. What are the students' perceptions of value? What characteristics might students add to the list of behaviors noted in the article?

Chapter 9 — Article Two
"Selling Savvy"
Make copies of the following article and discuss sales techniques. Sales training is a good use for video. Student role plays can be taped for review and analysis. Many students have never seen themselves as others do and will find seeing themselves on video an enlightening experience. Using sample brochures (tour, hotel, etc.), have students pair up and practice the various steps to a sale. Reverse the roles between client and agent. Once the pairs seem comfortable, videotape them and ask the class to offer constructive criticism and praise. This exercise works best once students become comfortable with the presence of the videocamera.

Chapter 9 — Article Three
"How Well Can You Sell?"
Make copies of the following article. Remind students that being an effective travel agent requires product knowledge and automation skills. However, these by themselves do not pay salaries or rent. A counselor must be able to convert these skills into sales. Surveys have found that at least 50% of the time it is the travel agent who chooses the client's hotel, cruise ship, air carrier, and destination spot. It is therefore vital that agents possess and develop selling skills. Good sales people are made, not born. The following article presents seven selling scenarios which can be divided over the course of several classes. After each one, stop and ask students how they would respond. Suggested appropriate behavior follows each scenario. There is always more than one correct answer.

Chapter 9 — Article One
Building Repeat Business

By Bob Losyk

If we asked everyone reading this article what it would take to make a $10 dessert a good value, each one would have a different answer. Everyone's perception of this choice morsel would be different.

The same is true of your customers. They define value in their own terms. That value arises out of their perceptions. These perceptions, whether positive or negative, determine whether they will buy from you or your competitor. And the overall perception of the experience determines whether they will come back again, or not.

Customer perceptions are often not at all the ones we think we have created. This is a fact that agency owner/managers must not overlook. For the customer, perception is the most important reality — and may be the one that continues to bring them back in.

Owners, managers and staff must begin looking at everything they say and do from the customer's point of view. Decisions should not be made without first considering what impact they will have on the customer.

If a potential customer walks in the door, and the first thing he or she sees is an agent at a desk cluttered with stacks of papers and stray notes, the perception is: This person is disorganized and might make mistakes with my travel plans. Or if your agency bathroom is dirty or brochure racks are sloppy, then your work must be sloppy, too. First impressions do last, especially the negative ones.

Every contact between a customer and a travel agency — whether with an employee or just the physical aspects of the agency's office — creates a perception in the customer's mind. Jan Carlzon, president of the Scandinavian Airlines System, calls these "moments of truth."

Keeping Score

The customer keeps a mental score card of these perceptions and adds them up. When an agency scores below the customer's standard level of expectations, the agency loses the customer. When the score is equal to the customer's expectations, service is only adequate or good. When the agency goes above the customer's standard, an overall positive perception is created that leads directly to repeat business.

What can we do as owner/managers to create positive perceptions? Our first task is to do a little brainstorming with our staff. Think about the experience your customer has from the first contact with your agency until the travel plans are completed. Let's call this the overall service package, whether for commercial travel or leisure travel.

List every "moment of truth" in the service package. Start with the first phone call or first visit. (Or better yet, start with the parking lot.) List these "moments" in the order the customer would normally encounter them. Go through the entire process, leaving nothing out. Anything that creates a perception, whether positive or negative, should be included.

Next, pick one of these moments of truth. For example, let's use the first phone call. List all the expectations for a first phone call. Remember, look at it from his or her point of view, not yours.

Now make a list of all the potential detractors — anything that creates negative feelings or perceptions. It could be that the phone rings 10 times before it is answered, or the voice on the other end says,"XYZ Travel, please hold," and abruptly puts you on "ignore" for longer than you care to be. If you have trouble thinking of detractors, call some other agencies and then list what you did not like about the experience.

Finally, list the service enhancers. These are all things that your agency can do to create positive perceptions, such as answering the phone within three rings, or putting a caller on hold politely and never for more than 40 seconds.

Choose one of these moments of truth each week and work it through with your staff. You will be shocked at some of the things your agency is doing wrong, and excited about some of the things being done right. Now you have a master list of all the experiences a customer goes through, and can precisely identify where you may be losing business.

The second task of owner/managers is to create a list of the customer service behaviors that are critical to building repeat business.

Behaviors are any actions that can be seen. Don't dwell on personality factors or attitudes, which we may not be able to change, but rather focus on actual behaviors that we can change.

Behaviors for Building Repeat Business

Appearance	Flexibility
Asking questions	Handling stress
Communication skills	Honesty
Consistency	Listening skills
Cooperation	Motivation
Creativity	Problem solving
Empathy	Punctuality
Enthusiasm	Reliability

We must make employees aware, however, of the attitudes they exhibit and how those attitudes affect the customer.

Our job then is to indicate, teach and reward the service behaviors we want our employees to exhibit. One aspect of that job is to become models of customer service behaviors ourselves. Let's look at some of the behaviors that employees must use in order to build repeat business.

The Greeting

Have you watched the faces of your employees, or listened to the greeting they give to your customers entering the agency? Are they making your customers feel recognized or important?

Among agents whose managers have called in a consultant to "mystery shop," a common trait is failure to make eye contact until they have finished the task at hand. When they finally meet the client's eye, their greeting is often cold, as if the customer's presence is an annoyance or just more work. The first critical impression often needs the most improvement.

Customers tell us that it is this first critical greeting that often makes them decide whether you or their competitor will get their business. People like to do business with people they like, and who are friendly and warm. Customers want a sense of rapport. They also like travel agents with enthusiasm and a sense of humor.

Observe your employees and coach them in this area. Do quick role plays during informal meetings. For one week, have your entire staff practice greeting their co-workers each morning with a firm handshake, eye contact and the words "Good morning. How are you?" It may sound hokey, but it creates enthusiasm and drives the point home.

Steer employees away from using the phrase, "May I help you?" This is a yes-or-no question, and usually gets a "no" answer. Instead, change it to an open-ended question such as, "How can I be a of assistance?" or, "What can I help you find?"

Looking and Listening

Another area that creates strong perceptions and is consistently mentioned on customer surveys is the appearance of an employee. Customer expectations about the quality of service to be received can be changed solely by the way an agent looks. Yes, there still are agents working effectively in jeans and T-shirts. But when in doubt, the general rule is to have them look as professional as possible.

How do your employees sound to customers when they are talking with them? Most people never think about the different qualities of their voice. But customers immediately notice the volume, tone and speed of a voice. Coach them to adjust the speed of their words to the rate of speed of their customer's. If the customer is a fast talker, employees should speed up their own speech slightly. If the customer speaks at a turtle's pace, have them slow it down. This develops rapport more quickly.

As we become experts in the places we have traveled, it is hard not to go on and on about the details. But listening carefully to your customers' wants and needs not only develops rapport, but gives you a greater assurance of fulfilling those wants and needs, with fewer errors.

A quick reminder you can teach employees to help them become better listeners is the old railroad crossing phrase: "Stop, look and listen." "Stop" means to stop talking. You cannot talk and listen at the same time. "Look" is the ability to look a customer directly in the eye while listening, encouraging them to think, "This person cares about me, and is paying attention." "Listen" means more than just hearing the customer. It means being able to understand what they are saying about their wants and needs. Only when you can accurately determine your customers' needs can you help solve their problems.

Never assume anything about the customer's level of knowledge. Employees should begin talking to new clients in basic terms, asking questions along the way to check for comprehension.

Some customers know so little about your products or destinations that they do not even know which questions to ask. The job of your employee is to ask the right probing questions to find out what the customer already knows, and then move the conversation along to determine needs.

Flexibility and Empathy

The companies that have become legends in customer service create policies that are flexible. They empower employees to make decisions and exceptions through constant training. Let your staff know when they can make exceptions in fulfilling customer needs or solving their problems. Tell them exactly what they can and cannot do.

Customers are often offended by rigid rules and regulations that cannot be bent, and for good reasons — they feel it is at their expense. They especially hate the words, "That's not our policy" or "We can't do that for you." Eliminate the negative words and phrases that drive customers away.

It is far better to spend a little extra time and money in the short run in order to build repeat business and long-term profits in the long run. The companies that give exceptional service go above and beyond by making exceptions and driving up perceptions.

Finally if there is one interpersonal behavior that is critical to service success, it is knowing when and how to show empathy. Empathy is not sympathy, but a sensitivity to the concerns, needs and feelings of the customer. It is being able to say truthfully, "I understand how you feel." It is being able to "walk a mile in another person's shoes." Expressing empathy is critical in calming unhappy or irate customers, and solving their problems.

By constant role modeling, observation, reinforcing and coaching, you can train employees to become experts in interpersonal skills and behaviors. These simple techniques take little effort, yet do a great deal to develop long-term relationships and repeat business.

How important is repeat business? It costs five times more to get new customers than to keep the old. You can save a lot of money and realize higher profits simply by managing customer perceptions and employee behaviors throughout your agency.

Reprinted with permission from *ASTA Agency Management* magazine, December, 1990

Chapter 9 — Article Two
Selling Savvy

By Lawrence J. Frommer

Office Memo
TO: The Typical Agency Staff
FROM: The Manager
RE: Selling

I don't have to remind you that expertise combined with people skills go a long way in this business. But while both are great assets, by themselves they pay neither the rent nor the salaries. First, they must be converted into sales.

Many agent tend to confuse knowledge with selling. Wrong. This is not to belittle knowledge alone, no matter how expertly dispensed, is not selling. It is merely the prologue to selling. You can proffer all the data in the world, but if the customer doesn't take out the checkbook or credit card, that knowledge is squandered.

Selling is what happens after all of the rhetoric between customer and agent has been exhausted and it's time to ask for the business. And it is at this crucial juncture that many agents, having acquitted themselves nobly in the knowledge department, have difficulty.

Not that any agent is expected to register a sale each time a prospect calls or walks into the office. In this league, if you sell one out of every six or seven, that's an impressive batting average. But here are a few techniques and tactics to enhance your odds.

Thinking about Selling

Don't think of selling as selling. For many in our business selling has a bad name. Whereas informing is clean and tidy, selling means getting the hands dirty. It means asking a client to buy. It means facing customer objections. It means asking a customer for money.

But if any of you have qualms about selling, remind yourself that you are not going to offend your customers. They expect you to ask for the business. Their clothiers do. Their insurance agents do. Why not their travel agents?

Try forgetting the word "sell" and thinking of the process as *helping people get what they want.* Your prospects wouldn't be talking to you if they didn't want to travel.

Listen first, talk last. Except for asking qualifying questions, put your mouth on hold for awhile and lend a good ear. Take notes. It tells the client that you are listening. And when you listen, you give your clients an opportunity to help you help them.

This is why it is ill-advised to distribute brochures too early in the discussion. They create a distraction and interrupt that all important qualifying dialogue between you and the client.

Find out all about client preferences. How many are travelling in your party? When do you wish to travel? How much time do you have for your vacation? What time of day do you prefer to depart and return? What are your flight seating preferences?

In qualifying a client, questions such as these are standard. They deal largely with the detail and structure of a vacation. But the answers to these questions may give no hint as to "satisfaction preferences."

So we dig a little deeper. What are your budget constraints? Are you inclined to beaches, mountains, lakes, rivers, cities? Do you prefer independent or group-escorted travel? What travel experiences have proved the most gratifying and which the least? What did you like and dislike about your last vacation?

You cannot ask customers enough questions, particularly those dealing with lifestyle, budget, and destination. It helps them analyze and articulate their own preferences. The more information you can derive, the greater the odds that you'll be able to plan appropriately.

Probe the budget, gracefully. Determining a client's budget is probably one of the most sensitive phases of the qualifying process. Do you automatically assume that the clients want what's cheap? Do you try to determine price levels from previous vacations? Do you just ask how much they can spend?

The last tactic can backfire. Probably the wisest course is to explain what is available within the various price ranges and let them choose. Above all, never assume.

A Wide Repertoire

Remember that you and your customer are different people. Some of you in the office are cruise buffs. You would be willing to take off and cruise yourselves at the drop of an anchor, and you're chafing to sell a cruise to the next client who walks in.

But perhaps that person is not the cruise type. Perhaps he or she is the Bermuda cottage colony type or the scenery of the Canadian Rockies type. Guide the customer, but don't force your preference.

Give an alternative. Suppose a couple walks into your agency eager to travel on designated dates. They've arranged their busy schedules around those dates. Then you find that the hotel they requested (or the cruise ship. or the tour package) is sold out for the requested date.

You must say no — but never without an alternative. For instance, if the hotel of preference is unavailable for the 26th but comes open on the 28th, can the clients shift two days? If not, how about two nights in a another hotel and a move to the property the couple originally requested?

Never let a customer out of your life without an option.

Win at name recognition. Name recognition of customers is a foundation of good salesmanship not only because it makes people feel important when recognized but also because it warms the relationship between clients and agency. (Remember, though, not to be too free with first names — your client may prefer the gracious formality of Mr. or Mrs.)

And while you're at it, give your name, too. Give the caller or walk-in a chance to call you by name, to affirm that he or she is not just talking to a corporation.

Boost a customer up the ladder. I am aware that many calls are budget oriented these days. This is the mentality of the marketplace. But there are customers who are used to better and who can afford better, even if they are attracted to the latest bargain.

If that bargain, in your estimation, is not compatible with the lifestyle of your customer, then you have got a selling job to do. You are obliged to caution him that the package or whatever is below his standards. You're not trying to gouge him. You're doing him a favor.

Do it subtly, with expressions such as, "You're accustomed to traveling better than that, Mr. Smith — may I ask why the change?" or, "The hotel on this package is not up to your usual standard — are you sure that's what you want?"

Friendly Persuasion

Selling sometimes means unselling. How would you handle a good client whose best friends are urging her and her family to join them on a cruise ship which you are convinced is not suited to them?

Sensitive handling is required here. After all, when friends recommend, friends listen. But if you harbor any doubts, it is your responsibility to your good client to articulate them. On the other hand, you don't want to force your client to choose between your agency and her friends.

Probably the safest route out of this dilemma is to indicate that there are other ships more appropriate to her lifestyle and more consistent with her previous vacations. She may not buy it. You may still find yourself booking the cruise about which you have doubts. But you have burned no bridges and you've done your job.

Don't overrule objections, meet them. Let's say that you suggest a particular trip to a client and he objects. Don't panic. Don't take it personally. Get those objections out on the table where you can deal with them.

Above all, don't belittle an objection, for it is important to the client even if it is based on misinformation. If you can counter the objection by giving the client additional or more accurate information, you stand a better chance of negotiating the sale.

For instance, a customer may be reluctant to take a cruise because she perceives cruise ships as floating homes for the aging. Don't scoff at this perception. Your reply could be, "I can understand your thinking, Mrs. Jones, because not so long ago people who cruised were elderly. But almost every ship today has young passengers, and some ships actually cater to young married couples like yourself."

A greater difficulty is the unspoken objection. That's the one at work when a prospective customer says, "I'll think about it" or "I need to sleep on it" or "Let me go home and talk it over with my wife."

Perhaps the real reasons Mrs. Jones was ambivalent about booking the cruise were not so much her perception of the clientele but price or a fear of seasickness — both of which could have been readily addressed.

Get to the unspoken objection. Try asking, "Is there still a question in your mind that we haven't answered yet?" or "Do you have any other doubts about cruising that you haven't mentioned?"

Don't let objections throw you. They are an integral part of any sales process.

Closing Questions

End it all. The preliminaries are over. You've done your homework. You've been helpful. You've been knowledgeable. You've been patient. You've answered many questions. You've met objections.

Now you must ask for the business.

How? As super salesperson Charles Roth writes, you start to do something that the prospect must stop you from doing in order to avoid giving tacit consent to what you are trying to sell. You can ask for a deposit to guarantee the reservation. You can solicit air schedules from the computer. You can begin writing up the order. You can use the often effective scarcity approach and call the supplier to determine if space is even available.

Or you can start asking questions that by their very nature presume that the client is going, such as, "If we can get this for you, is this what you want?" or "Do wish to pay cash or by credit card?" or "Shall I book Package A or Package B?"

And as former agency executive Victor Hilarov once pointed out, "The more selections you can get the client to make on subordinate issues, the more real the trip becomes to the client and the more likely he is to take it."

It is estimated that at least 50 percent of the time travel agents choose the hotels clients will sleep in, the ships on which they will cruise, the carriers they will fly and even the destinations they will visit. That's a lot of sales power.

But pushing our products and our services requires an extraordinary amount of time and talent, even with the tools of automation. There are constant barrages of questions and answers, incessant changes, busy work, conversations. Unless you are handling mostly commercial business, you rarely make a quick transaction. There is always a lot happening with nearly every prospect we talk to.

Yet nothing really happens, until we ask for the business.

Reprinted with permission from *ASTA Agency Management* magazine, December, 1990

Chapter 9 — Article Three
How Well Can You Sell?
Every Sale Has Key Junctures, Points at Which
the Deal Can Be Clinched — or Lost.
Take This Test to Uncover the Anatomy of a Sale.

By Dawn M. Barclay

In a little more than 15 years since the first large-scale CRS systems were introduced in the 1970s, computers have become the lifeline of most travel agencies — the link to airlines, hotels, rental cars, and ultimately profits. It's not enough anymore for a travel professional to be a destination specialist, a ticket dispenser, a troubleshooter, a visa procurer, an itinerary planner, a map decipherer, a current-affairs ace, and an accountant. You must be well-versed in all the latest computer enhancements, too.

Automation has become so important, however, that it too often eclipses a travel agent's seminal role: salesperson. If you aren't skilled in selling, the number of computer languages you know or countries you've visited are irrelevant. Without sales savvy you risk losing bookings, and in a business of slim profit margins, bookings are everything.

"In the last six years, the deregulated environment has fostered a shopper syndrome — travelers are looking for the best deal. As a result, sales techniques are what turn shoppers into buyers," says Robert W. Joselyn, president of Robert W. Joselyn & Associates, a Scottsdale, Arizona, industry consulting firm. "People want to be sold on travel. They're just looking for someone to sell them — someone who exudes confidence and is passionate and knowledgeable about his or her product."

Are you that kind of agent?

Test Your Skills
Think about what you'd do in each of the following scenarios and then see how your responses compare with the advice given following them.

Situation #1
After a long morning of taking reservations, you finally head to the back room for lunch. Five steps away from your desk, you hear your phone ring. Although a group of coworkers are chatting nearby, not one offers to pick up your line. What do you do?

The First Hello
Think of every incoming call as your paycheck, says John Dalton, author of the book *It's Time to Sell Travel* (Business Concepts Unlimited). Every call is an opportunity to begin selling yourself to a prospective client. **So if your phone rings as you head to lunch, put your lunch on hold, at least long enough to handle the call. Follow your greeting of "Good afternoon" with your agency's name and your name. Or answer politely and put the caller on hold momentarily — then ask a co-worker to take over.**

"But never answer, 'Busy, hold,'" warns Dalton. "You leave clients wondering if they've reached the right number. You also give them an impression of your agency as an abrupt, impersonal, and frantic place."

If after identifying yourself and your agency you must put callers on hold, never leave them for more than 30 seconds. "If no one can help immediately, ask if the caller would mind being phoned back at the earliest opportunity," Dalton recommends.

Never answer a call by just saying "Travel," advises Jim Smith, president of the GEM Travel Consortium in Massapequa, New York. Voice pride in your agency. "Just as the vacation begins for the client the moment they first contact the agency, so should their confidence in your abilities."

Once you've started to help a customer, try to avoid distractions, adds Robert Joselyn. "If you have two or three interruptions, a client will begin to feel uneasy about your competence — especially if you keep coming back to the phone saying, 'Where were we?'"

No matter what your mood (irritation, fatigue, boredom), keep it under wraps; as a salesperson, you must always appear helpful, enthusiastic, and articulate. If you're unsure of your phone personality or voice, record your conversations and then evaluate them, suggests Bridjette Powers March, owner of Werner Travel in Anchorage, Alaska. Her agency grades calls based on what tones come over the line — angriness, happiness, eagerness, and so on — as well as clarity of speech. "We had one Czech employee, for example, who spoke English fairly well, but her thick accent was hard to understand over the phone. After recording and listening to her own calls, she improved 50% in one week," says March.

Situation #2

A new client has made an appointment to come into the agency to discuss her travel plans. When she arrives, however, the office is at its most frenetic — everyone is on the phone, and you're with a client. What do you do?

The First Handshake

A client's impression of your agency is formed within the first 15 seconds after he or she enters, says Joselyn. That means professionalism is reflected in the way your visitors are greeted, the way your office is decorated, and even how each agent is dressed.

The worst thing you can do is fail to acknowledge a customer's presence, says Ellen M. Gill of AAA Western New York Travel in Buffalo, New York. **If you have no receptionist, excuse yourself from the customer at your desk and greet the incoming client. Graciously tell her you'll be with her as soon as you finish your current transaction. If you're on the phone and see a client walk in, at the very least, smile and whisper, "I'll be with you as soon as possible."**

Seat waiting visitors in a well-lit area and give them two of your agency's most essential sales tools — client profile forms and your agency's scrapbook, advises GEM's Smith. "The profile forms will allow you to get some important information — name, address, travel preferences. The scrapbook, filled with postcards from clients and letters of commendation, will whet prospects' travel appetites and boost their confidence in your firm."

At Gill's agency, a receptionist starts the sale process with walk-ins by obtaining names, addresses, and travel biases. She then gives them appropriate brochures to peruse until a travel planner is available. Because the agency works with a limited number of preferred suppliers, the receptionist needs little travel training to give clients the right brochures. (A receptionist could also show prospective clients generic tourism office brochures.) When an agent becomes available, the receptionist accompanies the clients to the agent's desk and introduces them. "Already, two persons at the agency know the clients' names. They've established a rapport before the actual sales process has begun," Gill says.

Just as essential as an agency's meet-and-greet techniques are its more cosmetic welcoming touches. Your office should be a place where you'd be proud to invite clients. Agents shouldn't eat in view of clients, have cluttered offices, or dress differently from their job-interview attire, says Joselyn. Nor should they be overheard asking, "Has anyone seen Mr. Jones's file? I've been looking for it for a week!"

Larry Gove of Miller-Gove Travel in Emeryville, California, recently gave each of his agents a $25 gift certificate to Nordstrom department store and asked them to study the salespersons. The agents were then asked what observations they could incorporate into their own jobs. Their findings: The office should always be adequately staffed to keep clients from waiting, agents shouldn't chew gum at work, and clients should be addressed by name.

Situation #3

"Send us to Bermuda," says the middle-aged couple across your desk who are here to plan their annual February getaway. "We're in the mood for an island in the sun." You know that Bermuda won't be as warm as they'd like in February, and you're sure they'd prefer the Caribbean island where you and your spouse occasionally escape. But these clients are experienced travelers and you're hesitant to disagree with them. What do you do?

Pinpointing the Desire

Giving clients what they really want (not what they think they want or what you'd like) is the difference between making a one-time sale and building a lifelong agent-client relationship. But don't take that advice literally. To find out what clients actually want, you may need to probe. "That means controlling the conversation — not by talking the entire time, but by asking questions that uncover what's unique about the client's vacation needs," says Christopher Hooson of Agenda Inc., a travel management consulting firm in Cambridge, Massachusetts. "Qualifying the client gives you the information you need to make appropriate recommendations."

So before you send a sun-seeking couple to Bermuda in February, even if that's what they've asked for, first pinpoint their dream. If you're not sure they'll be happy with their choice, politely explain why: "Bermuda is a lovely destination, but it may be under 70 degrees in February." From the information you garner, you can suggest suitable alternatives.

To successfully confirm a client's request, ask a series of simple questions such as the names of travel companions, dates of travel, and length of stay. Then follow with open-ended questions that dig deeper: Where have clients traveled before? What do they do in their spare time? Do they prefer traveling in groups? The combination of answers gives you a better understanding of what the client is looking for.

The idea isn't to grill clients but instead to put them in the best frame of mind to answer questions and ultimately to buy. Many successful sales professionals establish this ease with body language — behavior that psychologically relaxes clients and makes them feel special. Such techniques include repeating the client's name often, maintaining eye contact, and leaning slightly forward as you talk, thus physically entering the discussion.

Sit beside the client when going over a brochure or itinerary, suggests Rudy Ligtelyn of Ligtelyn Travel in Los Altos, California. "It makes clients feel like they're dealing with a friend in their living room."

Once you've qualified your clients, don't be afraid to present your opinion regarding their requests or to tactfully advise them that the destinations or hotels they've chosen may not best suit their needs, says Joselyn. "People come to you for your travel knowledge, just as they go to a physician when they're feeling ill. If you tell a doctor you think you have pneumonia but he prefers to run a few tests before making a diagnosis, do you take offense?"

Situation #4

You agree with your recently engaged clients that Hawaii would make a perfect honeymoon. They want something tropical, romantic, and isolated — not to mention far from the in-laws. Although you've had prior success selling a terrific package complete with secluded villa, gourmet dining, and activities skewed to the young and glamorous, you hesitate to suggest it because the couple are college students. How do you determine what they can afford?

Money Talk

Determining a client's travel budget is perhaps the touchiest part of the qualifying process. Although a customer's age, type of dress, and occupation can provide clues, they aren't always sure indicators. Nor is it wise to ask about a budget point-blank. Clients usually try to get the best possible deal and are likely to low-ball the figure.

You'd be much wiser to offer a choice of price ranges (high and low) and explain the difference in quality between the two. Then let the clients decide which they would prefer. Your engaged college students may wear jeans and drive a jalopy, for example, but they may come from well-to-do families or have sizeable honeymoon savings.

The art of successful selling is to recommend a package that doesn't insult the client by being too cheap or too expensive, Joselyn says. "If you've asked about past vacations and where customers have stayed, you should have an idea of what they're willing to spend."

Too often travel agents presume that clients want the cheapest possible vacation, Joselyn says. Ironically their own value system can keep them from selling up. "Because agents don't make a lot of money, they often neglect to mention the more expensive options to clients, assuming the costs are excessive. Meanwhile the client, who often earns more than the agent, might not consider a deluxe package to be extravagant at all," he explains.

Situation #5

After listening to a family describe what they're looking for in a Mediterranean cruise, you lay out a dozen brochures and begin to page through them. You offer comparisons of each line, pointing out relevant "early-bird discounts," "inside upper-deck berths," and "air-sea programs" to help convey that you really know your stuff. The would-be cruisers sit very quietly as you make your pitch. When you're finished, they thank you and leave. What went wrong?

The Pitch

Many agents jeopardize their own chances of making a sale by inadvertently overwhelming clients. "Never offer more than two choices — three, tops," says GEM's Smith. Too many options impede decision-making. Nor are you likely to impress customers by drowning them in travel jargon — you may know what "round-trip transfers" mean, for example, but your clients may not. They'll better understand if you explain that they'll be driven from the airport to the hotel and back again for departure.

To present the product in the way most likely to excite the traveler, the Institute of Certified Travel Agents' Travel Career Development manual suggests speaking the client's language. Sell the benefits of a package — not the features. Customers won't be motivated to buy unless the benefits are clear. **For instance, to sell a family cruise you should establish the desired itinerary, budget, and atmosphere before you haul out every brochure in your files. Then preselect one or two appropriate ships or lines and concentrate on selling those. Don't simply recite the ship's features — in clear and detailed terms point out the benefits.** A cruise cabin described as deluxe (a feature) means much less to clients than explaining how much more comfortable they'll be with more living space and an ocean view (two benefits). Practice using vivid descriptions — "cabins with sitting areas"; "four-course meals"; and "a deep saltwater pool' — instead of empty adjectives like "nice," "pretty," and "wonderful."

If your clients don't like the fist ships you present, you can offer one or two other options — but never more than a few at a time. Leisure travel is an important purchase, and the last thing you want to do is confuse or intimidate your clients.

When presenting a product, Ellen Gill describes each aspect of the trip in a positive light, followed by a question such as, "You did say you wanted an ocean view like this room rate offers?" That way she gets the client into the habit of answering yes. By linking the features of an itinerary to the client's self-proclaimed requirements, you've got them selling themselves.

Situation #6

A corporate client calls and tells you she needs to travel to Manaus on business. "What's the newest hotel in the city?" she asks, "and what kind of travel documents will I need?" You know that Manaus is in Brazil, but since you usually handle domestic reservations, you know nothing about the country's hotel or visa requirements. What do you tell her?

The Curve

It's impossible to know everything about every place. But do make the effort to learn where to find answers to questions beyond your expertise. **If a client wants to know about visa requirements in Brazil, new hotels, or other information you don't know, confidently explain that even though you haven't been there, you know how to find the answers and will call her as soon as possible.**

"Faking it ruins clients' confidence much more than admitting that you're not sure of an answer and then offering to look it up," says Joselyn.

At AAA Lehigh Valley in Allentown, Pennsylvania, Sally McCorrison's staff is well briefed on destinations, thanks to in-house training and fam trip reports. But questions still crop up. "When our agents are unsure, we consult a co-worker who has been there or we call a tourist board," she says. "Instead of being annoyed by our lack of knowledge, most clients are happy that we're willing to go that extra step."

When clients book travel in person, it's often more expedient to first determine which questions will hinder the sale, advises Hooson. "If you're booking clients at a certain hotel in Bermuda and halfway through the reservations process they ask, 'By the way, does the hotel have evening entertainment?' you probably don't need to interrupt the booking to find out, since nightclubs and discos may be located close by if not at the hotel. You can answer, 'When I finish your reservation, I'll find that out for you.'"

On the other hand, if you're booking a cruise for a client and his elderly Hispanic father and they ask whether there's a Spanish-speaking doctor on board, you should immediately ask if such a doctor is essential. "If the doctor is a requirement, you'd better find the answer before you proceed with the booking," he says.

Situation #7
After discussing ski-weekend options at length, you present your client with a popular package that meets his requirements and budget. He still seems hesitant to buy. What do you do?

Closing the Sale
If you've done a good job qualifying your client, the close should be simple. It's a matter of reviewing how the features and benefits of the vacation meet the client's specified needs — and asking for the client's business. Too many agents neglect that last, most crucial aspect of the sale for fear that they'll appear manipulative. They may even offer the client the option to postpone the decision, although it could cost them the sale.

"Listen to objections and then counter them," advises Joselyn. "If clients are worried about money, emphasize value ('You'll get seven nights for the price of five'), or downscale the package to meet their needs, perhaps by offering a shorter vacation or a less expensive hotel." Then ask them for the sale ("Would you like me to reserve your space now?")

Also if the situation warrants, create a sense of urgency, Dalton suggests. **If your ski client, for example, still seems hesitant once you've found a suitable package, you can speed up the sale by telling him that it's no problem to begin a booking. Point out how each part of the trip meets his travel objectives, and then stress that because ski packages — especially popular ones — sell out quickly, he'd be wise to put down a deposit soon. If he still hedges, offer to book a reservation to guarantee the package. If he prefers that you not book this trip, you can search for another one.**

Advise clients that they can always change — don't say "cancel" — a reservation if restrictions permit, suggests Dalton. "And if money seems to be the obstacle, promote the travel-now, pay-later option of using a credit card."

Remember, you're selling clients their dreams, providing them with things they have already professed that they want. "The question shouldn't be whether clients will travel, but how," Joselyn says. "Offer options, but not the option to drop the sale."

When dealing with a high-risk product like travel — one in which people invest precious time and money for something they can't see or feel ahead of time — clients need a personal touch. Computer knowledge and destination expertise are essential aspects to travel planning. But without the ability to sell, you may never get the chance to exercise any of the other skills your job requires.

Reprinted with permission from *Travel Life* magazine, September/October, 1990, a publication of Whittle Communications

Sales Techniques
Chapter 9

End of Chapter Review

Name _____ Date _____

Directions: Identify each question as being Open (O), Closed (C), or Feedback (F)

_____ 1. When will you pick up your air tickets?

_____ 2. Why do you want to go to Peru?

_____ 3. Will a 10:00 a.m. departure be suitable?

_____ 4. So, you prefer an escorted tour rather than an independent one?

_____ 5. When do you want to take the cruise?

Directions: Change these closed questions to open questions. Structure them so a client will give the most information possible.

6. Will you charge this trip on a credit card?

_____

7. Did you like the service on that airline?

_____

8. Do you want to depart on the 6:00 a.m. flight?

_____

9. Have you ever been to Hawaii?

_____

10. Do you think you can afford the deluxe hotel in Paris?

_____

Directions: Rephrase these negative statements positively to suggest a solution.

11. That excursion fare does not permit travel on weekends.

_____

12. Half-day tours of Zurich leave only in the morning.

_____

13. You have to connect at Denver to get to Colorado Springs.

_____

14. Sorry, we are closed on Saturdays.

_____

15. I'm sorry, all the flights to Honolulu are full on the 10th.

_____

Directions: List a feature after the following benefits.

16. The total inclusive cost is $1400.

_____

17. All meals are included.

_____

18. Optional land sightseeing is available.

_____

19. There are structured activities on board to participate in.

_____

20. Space is available on the date you want.

_____

Answers to End of Chapter Review Questions

1. C

2. O

3. C

4. F

5. C

6. What credit card would you like to use? OR How would you like to pay for the tickets?

7. What did you like about the service on that airline?

8. What time would you like to depart?

9. Where have you traveled previously?

10. What type of hotel are you looking for in Paris?

11. You can travel anytime Monday through Friday on that fare.

12. There is a half-day sightseeing tour of Zurich every morning.

13. You can reach Colorado Springs by connecting at Denver.

14. Our office is open Monday through Friday from 9:00 a.m. to 5:30 p.m.

15. I can confirm a flight on either the 9th or 11th and waitlist you for the 10th.

16. All costs are known in advance.

17. No searching for a restaurant.

18. There is an opportunity to see all the sights.

19. You won't feel alone.

20. We can reserve space now.

Customized Sales
Chapter 10

Review Chapter Objectives
- Describe the differences between inside and outside sales
- List two types of groups
- Define incentive travel
- Identify four local business clients
- Note the special needs of handicapped travelers

Review Vocabulary
- Affinity group
- Blocked space
- Charters
- Group profile
- Incentive trip
- Inquiry
- Inside sales
- Outside sales
- Pied Piper
- Specialization

Transparencies
- Chapter outline

Customized Sales
Chapter 10 Outline

I. Inside Sales

    A. Telephone Sales

II. Outside Sales

    A. Selling to Groups

        1. Incentive Groups

        2. Meeting Planning

III. Special Services

    A. Business Travelers

    B. Handicapped Travelers

    C. Families with Children

    D. Senior Citizens

    E. Religious Groups

    F. Honeymooners

    G. Charters

Answers to Textbook Review Questions

1. **Compare the needs of clients who come into a travel office and those who call on the telephone.**
   People who call an agency are usually shoppers, unprepared to discuss their plans in detail and merely wanting information, or buyers, definite in their plans and ready to book. People who come into a travel office need to spend time with a travel counselor to plan details, go over brochures, look at maps and brochures, and so on.

2. **What would you emphasize about your company to inspire confidence in its ability to handle a group's arrangements?**
   Answers could include: previous experience in handling groups, will work closely with the group contact to ensure that all the special requests and needs of the group will be satisfied.

3. **What special services do business travelers expect?**
   Answers could include: care and attention; quick, accurate, and efficient service; ticket delivery; a 24-hour WATS line in case of emergency or last-minute changes; a branch office in their company; up-to-date computerized reservation and accounting systems.

4. **Which forms of transportation appear to be the most adaptable to the needs of the handicapped traveler?**
   Each form of transportation has drawbacks for the handicapped traveler. None is ideal.

Answers to Discussion Topics

Telephone Sales

Answers will differ but may include: A. The counselor needs to first determine when the client is traveling before he/she can quote an accurate fare. B. Booking a group of 40 senior citizens requires special attention and special arrangements.

Recommendations

A. The counselor couldn't possibly book the Hartford after giving the description she did.

B. She would now have to book a hotel that isn't as convenient for the client.

C. An agent should avoid giving subjective judgments about hotels—particularly before the booking is made.

Special Client Needs

Answers will vary but could include

A. The senior citizens would probably require a hotel with room service, entertainment, activities, minimum of walking, and ambiance.

B. The junior high school students would require activities and entertainment

C. A wide range of activities would be needed to satisfy the equally wide range of ages.

D. The handicapped couples would require the most specialized services of all. The entrance needs to be level or have a ramp, and elevators must be big enough to accommodate a wheelchair. Within the room, the light switches, thermostats, air conditioning controls, and locks must be low enough to reach. The bathroom should have safety bars and enough room to accommodate the wheelchair.

E. It would seem unlikely that the same hotel would offer the diversity of all the above features.

F. Answers may vary.

Answers to Workbook Exercises

Worksheet 10-1

Affinity group	An organization formed by people with common interests
Blocked space	Group space reserved on aircraft, cruise ships, in hotels, and so on by retail agencies, wholesalers, or tour operators, that they hope to resell
Charter	A plane, ship, bus, or other form of transportation used for non-scheduled operations
Group profile	To determine the make-up of a group, one constructs a profile based on the average member in terms of age, economic status, background, social and cultural interests, and whatever other factors may have led the person to join the group.
Incentive trip	A trip offered as a prize or bonus for superior performance
Inquiry	A request for information
Inside sales	Sales efforts inside the travel agency
Outside sales	Sales efforts conducted outside of the travel agency
Pied Piper	A term used for the key decision-maker within a group
Specialization	To concentrate one's activities to one particular group

Worksheet 10-2

Answers will vary. These are some suggested responses:

1. "We can book all advertised airfares. Tell me when you are thinking of traveling and I'll find the the best airfare for you."

2. "There are many different air fares from Atlanta to Miami. When were you interested in traveling?"

3. "I'll send you brochures on Bermuda. There are many package trips to Bermuda that you may want to consider. Perhaps we could make an appointment to discuss it."

4. "There are many tours to Alaska. Perhaps we could make an appointment to go over all the information."

5. "No one in our office has been on a safari but we do have a lot of information on them. Did you have some specific questions that I could answer?"

Worksheet 10-3

1. Airplane — Most airlines permit a seeing-eye dog to travel in the passenger cabin free of charge. Some airlines do not permit seeing-eye dogs on long flights. Handicapped clients find it difficult or impossible to use the bathrooms on planes. Airlines treat wheelchairs as checked baggage and supply their own to take clients to and from the airplane. They try to leave the middle seat in a row empty if a handicapped client is occupying one of the others. By law, carriers may not exclude any qualified handicapped person from any seat in an exit row or any other location, except to comply with FAA regulations which govern the procedure for the emergency evacuation of the aircraft.

Worksheet 10-3 (continued)

2. Some Turboliner and Amfleet equipment provide seats specially designed for handicapped passengers and have storage space for wheelchairs nearby. There are also special bathrooms in these cars. Certain sleeping accommodations are adapted for the handicapped. Most seats are wide enough to negotiate a 26" wide wheelchair. Passengers can order food and drinks at their seats. Amtrak will carry seeing-eye dogs at no charge.

3. Some major car rental companies can, with advance notice, provide cars with hand controls for handicapped drivers. The car can also be waiting outside the baggage claim area if airport regulations permit. Some smaller cars may not have room for a wheelchair in the trunk.

4. Some tour operators specialize in tours for the handicapped and use motorcoaches with hydraulic lifts and enlarged baggage compartments. Most other tour operators will not accept handicapped passengers without a companion.

5. Many cruise lines refuse to accept the very elderly or passengers with a history of illness. Most ships will not carry seeing-eye dogs. On many cruise ships cabin doors are too narrow for a wheelchair. Tendering is almost impossible for wheelchair passengers.

Worksheet 10-4

1. Pros — Choose from: Business travelers frequently know what they want; business travel takes place year round and therefore can provide a steady source of income; business travelers often request straightforward arrangements; business travelers often extend their business travel to include meetings and conventions that can produce additional revenue for the agency; business travelers may decide to use the same agency for their pleasure travel.
   Cons — To properly service business travelers, agents need to be quick, accurate, and efficient; agencies need to be completely computerized for both bookings and accounting; agencies must study the costs involved in providing service to determine if it's worth it.

2. Answers will vary.

Classroom Activities

1. You have been asked by a local senior citizen group to put together a two-week trip to Europe for its members. The trip is scheduled for next summer and will be a motorcoach tour beginning in Amsterdam and ending in Rome. All trip arrangements have been set, and you are now to make a presentation to the group to encourage participation. Fifty people have RSVP'd to attend the meeting. You will be showing slides of the destinations.
   - List the steps you will take to arrange the meeting.
   - List the materials you will need to order or have with you.
   - What type of room set-up might you want to request?
   - Write a brief outline of the key facets you want to include in your presentation.
   - Deliver your presentation to the class (approximately 10 minutes).

2. Develop a sample sales presentation for each of the following groups: handicapped, senior citizens, junior high school students. How do the needs of these groups differ? What special considerations must be given in terms of accommodations, transportation, meals, and sightseeing?

Articles

Chapter 10 — Article One
"Motorcoach Travel"
Copy the following article dealing with the motorcoach industry. What specific groups does the motorcoach industry cater to? How can travel agents direct their sales to this particular market? How can this market be expanded? Why is service so important to the motorcoach market? Discuss client satisfaction as the key ingredient in a motorcoach tour operator's success.

Chapter 10 — Article Two
"Keeping Corporate Clients Contented"
What are the special needs of corporate clients? Why is service so important to this group? How can service be measured?

Chapter 10 — Article Three
"Incentive Travel: Superior To More Common Rewards"
How does incentive travel differ from other travel groups? Choose a destination that would be appropriate for this market. List the steps in qualifying an incentive client. What additional amenities might be necessary to provide for an incentive group?

Chapter 10 — Article One
Motorcoach Travel

By John P. Butters, CTC

An increasingly sophisticated U.S. riding public may begin to voice its opinion about motorcoach travel. Will the travel industry respond to these opinions and use them to create new ideas for bona fide motorcoach travel? In addition, does the travel community recognize a potential motorcoach traveler?

Potential domestic motorcoach clients do not usually walk through the doors of a travel office and shout the name of their preferred motorcoach operator. Nor have they pre-selected an itinerary. In fact, many individuals are unfamiliar with the features and benefits of an escorted tour or with the fact that it could be the type of vacation they seek. This market element represents a solid base for any organization.

Perhaps what tells a person most about the motorcoach traveler is what he or she doesn't say. A person rarely admits that traveling to a strange city, picking up a car rental, or finding a hotel intimidates him/her. Many times an individual does become extremely uneasy, nervous, and lonely. To this timid individual the benefits of an escorted tour become very attractive, especially with its built-in safety.

The stereotype of motorcoach travelers fall into two categories: the mature traveler (persons 55 years or older) and single or widowed women. Are these assumptions based on fact? Probably not. Motorcoach tours no longer attract just the senior market. Younger travelers in their 40s, 30s, and even 20s find motorcoach travel attractive. Travelers between the ages of 18 and 34 represent about one-third of the tour-going public. This hardly indicates a youth movement but does show a positive change. Even families enjoy themselves because the work and the worry are no longer their responsibility. The demographic mix has been changing slowly in recent years.

Tours include many benefits. Prepayment ranks high because the traveler can determine the entire cost in advance. The tour operator or wholesaler arranges for volume discounts making for lower costs, assured entrances to popular shows which avoids disappointments, and reliable sightseeing. The traveler can move around freely and without hassle which gives great peace of mind and complete relaxation. When the motorcoach leaves in the morning, the sightseeing begins. When it stops, it is situated in the right place for a visit, a meal, or an overnight stay. Airport arrivals and departures, hotel check-ins, and baggage are handled without the client's active participation. Escorted tours are planned by individuals who know their selected areas intimately. Each day's itinerary has been tested repeatedly, thus ensuring the maximum utilization of time. The presence of a tour escort expedites the handling of any unexpected incidents.

Motorcoach tours range from one-day excursions to itineraries lasting several weeks. Some set a leisurely pace with stays of two or three nights in major cities, while others cover more territory and visit new places every day. As more travelers demand highly specialized tours, tour operators will shift gears to meet this need. The creativity in motorcoach design together with the ingenuity of tour offerings makes the 1990s an excellent decade for motorcoach travel.

Motorcoaches of the 1990s will sport a new look in styling and seating configuration to replace present-day coaches. One popular European manufacturer, already selling coaches in the United States, designs a motorcoach with 27 polished wood and supple leather seats instead of the usual 45. The configuration is nine three-seat rows similar to the airlines' business class. The bus has a VCR system, closets for hanging clothes, and a full kitchen including a sink, microwave oven, a refrigerator/ freezer, and a roomy bathroom. Larger windows, fewer obstructed views, and bright, color-coordinated interiors describes Eurostyling. Even the seats are curved to fit the back and offer a firmer lumbar support. With coaches operating with a driver and a hostess; they offer all of the amenities of first-class travel.

To meet the the demand of discriminating travelers, motorcoach companies must maintain an inventory of coaches of various sizes, rather than just the 40-foot long, 102-inch-wide, 46- or 48-coach seat that has been the industry standard. Coaches range in size from 20- to 25-seat "minis" to a 60-foot, five-axle, 76-seat H5-60.

The National Tour Association brochure, which includes more than 100 commission-paying tour operators in every price category, is an important tool for selling motorcoach travel.

Reprinted with permission from *Travel Industry Marketing,* a publication of the Institute of Certified Travel Agents

Chapter 10 — Article Two
Keeping Corporate Clients Contented

By Carol Reddoch Kasper, CTC

As travel professionals, we should ask ourselves: Do my corporate clients use my agency because I deliver tickets free of charge? I doubt it, since most travel agencies today deliver corporate tickets free of charge. Is it because of the airline fares they get for their trips? I doubt it, since every travel agency has access to the same information, and most are adept at finding the lowest possible fares. Is it the quality of the product? I doubt it. Every travel agency sells the same products, and most are able to sell skillfully and knowledgeably. Is it your employees? Now we are getting close! Most travel agents have adequate training and good computer skills but what makes your employees better than your competitors? John Dalton calls the magic ingredient *"glue,"* that intangible commodity that makes your customers "stick" to you and not the agency down the street. In today's fiercely competitive environment, you must have a special kind of "glue" to keep your customers coming back to you. What is "glue?" Obviously, it is exceptional service. It is the perception that your clients have of the service they are receiving from your agency.[1]

That good customer service is the key to keeping your clients contented is substantiated by the fact that traditionally eighty percent of an agency's effort is spent in maintaining business, with fifteen percent spent in selling and five percent in finding new business.[2]

A company's customer service philosophy must come from the owner or president and be adhered to by all levels from management down to the lowest position in the company. Every time an employee has any personal contact with a client or potential client is an opportunity to provide quality customer service. Thus, the company's customer service policy becomes an integral part of the company's personality.[3]

The opportunity to provide quality customer service in a travel agency is available through two sources: the *"front line"* and the *support team.* Every travel agency has a "front line," those employees who answer the phones or greet clients as they enter the office. In a small agency, the "front line" is usually an agent or travel counselor. In a larger agency, a receptionist or secretary may initially greet the public. With today's high technology, an automatic attendant phone service may be a client's "front-line" contact with the company; however, since travel arrangements are very personal transactions, even for business travelers, the choice of an automated "front line" would defeat the purpose of personalized customer service.

Given that a company, or an individual for that matter, never has a second chance to create a first impression, what necessary skills should the agency's "front line" command? First, because corporate clients make their travel arrangements exclusively over the phone, excellent telephone manners, a pleasant tone of voice, and a positive attitude are essential, especially since this telephone contact may be the sole opportunity an agency will have to communicate with a client. When an employee is on the phone with a client, that individual is the single representative of the organization. In other words, this "front line" employee is the company.[4] To be sure, phone manners and techniques can be learned and improved. It is very important that all travel agents have such training.

In addition to appropriate telephone skills, other qualities needed by employees to provide exceptional customer service are:

- Anticipating the client's needs—providing a service without requiring the customer to ask for it;

- Good listening skills — most people tend to hear what they want to hear and filter out the rest. It is important to listen attentively to understand what is being said so that the response is accurate;

- Excellent communication skills — proper grammar and a well-modulated voice are indicative of a positive attitude;

- Willingness to help — even if all of the questions cannot be answered.

Just as there are positive qualities that agents need to provide outstanding customer service, there are also negative traits to be avoided.

Seven Customer Service Sins
1. Apathy
2. Brush-off
3. Coldness
4. Condescension
5. Robot attitude
6. Rulebook responses
7. Runaround[5]

Assuming that all "front line" employees have excellent customer service skills and the agents are all trained professionals, what else is needed? Unfortunately, most agencies feel good customer service skills are enough. In today's fiercely competitive environment, however, a pleasant voice, positive attitude, and good listening skills are not enough to keep a corporate account "glued" to the company. Going *"the second mile"* has become essential. Our company instituted a "second mile" program with our employees and advised our corporate accounts of its inception. When any of our employees, particularly agents, do something special or go "above and beyond the call of duty," we encourage our clients to let us know so that we can acknowledge the action and reward the appropriate person. By enclosing an airport map, offering to enroll the client in a frequent flyer program, calling the sales office directly to clear a seat or waitlisted fare, enclosing a drink coupon or free admission to airport lounges, or upgrading a V.I.P. to first class, the agent is going the "second mile" to provide exceptional customer service. When the president of our largest account personally phoned our president just to say, "Thanks for the drink coupon; I really appreciated it," we knew that our program was a success.

Our agents are motivated in several ways. They appreciate the compliments, obviously, but whenever we receive positive comments about a particular employee, that person is given a dollar bill and her name is placed in a drawing for free airline tickets, as well as acknowledged in the weekly company newsletter. This program is so basic and simple to implement that any sized agency would benefit by instituting such a program.

Regardless of the quality of the "front-line" customer service program, support personnel is a necessary element of an effective customer service program for corporate accounts. Most owners, managers, and agents are too busy to personally visit each account, write letters to suppliers that have not provided the service they promised, negotiate special meeting fares on behalf of the corporations, provide consultation services to accounts that are interested in instituting a travel and entertainment policy, work with sales representatives to advise corporations of new services, negotiate local hotel and car rates for corporate accounts, customize management reports, research and recommend the best third party billing system, organize seminars for corporate travel planners, provide V.I.P. services such as cocktail parties and golf outings as well as keep clients advised of any changes in the travel industry that may impact their business. Who then does see to each of these needs, needs that corporate clients expect to be met?

If an agency has at least ten corporate accounts and does not have such a person to provide these services, the agency probably will not have those ten accounts for long. Corporate clients are becoming very knowledgeable about services provided by travel agencies and accordingly are becoming very demanding that those services be provided to them.

While these services should be provided, an entire customer service department or even a full-time employee to handle those responsibilities is not necessary. Depending on the size of the agency and the person chosen for the job, a part-time employee may be able to provide excellent service to the agency's corporate accounts.

Whether part-time or full-time, what type of person should be employed as a customer service representative? Obviously, putting the wrong person in that position will not only be ineffective, but very probably will be counter-productive.

Personal qualities necessary for a customer service representative

- Patient
- Able to make quick, accurate decisions
- Flexible
- Personable
- Neat and clean in appearance
- Knowledgeable of customers
- Able to respond promptly to problems and requests
- Caring; sensitive, yet able to remain objective
- Mentally and emotionally stable
- Able to assess each situation and know when to involve top management.[6]

Selecting the right person for this job is critical. Your customer service representative is your company. He or she is the person your clients see personally and communicate with; therefore, this person must project the image you want for your company.

To implement a customer service program in a travel agency, however, requires more than selecting the right person. First, the following questions must be asked:
- How are complaints handled now?
- From a customer's viewpoint, what should be changed?
- What resources does the company have to work with?
- Can the company's present service system deliver on its promises?
- What are the main reasons for complaints?
- What parts of the previous system work and should be continued?
- How well does the company's complaint system function?[7]

When these questions are answered and the program has been designed, then the budget must be established. The costs to be incurred include salary, benefits, company car (if the budget allows), office supplies, phone bills, and monthly budgets for lunches, compensation for mistakes, and V.I.P. services.[8]

Introducing a new customer service program to the staff may be a sensitive procedure. Expect negative reactions initially from the agents. There will be resentment until the program is established and running smoothly. The customer service representative will be communicating problems from clients to the agents and asking why the problems occur. Even the most tactful, sensitive person will be greeted defensively by an agent who is being asked to respond to a problem, especially if he or she has made a mistake. Corporate agents are always working under a tremendous amount of stress and are not happy about being confronted by someone they perceive as an outsider to defend their actions, particularly when ninety-nine percent of the problems occur with suppliers. In fact, statistics show that as many as seventy-two people may handle a single trip.[9] No wonder problems occur. A new customer service program must be explained in a positive manner to be accepted by the existing staff, which must feel that the customer service representative is an extension of themselves to the clients.

A general misconception of a customer service program is that since it does not produce sales, it is unproductive. The truth is: "A satisfied customer is never unproductive."[10]

A customer service department is a unique idea in the travel agency community. Very few, if any, competitors have a true customer service department. Therefore, a detailed explanation of the customer service department is a valuable addition to a corporate proposal.[11] It can be the competitive edge you need to draw corporate business from the mega-agencies when clients know they will be serviced as a "big fish in a little pond."

The *benefits* of a customer service program far outweigh the costs. Not only does your customer service representative handle problems and complaints, but in the process, he or she is provided with the opportunity to improve existing services and operational procedures. By discovering problems, solutions may be found to prevent their reoccurrence.[12] For example, seat assignments are usually the number one service problem reported by travel agencies that handle corporate accounts. By insisting that every itinerary either has a seat assignment printed on it or an explanation as to why a seat could not be assigned, the agent assures the client that his preferred seat has been requested. Knowing how important seat assignments are to corporate travelers encourages agents to call the airline personally to try to clear the requested seat. Another example is that by providing additional information such as frequent flyer numbers in the computer history in an automatic move field, the information is printed on the itinerary and the client knows that his frequent flyer information has been given to the airline.

A good customer service program not only provides the opportunity to educate agents to the needs of the clients, but also provides the opportunity to educate the travelers and travel planners. A customer service department that plans seminars and familiarization trips for the travel planners is providing valuable service. The better educated the travelers and travel planners are, the more appreciated the travel agents will be and the easier their job will be.

A customer service representative who establishes good relationships with travel planners as well as sales representatives from the airlines, hotel companies and car rental companies will reap invaluable benefits not only through agency loyalty and ability to resolve problems, but through leads for future business.

By having a customer service representative who visits accounts regularly, an agency becomes aware of the opportunities for incremental business. If it is found that field offices exist, the account can be consolidated. If there are regular sales meetings that an agency is not handling, the agency's meeting planner can offer to assume those for the account. If there is a recreational association, the opportunity to plan its trips becomes available. The more an agency knows about the companies who use their services, the better it can service all of their needs.

Once a customer service department or program has been established, how can its effectiveness be evaluated? The first and most important criterion is also the one that takes the longest time to measure. "If you have maintained an account for more than three years, you are providing better service than your competition. Industry statistics advise that the average length of time a travel agency maintains a corporate account is three years."[13]

An earlier indicator that is simple and inexpensive is a survey. The surveys will be returned at a very high rate if an incentive such as a drawing for a free trip or getaway weekend is offered. Usually, an annual survey is sufficient to track service patterns.

The third and most immediate opportunity for evaluation is the postpaid critique card in each ticket jacket, asking the traveler to rate the services of the travel agent, airline, hotel, car rental company, emergency hotline, etc. and provide space for comments. An additional space to request information on vacation destinations will provide leads for leisure agents which can result in a noticeable increase in vacation business without any further expensive marketing efforts.

Such an evaluation of any new program is imperative to determine its effectiveness. Without an evaluation, the budgets and marketing plans for future years will be impossible to implement.

In summary, a dedicated, responsive customer service organization is one of the best investments that can be made in this era of heightened consumer awareness. Managed in the right manner by the right people, the customer service department can reap long-lasting benefits for a company—benefits that will be reflected on the bottom line.[14]

Reprinted with permission from *Business Management*, a publication of the Institute of Certified Travel Agents

238

Endnotes

1. John Dalton, "How to Find, Sell and Maintain Corporate Accounts," Travel Profits '88 seminar, September 8, 1988.

2. Ibid.

3. *Management of Sales Personnel*, I.C.T.A. text "Effective Customer Service," reprinted with permission from "Small Business Report," February, 1980, p. 252.

4. William B. Martin, *Quality Customer Service*, p. 16.

5. Dalton, Travel Profits '88 seminar.

6. Donna Thomas, "The Secrets of Keeping Your Accounts Happy," Travel Profits '88 seminar, September, 1988.

7. *Management of Sales Personnel*, I.C.T.A. text, p. 253.

8. Thomas, Travel Profits '88 seminar.

9. Ibid.

10. Ibid.

11. Ibid.

12. Ibid.

13. Ibid.

14. *Management of Sales Personnel*, I.C.T.A. text, p. 257.

Chapter 10 — Article Three
Incentive Travel: Superior To More Common Rewards

By Kathy Kaczmarek, CTC

Webster's definition of "incentive" is "to motivate or encourage beneficial behavior, performance or action that would not have otherwise occurred."

An incentive market is any situation where a tangible reward is offered in return for a desired behavior, performance and/or action. The incentive travel product is a program in which travel is the reward.

The incentive market offers a lucrative and sometimes non-competitive opportunity to those willing to design, market and manage incentive programs.

Incentive rewards used to motivate people include:
* Money
* Merchandise
* Recognition (employee of the month, most improved employee, etc.)
* Prestige (elite sales club membership, representing boss at outside functions)
* Authority/Responsibility (promotions, new responsibilities, training)
* Travel

Incentive Travel is
* An expandable market
* Interesting and fun
* Very Lucrative

Incentive travel is not
* Business as usual because it requires new skills
* Short term
* Easy
* Business that will be driven in the door by suppliers

Travel is usually a superior incentive to traditional non-travel alternatives, although it is the least used of current incentives, accounting for less than 1 percent of all incentives offered. This spells opportunity for both the client and the incentive travel company.

The travel experience provides a value and is usually remembered longer than any other incentives, especially if it is truly an exquisite experience. Money awards get mixed up with the achiever's "other money" and may be spent to pay bills. Merchandise wears out and high level achievers often own all the merchandise they want.

With a travel reward, prestige and recognition are realized because the achievers are on the trip with other winners. Association with other winners on the trip, sometimes referred to as "A Gathering of Eagles," benefits the achievers and the organization because the "eagles" will share their experiences and ideas and learn through each other.

The incentive travel opportunity is beneficial to the incentive travel company because of the high profit potential. The travel package sold is typically complete. It is a "cruises-plus" situation where not only are travel arrangements sold, but meals, gifts and special events are included in the trip to provide the achievers with an extraordinary experience.

The travel package is usually "first class." It is preferable to cut back on a destination before backing off on "first class" quality. In other words, if an exquisite Hawaii travel package cannot be arranged within the budget, an exquisite San Francisco travel experience should be provided. It should be an experience the achiever cannot buy and will not forget. If the achiever does not think the award is superior, he may not be motivated to earn it.

Planning incentive programs can be quite profitable as the sponsoring organization is typically willing to pay for incentive-program design and administration. The money that is made on the design and administration of the overall incentive program is almost always greater than that earned from the sale of travel itself.

Although there is aggressive and sophisticated competition for major incentive programs, there is far less and sometimes no competition for small- and medium-sized incentive programs. Commercially oriented agencies often lack the creativity and leisure skills required, while leisure-oriented agencies often lack the client relationships and disciplined approach needed.

In addition, most agencies also lack the direction. Almost all agencies lack the consulting and analytical ability to design incentive programs, the promotional ability to carry out an incentive target-marketing plan and the service capacity to execute and administer the program.

These obstacles can be overcome by creating a special team, complementing your travel skills and contacts with the specialized skills of an accounting firm and an advertising agency, with you, the travel counselor, serving as the incentive program coordinator.

Identifying specific incentive-travel prospects is the easiest part of incentive travel. Almost every relationship we have provides another incentive-travel prospect.

We should start with our current client base. The first potential clients should be among our existing commercial accounts, followed by our existing non-commercial, but "incentifi-able" organizations, such as the American Legion, national clubs, publications, etc. From there we turn to connected non-client prospects, which include our leisure clients' business firms or other membership organization.

In coordinating an incentive travel team to include an accounting firm and an ad agency, we broaden our incentive client base by including their current clients as additional selling opportunities. Our final prospects include unconnected, non-client prospects.

In promoting our incentive travel product, personal selling is much more productive than advertising. The personal-selling opportunity has three stages. Getting the attention of the organization is the first step. The second step is the initial call (or calls), which helps us to gather information and learn about the clients business, as well as determine whether the incentive concept needs to be sold. The third step is the sales presentation, which should be flexible. We can vary the destination or any part of the plan or minimize the risk involved to the client's satisfaction, if we are flexible. It is as important to sell our capability and approach as it is to sell a specific offering.

Let the client know that we are gathering information to help us custom-design a program specifically for them. Make them aware that any of our competitors who submit a ready-made, "guaranteed" program without completing this initial research are probably giving the client a "boiler-plate" or someone else's program. A program should be designed specifically for each individual client organization to meet its unique needs, goals and objectives.

The most important criteria for selecting the incentive destination are to research, profile and understand all we can about our potential achievers. If we know their age, marital status, income level, cultural and professional activities and general lifestyles, we can select an appropriate destination for them.

The most popular travel incentives are weekend packages — trips to Hawaii, the Caribbean, Bermuda, London, Paris, Hong Kong and cruises. Some new "hot" incentive destinations include family packages, golf or tennis packages, Club Med stays, spas or ski programs.

Many enhancements can be negotiated and included in our programs. In relation to transportation arrangements, we can negotiate and include first-class meals during coach flights, luggage tags, and "official" carrier, pre-boarding arrangements and/or a company motivational movie on the flight.

The hotel accommodations might include flowers in the individual's room, a 50 percent reduction on rooms one night before the group's morning arrival in Europe, theme party props, customized brochures and/or free delivery of "pillow gifts."

Pillow gifts are little incentive gifts left on the achievers' pillows each night, possibly ranging from a gourmet chocolate the first night and escalating in value to a set of crystal goblets on the last night.

Meals and social functions can include candles, decorations, distinctive menus, costumes or masks and/or free clean-up service. To create that exceptional travel award, the "little extras" and special events are a must. The key to a travel award is creating a trip that the customer cannot buy!

Some local businesses at the destination may be able to arrange dinner parties at the home of certain dignitaries. Someone once received approval to host a masked ball in a Venice canal house by donating money to the Canal House Restoration Fund. A photographer helps to keep the trip "memorable" long after the achievers have returned home. And those "pillow gifts" offer endless opportunities for creativity.

Another consideration in developing the travel incentive destination is to know about the destination so you do not "fight the site." In other words, make sure you leave time for shopping on a trip to Hong Kong and do not schedule a barbecue in Paris.

Reprinted with permission from *Travel Counselor* magazine, a CMP publication

Customized Sales
Chapter 10

End of Chapter Review

_____

Name   Date

Directions: Fill in the blanks.

1. What two types of clients will generally decide to telephone an agency rather than make arrange ments in person?

   1._____ 2._____

2. When selling to a group, what factors would you include in constructing a group profile?

   _____

   _____

3. A special interest group is
   a. a group of interesting people.
   b. a group entitled to a special hotel rate.
   c. a group sharing the same hobby, profession, or ethnic heritage.
   d. a group that a travel agency takes a special interest in.

4. Why should you arrive early if you are giving a presentation to a group?
   a. to check that there are enough chairs in the meeting room.
   b. to relax by having a drink at the bar.
   c. to order audio-visual equipment.
   d. to get a good parking space.

5. Amtrak carries seeing-eye dogs at no charge and on most trains offers a discount to handicapped passengers.   True   False

6. Most airlines will reserve the bulkhead seats or those near the emergency exits for handicapped travelers.   True   False

7. Most cruise ships will not carry animals of any kind, including seeing-eye dogs.   True   False

8. Most phone shoppers are a nuisance and should not be viewed as potential clients.   True   False

9. One advantage of having a lot of corporate accounts is that business travel takes place year-round.   True   False

10. Honeymooners and senior citizens have most of the same needs.   True   False

Answers to End of Chapter Review Questions

1. Shoppers — unprepared to discuss their plans in detail and merely want information.
   Buyers — They may be absolutely definite about what they want and are prepared to book.

2. Age, economic status, background, social and cultural interests, and whatever other factors may have led the individual to join the group.

3. C

4. A

5. True

6. False

7. True

8. False

9. True

10. False

Follow Up
Chapter 11

Review Chapter Objectives
- Explain three ways clients change plans
- Describe four emergency situations
- Discuss four types of specialized travel insurance
- Determine how much insurance to sell to a customer
- List the steps involved in a reissue
- Relate the importance of a client profile
- Compare the differences between a written and an oral contract

Review Vocabulary
- Contract
- Coverage
- Double indemnity
- Errors and omissions
- Itinerary
- Liability
- Policy
- Premium
- Principal sum

Transparencies
- Chapter outline
- Types of travel insurance

Follow Up
Chapter 11 Outline

I. **Changes After the Sale**

II. **Common Reasons for Changes in Plans**

    A. Strikes

    B. Bankruptcies

    C. Other Emergencies

    D. Death

III. **Client Protection Against Changes**

    A. Flight Insurance

    B. Travel Accident/Health Insurance

    C. Baggage and Personal Possession Insurance

    D. Trip Cancellation or Interruption Insurance

IV. **Selling Insurance**

V. **Record Keeping**

    A. The Profile System

    B. Reissues

    C. Itineraries

VI. **Contracts**

VII. **Handling Complaints**

    A. Misrepresentation

    B. Errors and Omissions

Types of Travel Insurance

- Flight

- Travel Accident/Health

- Baggage and Personal Possession

- Trip Cancellation or Interruption

Answers to Textbook Review Questions

1. **What items might be kept in a client file for a couple taking an escorted rail vacation in California?**
   Answers may include: deposit and final payment deadlines, information on the tour, client information.

2. **Do complaints have any positive features? What can we learn from them?**
   Agents can learn valuable first-hand information from their clients about suppliers or destinations.

3. **Should agents consider travel insurance primarily as a source of income, as protection for clients, or as a way for agents to protect themselves from liability if clients are assessed cancellation penalties, lose baggage, or suffer some other loss that insurance would have covered?**
   All of the above.

4. **What steps can agents take to reduce the risk of being sued by clients?**
   Answers may include:
   - Encourage clients to take out insurance.
   - Take out insurance themselves.
   - Ensure that clients are aware of the agency-supplier relationship and its implications.
   - Disclaim responsibility for the actions of suppliers.
   - Choose suppliers carefully.
   - Never misrepresent products, suppliers, or destinations.
   - If there is a problem, act quickly, decisively, and fairly.
   - Never assume and check everything twice.

Answers to Discussion Topics

Insurance

A. Neither the motorcoach operator, driver, tour operator, tour guide, or travel agent is responsible for the accident.

B. Health and accident

C. If the passengers did not purchase insurance, they are out of luck.

D. The tour passengers who were hurt would have to be treated, and the motorcoach would either have to be repaired or another one substituted. It is possible that the tour could go on.

Client Profile

Answers will differ.

Complaints

A. She should be handled with care and away from the other clients.

B. The manager should deal with her.

C. The phones and other clients should be dealt with by the rest of the staff.

D. It doesn't sound like anyone could have prevented her from coming into the office. Unfortunately, there are some clients (and people in general) who always complain. The owner of the agency may want to consider whether the client's six trips a year are worth the aggravation.

Answers to Workbook Exercises

Worksheet 11-1

Contract	An agreement between two or more people
Coverage	Inclusion within an insurance policy or the amount available to meet liabilities
Double indemnity	The insurance company will pay twice the principal sum if an accident is completely beyond the individual's ability to avoid.
Errors and omissions	A type of insurance to protect an agency by covering claims for damages suffered by the client for financial loss, inconvenience, embarrassment, or other injuries because of an error or omission on the part of the travel agent.
Itinerary	A planned route for a trip
Liability	Obligations or responsibilities
Policy	A document within which an insurance contract is included
Premium	The amount paid for a contract of insurance

Worksheet 11-2

1. 1. Flight insurance is a form of accident insurance. It provides short-term coverage for accidents that occur during travel.

   2. Health and accident insurance protects the client from travel and non-travel related accidents and sickness at all times while away from home.

   3. Baggage insurance protects clients against loss or damage to baggage and personal possessions while traveling and picks up where the responsibility of a carrier is limited.

   4. Trip cancellation insurance will reimburse clients for nonrefundable pre-payments if they must cancel for a covered reason.

2. Choose from: strikes, bankruptcies, civil wars, political violence, epidemics, natural disasters

3. Coverage begins when the client leaves home and includes the ride to the airport. Coverage ends when flights are completed or after 180 days, whichever comes first.

4. Choose from: any tour, cruise airfare, etc., with high cancellation penalties; all charter arrangements; all escorted tours where baggage may be left out overnight for early morning pick up; touring by car

Worksheet 11-3

1. Consular officials can advise him of his legal rights. The official can also arrange legal counsel and contact the person's family.

2. The Citizen's Emergency Center can transmit details of medical history and transfer funds to pay for medical care, if necessary.

3. An official from the American embassy or consulate will mediate to arrange local burial or shipment of the body.

4. Most U.S. embassies can issue temporary emergency passports and can arrange for funds to be transmitted quickly. They also can provide small government loans if necessary.

5. No assistance can be offered.

Worksheet 11-4

1. F

2. F

3. F

4. F

5. F

6. Answers will vary but may include: transportation information, accommodation, sightseeing, average temperature, clothing suggestions, shopping tips

Worksheet 11-5

1. The client expects the agent to confirm reservations, send deposits, check timings issue correct documents, etc. They also expect the agent to negotiate for the best possible arrangements at the best possible price. Because an implied contract can be open to misinterpretation, the agent must make sure that the client understands their relationship. Both agent and client must not assume anything.

2. Answers will vary.

Classroom Activities

1. Ask students to visit local agencies and obtain copies of suggested insurance coverage. Ask them what sort of coverage they would recommend for their parents? For their grandparents? For themselves? Why might these amounts differ? Would the amounts also differ depending on destinations? If so, why?

2. Ask students to research the effect of a recent strike, or a recent disaster, if appropriate. How does this impact the entire travel agency community? How long do these repercussions last? Is there ever a time that a disaster can increase tourism? Ask students to explain their opinion.

Articles

Chapter 11 — Article One
"Complaining 101" (First of Two Parts)
Chapter 11 — Article Two
"Grumbling Etiquette" (Second of Two Parts)
Ask students to discuss a recent example of poor service which would warrant a letter of complaint. Ask them to write such a complaint letter, being as specific as possible. Exchange letters and ask students to address their fellow students' complaints by responding to the original letters. Would all letters need to be followed up with a written response? When should other forms of follow up be used? In a travel agency, who should send follow up letters?

Chapter 11 — Article Three
"T.A. Law"
Ask students to list four ways they can protect themselves and their agencies from lawsuits. How can preferred suppliers provide additional protection? What is the importance of waivers? Ask students to visit three or four local agencies and see if they are protected by USTOA, ASTA, or NTA. Do these agencies use these affiliations in their print media advertising?

Chapter 11 — Article One

Complaining 101
How to get satisfaction for clients when a travel experience turns sour
(First of two parts)

By Phyllis Fine

Rats in a hotel room. A dog missing from a just-landed plane. Lost luggage, a noisy ship cabin, an undelivered refund.

Such complaints make up the dark underbelly of the travel industry, the opposite of the paradise promised in every ad and brochure. While you may not see this side of travel every day, you probably do field your share of consumer complaints. When a trip turns sour, chances are you're one of the first sources clients turn to.

But how involved should you get? It's "just good business" for travel agents to help clients get satisfaction for complaints against travel suppliers, says Wayne Caldwell, an associate in the office of travel attorney Alexander Anolik. But to avoid personal liability for such complaints, agents should print a disclaimer on trip materials, he notes. This statement should say, in effect, that you're acting as an agent for the supplier and are not responsible for any problems in actually providing travel services.

Realistically, though, what concrete steps can you take to help satisfy clients with a beef? There are essentially two parts to Complaining 101, the successful art of handling consumer gripes. First, you have to know how to deal with the complainer successfully; next comes knowing how to complain effectively on a client's behalf.

No part of the process is exactly easy, especially the initial personal contact with the complainer. According to Wendy Perrin, who mediates consumer complaints in her Ombudsman column in *Conde Nast Traveler*, you may be talking with people who are really "furious," especially if they've already tried to deal with the supplier directly and haven't gotten any satisfaction.

Gathering Evidence

Your strategy here is to let clients vent their anger first, while you listen with the neutral sympathy of a psychiatrist. Keep your ears tuned for the pertinent details, eventually following up with questions in the manner of a "lawyer gathering evidence," as Perrin puts it. Your agenda is to determine if the complaint is justified — and just how you can help.

Perrin's bottom-line formula for deciding the legitimacy of a complaint: Figure out exactly what was promised and then what was delivered. The client's complaint "is strongest if you can show that the company did not deliver something that was promised in the contract," she says.

If the problem is more complex, there are other issues to consider, especially that of fairness. For example, "if the client became ill and had to buy a ticket to get home early because of a medical emergency," he or she may feel it's unfair for the airline to keep all the extra money paid out, even though contractually the airline may not owe the customer any money.

Another criterion, according to Perrin, is the seriousness of the problem. Sometimes the client just wants to moan about bad food or poor service — complaints that you would reasonably pass on to the supplier, who should have an interest in quality control. But if the food problem went beyond cardboard pizza to a case of food poisoning, that's a distinct escalation justifying a formal complaint.

Complete documentation of the problem — from airline ticket stubs to, for example, a written statement from the doctor who diagnosed the food poisoning — can also help determine the legitimacy of a beef and the likelihood of its resolution. Tangible evidence is the best way to counter suppliers who may dispute a client's statements. Follow the rule of documentation for yourself as well, keeping copies of correspondence and careful records of just who you've spoken to in your efforts to help the complainer.

Once you've determined that your client's beef calls for some kind of response and possible compensation, your next step is to contact the supplier directly. You might also see if there are other possible sources of help, such as supplier trade associations.

When it comes to handling suppliers, Perrin says, "the bottom line is having good contacts and good relationships."

Your agency's individual clout with a supplier is probably based on the agency's sales record and the supplier's view of its sales potential. But if you want to jumpstart the complaint process, you might look to the strength that's in numbers. Belonging to any group of agents — from a trade association to a mega-agency network — can help add some substance to your clients' complaints — and your own. The following are typical of the ways major agent groups handle consumer complaints:

- If you're a member of ASTA, the association's Consumer Affairs department will help mediate your client's complaints against suppliers, as long as you (or the consumer) have already tried to solve the problem first; your complaints are not more than six months old or in litigation; and there is complete documentation to substantiate the claim. The department will also work directly with consumers, so if you're not an ASTA member, you might have your clients initiate the first contact with this ASTA department.
"We can't guarantee results," says Stan Boscom, the department's manager, but there's a good chance a problem will be resolved, especially if both the agent and the supplier are members of ASTA (currently there are 4,780 ASTA supplier members, who include most major companies). But, "in the rare times when a case reaches a stalemate," a supplier will face possible expulsion from ASTA.
- The AAA (American Automobile Association) has a less formal structure for troubleshooting, but "at times we do act as a mediator" on behalf of clients of member agencies, according to a spokesperson.
- Mega-agency Rosenbluth Travel "will stand behind the client" and work with the supplier when the client has a beef about a trip, according to spokesperson Regina Schneider. In the "unusual cases" when a supplier doesn't settle a complaint to a client's satisfaction, the customer's Rosenbluth agency is entrusted to provide him or her with an "equitable" amount of credit for future trips.
- "We tell an agent, 'Try and settle it yourself first, then we'll go to bat for you,'" using the clout of 1,900 agency members, says Sue Shapiro, president of the GIANTS consortium. "We have dropped vendors from our organization if the number of complaints against them became disproportionate to the number of bookings," she adds.

Who Ya Gonna Call?

One of the first rules of efficient complaining is knowing who to call. Beyond the obvious — the direct supplier of travel services — there are usually other alternatives to help handle a client beef, according to Wendy Perrin, editor for the Ombudsman (consumer complaints) column of *Conde Nast Traveler* magazine.

One general rule is to find the organization that deals with the kind of travel supplier being complained against — a dude ranch trade association for a dude ranch complaint, for example. However, this rule doesn't always apply, says Perrin. For example, if the problem is with a cruise," there's nowhere you can go except the cruise line," she says. The Cruise Lines International Association is strictly a marketing group and steers clear of dealing with any consumer complaints. (However, if you're a member of the National Association of Cruise-Only Agents, the group's executive board can help "put you in touch with the right people," says Ron Bitting, the association's president.

There's no overall regulatory body to contact for hotel complaints, either. Perrin will often ask the American Hotel and Motel Association for a comment she can use in her column, but for solid help, "I might go to the tourist board of the country, especially for Caribbean hotels."

You'll have more overall choices if the problem is with an airline, since this segment of the industry is more tightly regulated. If your client's complaint has to do with service — lost luggage, denied boarding and the like — you can contact the DOT's Office of Consumer Affairs at 202-366-2220, 400 Seventh St. S.W., Washington D.C. 20590. If the complaint concerns safety issues, the FAA has an aviation Safety Hotline, 800-255-1111.

Other general sources to keep in mind are the Better Business Bureau or the consumer protection division of the supplier's state attorney general's office, both of which can tell you if a company has received many other complaints. If a company goes belly up, another good source is the local Bankruptcy Court.

Again, if one group doesn't respond, "there usually are more choices," says Perrin. It helps to think of all the different groups ultimately involved in a travel transaction — from the credit card companies to the airports to the countries visited.

Finally, there's always Wendy Perrin herself - members of her department personally deal with every complaint sent to Ombudsman, *Conde Nast Traveler*, 360 Madison Ave., New York, New York 10017. Include a daytime phone number; you can also fax letters to 212-880-2190.

Chapter 11 — Article Two
Grumbling Etiquette

(Second of Two Parts)

By Phyllis Fine

There's more to fielding a client complaint than knowing a) how to handle the complainer gracefully and b) just who to grumble to. While points a. and b. were covered last week ("Complaining 101," *Travel Agent*, March 23), there's another aspect to consider: the style of your (or your client's) complaint to a supplier can affect how quickly and efficiently it's handled.

So, here are some easy tips on the fine art of grumbling most effectively, passed on by knowledgeable supplier sources and Wendy Perrin, who mediates consumer complaints for *Conde Nast Traveler*.

- *The best time to complain is when the problem is actually occurring, or immediately afterward.* If clients speak up while the waiter is spilling soup or the marching band is practicing next door, they can try to get the offending behavior stopped. If it's too late to solve the problem right then and there, clients can at least register the complaint to the appropriate authorities and "lay the groundwork for later on," says Perrin. "Try to get documentation on the spot," she adds. "If the manager says, 'Write to us and we'll send you a refund,' then get his promise in writing."

This is a tip you may want to mention to clients during your pre-trip briefing, prefacing it with a statement on the order of, "Of course everything will go perfectly on your trip but just in case … ."

- *Put the initial beef in writing.* Making a complaint is one situation where it's important to begin with a letter, not a phone call, says Carnival Cruise Lines spokesperson Jennifer De La Cruz. "We need it in writing because we carry so many passengers," she adds — a point that most major suppliers will heartily second, since it's more time-efficient to start with something on paper and proceed from there.

To speed up the process as much as possible, the complaint letter should feature "as many pertinent details as possible," says De La Cruz, including, of course, the bare-bones facts such as the exact dates of the trip. Then proceed to a summary of the problem that's as brief as possible. While it's important to include everything you think is essential to the story, extraneous details (such as my mother passes your office every Wednesday on her way to the YMCA," a fascinating fact included in an actual letter sent to Travel Agent's offices) can distract from the matter at hand.

And, probably, most important, include as much paper documentation as possible with the complaint letter. As we mentioned in part one of this series, any kind of tangible evidence of the problem — from airline tickets to written testimony from witnesses — is especially necessary if the supplier disputes the client's claims. And "anytime you come into contact with someone, get his or her name," and write it down for your records, suggests James Faulkner, a spokesperson for Northwest Airlines.

- *Control the tone of all communications with the supplier — and be as polite as you can.* "Sometimes it's hard (to be nice)," admits Perrin. "You might have forwarded the fax to them five times and they've lost it every time, left 20 messages and not one has been returned. But don't be nasty — it won't help you in the long run."

The person who first reads your letter or takes your phone call probably isn't the person responsible for the problem, and may react to angry words with defensiveness, responding to the tone of your message instead of its content. How inclined to help someone are you when the other person starts off with an insult?

Another tip on tone: Drop any hints of self-pity or whimpering. Though Perrin says she's a patient person, she admits she feels less like helping those who send long-winded letters" and whine "about how this was their dream vacation, etc., etc." Complainers will get a lot farther by using calm, matter-of-fact language and a business-like tone.

- *Avoid idle threats, which tend to destroy your credibility.* How seriously can the customer service department at a large, well-known airline take statements such as: "I'm going to tell all my friends and family, and we're going to make sure no one on the Eastern Seaboard ever books Gigundo Airlines again."

"Making threatening statements won't accomplish anything," adds De La Cruz. "If passengers write that they'll be contacting their lawyer, [all that happens is] the letter is automatically forwarded to our legal department" — which doesn't necessarily speed up the process of handling the complaint.

- *Do ask for compensation for your clients if you think it's called for — but make your requests reasonable.* Bruce Rosenberg, director of Hilton's travel agency marketing, finds it useful to get specific suggestions about the kinds of help he can provide to specific customers — whether they "want a refund or an apology letter. And sometimes there are times when we concurred that there was a problem but didn't know what we could do to fix it, because the client didn't suggest anything — so it took two or three phone calls just to sort out what was needed."

However, do make sure your client's requests are within the bounds of reason. "It's not going to be beneficial or productive for clients to say they want a refund for the whole cruise when they didn't like the food served on the ship," says Perrin.

- *Give suppliers a deadline for their first response to a letter,* suggests Rosenberg. Make it a reasonable amount of time — at least 30 days from the date you expect them to receive the letter, for example. You might write something like, "I expect a response by _____." "That way there's a deadline, and people do respond well to deadlines," since it gives them something to work toward, Rosenberg adds.

- *To save time, find the right department to deal with the problem — and always get the name of a particular person to call or write to.* (*Travel Agent* has received copies of complaint letters addressed "To whom it may concern — For your immediate attention!" — guaranteed good for a laugh, but not for a quick response.) Exactly who to target "depends on the nature of the complaint," says Perrin. "If it's a niggling problem that can be solved by calling the frequent-flyer customer service [department], do so. If it's touchy or it's related to corporate policy, go higher." Use any contacts and relationships you've built up, from DSMs to the Major Hotshot Honcho who's your buddy. If the big honcho doesn't know you from Adam, though, your indignant letters addressed to the president or CEO are usually forwarded right back to the customer service department, Perrin says.

If it's beginning to sound like following up on your supplier complaints is a full-time job in itself, take heart. One way to handle the task may be to steal an idea from suppliers and create your agency's own informal customer service division. All complaints can be funnelled to this department, which should be staffed by your most patient, cheerful and enthusiastic agents, ones who won't mind dealing with sometimes angry clients.

You can also borrow from the technique used by *Conde Nast Traveler's* Ombudsman department: "We use our expertise to tell people who to complain to, and how to complain — on the theory that if you give people a fish, they'll eat for a day: if you give them a fishing pole, they can eat for a lifetime," says Richard Levine, the magazine's senior projects editor, who oversees the Ombudsman column.

So, if your agency played no part in the problem, and you're too busy to do much for your clients, you can listen very politely and send them on their way with some gentle guidance — as above.

Gripe, Gripe, Gripe

Getting more and more complaints about bad trips lately? You're not alone. *Conde Nast Traveler's* file of consumer gripes on travel is bulging as well. The magazine's Ombudsman complaint column usually publishes six to eight letters an issue, but there's been a noticeable increase in the number of letters the Ombudsman department has actually received — from an average of 120 letters a month in 1990, to 150 a month in early to mid-1991, to the current count of roughly 220 a month.

Why the upward surge in complaints? According to Richard Levine and Wendy Perrin, the editors in charge of the column, the major reason is travel suppliers' recessionary belt-tightening. With many airlines going bankrupt and others cutting back, "the jobs that airlines get rid of first are those that deal with the public and resolve complaints," says Levine. Perrin sites a "backlog in customer relations departments of sometimes several months worth of mail."

And, even when travel suppliers do make restitution to complaining consumers, "there's less money to give out," adds Perrin. "In situations where a year ago they may have given out a $500 certificate, now it's $200. You can see the results of the recession everywhere."

But suppliers assure *Travel Agent* that they very definitely still want to know when someone is dissatisfied with their product or services. "If we have an unhappy client, let us know," says Bruce Rosenberg, director of Hilton's travel agency marketing. "How else can we make improvements?"

Chapter 11 — Article Three
T.A. Law

By Dawn Barclay
(All the case histories described in this article are real.)

A couple sued a travel agent for $50,000 after they were booked into a resort that was being renovated.

The estate of a woman killed by a water buffalo while on safari won a $1 million suit after claiming the woman's travel agent didn't warn her of the trip's dangers.

Sound preposterous? Sure, but more and more disgruntled clients are hauling agents into court for incidents as absurd as a hurricane hitting the Caribbean during their stay — and they're winning.

Now more than ever, preventive measures are essential when dealing with clients. Wholesalers are having a harder time staying afloat in today's precarious economy, and penny-pinching clients are putting a higher value on hard-earned vacations and business trips. If something goes wrong, travelers aren't simply willing to forgive; they want compensation.

Unfortunately, as consumers start winning more cases, the domino effect kicks in. "Travelers hear of other travelers' settlements for outrageous sums and want to follow their lead, no matter how frivolous the complaint," says Paul Ruden, senior vice-president of legal industry and government affairs for the American Society of Travel Agents (ASTA).

And though the cases may seem ridiculous, consumers sometimes win in small-claims court where only a limited amount of money is involved, says Jeffrey R. Miller, a travel attorney in Gaithersburg, Maryland. Judges, in his opinion, are "pro-consumer and don't take the time to look deeply into the law and understand the agent's side of the business."

But while owners wrestle with self-defense questions like whether to incorporate or if they should but error-and omissions insurance, front-line sales agents deal with a different predicament: how to provide good service without becoming paralyzed by paranoia.

Compounding the dilemma is the fact that as agents seek more professional images as consultants, instead of being mere order takers, they open themselves up to even greater liability. Many courts rule that agents have a fiduciary responsibility to their clients. Thomas Dickerson, a New York lawyer who specializes in consumer-travel cases, explains: As fiduciaries, "agents are entrusted to do something that clients cannot do themselves. Under law, courts hold fiduciaries to a higher standard of care." Since you accept responsibility for planning a customer's trip, goes the common logic, you must be accountable for your recommendations. And if you change fees for your services, you may be held to an even higher standard because of the dollar value put on your assistance.

"We're all living in paranoia-land," says Anne Sullivan of Hill and Dale Travel Ltd. in New York and an ASTA national director. "Even if cases are frivolous and the client doesn't win, it's still costly and time-consuming to go all the way to court."

Although you won't always be able to protect yourself — sometimes agents do everything right and still lose — your chances of being on the receiving end of a subpoena will diminish if you take preventive action.

Know Your Suppliers

A travel agent sells a couple a tour to the Orient, offered by a reputable deluxe-tour operator. Later, rumors surface in the trade press that the company may have financial problems. When the operator changes the hotels for the tour, the agent contacts the tour company and the new hotels and assures the clients that all will proceed as promised. When they arrive in Japan, the couple finds that their hotel stays were never paid for by the supplier, which had ceased operations the day before. Realizing that the remainder of their hotel vouchers will be worthless, the clients return to the U.S. and sue the travel agent for $50,000, citing negligence.

The above case, Marcus v. Zenith Travel Inc., has yet to be resolved. But whatever its outcome, the lesson is clear: Thoroughly research what you sell. Although you won't often be successfully sued by a client with an off-the-wall complaint ("I didn't like the hotel's wallpaper"), travel attorneys warn that nothing protects against blatant negligence.

But how do you define negligence? It's a thorny issue. Dickerson, the plaintiff's attorney in the above case, claims agents should do research and tell clients about anything that will or could have an adverse effect on their trip. "They have duties and obligations similar to a trusted person, such as a doctor or lawyer," he says. Under these terms, negligent behavior could include selling a tour offered by any wholesaler that is widely known to be faltering financially; booking a tour from an operator unknown to your agency without any investigation; or blindly recommending properties without considering a client's specific request (such as booking a hotel in downtown San Juan for a client who requested an oceanfront resort).

Ruden and ASTA hold that Dickerson's view imposes unfair obligations on agents. "Agents can't reasonably be held responsible for knowing the financial condition of privately held companies," he says.

Andrew Pesky, president of Zenith Travel (the defendant in the above case), maintains he did everything he could to protect his clients. He says he had read in the trade press that the operator he'd booked them with had been sold, but claims he'd received confirming telexes from most of the hotels involved just days before the client's departure. "There was no reason for me to think there was anything wrong," Pesky says.

You can ward off possible lawsuits by taking the following steps:

- Keep abreast of industry developments by reading the trade press and any information from suppliers that reaches your desk; share relevant update with clients.

- Follow world events and consider how they may affect your clients' travels. For example, the recent default of KLR International Inc. following the outbreak of the Gulf war may have surprised agents who knew it to be a leader in East Africa travel. A closer look at its tour offerings, however, reveals that it was heavily invested in Egypt, a country severely affected by the war. If an agent had been sued by a client left stranded on a KLR tour to Kenya, it could have been a close call, considering the information about KLR's trip destinations that was publicly available.

- Sell tours offered by companies that are bonded by the U.S. Tour Operators Association (USTOA). ASTA's Tour Protection Plan, or the National Tour Association. Clients booked with such affiliates are better protected against agency default. The USTOA has a $5 million annual budget from which it reimburses clients if members go under. At the very least, follow the lead of Ann Geraci, CTC, of Anspach Travel Bureau, Inc. in Highland Park, Illinois. She always asks unbonded tour operators if they place client funds in an escrow account. If so, payments aren't touched by the operator until travelers return, and clients have a better chance of recovering their money if the company folds.

- If someone requests a tour by an unfamiliar operator, investigate the company's reputation. Ask colleagues if they've ever dealt with it and find out if it's bonded with any of the above agencies. Call the company to ask about its history and request a financial statement. "Reputable operators are proud to share their bank (information) and to trade references," Geraci says.

- If after taking these precautions, you're still unsure of the wholesaler's credentials, recommend a similar tour offered by a supplier you do know. If the client insists on the unfamiliar operator's tour, either turn away the business or have him sign a waiver absolving you of responsibility for the choice of tour operator.

- Be especially careful when booking hotels in foreign countries. Three out of four consumer claims involve the quality and/or location of foreign accommodations, says Mark Pestronk, a lawyer in Washington, D.C. He suggests booking rooms for clients in foreign hotels only if you're also booking the client's air fare. "At least if you make some money from the airline tickets, you'll have made some money to recompense disgruntled clients," he explains. If clients want you to book only their hotels, Pestronk advises that you urge them to sign a waiver acknowledging that foreign hotels may not be modeled after American standards and thus won't hold you responsible.

Alexander Anolik, a San Francisco attorney and author of travel law books, takes this one step further. His recommendation — anytime you send a check to an overseas supplier, write on the back: "Any disputes arising out of this transaction shall be settled in the [client's hometown and state] U.S.A." This spells out which country has jurisdiction if problems do occur.

- To avoid booking clients in hotels under renovation, make a quick monthly call to tourist boards of the countries and cities you sell most often.

Don't Promise The World

After clients buy an airline vacation package, they hear that the airline is on shaky financial ground. When they ask the agent who worked with them whether they should cancel their plans, the agent assures them of the airline's solvency. But the airline does go under during the trip, and the clients — left with worthless vouchers — sue the agency and win.

No smart agent should guarantee anything regarding a trip, especially those things that are completely out of the agent's control, such as a supplier's solvency. "The travel business is based on dreams, non-reality, hyperbole," Dickerson says. "You have to be more and more careful about how you describe what you're selling. The more accurate you are, the better off you are." That's true even if it means warning clients about potential negatives — such as the fact that Phoenix is stifling in the summer or that gypsy thieves hang out in Rome train stations and rob unsuspecting tourists.

More rules of thumb:

- Never puff a destination or supplier ("It never rains in April there," or "Everyone meets someone special on singles tours").

- Never make promises unless you're repeating the claims of the suppliers, and then "make it clear that it was the supplier who made the guarantee," says attorney Rodney Gould of Framingham, Massachusetts.

- Know the produce you're selling, and if you don't, tell the client so. "Don't be afraid to ad,it you're unfamiliar with an area or a supplier," Gould says. "If the client wants to book something you're unfamiliar with, make it clear you're booking it based on his/her request, not on your recommendation."

- Arm your client with as much information about a destination as you can — photocopies of articles, tourist board information, guidebooks. "This prevents clients from coming back and saying something preposterous such as, "You didn't warn me that the sun would be hot in the Caribbean,'" ASTA's Ruden says.

Disclose Your Suppliers

A woman requests a three-day tour to Las Vegas advertised in a flier she's brought with her. The agent books it but doesn't disclose the name of the operator (even though it's on the flier). When the client arrives in Vegas, she finds out that the operator has switched the hotel from the promised one on the Strip to a property a half-mile out of town. Upon returning, she sues the agency for her inconvenience and wins $106.

Although it's obvious an agent doesn't own the airlines, cruise ships, hotels, or ground transportation she's booking, it's less clear whether an agent or a supplier has created a vacation package. In this case, even though the client simply had to read the company's name on the brochure, the agent was still liable because she hadn't explained to the client that a third party had put together the package.

According to ASTA's *Travel Agent Manual*, if an agent doesn't tell a client that she is booking him through a wholesaler and the company doesn't perform up to snuff, the agency may be responsible. So it's always a good idea to do the following:

- Make it standard office procedure to tell clients which suppliers you're using and to get their consent. Add this policy to your agency manual to show that it's common practice. New York attorney Arthur Schiff suggests that when you book a client, you write on the final documents "As explained at the time of reservation, this vacation has ben booked through XYZ Tours, which is responsible for ... ." You may even want travelers to sign a waiver acknowledging that they know they've been booked with an outside operator. "As long as the wholesaler was chosen with care," Schiff says, "disclosure shifts the responsibility from the agent to the supplier."

- Hang a disclosure on a sign in your office, in full view of every customer: Please be aware that ABC Travel acts only as an agent. We are not the actual supplier of the travel services you are booking.

Insurance: The Best Policy

An agent books a mother and her four children on a charter flight to Puerto Rico, and the carrier goes bankrupt prior to the family's return trip. The woman sues the agency and wins.

In ruling against the agency, the court considered that the agent didn't warn the woman of the risk involved in a charter and also didn't offer the client insurance. You should always pitch insurance. Besides offering a high commission (usually about 35 percent), insurance protects both you and your client. And if travelers decline to buy it, make them sign a waiver proving that you offered it.

Some marketing tips:

- Sell the insurance that is most appropriate. "If there is an illness in the family, offer trip cancellation insurance," says attorney Miller. "If you're booking a student heading off to college with an entire wardrobe of new clothes, offer baggage insurance." But make sure you know what the policy you're selling covers. Most insurance companies won't cover pre-existing conditions, and agents often get tripped up by these clauses. For a clear definition of what the conditions are, consult the insurance company.

- Pitch insurance as a positive addition to a client's trip. Some agencies automatically include the insurance cost with the price of a client's tour and tout it as an extra.

- Be wary of insurance sold along with vacation packages by tour operators. Though the coverage may be cheaper, "if the operator goes under, the protection will be worthless," Dickerson explains.

- Stamp Insurance Always Recommended on all travel documents, offer it by mail, or enclose insurance forms in tour documents — all constitute legitimate offers.

- Suggest that clients charge travel on major credit cards, most of which offer automatic accidental death and disability protection. Also, since clients who use plastic usually pay after their trip, they have a chance to complain and refuse to pay for inadequate service. This means the charge card company must take up the dispute with the supplier. Be especially wary, though, about having clients charge tickets on airline credit cards. "If the airline defaults, there's no protection," attorney Anolik says.

Let Waivers Do You a Favor

An agent books a couple on a tour and later warns them that she has learned the operator is having financial problems. The clients choose to go anyway. She offers them trip cancellation/interruption/default insurance and claims they refused it (they deny it was offered). When the operator folds, the couple sues the agency and wins $4,056.

June Jackson, the owner of the agency involved in the case, offered insurance but failed, she admits, to get a signed waiver of refusal. Waivers — signed forms that absolve agents of responsibility in certain situations — have become a safety net for many agencies. Clients may be asked to sign waivers showing that they've been warned about a travel advisory or that they won't hold the agency responsible if they suffer an injury on the trip. Although waivers can protect you (in court, paper generally stands up better than your word that you discussed a situation verbally with your client), the sheaves of release forms may also annoy or even scare off some clients.

Most attorneys admit that signing a waiver doesn't provide absolute protection for the agency in court, and no waiver will protect against an agency's negligence. But, according to Kansas City, Missouri, attorney Jack Z. Krigel, "it acts as a deterrent and may place the agent at a psychological advantage. Clients may be less likely to sue if they've signed the disclaimer."

In the end, you'll have to decide if they're worthwhile, but here are some considerations:

- At the very least, use waivers on a selective basis, suggests attorney Miller: with clients you don't know, those who disregard your advice regarding tour operator selection, or travelers leaving on exotic or adventure tours. Jackson mainly uses waivers for clients who decline insurance on international or very expensive trips.

- Always get a signed waiver when you book a charter air product, says attorney Gould. Clients should acknowledge that charters operate under different rules than major airlines. "If a charter is 47 hours late, the client has no recourse against anyone and clients should be made aware of this, " Gould says.

Keep Working After a Booking

An agent books a client on a flight from New York to Hawaii via Seattle. But the CRS information is incorrect. The second leg of the flight has been cancelled, and the agent hasn't been informed. The client sues the agency for not reconfirming the reservations directly with the airline and wins $1,894.

Many post-booking procedures help protect you from lawsuits, but this case illuminates an extremely controversial issue — reconfirming reservations. Since CRS contracts limit the airlines' liability in the event of misinformation, the burden in this case was dumped solely on the agent. The court ruled that the agency should have been responsible for confirming reservations with the airline directly: "This defendant was negligent."

But how is an agency with numerous pending reservations expected to reconfirm every one, asks ASTA's Ruden. And when and how often should reconfirmation occur? In many agents' minds, this defeats the entire purpose of leasing CRTs — to avoid making phone calls to airlines. Besides, Ruden says, most flight cancellations happen at the last minute, so that even if agents reconfirmed a few days before a client's departure, they likely wouldn't know about many changes.

According to attorney Schiff, the ruling in the above case was partially fair because the client assumes the reservation was made properly. But he says that agents shouldn't be responsible for reconfirming every reservation (unless specifically asked by the client to do so). "The definition of negligence is failing to act up to the level that the ordinary, prudent travel agent would have done," he says. "And the ordinary, prudent agent in today's marketplace would rely on the computer to properly make the reservation and therefore would find it unnecessary to reconfirm."

While reconfirming reservations remains debatable, attorneys do agree that other post-booking procedures should be common practice. "If the agent can, within reason and without undue effort, get information [about a situation] that would adversely affect the client and does not, the agent is liable," says Dickerson. So if you aren't doing all of the following, you should be.

- Act immediately on any schedule change that appears on the CRT. Include the passenger's home phone number in bookings that require an early departure so the airline can call him if the schedule changes at the last minute.

- Check your CRT for State Department advisories and forewarn clients about trouble spots.

- Alert clients to outbreaks of disease and necessary inoculations as reported by the Centers for Disease Control.

- Explain any necessary visas required for the destination by checking with the country's consulate.

- Act on any complaints relayed to you by colleagues and/or clients (for example, advise a client if the tour company booked is known to be experiencing difficulties).

- Repeat any warnings you make to clients in writing and have clients indicate that they have heard your warning, especially if they decline to heed it.

Is all of this tiptoeing and tip-following worth the bother? At the very least, most of the advice is common sense and easy to adapt. And you'll be glad you followed it one day when a dream client comes back from a lousy trip and suddenly turns into your worst nightmare.

Remember, too, that you have one final protection against being sued: If clients are unreasonable or refuse to take advice or sign waivers, you always have the right to turn down the business. Says Miller, "Ultimately, you must question whether $100 in commission is worth $1,000 of heartache in court."

Reprinted with permission from *Travel Life* magazine, July/August, 1991, a publication of Whittle Communications

Follow Up
Chapter 11

End of Chapter Review

_____

Name   Date

Directions: Fill in the blanks.

1. Name three reasons why travel agents offer insurance to their clients.

    1._____   2._____

    3._____

2. List the four types of travel insurance.

    1._____   2._____

    3._____   4._____

3. Your client casually mentions that he needs to buy trip cancellation insurance for his tour. He tells you that his father is terminally ill and that he may have to cancel his trip. Would he be covered if he cancelled his trip due to his father's death? If not, why?

    _____

    _____

Directions: What advice would you offer clients in the following situations?

4. You are escorting a student tour to France during spring vacation. One of the students is arrested for shoplifting in the Galaries LaFayette, a famous French department store. Where do you begin?

    _____

    _____

    _____

5. Mrs. Messer comes into your office. Mr. Messer has had a serious accident, and she is trying to locate her daughter, on summer vacation in Europe. The daughter bought her air ticket from you, a round trip on Lufthansa from MIA to FRA. Is there any way you can help?

    _____

    _____

    _____

Answers to End of Chapter Review Questions

1. To protect clients, to earn commissions for their agencies, to provide liability protection for their agencies.

2. Flight, health and accident, baggage, trip cancellation or interruption.

3. No — there is no coverage for pre-existing conditions.

4. Contact the United States Embassy. Although they can not intervene, they can help arrange legal counsel and contact the student's family.

5. Yes — Contact the Citizen's Emergency Center in Washington, D.C. You can give them the dates of arrival and departure in Germany. Notify Lufthansa as the daughter will be calling to reconfirm flights.

Marketing
Chapter 12

Review Chapter Objectives
- Identify the steps involved in marketing
- Describe the relationship between a travel counselor and a supplier
- Relate the importance of service to the travel industry
- Differentiate between sales and marketing
- Analyze market segmentation
- Discuss the importance of agency image
- Summarize the advantages and disadvantages of using direct mail

Review Vocabulary
- Advertising
- Demographics
- Direct mail
- Distribution
- Image
- Marketing
- Primary data
- Publicity
- Public relations
- Secondary data

Transparencies
- Chapter outline
- External factors that affect market research
- Types of segmentation
- The four Ps
- Eye flow pattern
- Direct mail tips

Marketing
Chapter 12 Outline

I. Marketing and Selling

A. Inventory

B. Representing Suppliers

C. Flexible Pricing/Dual Distribution

D. Image/Intangibles/Service

II. The Process of Marketing

A. Market Research

B. Market Segmentation

C. Marketing Strategy and Market Plans

D. Segmental Analysis

III. The Four Ps

A. Place

B. Price

C. Product

D. Promotion

External Factors
That Affect Market Research

- Social Change

- Legal Change

- Political Change

- Economic Change

- Technological Change

Types of Segmentation

- Demographic

- Psychographic

- Benefit

- Geographic

- Usage

- Price

The Four Ps

- Place

- Product

- Price

- Promotion

Eye Flow Pattern

1. Photograph — no matter where located on page

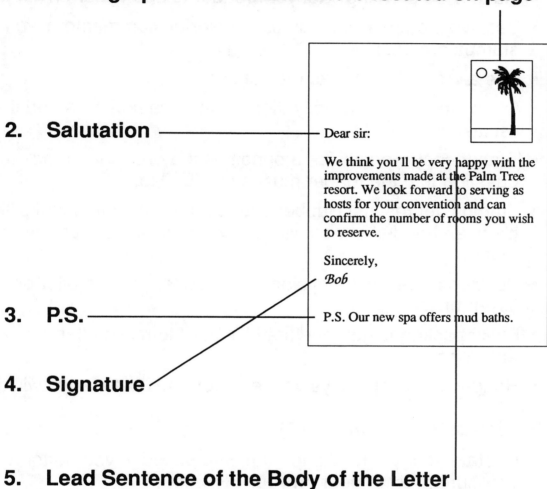

2. Salutation ——————————— Dear sir:

We think you'll be very happy with the
improvements made at the Palm Tree
resort. We look forward to serving as
hosts for your convention and can
confirm the number of rooms you wish
to reserve.

Sincerely,

Bob

3. P.S. ————————————— P.S. Our new spa offers mud baths.

4. Signature

5. Lead Sentence of the Body of the Letter

It is most important to understand and take into consideration the eye flow or eye movement of people while they are reading your letter. Remember — you have six to eight seconds to attract the attention of your readers.

Direct Mail Tips

1. Outer Envelope

- Make it look inviting! Get your reader to open your envelope.

- Use live stamps when you can. Colorful, commemorative stamps are best.

- Use a credible name as the sender.

- Avoid labels — especially those with code numbers and that list last name first.

- Teaser copy works! Use a benefit, set a deadline, or ask a question that the reader must say "YES" to.

- Stamps get results! Rubber stamps or printing that looks like it's been hand-stamped will give your envelope that human touch.

- Business-sized #10 envelopes pull better than smaller or larger ones.

- Bulky packages get read first! It's hard to resist a lumpy envelope!

- Hand-written copy says you're important! Just a word will do.

2. Business Reply Card (BRC)

- Restate your offer. All important info stated in your letter and brochure must appear on your BRC, too!

- Make it complete and simple. This piece must stand alone.

- Make it look positive! Almost any BRC you read says "YES" as its first word, usually in big letters.

- Always use a deadline!

- Supply postage. Make it easy for your reader to respond.

- Make it look official and important.

Direct Mail Tips (continued)

3. Sales Letter

- Use a name or title. Address your reader as an individual — names are best. *(Spelling counts!)*

- Use YOU as the first word — and use YOU as often as you can throughout the letter.

- Emotional lead. Involve your reader fast! Appeal to the EGO. Mention MONEY.

- 25-word limit in first sentence.

- Credible signature — in a second color, preferably blue.

- Use a PS! Re-state your best reader benefit. Remember — it's being read twice.

- Benefits, Benefits, Benefits! Tell your reader over and over what's in it for him!

- Indent paragraphs — always. Much easier for the eye to follow.

- Call to action. Ask the reader to respond and tell how.

- Avoid word breaks at the end of a line.

- Use ample margins — at least one inch.

- Single space. Letter should look like letter.

- Use a typewriter. Don't have letter typeset.

- Use dots, dashes, and bullets. Liberal use of these symbols adds life to your letter!

- Create a deadline for response.

- Be conversational. Don't use a big word when a small word will do.

- KISS! Keep It Short and Simple.

- Visuals. Use photos or graphics to support your offer.

Answers to Textbook Review Questions

1. **What is the relationship between an agent and a supplier?**
   An agent acts on behalf of suppliers, usually with the power to commit them to agreements with clients.

2. **What distribution channels might exist for airline tickets besides travel agencies and the airlines themselves? What possible benefits can travel agencies offer the consumer compared to other distribution channels?**
   Ticket machines and satellite printers. Travel agencies offer services machines cannot provide.

3. **What do you think a travel agency sells?**
   Answers will differ but may include: travel arrangements and products — transportation, accommodation, travel insurance, luggage, passport photos.
   Intangibles — dreams, credibility, trustworthiness.
   Service — themselves, counsel, information, expertise.

4. **What are the main differences between selling a tangible product and an intangible one?**
   Selling a tangible item is easier because it can be seen, tried, and touched. When you sell an intangible item, your clients are buying something before they see or try it and with no guarantee that they will get their money back if they are not satisfied.

5. **What is the difference between marketing and selling?**
   Marketing is determining what product to sell. Selling is convincing a client to buy that product.

6. **Can you give an example of social change that is affecting travel right now? Legal or political change? Economic change? Technological change?**
   Answers will differ.

7. **What is the major purpose of segmental analysis?**
   To study divisions of the agency's business to determine which ones are the most profitable.

8. **According to some opinions, direct mail is the best for reaching former clients, and other forms of promotion are more likely to attract new clients. Do you agree?**
   Yes. Direct mail can be tailored to clients whose individual needs and preferences are known to the agency.

9. **What, in your opinion, constitutes an effective direct mailing?**
   Answers may differ but can include: One that encourages a current client to contact the agency and make a future booking; One that reaches new clients and generates new business.

10. **Publicity is really free advertising. How could a travel company get publicity?**
    By publicizing special travel nights such as cruise nights, bridal shows, or get togethers with speakers and films. By submitting press releases to newspapers or other media outlets

Answers to Discussion Topics

Niche Marketing
Discuss the concept of niche marketing. Have students choose a niche market and have them discuss ways of designing their office to correspond to the market. This would include colors, posters, office displays, or window displays. What sources could be used to obtain displays or promotional materials? What direct mail promotional pieces would be most appropriate to use in conjunction with the chosen niche market — letters, postcards, flyers, brochures, newsletters, questionnaires? How would students develop a mailing list? From what sources?

Answers to Discussion Topics (continued)

Image
Have students give their definition of an image. As defined in the text, it is the impression a company makes and the associations the company's name evokes in the mind of the individual consumer. Students should then assume that they are opening a new travel agency. Have students design a business card for the agency reflecting the image they would like to project. They should consider element such as shape, name, lettering, size, logo, color. Students should critique each other's cards.

Promotions
Using the newspaper, *Yellow Pages*, and a magazine, have students compare the usage of various types of advertising promotions. Discuss the effectiveness of each of them and whether you agree that the information was appropriate to the outlet.

Marketing Research
Market research is the process of surveying and questioning clients, reviewing past bookings, and trying to predict social and economic trends in an attempt to predict what clients will buy. Factors that influence market research include social change, legal and political change, economic change and technological change. In an ever-changing world, travel agencies must be able to react to events with a marketing strategy. Using the Sunday edition of the local newspaper, have students select two stories that relate to the above named factors and have them discuss marketing strategies to deal with them.

Answers to Workbook Exercises

Worksheet 12-1

Advertising	The use of different media to promote products or services
Demographics	Statistics and facts, such as age, sex, marital status, occupation, and income, that describes a human population
Direct mail	The sending of letters, postcards, flyers, brochures, questionnaires and newsletters directly to past and potential clients
Distribution	How one delivers and sells a product
Image	The impression that a company makes and the association its name evokes in the mind of the individual consumer
Marketing	Determining what product to sell, how, where, and to whom
Primary data	Information originally collected for the specific purpose at hand
Publicity	Advertising used to get the message out to the target audience
Public relations	Any activity that an agency conducts to establish recognition and respect within the local community
Secondary data	Information that already exists somewhere, already having been collected for some other purpose

Worksheet 12-2

1. Determining what product to sell — how, where, when, and to whom — is the function of marketing, while convincing a client to buy is the function of selling

2. Travel agencies normally maintain no inventory unless the agency pre-purchases blocks of airline seats, cabins, hotel rooms, etc. for resale. They place an order only when the client is ready to buy. Most retail stores purchase inventory at net cost to sell at a profit.

3. Choose from: to retain some method of selling whatever agents do not sell; to make the product as available as possible; to reduce its selling costs.

4. Choose from: dreams, credibility, service, themselves

5. Choose from: social change, legal change, political change, economic change, technological change

Worksheet 12-3

1. Developing statistical profiles of the human population based on characteristics such as age and income

2. Identifying groups with similar travel needs within the total population

3. Marketing a particular type of travel

4. Choosing a product to sell and then searching for people to buy

5. Finding needs within a group and then choosing the product to sell

Worksheet 12-4

1. Price

2. Product

3. Promotion

4. Promotion

5. Product

6. Promotion

7. Promotion

8. Place

9. Product

10. Product

11. Answers will vary.

Worksheet 12-5

1. Choose from: answering telephones promptly and courteously, decorating and furnishing the agency well, having a knowledgeable, well-groomed staff, designing appropriate business cards

2. Advantages: reaches identifiable segments of the total market, permits an agency to advertise when it needs to, the effectiveness can be measured

    Disadvantages: it requires time, effort, and expense

3. By inserting a response card or return reply envelope

Worksheet 12-5 (continued)

4. Choose from: special travel promotions, staff news, agency news, client news

5. Conventional information that will be valid for a year — for example, general statements about service, experience, and expertise.

Worksheet 12-6
Answers will vary.

Worksheet 12-7
Answers will vary.

Classroom Activities

1. Bring in — or design — travel agency business cards. What image do they suggest? Consider such elements as design, shape, name, lettering, size, and logo. Compare the cards and ask students to consider what markets the cards suggest the agency is trying to attract.

2. Divide the class into teams and ask students to choose a particular supplier and product line, then devise a written marketing plan for it. If appropriate, have them interview representatives and obtain pamphlets such as shareholder reports or financial statistics. Have them include sample ads, promotional materials, and sales tools such as videos or brochures. Have each team present their recommendations to the class.

3. Ask students to consider the differences in reaching each of these target markets — the weekend tourist, children and families, budget - stay now, pay later - travelers, and businesswomen. How can hotels better market their food and beverage divisions, restaurants, entertainment centers, room service? Visit area properties and collect their promotional material. What do they provide in the way of theme parties, contests, cocktail specials, etc.? Visit local travel agencies, restaurants, and see what they provide in these areas. Compare this information. What does this tell students about the competitive nature of these sectors of the industry?

4. Focus group: Ask students to choose an issue in the travel industry, then design a series of ten to twelve questions relating to opinions about that issue. Next, ask them to choose six to ten members to be part of a focus group on the issue. Choose one person to be the facilitator and another to record the responses on the board or on a flip chart. Ask students what they have learned from the experience. What are some positive and negative results of focus groups. Many focus groups are videotaped. How comfortable would they feel under those conditions? How might this affect their responses?

5. Ask students to design a survey or questionnaire about an industry topic that interests them. Next, ask them to distribute the document and correlate the results. What did they learn about the value of surveys and questionnaires? What was the return rate? How accurate is the information? How willing were the respondents to answer questions?

Article

Chapter 12 — Article One
"Don't Guess — Investigate"
Ask students to read the following article. What are some common research mistakes? Misconceptions? How can smaller agencies market themselves and be competitive?

Chapter 12 — Article One
Don't Guess — Investigate

By Robert W. Joselyn, Ph.D.

If you think that marketing research is somewhere between a corporate jet and an executive dining room on the list of likely expenditures for your agency, think again. There are marketing research options open to even the smallest agency that fall within reasonable limits in terms of both finances and expertise.

But why bother? For at least three reasons: Market information will often help a travel agency to plan better; it can lead to better execution of agency plans; and it enables an agency to monitor how well its plans are working.

Better Planning

Travel agencies are increasingly finding it necessary to "position" themselves relative to direct competitors. Rather than making educated guesses about positioning, it is often beneficial to base such decisions on market research data.

A number of years ago, a brand-new travel agency conducted a market survey profile of area residents before developing its initial marketing plan. It then matched the findings against customer profile data provided by a number of potentially important suppliers. While a number of useful conclusions were drawn from the results, one match jumped off the pages of the analysis.

A significant number of respondents had the same characteristics as the typical Club Med customer of the time. Therefore, this agency established a stated objective to become known in its primary geographic market as the area "Club Med store" within three years. The agency was able to work toward this long-term goal with a degree of confidence that could not have existed without the research.

Another recent example of the value of market research for agency planning involved a commercial travel agency on the West Coast. While agency managers worried about how the Middle East conflict, on top of an already weak economy, would reduce their commercial sales, this agency conducted a number of focus group sessions with its commercial clients to determine what their reactions actually were.

The agency discovered, far sooner than it would have by waiting for negative sales results, that its commercial sales were likely to fall by 40 percent as a result of client restrictions on international travel. It also learned that a number of its commercial accounts were willing to ease their restrictions once they understood the increased security measures being taken by airlines and airports around the world.

The agency responded by preparing a "Travel Security Advisory" that outlined these security measures, and included the agency's own tips for U.S. travelers to international destinations. This "advisory" was then distributed to all of the agency's commercial clients. It also found out which of its own employees were interested in working fewer hours and reduced their schedules.

Thanks to simple and inexpensive research, this agency was able to reduce commercial sales losses in advance and to lower its costs quickly in anticipation of lower commercial sales.

Execution and Results

Market research also can be of tremendous value in the pursuit of agency objectives.

For example, the agency whose goal was to become the area "Club Med store" in the minds of a targeted group made an additional effort to learn more about this group. One discovery was that a sizable percentage of those who fit the Club Med profile belonged to health and athletic clubs.

The agency then approached local health and athletic clubs with the idea of sponsoring "Club Med" events, such as volleyball tournaments, in exchange for promotional exposure at the clubs and access to club mailing lists.

While only one component of a very successful promotional campaign, this effective tactic was the direct result of market research information put to use.

As any experienced manager knows, plans are not self-fulfilling. When agency actions (and investments) are not yielding the results desired, it is far better to know this sooner than later — in time to stop an efficient use of resources, and adjust plans or execution for better results.

Market research techniques can be used to monitor agency performance. While most agencies extol the virtues of customer service, for example, few measure it systematically. One recommended method of doing so is a short telephone survey of a random sample of agency customers.

After a brief introduction stating the purpose of the survey, a few simple questions may yield instructive answers (see below). This can be done for the agency as a whole and even for individual agents, to determine where pats on the back, further training or changes in procedure might be warranted.

Using research for evaluation could also help the agency pursuing "Club Med store" status. Rather than wait for, or solely depend on sales results, which may take a long time to show conclusive evidence, the agency could survey a sample of the target customer group from time to time to determine whether its efforts to create an association with Club Med were actually working.

A Sample Phone Survey

Hello, Mr. Smith? I'm Sally Thompson from Thunderbird Travel. As part of our commitment to customer service, we would like to conduct a two-minute follow-up with select customers. Do you have two minutes now for five short questions relating to your recent trip to New York? Thank you.

I'd like to ask you to rate the service Thunderbird Travel provided to you in the following areas as excellent, good, fair or poor.

1. How would you rate the courtesy of the agent who handled your travel arrangements? (Read options.)

2. How would you rate the efficiency or timeliness of the handling of your travel plans? (Read options.)

3. How would you rate the accuracy of your travel plans? (Read options.)

4. How would you rate the knowledge and professionalism of the agent who handled your travel arrangements? (Read options.)

5. Finally, how would you rate your overall satisfaction with the service provided by Thunderbird Travel on this particular trip? (Read options.)

Thank you, Mr. Smith, for taking the time to help us monitor our customer service.

A pattern may be evident without further examination of the results. But values can be assigned to the responses obtained — for example, 10 for "excellent," 7 for "good," 3 for "fair," and 0 for "poor" — and an average rating on specific issues as well as overall customer satisfaction can be calculated. While this process is not strictly scientific, it may nevertheless provide helpful insights.

Data: Processed or Raw

Primary data collection means that you directly collect data from the target source of information. Secondary data collection refers to the acquisition of data which someone else has already collected. Although each of the examples given so far involved the collection of primary data, the general rule should be: "Never collect primary data before determining whether secondary data is available."

There are two good reasons for this: acquiring secondary data is usually less expensive, and it is usually faster.

On the other hand, great care must be taken to evaluate the data's applicability and accuracy. To be useful, secondary data must answer the questions you are interested in, apply to the target you are interested in, have been collected in a trustworthy manner, and be timely.

All four of these conditions must be met for the secondary data to be perfectly useful. But as long as you are aware of its limitations, even data that doesn't qualify on all four counts may be somewhat helpful.

Consider the agency that wants to identify every business firm within a geographic area that does international business and has its own sales force. It could try to conduct a survey of all businesses in the area — or it could check with the chamber of commerce, which quite probably has such a list and will provide it for a modest fee. Often such organizations will add other details that might be useful in developing a commercial sales call list. While not every relevant firm may belong to the chamber, the agency probably will miss fewer organizations this way than by conducting a survey to which some companies do not respond.

To select appropriate secondary data, as well as to design your own research devices, you should understand two criteria of market research evaluation: validity and reliability.

Validity is a function of whether the data answers the questions it is meant to. For example, suppose questions designed to measure respondents' attitudes about hoping to take a cruise someday actually elicit responses about the respondents' perceived ability to afford a cruise at present. In this case, the results would lack validity.

Reliability is a function of whether the research findings are representative of the population about which the researcher wishes to generalize. If the agency surveying the preferences of potential Club Med customers received responses from individuals whose age, income or lifestyle do not match the Club Med profile characteristics, that survey's reliability could be seriously questioned.

If secondary data is unavailable, you don't have to stop there, no matter what kind of budget you have. There are two useful research techniques every agency can afford: the focus group and the simple survey.

Sharpening Focus Groups

A focus group can be described as a data collection session that blends "group interview" and "group brainstorming." Because the number of participants is small, and because participants are seldom selected by random sampling of a defined population, the reliability of focus-group results cannot be guaranteed, even when a number of sessions are involved.

Technically, the focus-group technique is best used to generate ideas rather than to test them. With a full understanding of the risks, however, focus-group research is often used to test ideas and to draw conclusions as well. This typically occurs when the organization doing the research lacks the time or money to conduct more technically correct research and is usually far better than none at all.

Travel agency focus-group research typically involves gathering a small group of agency customers and/or non-customers together for discussion of one topic or several. Though informal, the discussion is not entirely unstructured. On the contrary, it is recommended that the agency owner, manager or group leader develop guidelines to help keep the conversation on track and to ensure that all the topics the agency is interested in are at least introduced

Consider the following possibilities:

- A focus group of female business travelers to determine whether they have specific travel needs or desires which the agency can do something about.

- A focus group of retired senior citizens to determine whether there is a market for grandparent/grandchild travel in your community.

- A focus group of commercial client travel coordinators to determine what your agency might consider doing to help them in their jobs.

- A focus group of newcomers to the area to determine how a newcomer selects a travel agency.

Because focus groups allow interaction, there is less chance that participants will misinterpret questions and reduce the validity of the results. The main validity problem in focus groups is that participants may not express their true feelings because of the other participants' presence. This problem usually can be avoided by staying away from issues that involve personal or socially significant subjects.

A second validity concern with focus groups relates to the dynamics of a group discussion. A natural tendency to want a unanimous conclusion is often fostered by a dominant personality in the group. This problem can be minimized by having participants fill out individual questionnaires before the discussion and by having the group moderator control the discussion so that no one person dominates.

The final validity concern relates to data recording. People are always somewhat more inhibited when it is obvious that what they say is being recorded.

It is generally best to tape-record sessions rather than take notes. Once it is explained that tape recording enables the focus group moderator to take notes later while paying attention now, the tape recorder can be placed out of view more easily than someone taking notes. In a few minutes, out of sight will be out of mind.

The possibilities for focus-group research are endless. They can be conducted in the office conference room or after lunch at a quiet restaurant table. And getting participants will probably be the least of your problems. Most people feel that businesses don't ask them for their opinions and ideas nearly enough and are pleased when one does. And, though we all know there is no such thing as a free lunch, being fed just for putting in one's two cents' worth comes close.

Simple Surveying

Scientific survey research can be very complex with the issues ranging from sampling and question design to data analysis and interpretation. But this is no reason for a travel agency to avoid doing simple surveys that can be of great value, such as the telephone survey already mentioned.

Another example of extremely useful travel survey research is the customer-profile survey to be used in developing a customer database, which can be a valuable aid in planning and promotion.

The first task is to determine what information you want to have about your customers. A possible list of desired information might include:

• Basic information such as name(s), address and phone number.

• Place of work (for future cross-selling of commercial travel services).

• Past travel experiences and future preferences, including type of travel (cruise, escorted group, adventure travel, destination resort, etc.) and destinations (Europe, Hawaii, etc.).

• Local publications read, radio stations listened to, etc.

• Special interests (golf, tennis, theater, scuba diving, art, classical music, etc.).

• Demographic information (age range, marital status, family status, etc.).

The customer profile involves the development of a questionnaire to be distributed to "qualified" customers of the agency. (Criteria should be established that make customers "earn" their way into your database.)

Some data collection devices, such as following up on customer satisfaction by telephone, may be within your competency and comfort level. But when in doubt, and if at all possible, enlist the help of someone with at least a little training in questionnaire development and design. The wisdom of this investment may be measured by the importance of future decisions to be based on the data collected. And the appropriate talent to design your data collection device may be as close as a high school teacher or college professor, or a phone call away at an industry consulting firm.

A simple survey is indicated rather than focus groups if information reliability is paramount. And reliability requires a definition of the population, or particular group of people, about which you want to generalize.

It also requires the acquisition of some sort of list of this population or of a larger population that includes the one you are interested in. And an appropriate method for sampling this population must be selected. (In the case of a customer profile, the sample may actually be a 100 percent census.) None of this is as difficult as it may first sound.

Only a few travel agencies ever give market research more than a passing thought. That's a shame. It is an irony of business that those who can least afford to make a mistake caused by a lack of market knowledge are often the least likely to take preventive action, such as market research. By using existing data, focus groups and simple surveys, your agency can plan smarter, execute better and monitor progress in a more timely manner. No matter what your agency's size, it's never too late to start.

Reprinted with permission from *ASTA Agency Management* magazine

Marketing
Chapter 12

End of Chapter Review

Name _____   Date _____

Directions: The marketing mix of a company consists of four main elements — product, place, price, and promotion. Indicate the element each of the following helps identify.

_____   1.   What is our company image?

_____   2.   Should we specialize in cruises and luxury travel?

_____   3.   Do we charge service charges?

_____   4.   Will we sell travel through television advertising?

_____   5.   Do we offer our own tour packages?

Directions: Fill in the blanks.

6.   Define marketing and distinguish it from selling.

     _____

     _____

7.   What is exclusivity?

     _____

     _____

8.   Why do travel suppliers prefer to offer their products through travel agencies rather than selling directly to the public?

     _____

     _____

9.   Name four ways a travel agency can reach prospective clients.

     1._____   2._____

     3._____   4._____

10.   What are some disadvantages of direct mail?

     _____

     _____

Answers to End of Chapter Review Questions

1. Promotion

2. Product

3. Price

4. Promotion

5. Product

6. Determining what product to sell — how, where, when and to whom — is the function of marketing. Convincing a client to buy is the function of selling.

7. Only those appointed travel agencies that continue to meet conference standards may sell the products of conference members and receive a commission.

8. Suppliers would prefer not to have to employ large sales and reservation staffs of their own.

9. 1. direct mail 2. print advertising 3. radio and television 4. special promotions and public relations

10. It requires time, effort, and expense. More staff time is required to prepare the message, organize the mailing lists, address labels and stuff envelopes.

Automation
Chapter 13

Review Chapter Objectives
- Explain the various components of a computer
- Describe why computers are important in the travel industry
- Relate the history of automation in travel
- List three widely used computer reservations systems
- Define bias and how it can affect airline bookings

Review Vocabulary
- Access
- ARINC
- CPU
- CRS
- Hardware
- Input
- Keyboard
- Memory
- Modem
- PNR
- Program
- Software

Transparencies
- Chapter outline
- Components of a computer system
- CRS ownership
- Components of a PNR
- Automation's capabilities

Automation
Chapter 13 Outline

I. Components of a Computer System

A. Hardware

B. Software

II. History of Automation

A. ARINC

B. Hosts/Co-Hosts/Multi-Hosts

C. Bias

D. Access

III. Computer Reservations Systems

A. The PNR

B. No-Recs and Unable to Sell

C. Other Participants in CRS

D. Back-Room Systems

IV. Computers and the Future

Components of a Computer System

- **Hardware**

  The Physical Components That

  Can Be Touched, Seen, and Heard

- **Software**

  The Program or Instruction

  That Tells the Computer What

  To Do with the Information It Has

CRS Ownership

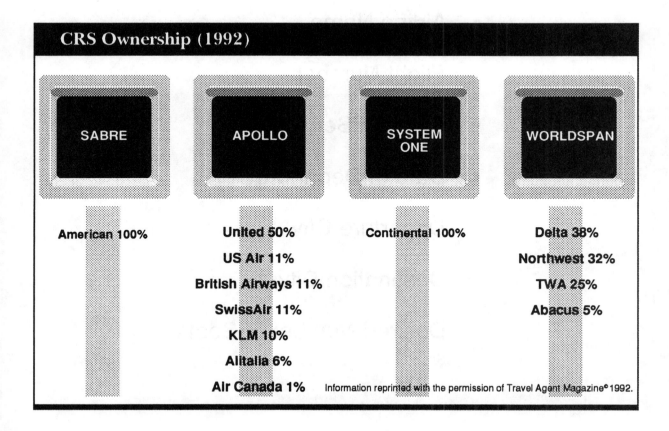

CRS Ownership (1992)

SABRE	APOLLO	SYSTEM ONE	WORLDSPAN
American 100%	United 50%	Continental 100%	Delta 38%
	US Air 11%		Northwest 32%
	British Airways 11%		TWA 25%
	SwissAir 11%		Abacus 5%
	KLM 10%		
	Alitalia 6%		
	Air Canada 1%		

Information reprinted with the permission of Travel Agent Magazine© 1992.

Components of a PNR

- Airline Name

- Flight Number

- Class of Service

- Date of Departure

- Departure City

- Destination City

- Desired Number of Seats

Automation's Capabilities

- Check Flight Availability

- Display Schedules

- Quote Domestic Fares

- Book Reservations and Price Itineraries

- Assign Reservations to Queue for Ticketing

- Print the Ticket/Provide an Invoice/
  Prepare an Itinerary

Answers to Textbook Review Questions

1. **How can current computerized reservations systems help agents sell travel arrangements other than air transportation?**
   Current computer systems were developed to handle airline reservations, fare questions, and ticketing. Systems and procedures were designed with the airlines' needs in mind. The airline product is similar from one airline to another. Airlines were able to put inventory into the computers and work toward standardizing the booking process. Car rental firms were quick to follow. Other industry suppliers (hotels, cruise lines, tour operators) have more complicated products with many variations.

2. **Explain the difference between hardware and software.**
   Hardware includes the physical components that can be touched and seen. Software is the program or instruction that tells the hardware what to do.

3. **What features do you most appreciate about the reservations system with which you are the most familiar?**
   Answers will differ.

4. **If you had one wish, which feature or program in a computer would you ask for?**
   Answers will differ.

5. **If clients could book certain travel arrangements directly with suppliers through their television set at home, would travel agencies be radically affected?**
   Yes! Travel services available over public networks may ultimately change the nature of the business. Encouraging travelers to do their own shopping on-line results in tremendous savings in labor costs. Costs of providing ticket outlets have been reasons airlines have permitted the agency distribution system. If labor costs could be reduced, airlines might want to control their own ticket distribution process.

6 **Do computers enslave or free their users?**
   Answers will differ.

Answers to Discussion Topics

Unable to Sell
Messages sent by B's computer for flights on A's old schedule are returned — "unable to sell." This difficulty can be avoided by an understanding of direct access, access to the inventory of needed airline.

PNR
Answers will differ. Students must supply city of departure.

Record of Changes
Miss Nomind is going from Boston to Bermuda on June 7 on American Airline's flight 615. She is in coach class. Her flight is scheduled to depart from Boston at 9:50 a.m. and arrive in Bermuda at 12:49 p.m. She returns on June 14 on American's flight 632, coach, departing Bermuda at 4:45 p.m., arriving Boston at 5:32 p.m. The history will show the original PNR and its changes.
AA 615Y 07 JUN BOSBDA 950A 1251P
AA   63Y 14 JUN BDABOS 445P 547 P

Answers to Discussion Topics (continued)

Automation

Today most travel agencies are automated. Clients expect and need instant confirmation of their travel plans. The access to information that the systems provide is invaluable. Persuade Mr. Fussbudget that he needs the machines to be competitive.

Answers to Workbook Exercises

Worksheet 13-1

Access	The ability of an agent to make use of the information in airline systems
ARINC	The communication network owned by major airlines that links different airline computer systems with each other
CPU	The central processing unit or the operations center of the computer
CRS	Computer Reservations Systems
Hardware	The name for pieces of physical equipment used in the automation process
Input	That which is entered into the computer
Keyboard	Looks like a typewriter and is the computer operator's way of communicating with the computer system
Memory	The place where all of the information and instructions about what to do with information are assembled
Modem	A type of transformer that permits signals to travel over normal telephone lines
PNR	Passenger Name Record — The computer term for the automated client file
Program	A computer term that means instruction
Software	Computer programs that tell the machines how to manage data

Worksheet 13-2

1. When airlines lease their systems they deliberately program characteristics to influence the user's choice. They do this by positioning their own services more prominently. Since most bookings are made from the first displays, the leasing airline has an advantage.

2. A PNR is the complete record of a reservation displayed on the computer screen. Its components are airline name, destination city, flight number, number of seats, class of service, departure date, departure city.

3. Back-room systems are computerized accounting systems that perform back-up tasks and are often found in the back room. Choose from: print invoices, maintain agency payroll, record client payments, compile employee productivity reports, keep accounts receivable and payable, report supplier volume, keep an inventory of tour and group programs, trace override commissions, track hotel and car commissions, produce financial reports, prepare management reports.

Worksheet 13-3

1. S
2. S
3. H
4. H
5. H
6. H
7. S
8. H
9. S
10 S

Classroom Activities

1. If your school has a CRS or simulated system, this is a good opportunity to go further into the merits of that particular system —why it was chosen, how it works, what the various components are, and so on. This is also an excellent chance to have students practice building PNRs. If systems are not available, but a standard computer lab is, ask students to meet there and demonstrate a simple program such as Wordperfect or Microsoft Word. In this way students will become familiar with various pieces of hardware and one software package.

2. Invite local automation representatives to be guest speakers. Ask them to discuss the newest automation changes and future outlook for the industry. Ask them to discuss the role and importance of training in automation.

3. Ask students to research and discuss the expanding role of automation in the following areas: interoffice E-mail, message queues, computer searches, desktop publishing, accounting functions, vendor reports, and commission tracking. How else do computers help agents in their daily routine? For example, ask students to compare the time it takes to look up information in the *OAG*, call the airlines to check the reservation, then return the call to the client versus checking availability on the computer screen and confirming directly. How much time does this save on a daily basis?

Articles

Chapter 13 — Article One
"The Newest Automation Products"
Ask students to visit two local agencies and compare their systems. Interview one agent from each location and ask why the agency chose that particular system. What advantages does it offer over other systems? Ask them to consider bias and accessibility. If they could add one feature to improve the system what would it be? Then ask students to use this practical information and compare it to the information found in the article. If they were owners of an agency, what system would they choose? Why?

Chapter 13 — Article Two
"The Proliferation of Automated Accounting Systems"
Why are back office systems becoming more popular? How practical are customized systems? Why is computer literacy so important to today's agent?

The Newest Automation Products

By Jim Glab

Christmas is over, but the elves in the workshops at the four airline computer res systems are busier than ever, designing new toys for travel agents to use in the New Year.

Much energy is being devoted to new personal computer applications for agents, as PCs continue to proliferate in place of dedicated CRS terminals. Vendors say they will make life easier in the future for third-party software suppliers and the agents who want to use their products, by developing enhancements that allow such non-vendor programs to be more readily integrated with the CRS's proprietary functions.

Considerable development is also going on in automating cruise and tour transactions, in so-called "seamless" connections through the CRSs to other host systems, and in international data transmission.

Following are some of the more significant innovations and improvements retailers can expect to find in their electronic stockings this year.

Opening Up SABRE

A major focus of SABRE for 1992 will be "to make better use of our installed base personal computers," which are now used by about 60 percent of its subscribers, says Eric Speck, vice-president of marketing. "Using that technology, we'll be able to move to graphic user interfaces, new operating systems such as Windows, and a whole host of things to improve the ease of use in the system."

Speck says the SABRE workstation will be the platform for an increasingly open system. "We're looking forward to providing a very high level of support and consulting to subscribers who want to make use of third-party software," Speck says — a "policy progression," he adds, from the previous "use-it-at-your-own-risk approach."

A graphic user interface "allows you to use icons and point-and-click, to bring up windows and things like that," he explains. "It's a whole new generation of interaction between the user and the screen. There are examples where something that used to take eight screens can be done in a few clicks — that type of productivity improvement will come."

SABRE will bring out an application program interface, he says, "whereby third-party software can interact with SABRE at a much closer level, at the system level." As part of this new direction, he says, SABRE will introduce in 1992 a new product that represents "a significant breakthrough in terms of back-office systems and the types of things they can do for corporate clients," but details are not yet forthcoming.

One of the company's first new products for 1992 is SABRE Help, an interactive/reference program for PC users. "If the agent is in the middle of making an entry in SABRE and can't remember how to complete it, the personal computer workstation will kick in and assist the agent," Speck explains.

SABRE is also proceeding toward "full functional equivalency" for hosted and non-hosted airlines in SABRE and is continuing to develop "seamless connectivity" not only with other airlines but with non-airline vendors as well — something it started in 1991 with its direct connect service for airlines. Seamless connectivity means that when the agent decides on a particular flight from the main display, SABRE will automatically connect to that airline's host system, without extra keystrokes, for a real-time booking and confirmation.

Subscribers who use the CD-ROM SABRE*Vision* product — and they number well over 5,000 now — will have new video disks in 1992 that cover cruises as well as hotels. For cruise lines that don't buy advertising space on the disk, only basic textual information will be available. But for those that do advertise, such as Royal Viking, NCL and Princess, a variety of visual images will be offered, including deck plans and cabin layouts, "as well as photographs and images of the vessels and public rooms and cabins," Speck says.

SABRE *Vision* users have demonstrated "an insatiable demand for more and more images," according to Speck, so SABRE will keep expanding its disk contents to include destination information and other kinds of suppliers.

Also in the cruise area, SABRE has just finished making Royal Caribbean's CruiseMatch 2000 automated booking system available to its subscribers and hopes to come out by the end of 1992 — or shortly thereafter — with its own cruise booking product, which it has been developing with Kloster Cruise Ltd. and Princess Cruises. That system, capable of full integration with SABRE *Vision*, will initially feature the inventory of its two sponsoring cruise companies, but it is intended as an industry system open to other lines as well, Speck points out.

A new tour booking system is also under development, he reports, and should come out at about the same time.

Other SABRE product development for 1992 includes more affordable satellite ticket printers for low-volume users, the extension of Direct Connect to Commercial SABRE, and increasing globalization — such as its recent agreement with the SERTEL system of Aeromexico and Mexicana, which should give SABRE subscribers access to an expanding range of international suppliers and services.

Apollo's Platform

Covia will supply Apollo subscribers in 1992 with its newest Focalpoint product, Focalpoint 2.0, "a whole new generation of the Focalpoint product," says Lynn Rosenbaum, vice-president of subscriber sales and marketing. "It's based on Windows 3.0, and it brings to the customer all the advantages that come with Windows. It makes it easier for the customer to utilize the workstation as a computer instead of just a reservation terminal."

Focalpoint Product Manager Sarah Schiller adds: "With the introduction of Focalpoint 2.0, we are embracing an open-platform philosophy, We are very pleased if agents can add other software, can make their own choices about the tools that make sense for their own business environment rather than always relying on our selections."

Windows will permit agents to "have Apollo windows and other application windows open simulta-neously," she continues, "and they can use a Focalpoint feature called Copy & Paste to take information straight out of Apollo and enter it directly into the other application without doing any additional typing." Covia's 3,500 users of Focalpoint will be upgraded to the new version at no cost.

This year Covia will also roll out its Spectrum product, a hotel database that will include locator maps as well as hotel information for companies that pay to be included. Available as a CD-ROM product or a hard-drive up-grade, it will enable agents to pinpoint on its maps not only the hotels that advertise in the product, but also any of the 20,000 properties in Apollo's Roommaster hotel database, if the agent requests them.

"Spectrum will present the information in a different way, but the information will be entirely consistent with what's in Roommaster," Rosenbaum says. It will also be fully integrated with Apollo's hotel booking capability.

A new pricing program for Apollo subscribers in 1992 is called Global Fares, jointly developed by Covia, Europe's Galileo and Canada's Gemini systems. Format entries are similar to the earlier Interna-tional Fare Quote, but data will be updated daily instead of three times a week as before; and the system has the ability to do its own dynamic fare construction instead of relying on preconstructed fares as the earlier version did.

Selective Access, a new product also developed jointly with Covia's international partners, is a data-sharing program that enables agents to specify what kinds of information and functions they want to share with affiliated locations.

The earlier Group Code capability "is very non-specific; it's almost an all-or-nothing kind of situation," Rosenbaum says. But with Selective Access, agents can specify that only certain PNRs — such as those of a single corporate client — will be accessible to another location, or that all PNRs will be accessible to some offices but not others. "They can also specify what they want the affiliate to be able to do with the PNR," Rosenbaum adds.

LeisureShopper, due to debut in the third quarter of 1992, is Covia's entry in the cruise-and-tour booking sweepstakes. "The whole purpose of the product is to provide a dynamic shopping environment," Rosenbaum says. "We don't want the travel agent having to sequentially look first at one tour and then another tour; we'd like to dynamically present them with all their options and have the system do their shopping for them, based on their criteria." The product will also have "total booking capability, fully integrated into the rest of the PNR," she adds.

For commercial agencies, Covia will unveil the OSDP Manger (On-Site Document Printer), which will "make STPs more reliable and more affordable from the agents perspective," she says. "It's technically a dial-up product, but the user experiences it as a dedicated product," without having to pay for a dedicated line. It also has a feedback mechanism to let the agency know if the remote printer runs into trouble, such as a lack of ticket stock.

New Worldspan Order

The big job at Worldspan this year will be the continued development of its totally new Worldspan CRS, which in 1993 will replace the company's existing PARS and DATAS II systems. But in the meantime, the company is also rolling out more new products and crossing over more existing products from one system to the other.

By January, all DATAS II users should have access to the Worldspan International Fares and Pricing Program familiar to PARS subscribers, with daily updating, low-fare searching, and other improvements. "Two other things are ongoing now that should happen in 1992, prior to migration" of all subscribers to the new Worldspan CRS, says Dick Lee, director of airline and associate sales.

"We have selected PARS [rental] car system to be the new Worldspan car system, and it will be accessible by DATAS accounts prior to migration. And we have selected the DATAS hotel system as the Worldspan hotel system, and it will be available to all PARS subscribers prior to migration."

Coming up for PARS subscribers in 1992 is a hotel search capability in cooperation with THISCO as the second phase of the latter's UltraSwitch. It will permit agents to search and shop for hotels with real-time access to information on availability, rates, room types, and the physical specifics of an individual hotel as well as its policies on checkout time, credit-card acceptance and so on. Of course, they'll also be able to make the bookings.

The system includes a roster of 30,000 hotels that represent more than 90 percent of all hotel rooms booked electronically by U.S. travel agents, and the UltraSwitch shopping capability should give retailers much more confidence in the hotel data and confirmations, making them more likely to book through the system.

The hotel search function is coming out in PARS this year, but "a final decision on whether it will be available to DATAS subscribers before migration [to the new Worldspan system] hasn't been made yet," Lee says.

Also coming up in PARS in early 1992 is a new direct-link tour booking system that will initially include connections to MLT Vacations, Certified Vacations and World ComNet's TourFile system, and will add more wholesalers during the year. "It's a true tour booking system that will allow the tour operator to display their full product line in a much better environment," Lee says. "I think all of them will have booking capability, but some will be on a request basis, some will be on free sale, some of them will have direct-link capabilities."

A companion cruise booking system is also under development and will probably be introduced in early '93, Lee says. The company has already made Royal Caribbean's CruiseMatch 2000 available to both DATAS and PARS agencies.

Other new projects at Worldspan include an improved dial-in product for work-at-home agents, and new software that will enable agents who convert from other vendor to translate their accounting, customer profile and other in-house data to the new system.

"Looking at both the DATAS II and PARS systems, there are probably a couple of hundred enhancements in process right now," a spokesperson says, "and many of those are designed to ease the migration process, to make it as painless as possible."

Spreading System One

"We're looking at a lot of third-party vendors," says System One Director of Marketing Jim

Davidson. "There's a lot of third-party software out there, and we're trying to develop an avenue where we can make those products available in an easy environment for System One users.

"Right now it's very difficult to buy a third-party product such as WorldView, JetReady or TripFinder and to install them in an environment that's convenient for the travel agency. We're trying to come up with a program that allows them to integrate those into the res system. It will be a combination of some host-based stuff and some distributed stuff."

Specific new products for 1992, he says, include a credit-card verification program "that will hopefully help reduce some of the fraud and liability that the agencies face," and a work-at-home product called System One HomePro. "It allows the travel agency to really utilize professional agents working out of their homes, who dial into the home office reservations system, and it provides the home office with complete monitoring capabilities," Davidson says.

"On the leisure side, we're looking at developing a lot of database interconnectivity, particularly with the cruise lines," Davidson continues. "We handle about 75 percent of the air bookings for the cruise industry, so they're a major customer for us." For the agent, this will mean "more efficient transactions" with the cruise lines, he points out. Meanwhile, System One now has all of its subscribers on line with Royal Caribbean's CruiseMatch 2000 booking system.

A new System One program designed for agents who want more commercial business from small and mid-size companies is called Corporate Circle. "We've developed a program that includes training, specific products — primarily the new System One low-volume STP and our Access products — and a new form of lead generation," Davidson says. "It includes a combination of direct mail, advertising and telemarketing."

Agents pay a membership fee and go through a training course and get the above products as well as new-business leads generated by the Corporate Circle solicitation efforts.

Prism, the vendor's front-office agent productivity software, will have "a lot of enhancements that really streamline some of the efficiencies and add to the functions in quality control," Davidson notes. "Our System One Access product and our STP are also being updated so that we can really proliferate in the marketplace with those." Also, the proposed electronic ticket delivery network concept is "a big issue for us; we really want to push that along," he says.

After some uncertain times due to the financial troubles of its owning company and its new partnership with EDS, "we've finally gotten through a lot of the hurdles," Davidson says. "People aren't counting us out any longer. We ended 1991 in a real favorable position, and we're looking forward to a real positive 1992."

Reprinted with permission from *ASTA Agency Management* magazine, January, 1992

Chapter 13 — Article Two
The Proliferation of Automated Accounting Systems

By Jim Glab

The automation revolution in ASTA member agencies continues, according to the society's 1991 membership census, but nowadays the focus is on the back office.

Survey results indicate that member agencies are not becoming more automated in terms of adding more terminals from the major airline systems, but rather in adding more PCs, communications equipment and software in their offices for internal agency use.

Indeed, the number of CRS terminals per agency seems to be relatively constant no matter which vendor the agency uses. Tabulation of the 1991 ASTA results puts the median number at four terminals per ASTA agency for System One, Datas II and PARS agencies, and at five for SABRE and Apollo subscribers, so overall the average would be between four and five sets per office.

A question on the number of terminals per agency was not included in ASTA's 1985 membership census, but the Louis Harris/*Travel Weekly* survey conducted in 1987 found that the average agency location also had between four and five CRT's in that year, with the average slightly higher for SABRE and Apollo agencies than for those associated with other vendors.

The Golden Median

In evaluating these results, it is important to keep in mind that the numbers of terminals per agency in the ASTA census is a median, not a mean; as such, it is less likely to be rendered statistically misleading by the huge numbers of CRTs on the premises of a small number of mega-agencies. The median indicates that in any gathering of ASTA agents, you can pick one at random and the odds are greatest that he or she will work in an agency with four or five CRTs.

Since the overall volume of travel in the United States has continued its inexorable upward trend in recent years, wouldn't the number of terminals per agency be expected to increase? Not necessarily. The CRS vendors may have more terminals in the field, but there are more agencies in which to put them. The number of Airlines Reporting Corporation agency locations in the United States jumped from 27,193 in 1985 to 30,169 by the end of 1987, and to 38,057 by March 31,1991.

Moreover, "you have to remember that the average ASTA member is a smaller agency," with a substantial number of them doing $1 million to $2 million in annual volume, says Warren M. Erbsen, CTC, of Travel Gallery in Denver, chairman of ASTA's Automation Committee.

Another trend that tends to preclude the addition of more terminals per agency location is that agency employees are becoming more efficient in the use of the terminals they already have.

This is in part because the terminals can be used for more different kinds of booking each year, as vendors continue to expand the number of suppliers available through them and the efficiency of communications links to those other vendors, including a much greater degree of direct access. And part of it is due to the heavier emphasis that CRS vendors are putting on agency productivity per terminal, with an increasing use of CRS cost-reduction incentives that meet and exceed productivity goals.

The 1991 ASTA membership census did not ask whether responding members subscribe to more than one CRS system. Nor did it get into the question of what percentage of members are affiliated with which systems, although it is likely that ASTA member agencies would reflect the general retail industry averages. Recent CRS industry estimates in terms of air bookings made through the systems are that SABRE has some 42 percent of the market, Apollo 28 percent, Worldspan 18 percent (through its Datas II and PARS operating units combined) and System One about 12 percent.

Affordable Accounting

Perhaps the biggest surprise in membership census was the rapid deployment of other kinds of automation in agency offices — especially automated accounting systems.

The 1985 ASTA survey results indicated that about one-quarter of all member agencies were using back-office automated accounting systems. The 1987 Harris/*Travel Weekly* poll found that the figure for all travel agencies by that year was up 38 percent. Now the tally of the 1991 ASTA membership census puts the proportion of agencies with automated accounting systems at just over 52 percent.

"That's a factor of both greater affordability of the systems and the number of PCs that are being installed as part of the [airline] automation systems, as well as the greater ease of interfacing [your accounting system] with your automation systems," notes Erbsen.

Again, the dominant product for the back-office accounting was SABRE's ADS system, with more than 30 percent of the respondents on the accounting question claiming to use the brand. Apollo/Covia's TS2000 ranked second with 15.8 percent of the responses.

Exact tracking of specific products is difficult, however, since responding agencies used different names for the same accounting product or family of products. For instance, the results show at least 13 variations in the names that responding agents gave to Worldspan accounting products.

One noteworthy fact was that one in nearly 25 respondents claims to use a customized program designed specifically for his or her agency, rather than an off-the-shelf product.

As Erbsen says, there is an increasing reliance on personal computers among agencies, an observation borne out statistically by the membership census. In the 1985 membership poll, fewer than one in four ASTA agencies had one or more PCs. In 1991, the proportion had risen to 67.4 percent, or more than two out of every three agencies.

The questionnaire did not ask what portion of those PCs came into the office as new CRS equipment — replacing "dumb" dedicated reservations terminals with multifunctional PC work stations — but that trend on the part of CRS vendors has undoubtedly been the major contributor to the increased presence of PCs. Automation experts predict that the efficiency of PCs for all sorts of office activity — from fax mail to word processing to training to accounting to mailing-list management and electronic publishing — will mean a continued increase in their use by retail agents in years to come.

Will all dedicated CRS terminals in agencies ultimately be replaced by PCs? "I don't know about all of them," Erbsen says, "but a significant portion will be. There will always be a few agencies where it isn't worth it to upgrade, so they won't get into that technology, but a higher and higher percentage will be PC oriented."

The Fax Takes Over

When it comes to new office equipment, perhaps nothing has proliferated as quickly in the past decade as the fax machine, and the ASTA membership poll certainly bears this out. When the 1985 census form was sent out, the question on office equipment didn't even include a box for fax machines, since they were not considered essential for small businesses in those days.

But the 1991 results indicate that more than 78 percent of ASTA agencies now have one in the office — more than any other piece of equipment, with the exception of a copying machine, which is now in use in more than nine out of every 10 ASTA agencies, according to the 1991 results.

The breakup of the telephone company has led to new kinds of communications products and services available at lower costs to small businesses, and ASTA agencies have not hesitated to take advantage of those opportunities. In 1985, according to that year's survey, only 18.4 percent of ASTA member agencies used an inbound WATS telephone line, while 8.8 percent had an outbound WATS facility.

Today, according to the 1991 poll, the proportion of ASTA agencies using inbound WATS lines has jumped to more than half, at 56.8 percent, while 13.5 percent now use outbound WATS lines. In addition, 23.5 percent say they now use automated call-direction phone systems in their offices.

The growing reliance of the typical agency on commercial business can perhaps be seen in final statistics in this category: More than one-quarter of all ASTA agents responding to the poll, or 26 percent, say they now offer 24-hour service to their clients — another option that was not even considered worth asking about in the 1985 survey.

ASTA is trying to keep members tuned in to the changes in agency automation and communications by offering a range of professional seminars devoted to those topics. "We have them going virtually year-round now," Erbsen says, "with seminars on more efficient use of the airline CRS systems and more efficient and broader use of the PC, for things as diversified as accounting to desktop publishing to newsletters, and so on."

Does Erbsen think ASTA members are generally more knowledgeable about automation products now than they were a few years ago?

"Oh, yeah," he replies. "They have to be."

Reprinted with permission from *ASTA Agency Management* magazine, August, 1991

Automation
Chapter 13

End of Chapter Review

Name _____ Date _____

Directions: Identify each item as either hardware (H) or software (S).

1. Modem _____

2. PNR _____

3. Keyboard _____

4. Memory _____

5. CRT _____

6. Bias _____

7. Program _____

Directions: Answer the questions in the spaces provided.

8. What is bias and how does its elimination affect the marketing of airline reservation systems?

_____

_____

_____

_____

9. What is meant by the term "back room system?"

_____

_____

_____

10. What are some features of a back room system?

_____

_____

_____

Answers to End of Chapter Review Questions

1. Modem = H

2. PNR = S

3. Keyboard = H

4. Memory = H

5. CRT = H

6. Bias = S

7. Program = S

8. Bias is preferential positioning of an airline's schedule in its own computer system so that reservations agents sell the visibly-positioned flight first. With bias eliminated, airlines must compete on other levels.

9. An automated accounting system, purchased or leased, either from an airline or from a vendor.

10. Able to print invoices and itineraries, record payments, track accounts receivable and payable, track commissions, maintain payroll, generate management and financial reports.

Industry Communications
Chapter 14

Review Chapter Objectives
- List five instances when a travel counselor should use a letter
- Recall the most crucial step in letter writing
- Review five guidelines to letter writing
- Explain when to use overnight mail
- Summarize the ways fax machines are used in travel agencies
- Demonstrate proper telephone etiquette
- Explain the purpose of a policy and procedure manual

Review Vocabulary
- Deadline
- Fax
- Jargon
- Prepayment
- Refund
- Telegram
- Telex
- Voucher

Transparencies
- Chapter outline
- Client information
- Agent information
- Letter writer's guidelines

Industry Communications
Chapter 14 Outline

I. Oral Communication

   A. Preferred Suppliers

   B. Consortiums

II. Written Communications

   A. Vouchers

   B. Letters

III. Mail Services

   A. Telegrams

   B. Telex

   C. Overnight Mail

   D. FAX

IV. Interoffice Communications

   A. Telephone Techniques

   B. Staff Meetings

   C. Policies and Procedures Manual

Client Information

In most reservation situations, the following information is needed by the agent from the client

- Name(s) Complete with Appropriate Title(s)

- Home and/or Business Address and Telephone Number(s)

- Number of People Traveling

- Ages of Clients (if applicable)

- Dates and Times of Reservation

- Specific Reservation Information

- Method of Payment

- Special Requests or Restrictions

- Special Discounts

Agent Information

In most reservation situations, the following information is needed by the agent from the supplier.

- Reservation or Confirmation Number

- Name of Reservationist and Date

- Price Quote

- Hidden Extras

- Cancellation Policy

- Deposit and Final Payment Dates

- Commission Amount

Letter Writer's Guidelines

- Try to limit letters to one page

- Try to avoid sentences with more than seventeen words

- Use short paragraphs written in simple language

- Use active verbs

- Put important words and thoughts at the beginning

- Avoid beginning a letter with "We are in receipt of your letter"

- Describe rules and procedures in your own words

- Avoid industry jargon

- Use the first person "I/we" rather than "this agency"

- Choose short words instead of long ones

Answers to Textbook Review Questions

1. **The text suggests seven situations in which you might write a letter. Can you suggest any others?**
   Answers will vary but may include letters to
   - A client requesting payment.
   - A client accompanying documents.
   - A supplier requesting brochures.
   - A hotel requesting special services.
   - A hotel thanking them for accommodating special requests.
   - A tourist office requesting information.

2. **When do you think three-part messages/reply forms would be inappropriate?**
   When the information being transmitted is of a lengthy or detailed nature or when the format should be more formal and the appearance more professional.

3. **What major features would you want in a telephone system?**
   Answers may vary but could include: music on hold; a recording of agency information; while clients hold; speaker phone; speed dialing; call forwarding; three-way calling;automatic redial

4. **Putting callers on hold courteously is a key part of telephone etiquette. Can you summarize the major procedures without referring back to the text?**
   - Ask callers if they wish to hold and wait for a reply.
   - Explain why you are putting a caller on hold.
   - Estimate how long the caller will have to hold.
   - Reassure callers when they are on hold that they have not been forgotten.

Answers to Discussion Topics

Letter Writing

Letters will vary.

Telephone Messages

A. Receiving incomplete messages can result in not being able to return calls.

B. You must impress on your employees that they are the first voice a prospective client hears, and the way that the call is handled can create either a positive or negative image. If clients do not get phone calls returned, they may assume that the agent didn't care enough to call back. Instead, it may have been a case where the agent couldn't understand the message from the switchboard operator.

Staff Meeting

Answers will vary.

Answers to Workbook Exercises

Worksheet 14-1

Deadline	The date at which something is due
Fax	A machine that allows the transmittal of facsimiles of documents from one location to another
Jargon	The special language or communication of a particular field
Prepayment	The payment of products or services in advance of using them
Refund	To return money for prepaid unused services
Telegram	A form of written communication. Because it is costed by the word, symbols and abbreviations are often used
Telex	A message that can be typed, transmitted, and received in an instant by parties who each have a teleprinter
Voucher	A document issued to confirm arrangements. They may be used to introduce clients, confirm a deposit, or indicate full payment

Worksheet 14-2

1. accommodation
2. itinerary
3. luxury
4. computer
5. commission
6. cancellation
7. insurance
8. occupancy
9. guarantee
10. deluxe

Answers will vary but may include:

11. Thank you for your letter of July 10.
12. The representative confirmed a deluxe room.
13. We are sorry.
14. Please send payment as soon as possible.
15. The computer cancelled your reservation by mistake.

Worksheet 14-3

1. Using preferred suppliers means that travel agents will concentrate their bookings on a small select group of tour operators or suppliers

   Benefits to travel agents — allows agents to know a few select products very well and eliminates the problem of having just a vague familiarity with a vast number of products; agents become secure in their selling techniques; agents provide financial incentives

   Benefits to suppliers — The supplier will receive a higher volume of bookings from agents with whom they have a preferred supplier agreement.

2. Choose from: Ask callers if they want to be put on hold and wait for a reply, explain why callers are being put on hold, estimate how long the caller will have to wait, check with callers to reassure them they haven't been forgotten and see if they want to continue to hold.

3. Choose from: office procedures and changes, recent staff trips, upcoming promotions and advertisements, complaints

4. Choose from: offer to help the caller, find out why the client is calling, clearly record the caller's name, number, day, and time

5. A form of electronic mail — part telephone, part copier, part computer. They scan, digitize, and transmit images over phone lines and reprint a hard copy at another fax station. They can transmit handwritten, typed or printed data, photos, or illustrations. Choose from the following ways that they can be used in a travel agency: making reservations with foreign vendors, sending rooming lists or other last-minute information, preparing itinerary proposals, following up on proposals or commission requests, ordering ticket stock, booking cruises, banking and invoicing

6. Answers will vary. Choose from: history of the company, the company's philosophy and mission, an organizational chart, smoking policy, performance appraisals, liability, outside employment policy, and so on

7. Telephone tag is the situation when two people try to get in touch with each other by phone but keep missing each other. Some ways to cut down on the time spent with telephone tag are to call busy people early in the morning, develop secondary contacts, ask when the best time is to return a call, leave detailed messages, be available when you tell others that you will be.

8. A consortium is an organization formed to provide collective buying power and remuneration to its members. Through the consortiums' ability to negotiate on behalf of its membership, a small-volume agency can enjoy the same overrides as a larger one.

Classroom Activities

1. Bring in three or four staplers. Divide the class into teams and ask each group to develop an SOP (Standard Operating Procedure) for using a stapler. Demonstrate use of the stapler by following exactly and only the directions given. This will demonstrate the necessity of providing clear instructions. Once this in-class activity is completed, ask students to develop a standard operating procedure for answering the telephone, taking a message, putting a customer on hold, and ending a telephone conversation.

2. Write a letter for any of the special circumstances listed in the text. How does style differ in a complaint letter to a supplier, confirmation letter, or brochure request? What else would differ besides style? (Tone, length, address, signature, etc.?)

3. Ask students to purchase the Sunday edition of the local newspaper. Using the articles and advertisements, ask students to develop the written agenda for a typical Monday morning staff meeting. What articles and ads were most important to them? Did students begin with these items or end with them? How long is the time frame for each meeting? Where would such a meeting be held in an agency? How often? Who would attend?

4. Listening is a key part of communication, yet most of us are very ineffective listeners. To improve this skill, a fun practice activity is to "gossip." Begin a simple statement, preferably a tongue-twister but not one that is well known, and whisper it in one student's ear. Ask that student to repeat what he or she has heard to the next student, and so on, until the last student has heard the statement. Students may not repeat the statement. Compare the final outcome with the original statement. How do they differ? If this can become so different when students are trying to listen, consider the consequences in communication when we aren't listening effectively as usual. Another similar exercise is to read a short article to students and then ask a series of eight to ten questions. Have students write down their answers and then compare the number correct. If you repeat the activity, students' scores should increase.

5. What key issues do students believe should be addressed in a policy and procedure manual? Ask them to list the areas in a typical agency, hotel, tour operator, transportation supplier, and so on. Do these areas overlap or differ by supplier? Prioritize the areas, then develop a sample procedures manual for class.

Articles

Chapter 14 — Article One
"Preferred Suppliers - The Key to Agency Profitability"
How can preferred suppliers help an agency's bottom line? What disadvantages are there, if any, to using preferred suppliers? Visit a local travel agency (if appropriate) and ask them if they use preferred suppliers. Why or Why not? Compare results.

Chapter 14 — Article One
Preferred Suppliers — The Key to Agency Profitability

By Robert W. Joselyn, Ph.D.

A preferred supplier used to be an airline, hotel, car rental company or tour operator favored by an agency owner, manager or frontline travel consultant because it provided a consistently better product to its customers than the alternatives.

While there may have been some modest pressure on the frontline counselor to sell suppliers preferred by the agency's management, more often than not frontline counselors had the autonomy to choose and support their own selection of favorite suppliers.

In today's intensely competitive marketplace, there is nothing casual about a travel agency's preferred supplier relationships. It is virtually unthinkable for any profit-oriented travel agency to conduct its business without a carefully conceived and executed preferred supplier strategy.

One consequence has been the growing pressure on the travel counselor to conform to an agency's preferred supplier policy. This raises a number of questions:

1. Is a preferred supplier strategy in the best interest of the customer who trusts their travel plans to a professional travel counselor?

2. Is it ethical to favor a supplier from whom additional agency benefits are received?

3. Is a preferred supplier strategy fair to other suppliers?

4. What obligations does a professional travel counselor have when he or she believes a preferred supplier is not the best choice for the customer?

The business rationale for preferred supplier relationships is a compelling one, and the reasons go far beyond the income generated from override commissions. A well-conceived preferred supplier strategy can:

• Increase the travel counselor's sales effectiveness.

• Increase customer satisfaction with travel purchases.

• Foster supplier relationships that result in improved service for both the customer and the agency.

• Help the agency manage the travel industry's information explosion.

• Make a significant contribution to the bottom line.

Is Selling Preferred Ethical?

If there is a moral or ethical issue for the frontline counselor who is required to sell preferred suppliers' products, it is to make certain their opinions about suppliers are conveyed to agency management on a continuing basis. To have the selection of preferred suppliers controlled by management is not an ethical question. To withhold personal opinions from the decision makers about which suppliers should and should not be preferred, is.

However, there can be no question about the ethical issue raised when the travel counselor strongly believes one of the agency's preferred suppliers is not the best choice for the client. When the counselor's objection to a preferred supplier is based on relatively minor factors, personal opinion or unverified information, there is no basis for a claim of ethical conflict.

When the objections to a particular supplier are verifiable, however, what then? The travel counselor is in the difficult spot of being responsible both to the agency's ownership and the agency's client. This is not the conflict it might first appear to be if you believe what is best for the customer is also best for the agency in the long run. When the travel counselor believes a preferred supplier isn't the best choice for the customer, they have a professional obligation to both their agency ownership and the client to raise the issue with management.

What is the counselor's obligation to the client if the decision is to still use the preferred supplier?

If other professions are to be used as a standard, the answer is clear. The travel counselor's professional responsibility is to the client.

Given the benefits to the travel agency of a long-term preferred supplier strategy, a travel counselor must carefully weigh his or her objections before engaging in confrontational behavior with agency management. Only when convinced the client is paying too high a price for such a strategy, should the counselor confront management with a refusal to sell that supplier, either in a specific situation or as a general practice.

The travel counselor must recognize taking such a stand may put continued employment with the agency into question. Many owners will argue that if you work for a Ford dealership, "You either sell Fords with enthusiasm or find another brand of car to sell." As long as it's their business, that is their prerogative.

Most owners/managers will try to work something out with the counselor but when that isn't the case, the frontline counselor is faced with the personal choice between a sense of ethical responsibility and the potential short-term impact to his or her own wallet. In the final analysis isn't this often the final test of professional ethics?

Effective selling begins with knowing the product. Because it's not possible to "know the world" and all of the options for traveling it, the task must be simplified by narrowing the range of information to be mastered. With a tailored list of options, travel counselors will know those products better — and sell them better. Knowing the product better also increases clients' comfort with the purchase because the travel counselor is able to sell with increased competence and confidence.

A preferred supplier strategy can be an important risk management tool which leads to improved customer satisfaction. Some suppliers are better than others. If value and reliability are among the criteria used to select preferred suppliers, client satisfaction will increase.

Most businesses will go the "extra mile" for a valued customer, and travel suppliers are no exception. Over the past few years, travel industry suppliers have become far more sophisticated in tracking the source of their business. This process identifies the agencies producing the most sales and can lead to better service interactions, client travel enhancements at no additional cost, more responsive problem solving, and cooperation in educational and promotional efforts.

Working with preferred suppliers can foster a relationship which often results in improved service for both the customer and the agency.

Committing to preferred suppliers also helps counselors cope with the information overload of today's travel industry. Once the scope of travel products is narrowed down, it is possible to assign various counselors to keep up to date on specific suppliers.

Travel agencies with a strong commitment to preferred suppliers often limit familiarization trips and attendance at industry functions to the suppliers they sell most actively. These agencies also control the agency's resource material by only keeping the brochures and sales manuals of preferred suppliers with a secondary list of acceptable companies as back-up. The truly committed even restrict sales representatives' access to their employees.

Only the newest or most naive participants in the travel agency business fail to recognize the profit margins are extraordinarily low and, as a result, most agencies are marginally profitable. This means any action that can impact a travel agency's yield-per-transaction can have a dramatic impact on its bottom line.

Travel industry suppliers are willing to make investments that produce incremental business. One of the most common forms of incentive is the commission override (although special price and product enhancements have increasingly become part of the "package").

However, most frontline counselors fail to recognize the full significance of overrides. All too often the difference between a 10 percent and a 12 percent commission is thought of as an increase in income of 2 percent when it actually represents 20 percent more income for doing exactly the same amount of work.

Even this understates the true potential impact of overrides. For an agency operating near the break-even point, overrides can result in a 40 percent, 70 percent or 100 percent or more increase in the agency's profits. For some agencies, override income is the difference between profit and loss.

Inherent in the concept of a preferred supplier strategy is a commitment to direct the agency's sales toward selected companies. This narrowing of supplier options means travel counselors may not find their personal first choice of suppliers on the list.

A travel agency is not a democracy, it is a business. While the opinions and experiences of an agency's frontline sales staff should be given considerable weight in the selection of preferred suppliers, the final decision must be made by the agency's management. A list of "preferred suppliers" compiled by individual travel counselors, based solely on their personal preferences, would be unlikely to match the clout of a management-designated roster, selected with the agency's overall business mix and total sales volume in mind.

The evolution of an increased importance of preferred supplier relationships raises a lot of questions for travel counselors.

Is a preferred supplier strategy in the best interest of your client?

When preferred suppliers are selected, and retained, for the right reasons, the answer is almost always yes. In fact, it could be argued that an agency with an avowed policy of having no preferred suppliers is not fulfilling its professional responsibility to its clients, the responsibility to get the best possible product and service for the client's money.

However, if a preferred supplier is selected for the wrong reasons — for example, the only criteria applied was that the supplier offers the biggest overrides — then, the answer is often no.

Is it ethical to favor a supplier from whom additional agency benefits are received?

Yes, as long as it is the client who is preferred first.

Is a preferred supplier strategy fair to those suppliers not chosen?

Absolutely. It is the essence of free enterprise to patronize the best alternative.

What obligations does a professional travel counselor have when believing a preferred supplier is not the best choice for the customer?

Their first obligation is to raise the issue with agency management. If the conflict cannot be subsequently resolved through dialogue with management, the professional obligation of the frontline travel counselor is to the client.

Reprinted with permission from *Travel Counselor* magazine, a CMP publication

End of Chapter Review

Name   Date

Directions: Each of the following sentences contains one or more mistakes. See which ones you can find and correct them.

1. Each pronoun must agree with their antecedent.

    _____

2. Just between you and I, case is important.

    _____

3. Verbs is supposed to agree with their subjects.

    _____

4. Don't use no double negatives.

    _____

5. Leisure travel is different than business travel.

    _____

Directions: Fill in the answers to the following questions.

6. List three additional pieces of information an agent would need when selling a cruise package.

    _____

    _____

7. Define preferred suppliers.

    _____

    _____

8. What are three letter writing tips?

    _____

    _____

    _____

Answers to End of Chapter Review Questions

1. Each pronoun must agree with **its** antecedent.

2. Just between you and **me,** case is important.

3. Verbs **are** supposed to agree with their subjects.

4. Don't use double negatives. (**eliminate the word no**).

5. Leisure travel is different **from** business travel.

6. Choose from: category, deck, or cabin number preference; early or late seating; special meal restrictions, if any; optional tours

7. Those suppliers used frequently due to a positive past experience or an override agreement.

8. Answers will vary but may include: Limit to one page; avoid long sentences; use short paragraphs; use active verbs; place important thoughts at the beginning; avoid industry jargon.

Money Management
Chapter 15

Review Chapter Objectives
- List five sources of agency commission
- Explain three types of expenses
- Understand the influence of time on money
- Analyze credit-card and check payments
- Compare financial statements
- Review a balance sheet

Review Vocabulary
- Asset
- Balance sheet
- Cash flow
- Commission
- Debit memo
- Equity
- Invoice
- Liquidity
- Profitability
- Receipt

Transparencies
- Chapter outline
- Expenses
- Area-bank settlement plan

Money Management
Chapter 15 Outline

I. Bookkeeping and Accounting

II. Basic Financial Statements

    A.   Income Statements

        1.   Expenses

            a. Fixed

            b. Variable

            c. Semivariable or Mixed

    B.   Balance Sheet

III. Time Value of Money

    A.   Cash Flow

    B.   Handling Money

        1.   Invoices, Receipts, and Extended Billing

        2.   Payment Options

            a. Credit Cards

            b. Checks

    C.   Sending Payment to Suppliers

        1.   The Area-Bank Settlement Plan

        2.   Agency Checks

        3.   Service and Cancellation Charges

        4.   Security

IV. Negotiable Documents

    A.   MCOs/PTAs/Tour Orders

Expenses

Fixed — Remain unchanged despite changes in volume. They are predictable and can be controlled to some degree.

- Telephone (basic monthly service)
- Utilities
- Rent
- Insurance Premiums
- Subscriptions
- Computer Equipment Lease

Variable — Costs that increase and decrease directly and proportionately with changes in volume.

- Fam Trips
- Corporate Dividends
- Part-time Salaries
- Commissions of Outside Salespeople

Semi-variable or mixed — Change in response to a change in volume, but they change by less than a proportional amount.

- Office Supplies
- Cost of Advertising
- Postage
- Professional Fees

Area-Bank Settlement Plan

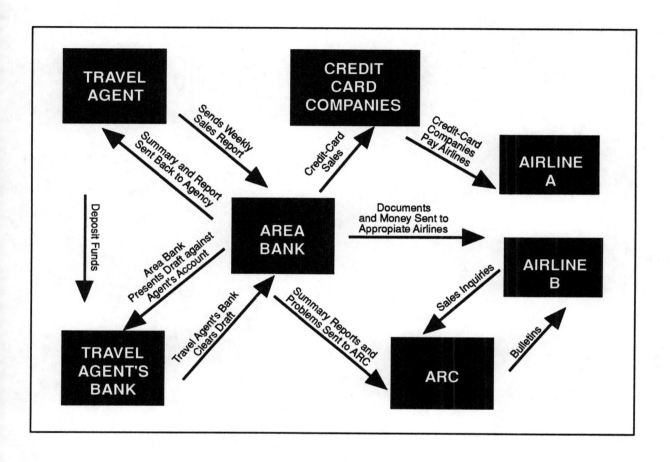

Answers to Textbook Review Questions

1. **What can an individual do to control company costs?**
   Answers will vary and may include: Control the cost of supplies, telephone charges, and postage.

2. **What can an individual do to increase company income?**
   Encourage clients to purchase commissionable products; keep track of suppliers who pay commission after the client's travel date; collect payments in a timely fashion.

3. **If a company were to hire one new employee, what extra expenses might be incurred? Would you characterize each of these expenses as fixed, variable, or semi-variable?**
   Answers may differ and may include:
   Salary — fixed; Bonuses or incentives — variable; Familiarization trips — variable; Corporate dividends — variable; Commissions — variable; Additional office supplies —semi-variable; Additional postage — semi-variable

4. **Summarize the dangers of extending credit.**
   It can eliminate cash flow.

5. **Why do companies need cash readily available?**
   Answers may include: to meet short-term cash expenses; to invest in future business; to repay loans; to pay day-to-day expenses

Answers to Discussion Topics

Credit Cards
Answers may differ. To avoid being put in the middle of an awkward situation, the agent could let the Diners Club representative speak directly to Mr. Visa to review the potential problem. It will then be an issue between the client and Diners Club and should have no adverse affect on the relationship between the client and agent, or the commercial account and the agency.

Negotiable Documents
Mr. and Mrs. Lightfingers seem like the culprits. The agency should contact the police. They should also report the burglary to The Airlines Reporting Corporation (ARC). Unless the thieves are caught with the unused tickets, the agency will not recover its loss. Agents can be held liable for stolen tickets unless theft by persons other than the agency employees is proven.

Cash Flow
The agency should consult with its lawyer to check the legalities. It will depend on the legal action taken and how successful it is. The amount may not be recovered and will be written off as a cost of doing business. Answers may differ. One option may be to have one person, perhaps the manager, responsible for the petty cash.

Answers to Workbook Exercises

Worksheet 15-1

Asset	The economic resources owned by a business
Balance sheet	A statement that shows the financial position of a business at a particular point in time
Cash flow	The rate at which a supplier receives money
Commission	The amount that a travel agent receives from a supplier for selling transportation, accommodations, or other service
Debit memo	A form used by airlines to recall commissions that were incorrectly taken
Equity	The resources invested into a business
Invoice	A statement that indicates the amount due
Liquidity	The ability to convert assets into cash
Profitability	The excess of return over expenditure
Receipt	A statement that indicates the amount paid

Worksheet 15-2

1. Fixed expenses remain unchanged despite changes in volume. Examples will vary.

2. Variable expenses are costs that increase and decrease directly and proportionately with changes in volume. Examples will vary.

3. Semi-variable expenses change in response to a change in volume, but they change by less than a proportional amount. Examples will vary.

4. Answers may vary.

Worksheet 15-3

1. An **asset** is a usable resource that the agency owns. Examples include cash in a checking account, short term investments, and money owed by clients. Other assets could include office furniture, supplies, company car and so on. A **liability** is a claim that other companies or individuals have against the agency. Examples include money owed to a bank, office supply company, suppliers, or airlines. Other liabilities include salaries, payroll taxes, and so on. An **equity** is the excess of assets over liabilities. An example of this is stocks and bonds.

2. An income statement is a statement of revenues and expenses. It summarizes the results of business activities and can be prepared for any period. A balance sheet lists assets and liabilities. It presents a financial picture of an agency at a given moment in time.

3. Accountants design accounting systems or advise agencies that design their own.

   Bookkeepers record daily transactions.

4. An invoice indicates an amount due. A receipt indicates an amount paid.

Worksheet 15-4

1. An agency can invest the money to increase its worth.

2. By using a credit card, a client can obtain 30 days credit with a payment schedule.

3. An agency can get an authorization code on a credit card. Checks can take up to two weeks to be processed. Clients could have sufficient funds the day they write the check but could close the account the next day.

4. When an agency writes a ticket they have to pay the airline within a week. They should not pay out money before receiving it.

5. Choose from:

   1. Compare the signature on the credit card with the signature written in the agent's presence.

   2. Check to make sure the credit card hasn't expired.

   3. Call for a credit card authorization.

   4. Do not give cash refunds for tickets originally charged to a credit card.

6. Choose from:

   1. Require proper identification.

   2. Have client sign check in the agent's presence.

   3. Do not accept checks that are larger than the amount of the sale.

   4. Do not accept checks from out of state.

   5. Do not accept second-party checks.

   6. Accept checks far enough in advance to clear the bank.

   7. Write client's address, phone number, and driver's license number on the back of the check.

   8. Do not accept checks that do not have a printed name, address or check number on them.

Worksheet 15-5

MCO	It is most often used to record deposits and full prepayments for air transportation, surface transportation, tour packages, supplemental charges, car rentals, hotel accommodations, or additional collection.
Tour order	It records payment for advertised tours. In most cases it serves as the actual document.
PTA	An authorization that allows the issuance of an airline ticket at a point other than the point of payment.

Classroom Activities

1. Prepare a sample week-long FIT package including air transportation, ground transfers or car rental, accommodations and sightseeing for a couple traveling throughout Europe. (Choose your own favorite itinerary.) Ask students to calculate the commission to the agency from such a sale. Next, ask students to consider a similar vacation offered by an established tour operator. Again, ask them to calculate the commission. In terms of time and money, which is the most profitable? Why?

2. This is a good opportunity to develop exercises using MCOs, PTAs, and Tour Orders. Such activities can be combined with tour brochures and the information provided in the CRS.

Articles

Chapter 15 — Article One
"The Tip-Off on Ticket Rip-Offs"
Ask students how agencies can protect themselves against this monetary loss. How can automated boarding passes help? Visit a local agency and ask if they have ever been the victim of some type of theft. How could it have been avoided?

Chapter 15 — Article Two
"The Cost of an Agent"
How can you measure productivity? How much is a first-year agent worth. How much is a 20-year veteran worth? What type of agent is more profitable — leisure or corporate? Why?

Chapter 15 — Article One
The Tip-Off on Ticket Rip-Offs

By Jim Glab

A new round of debate over who should be responsible for the cost of stolen airline tickets is still resolved, but one thing remains constant: The best way for agents to avoid liability is to prevent thefts in the first place.

ASTA has been putting pressure on the airlines for a change in liability rules so that agencies hit by thieves won't face bankruptcy. Under the current system, a retailer who is victim of a theft could be billed for tens of thousands of dollars by carriers if found negligent in his or her handling of blank ticket stock, and if the stolen tickets are sold or used for travel.

The Good News

According to the Airlines Reporting Corp., the good news about ticket thefts is that they appear to be gradually decreasing. "There has been the implication that all of a sudden there is a crisis," says ARC President David Collins. "But don't get the impression that suddenly things have dramatically changed—they have not."

In fact, he says, during the first 10 months of 1991, the number of tickets lost in thefts, burglaries and robberies was about the same as for the January to October period a year earlier. Over the longer term, the number of stolen or missing tickets each year has been quite consistent for the last five years. In 1986, about 51,000 were stolen or missing, and the total was about 56,000 last year.

The only exception to the level trend was in 1989, which was "a bit of a hiccup," Collins says, with 72,746 tickets not accounted for. "That was the year in which we had 24 armed robberies, and 21 of those were in the Southern California area."

From 1980 to 1990, stolen and missing tickets as a percentage of all the tickets shipped to agents has dropped substantially, from 0.066 percent in "80 to 0.032 percent last year.

"We're never happy to lose any tickets, but this is not suddenly a big crisis in the fall of 1991, and we are talking about a very, very small percentage of the tickets shipped," Collins says, noting that 175 million were sent to agents in 1990.

Creating a Diversion

There are three types of theft: nighttime burglaries, armed robberies and daytime thefts. In the case of nighttime burglaries, the question of agency liability is usually clear-cut, Collins says, since ARC rules spell out specific security procedures to be followed with ticket stock when the office is closed. And in the case of armed robberies, ARC never holds the agency liable for the value of the tickets.

The current controversy surrounds the third type, the daytime theft, "because the rule says they must take reasonable care, and it is not always so easy to come to an agreement on what is reasonable care and what isn't in a daytime operating environment," says Collins.

In the daytime theft, "the basic scenario is that people come into the agency and try to distract the agents in one way or another," Collins says. They probably have already checked out the agency, and the agent isn't aware of it. They look to see what the routines are in the agency, where the machines are, how many people there are, whether there are times in the day when there may be only one person there."

Once they have settled on a target agency, he continues, thieves use various diversionary techniques, such as dropping tennis balls on the floor. While the agency employees help to pick up the balls, an accomplice quietly lifts the exposed ticket stock.

"Probably a more common one is the pregnant lady," Collins notes. "She needs to use the bathroom in the back; somebody helps her, and while they are doing that, somebody else grabs the tickets off the machine."

The rapid growth in STP locations has not contributed to more thefts, Collins says, because most of those devices are located in secure corporate offices, and thieves tend to look for ground-level storefront agencies as their targets. "They want something that has easy access and easy egress," he says.

Automated tickets account for the majority of those stolen, since they represent about 95 percent of all tickets in circulation, according to ARC. That has helped create a generation of clever thieves, because when they issue the ticket for the buyer, "they have to be able to do it in a way that looks like it's been done on a printer," Collins notes. "They're relatively sophisticated people in that respect. In fact, that's probably one of the main reasons we don't have more tickets stolen — because you have to know what you are doing to be able to issue them."

Checking at Check-In

ASTA maintains that since the airlines are the ones who accept the stolen tickets for transportation, and since the carriers have the ability to detect stolen tickets at check-in if they would just bother to look, it is the airlines who should bear the brunt of financial responsibility.

"When a travel agency notifies an airline of the theft of ticket stock, and the airline has the reasonable opportunity to create a computer record of the stolen tickets by number, so that the airport counter personnel can check the legitimacy of proffered tickets with a minimum of difficulty or delay, the airline should create that record and direct its counter personnel to use it." ASTA Senior Vice President of Legal Industry and Government Affairs Paul Ruden wrote in a letter to carriers.

This is especially important — and easier — when checking in international passengers, since they must report to the check-in counter for processing instead of going directly to the gate, Ruden notes.

Collins concedes that the bulk of stolen tickets are probably used for international travel, since that is where thieves can get the biggest return on the stock. "I would say the preponderance [of stolen tickets] are used for the higher-priced end, and probably primarily for international travel," Collins says. "If you're selling a stolen ticket, obviously you don't sell it at the correct tariff. So you are not going to sell a $100 ticket on the shuttle for $50; its not worth the risk to you.

But Collins says it is not true that airlines never check for stolen tickets during the check-in process. Agents who lose tickets to thieves are required to report the ticket numbers to ARC immediately, and ARC stores them in a computerized list that is accessible to all airlines. Some carriers take automatic feed from ARC so the numbers are downloaded into their internal systems almost immediately. But once they are there, it is up to each carrier to decide what to do with them.

"A number of airlines are checking them," Collins maintains. "They all have their own methods of doing it, but it is a manual process. It does depend on the check-in agent inputting the number, and in the days of deregulation, we all know the pressure they're under when they check in a 747. So there is a human element there."

He says airlines may have procedures in place by which their counter personnel will check for a stolen ticket only if a passenger fits a certain profile, or only if he is traveling on a particular route or flight that may be a favorite of stolen ticket buyers. "There may be characteristics they watch for, and I really can't comment on that," Collins says. "But I think the airlines would say they're making a much greater effort today to do that than they perhaps have done in previous years."

Handle with Care

In his letter, Ruden argued that "the failure of an airline to take reasonable and practical steps" to catch stolen tickets before they are used, whether the agent was negligent or not, "reflects a choice by the airline to assume the financial consequences of the theft." To charge the retailer for the full value of the stolen tickets "could be fatal to a travel agency, a result which makes no sense from the perspective of either airlines or travel agencies," he wrote.

But Collins maintains that to grant retailers total immunity from financial liability might make some of them less cautious than they should be with blank tickets.

"That essentially says the agent can be negligent as hell — they can leave 1,000 tickets sitting on the counter and go out to lunch, and if those tickets disappear during the lunch hour, all the agent has to do is phone the airlines and he's off the hook," he argues. "If you're going to put the entire liability on the airline, what incentive is there for the travel agent to be prudent in looking after those tickets?"

The ARC president says travel agents should treat each blank ticket as if it were a $1,000 bill. "You would not leave a thousand $1,000 bills sitting on a counter," he says. "You wouldn't leave 200 of them or even 10 of them sitting on a counter."

While he emphasizes that the vast majority of agents are extremely careful with their blank stock, Collins says one statistic from ARC's investigations of ticket thefts is especially revealing: "Of all the stolen tickets, 25 percent of them are detected by the airline through usage before the agent has even missed them," he says. "I think that statistic tells you that there are some agents out there who are not taking good precautions to look after the ticket stock."

Automated Boarding Passes

Both ASTA and ARC are hopeful that technology will again come to the rescue in the future with the ATB-2, the new automated ticket/boarding pass that will encode data electronically in a magnetic strip on the back of each document. The airlines have agreed to phase in that technology over the next few years, and all agency ticket printers will be upgraded or retrofitted to make them capable of magnetic encoding, if they aren't already.

When a passenger checks in for his flight with an ATB-2, he will have to insert it into a machine that can read the encoded data, and improved software will make it possible to check every ticket electronically against an automated stolen ticket blacklist without human intervention.

"Here in ARC, we think that ATB-2 will represent a quantum leap forward in the ability to check for stolen tickets," Collins says.

Reprinted with permission from *ASTA Agency Management* magazine, January, 1992

The Cost of an Agent — How to Figure Sales Employees' Break-even Point

By Laura Del Rosso

The difference between a profitable and unprofitable travel agency often comes down to employee management, according to Doris Davidoff, agency owner and industry lecturer. With more than 50% of the revenues of a typical travel agency going toward staff salaries, it becomes critical that the owner or manager know how much it actually cost the agency for an employee to perform his or her duties, she said. When such productivity is analyzed, the responsibilities within an agency can be divided up more effectively, she added.

Davidoff told an audience at the ASTA World Congress that often neither the employee nor the manager knows actual productivity but relies on guesswork or conjecture. "If an employee makes $18,000, they might think that once they make that in commission the rest is profit for the owner," she said. "But you cannot know who is profitable unless you measure the productivity. You cannot go by a gut feeling or how they appear to be working."

Once their productivity is analyzed, the owner or manager can divide responsibilities according to the cost of the employee. (See chart)

For example, many small agencies are operated with employees performing sales functions, the all-important work that generates revenue for the agency. But those employees also perform other tasks such as bookkeeping, brochure filing and what Davidoff calls "rip and tear" chores that involve processing tickets. Davidoff suggests that these basic tasks are better performed by a support person, such as a receptionist, instead of the salesperson. In many cases the salesperson receives a higher salary, and his or her time would be more productively spent meeting clients and booking travel.

It is an efficient agency that combines the sales and support functions with each person performing his or her own backup paperwork, Davidoff said. The salesperson is probably a "people person" whose talent lies in meeting people and selling travel, but he or she may be interrupted by having to take a phone call for others in the office or by opening the mail.

In this case, the agency is also spending too much money for performing these support services, which could be accomplished by a lower paid receptionist, she said.

Davidoff's rule is to have the "least expensive person capable of doing the job do the job, except in an emergency." "The top salespeople shouldn't handle $149 tickets. They should be handled by the least expensive person. If you have a person making $20,000 a year handling the $149 tickets, instead of the $10,000 person, it costs you double to handle that transaction," she explained.

Most agencies — usually the large companies — that have separated their sales and support functions have found that the average productivity of sales agents rises as a result, she said.

The break point for agency size seems to be four or more staff members, she said. At that point, one full-time person should be responsible for support services, such as greeting clients as they enter the agency and answering the telephone. This person should also be designated to process the paperwork, including refunds, which also takes the salesperson's valuable time.

One common agency strategy is to use the support work as training for new employees who want to become travel agents, she said. But at her agency, Belair Travel in Bowie, MD, Davidoff has found that using the support position as a training ground can cause frustration for all in the agency, particularly that employee. The employee is often not focused on the support work at hand and is prone to mistakes, and, if no agent position opens up soon, becomes unhappy at the agency, she said.

Several years back, Davidoff said, she hired a receptionist who was satisfied with that position and did not aspire to travel agent work. There has been a marked improvement as a result, she said, with the receptionist enjoying her job and the rest of the staff according her more respect than they would be likely to give a trainee.

The support personnel should not necessarily be the lowest-paid staff people, especially if they have worked at the company for many years. Davidoff suggests that, when sales bonuses are earned in the agency, support people should receive a share of the income or any prizes won by the agency.

Davidoff said those in support positions should be given respect like any other employee, because each side — sales and support — is dependent on each other. If the salespeople cannot do the job, revenues will be down. If the support people cannot effectively back them up, the salespeople will not be able to sell, Davidoff said.

To get an idea of how much it costs to maintain an employee and how that person's time can be most effectively spent, agency owners should analyze an employee's profitability periodically, she said. The information can be obtained automatically through accounting systems or manually by taking the invoices and adding up commissions, not gross sales, she said. If the employee has assignments other than commissionable sales, such as the support responsibilities, they should be prorated into the equation.

The owner's salary should be included in the total office sales salary," assuming that the owner is making and earning a salary," she said.

Davidoff recommends sharing the information with employees to demonstrate to them the importance of productivity and to encourage them to help if changes or cutbacks are needed.

There may be some disagreement over whether the agent can bring in the amount of commission needed for profitability, she said. "When people say to me a leisure agent can't [generate the amount of commission], I say that they have to."

Employee Profitability Analysis

Description	Sub.Cat.	Totals
Annual Sales Salary		$15,000
Fringe Benefits		
Pension contribution		
Insurance (Life/Med)	$1,200	
Social Security (7.65%)	$1,148	
Unemployment (4.3% on first $7,000)	$ 300	
Other (Fams,parking etc)	$ 500	
Total Fringe Benefits	$3,148	
Total Annual Employee Cost		$18,148
Work Days Available Annually(5x52)	260	
Days Off with pay:		
Holidays	8	
Vacations/Sick Leave	15	
Fam Trips	5	
Other		
Total Days Off	28	
Total No. Days Worked Annually	232	
Employee Cost Per Day	$78.22	
Total Office Expenses	$350,000	
Total Office Sales Salaries	$115,500	

(Divide total office expenses by total office
  salaries.Multiply sales employee cost above
  by resulting number to calculate break-even
  income for this employee.)   3.03

Total Employee Cost Per Day $237.01

Annual Commission needed for office to break even from this employee

Per actual day worked		$ 237
Per five-day work week		$ 1,185
Per year		$54,984

Cost Per Hour For Employee $ 31.60

Average commission earned   11%
Bookings needed annually at average
commission rate for break even $499,885

Reprinted with permission from *Travel Weekly*

Money Management
Chapter 15

End of Chapter Review

Name _____   Date _____

Direction: Answer the following.

1. Name four sources of income for a travel agency.

   1. _____   2. _____

   3. _____   4. _____

2. What are the three categories of travel agency expenses.

   1. _____   2. _____

   3. _____

3. An expense incurred regardless of the level of sales or the amount of income an agency

   generates is a _____ expense.

4. Briefly explain cash flow and why it is important to a travel agency.

   _____

   _____

   _____

5. What can an agent do to help an agency maintain a positive cash flow?

   _____

   _____

   _____

6. What is the basic function of an accountant?

   _____

   _____

7. Agencies may impose their own service charges.   True   False

8. Money received immediately is worth more than the same
    amount received at a future date.   True   False

9. Commissions are generally deducted from deposits sent
    to suppliers.   True   False

10. A profit and loss statement can be prepared for any period.   True   False

Answers to End of Chapter Review Questions

1. Answers will vary but can include: commission on air transportation, cruises, tours, and accommodation; income from cancellation penalties; service charges; accessories; overrides; bonus payments from suppliers.

2. A— fixed B—variable C—semi-variable

3. fixed

4. Cash flow refers to a company's control of its cash so money is available to pay bills in a timely manner and excess funds are put to work to earn more money.

5. Answers may include:
   - Request credit card payment for airline tickets.
   - Issue tickets only if payment has been received.
   - Request early deposits.
   - Do not send payments to suppliers until payment has been received.

6. Accountants design accounting systems or advise agencies that design their own. They prepare financial statements using the data furnished by the accounting system. They also counsel agency owners on investments, sources of financing, and tax reduction techniques.

7. True

8. True

9. False

10. True

Career Development
Chapter 16

Review Chapter Objectives
- Identify types of resumes
- List four main parts of any resume
- Create a useful cover letter
- Explain the importance of follow-up
- Discuss three prospective job search sources
- Choose three personal and two business references
- Develop five questions to ask during an interview

Review Vocabulary
- Application form
- Benefits
- Career path
- Follow-up
- Information interview
- Interview
- Leads
- References
- Resume
- Screening
- Support services
- Training

Transparencies
- Chapter outline
- Where to find a job
- Guidelines for resumes
- Guidelines for cover letters
- Guidelines for interviews

Career Development
Chapter 16 Outline

I. Career Planning

II. Components of the Job Search

    A. Resume

    B. Cover Letter

    C. Interviews

    D. Other Written Documents

    E. Thank You Notes

III. Nine to Five

IV. Building a Career

    A. CTC

    B. Destination Specialist

Where to Find a Job

- Employment Agencies

- Newspaper Ads

- Friends in the Industry

- Industry Representatives

- Travel Industry Trade Shows

- College Placement Services

- Telemarketing

- Temporary Part-Time Positions

- Direct Mailings

- Cold Calls

Guidelines for Resumes

- Stress accomplishments and results

- Use short paragraphs and phrases

- Have other people proofread the final copy

- Avoid gimmicks

- Avoid exaggerated claims

- Avoid jargon and slang

- Avoid unnecessary information

- Organize and highlight information

- Don't use abbreviations

- Don't be repetitious with details

- Design the resume for easy scanning

- Center and balance with plenty of white space

Guidelines for Cover Letters

- Limit to less than one page

- Be specific

- Sell yourself

- Be aggressive but polite

- Be creative and professional

- Note the date available to begin work

- Use the active — not passive — voice

Guidelines for Interviews

- Relax but remain alert and interested

- Be confident

- Listen carefully and ask appropriate questions

- Do not smoke or chew gum

- Do not criticize former employees

- Respond with more than a yes or no answer

- Be sincere

- Use the interviewer's name during the interview

- Ask when the position will be filled

- Don't ask questions about benefits

- Speak correctly

Answers to Textbook Review Questions

1. **Why are good writing and speaking skills so important in the job search?**
   Writing and speaking skills give job applicants a competitive edge. Applicants with effective communications skills appear better prepared.

2. **How does information on a resume differ from that on an application form?**
   Application forms typically request the same information found on a resume, except in more detail.

3. **Under what circumstances would you feel more comfortable using a formal thank you note? An informal note?**
   Depends on the organization. A formal thank you might be more appropriate after an interview with a large organization.

4. **Whom would you choose as personal references? Professional references? Would they differ depending on the job being sought? Why or why not?**
   Answers will differ.

5. **Where might you consider going for an information interview? What criteria did you use for choosing this company?**
   Answers will differ. Students might respond with names of companies or areas of the industry that they are curious about but have no real career interest in.

Answers to Discussion Topics

Myth vs. Reality
Answers may vary. Students should discuss the fact that most individuals outside the industry believe this perception is true. However, students should also recognize that both of these situations should be mythical.

Interview
Answers may vary. Some include: directions and a trial run to the company to consider timing, printing of additional resume copies, researching company information, and so on.

Self-Appraisal
Answers may vary.

Answers to Workbook Exercises

Worksheet 16-1

Application form	A form that a company has applicants fill out prior to employment
Benefits	Those advantages offered by a company on behalf of its employees
Career path	The progressions and advancements people make in their profession
Follow-up	After an interview, sending a thank-you note to the interviewer
Information interview	The first interview in the interviewing process
Interview	The process where an employer evaluates the qualifications of an applicant
Leads	Avenues to follow for employment. These often come in the way of suggestions from friends and colleagues
References	A list of people who will recommend the applicant
Resume	A personal data sheet presented to an employer that introduces applicants through a summary of experience and qualifications
Screening	The process whereby applicants are narrowed down to the best few
Support services	Companies or programs through which employees can continue education and training
Training	Programs that increase education

Worksheet 16-2

1. 1. a heading 2. an objective 3. an education summary 4. work experience

    5. other relevant information 6. references

2. A cover letter is a letter of introduction that accompanies a resume and is designed to obtain an interview or an application form for the applicant.

3. 1. employment agencies

    2. newspaper ads and trade publications

    3. friends in the industry - network

    4. industry representatives

    5. travel industry trade shows

4. Sending a thank-you note is common courtesy. It reminds the interviewer of continued interest and brings the applicant's name back to the interviewer's attention.

Worksheet 16-3

1. F
2. T
3. F
4. F
5. T
6. F
7. F
8. F
9. T
10. F

Worksheet 16-4

Answers will vary.

Worksheet 16-5

Answers will vary.

Classroom Activities

1. Have students choose one of these ads and respond with a positive cover letter that includes a reference to experience, education, and skills. Include a copy of a resume and a properly addressed envelope that will contain both written documents.

   WANTED: Travel Agent — Seeking counselor for small branch office. Competitive salary, insurance, incentives. Candidate must have 3 years experience w/Sabre and must be aggressive. #4375

   WANTED: Salesperson — Fast growing travel company seeking fulltime help. Experience a plus but if you have an outgoing personality and are willing to learn, call now and grow with us. #800-555-1212

2. Divide the class into teams and have them debate the following issue: "Should agents be licensed?" In Ontario, British Columbia, and Quebec, legislation has been passed as a form of consumer protection that requires agents to adhere to certain standards. In the United States, most regulation is at a state level. Rhode Island, Ohio, Hawaii, and California are a few of the states that set standards for agents. Should government control licensing? What standards are needed?

3. Bring in the books, "Color me Beautiful" and "Dress for Success." Ask students to discuss the importance of looking professional for the first interview.

4. Practice sample interviews with the students. The best way to effectively improve their self-image is to continually practice and videotape their interviews. Class members and additional faculty or administration may volunteer to help. Students should feel comfortable enough to answer questions, but not so practiced that their answers appear to be rote. It is interesting to compare the first practice session with the last to demonstrate improvement.

Articles

Chapter 16 — Article One
"Questions of Ethics"
By definition, professional ethics constitute moral standards of commonly accepted values of right and wrong. However, universal professional standards of conduct are not always written or condoned by all members of the travel agency community. Many counselors consider ethical behavior to be that which is legally acceptable, while others strive for even higher principles in business. Conversely, when profit is involved, many agents tend to rationalize actions which might otherwise be considered wrong. Should we have laws to govern ethical practices? Why or why not? Use the following article to support your claim.

Chapter 16 — Article Two
"Empowerment"
Empowerment is one of the newest buzz words of the '90s. Why is this concept so important to travel agencies? How can managers instill this vision and help boost their employees' self-confidence? How will this in turn aid in increasing profits, employee satisfaction, lowering turnover and absenteeism? Ask students to research a national company that embraces this philosophy. Does this company have one individual who epitomizes the image of the company? How does this relate to the company's success?

Chapter 16 — Article Three
"Fast Ways to Sidestep Burnout"
Introduce the concept of burnout through personal life experiences or with a guest speaker. How can this be avoided? Ask students to create their own list of solutions to this problem. Share some of the suggestions in the article and ask students how realistic these possibilities are for smaller agencies. Many excellent videotapes are available on the topic of stress — one of the leading causes of burnout — any of them could be used as a follow-up activity.

Questions of Ethics
Temptations abound in travel agencies today, but how do you decide what's fair, what's foul? Put your scruples to the test.

By Rebecca F. Sox

Doing what's right. Sounds simple, until you try to define what you mean by "right," then put it into practice and stick to your instincts no matter what the cost.

Questions of ethics confront professionals everywhere, from the White House to Wall Street to the local travel agency. Though professional ethics — the principles and judgments that govern the way you do business — may be spelled out by laws or institutional codes of conduct, the subject is ultimately personal. What do *you* believe to be honest, fair, or justifiable in a given situation?

"You cannot be a professional without taking an ethical approach to your occupation," says Cord Hansen-Sturm, who teaches travel-industry ethics at the New School for Social Research in New York. "A travel professional must not only be an expert but must maintain high moral standards."

But the high road often conflicts with the bottom line. Keen competition among agencies, slim profit margins, and a lack of industry policy can make it tough for travel planners to clearly identify what's fair or unfair practice in travel agencies today. Deregulation has further clouded many issues. Hansen-Sturm says, "As laws changed under the new system of deregulation, many old ethical standards ceased to exist." One example: rebating. Once illegal, it's now considered a fair business practice. Yet even legal acts can be viewed by some as unethical.

As a result, ethics debates rage: Should agents accept overrides from carriers with whom they do a high volume of business? Is it right or wrong to bend airline rules to get a client a better fare? Or to take advantage of a hard-earned fam trip just for fun?

Put your own code of ethics to the test with the following hypothetical situations. There are no right or wrong answers.

Freebie Frenzy

One of the rental-car companies you frequently recommend is giving mink coats to travel agents who book 50 clients in one month. You need only one more booking to win, but it's the last day of the month. Just in time, a corporate traveler calls. When you suggest the rental company that's offering the coat, he says he prefers Firm X instead. What do you do?

A. Tell the client that your agency has had favorable dealings with the company in question and that you recommend them highly. Then let him decide.

B. Fabricate a reason why that company is his only option and book him anyway.

C. Book the client with the company of his preference and hope someone else will call so you can win the coat.

Gimmicks. Your clients get to take advantage of them in the form of frequent-flyer and frequent-stay discounts. Why not you? Many hotels and transportation companies offer agents special bonuses as incentives to book with them. Perks are tempting, but there are ethical aspects to getting "paid" for your business.

Although offering a prize is a legitimate way to attract the attention of agents who are bombarded by product information, many agents argue that the pursuit of an award can affect your ability to offer your clients the best service. The customer-is-always-right philosophy should take precedence, they say.

After National Car Rental distributed more than 18,000 prizes to agents and owners in their first sweepstakes last year, travel agency bookings increased dramatically over the previous year's figures.

Contests and awards can put agencies in awkward situations with their preferred suppliers. By booking a company with whom your agency does not have a contract, you potentially hinder the effort to meet a quota designated in the agency-supplier agreement. The consequences? Your agency may not receive the predetermined overrides from the supplier and, in the long run, could lose money.

There's nothing wrong with booking to win the prize when two suppliers are offering the same product, quality, and price — as long as the company you book is the one the client wants. If you know the client well, you might ask if he or she would mind booking with a particular company this time in order to help you attain your goal.

Release Rights

After you've spent three hours researching and booking a high-commission European vacation, the client calls to say he wants you to transfer his reservations to another agency. When you ask him why, he says he likes them better and that they are located nearer to his home. Though you offer to deliver his tickets, vouchers, and any other information he may need, he still wants to switch agencies. You know you reserved the last two seats on his departing flight, and if you don't release him to the other agency, he probably won't be able to rebook. What do you do?

A. Refuse to release, telling him it's against company policy (whether your agency has such a rule or not).

B. Tell him sure, you'll release. But after you hang up you cancel all his bookings.

C. Release him.

To release or not to release? Some agents argue that you should never give up space you've worked hard to book. Others feel that transferring a booking to another agency at a client's request is a basic courtesy (even though no one likes to lose the business). No industry-wide policy exists to tell agents when they should or shouldn't release a booking to another agency. An emergency situation could arise that would require circumventing established policy.

In many cases, the decision about whether to release may be out of your hands because of your agency's rules. Some travel agencies won't allow employees to release space to anyone for any reason. One rationale is that when you release a booking, you're giving up space that another client of yours may need. Not all agents agree. Even if there were no problems with the service you were offering, you create a negative image of the agency in the client's mind by refusing to release.

The choice between releasing or not has no legal ramifications. A logical solution lies in how you define the travel planner's function. As long as the agency is working as the agent of the supplier, the traveler is the owner of his reservation and has a right to pay for that reservation wherever he chooses.

Creative Booking

An important client has a meeting one hour before his departing flight. He's not sure he will make it, though, so he asks you to arrange a second reservation on a later plane just in case his meeting runs long. Both flights depart during peak hours, and you don't like to block space you know you aren't going to use. You decide to

A. Tell the client not to worry. You'll book both flights. You value his business and are willing to take that extra step to keep it.

B. Explain that you'd be blocking space during peak time and that someday he'll be one of those unfortunate travelers unable to get on an overbooked flight. Ask him to choose one or the other.

C. Tell him you'd rather book him on the later flight since it's unlikely he'll make the early flight anyway. But emphasize that it's his decision.

Call it creative booking: You find yourself bending corporate policies or airline rules to accommodate a valuable client. Making duplicate reservations is just one example of the iffy requests you may receive. Other examples include booking a cheaper round-trip ticket for a client who plans to fly only one way, booking a corporate client on a circuitous route in order to help him rack up frequent-flyer points, or helping him get around a company policy he doesn't like, such as a requirement that he fly coach instead of first class.

374

When a client asks you to do something you consider unethical, you have a choice between honoring the traveler's wishes or possibly losing him to an agent who will. Some clients, honest people, don't understand the reasons why you can't do certain things like making two separate reservations for them. On the other hand, many agents feel that they owe their first allegiance to the customer. If creative booking means saving the client money, some agencies are all for it.

The airlines are primarily at fault for promoting nonchalance about creative bookings among travel agents, because they occasionally bend the rules themselves. For instance, carriers sometimes waive advance-purchase requirements or other fare restrictions for corporate clients or loyal travel agencies. But when agents try to jockey fares without permission, they risk having their airline plates removed or receiving full-fare debit memos as punishment. Thus travel planners often finds themselves in a double bind, working to get the best deals for clients while they're strait jacketed by complicated and sometimes confusing restrictions.

Business travelers who ask agents to help them skirt their corporate policies present a less complicated quandary. The company that pays the bill has the right to determine what levels of service and policing they want the agent to provide. If it is specified in the agreement with the corporation, then all agents must be policemen for the agency's corporate clients. You risk damaging the agency's relationship with the corporation if you act as an accomplice to a client who breaks his company's travel policy. When you're dealing with a corporation on a contractual basis, your agreement is with the management, not the individual traveler.

But if no instructions have been given to the travel agency through a formal agreement with the company, go along with the traveler's request. It may be ultimately unfair to the company and its stockholders, but no problem exists between the agency and the client in such situations.

Fam Flim-Flam

Your best friend has always dreamed of taking a Caribbean cruise. She knows about familiarization trips and how cheaply you can travel on them. Please, she asks, can you book her on one these trips? All it will take is a request on travel agency letterhead verifying that she is an employee. She's a longtime friend who has done special favors for you in the past. You decide to

A. Sneak her on an upcoming cruise as long as she promises not to tell anybody that she's not really a travel agent.

B. Tell her you're sorry, but you could lose your job if you got caught.

C. Offer to find her an economy cruise she can afford instead of a free fam trip.

Even though they are considered working trips, fams are widely viewed as one of the nicest perks in the industry. When travel consultants sneak their friends along, other agents invariably call foul.

This happens frequently. Occasionally agencies put mothers, fathers, sisters, brothers, and friends on their ARC/IATA lists. Non-agent travelers don't follow the itineraries, and it makes the other agents angry because another employee could have participated instead.

Because fam trips are meant to generate business and to educate travel agents, those who send friends on fam trips are, in effect, robbing the tour operators. Although you may be doing your friend a favor, these trips cost the suppliers enormous amounts of money.

Sending non-agents on fam trips also damages the professional agents who take the working trips seriously. Tour operators will stop offering fams if we keep sending our friends. Or they will stiffen the screening process to make it more difficult for agents to go on these trips.

Many agencies require consultants to fill out a request form to justify each fam trip. Upon returning, the agent must submit a detailed trip report for tax purposes.

Every rule has an exception. Sometimes tour operators allow or even encourage you to bring a spouse or friend with you. Ask suppliers what their familiarization policies are and whether they would allow you to send a non-agent friend on occasion. If a supplier says no, you should adhere to the policy.

List Loss

You've been offered a better salary and an opportunity for rapid advancement at a new agency. You accept. But alone in the office one evening, before you've given notice to your current employer, you realize it would be easy to copy your agency's client list off your computer without anyone finding out. The list would help you show your new boss that you know how to generate business. What do you do?

A. Copy the list.

B. Copy only the names of the clients you know are coming with you anyway.

C. Decide you'd rather leave on the up and up, even though you're not particularly fond of your current boss.

The problems created when an employee takes off with an agency's entire client list can be devastating: lost reservations, lost relationships, lost profits. Because clients are legally viewed as the property of an agency, many people consider taking a client list to be theft.

Agencies spend a great deal of money to solicit clients. When an employee takes them away, a substantial amount of income can be lost. For example, an agency owner lost $8,000 in cruise bookings when an employee transferred to another agency and took a copy of the agency's client list. The owner sued the agent and won what she had lost in bookings. The agent's new boss paid the settlement.

Another instance: a travel agency was sold to a new owner, who took over the business on a Monday. The following Saturday, when the agency was closed, the senior agent (who had been hired by a competitor) came in, accessed the reservations in all but one of the computers, and switched them to the new agency. When the old agency opened for business on Monday morning, the employees discovered no record of most of their reservations.

There's nothing wrong with taking clients with you when you transfer to another agency if you can prove that you brought those clients to your former agency in the first place. If you've dealt with someone for 10 years and they always ask for you, there is nothing wrong with telling them you are transferring.

List-taking is not a black-or-white offense. If a client list is readily available and not kept under lock and key, it is probably not illegal to take it. If, on the other hand, it's locked in a safe or protected by a secret computer code, then taking the list borders on the criminal.

Some agencies now ask employees to sign agreements called *noncompetition clauses* that prohibit them from selling trade secrets. Besides protecting the client list, such agreements often bar employees from sharing information about the agency's supplier contracts, override-commission levels, or special marketing plans. Unfortunately, such agreements are sometimes difficult to enforce because interpretation can vary from state to state. At best these noncompetition clauses can serve to discourage agents from taking clients with them when they transfer to another agency and can provide proof in court that the agency tried to protect itself.

Of course, one could try this compromise: Send out announcement cards informing your clients when you are leaving the agency. Don't ask for the client's business, but if he or she chooses to follow you, fine. Be careful about soliciting business from clients whom you did not bring to the agency, though; you could be liable.

Ticket Brokering

One of your best clients asks you to sell a ticket he has earned with bonus frequent-flyer mileage. It would be easy for you to sell the ticket — in fact, you know just the buyer. Your chances of getting caught are slim, and your boss has never told you not to broker free tickets. You decide to

A. Sell the ticket. If you don't, somebody else will.

B. Ask your boss what to do.

C. Tell the client you'd love to help him, but it's against airline policy and you'd be in trouble if you got caught.

This one's easy. Most airlines' tickets, whether frequent-flyer awards or nonrefundable tickets that clients can no longer use, are nontransferable. An agency that knowingly allows a ticket to be transferred or suggests to a client that a ticket can be transferred could be held liable.

The airline policy hasn't stopped some agencies and coupon brokers from selling frequent-flyer awards though those that do may not fully understand the consequences. If airport ticket agents find that a flyer's identification doesn't match the name on his or her ticket, they can confiscate the ticket with no refund. What's worse, the traveler could then sue the agency for the cost of the trip. Or the airline could honor the ticket but charge the entire cost to the travel agency that sold it. Additionally, if airlines suspect that you are brokering tickets, your supplier-agency relationship could be permanently damaged. Repeat offenders have had their plates lifted.

If you found these questions tough to call, you're not alone. Travel agents across North America face ethical dilemmas every day, seldom with clear-cut, right-or-wrong answers. Even in situations in which laws dictate proper conduct, there are exceptions, multiple interpretations, or ulterior temptations that can influence how you'll act.

Try comparing your responses to the scenarios presented here with your co-workers'. Are you all operating under a collective set of scruples? Do travel agencies need clearer guidelines — or simply more ethical representatives? The state of the industry is in your hands ... er, your conscience.

Reprinted with permission from *Travel Life* magazine, May/June, 1989, a publication of Whittle Communications

Empowerment!
Empowering Employees with the Authority to Make Decisions Can Be the Key to Better Customer Service, Happier Travel Counselors and Smoother Management

By Susan Gibson Breda

Consider the case of a huge travel agency in California which believed it was rendering quality service to satisfied customers. The agency attached cards soliciting customer input on service to its clients' tickets. Only a few of the comment cards were returned, but most were favorable so the agency assumed all was well.

However, when the agency probed further, it discovered its bread-and-butter corporate accounts were not so sanguine. Travelers frequently felt hampered by travel counselors' inability to clearly define corporate travel policy and answer questions concerning the restrictions imposed by their companies' travel coordinators.

The solution: "Empower agency personnel to provide on-the-spot answers to corporate travelers by conducting thorough cross-training with the client, deciding which waivers of policy were acceptable, which were not and which needed to be bounced back to the travel coordinator for resolution."

The result: happy travelers, happy travel coordinators, happy clients. If this agency had not gone the extra step in defining customer expectations, it would have discovered far too late that its travel counselors needed further empowerment to satisfy the customers' needs and wants.

Empowerment. The word connotes strength in decision-making and action, solidity and wisdom. Empowering employees by giving them the authority to solve client problems can be extremely rewarding for agencies, customers and travel counselors.

The counselor is in a unique position to answer immediate problems of clients. If handled well, the counselor's professional skills are respected and used to the fullest, the customer is satisfied and the agency has increased its chances to build repeat business because its customers are satisfied.

It may sound easy enough, but empowerment can't be employed in a haphazard manner. Ad hoc decision-making that runs counter to the agency's goals will create more problems than it solves.

Travel agency management, travel counselors, and customers see empowerment through different eyes.

Travel agency owners and managers envision empowered employees as well-trained professionals, individual travel counselors imbued with common sense, good judgment and customer service savvy. These stalwarts embody company philosophies and policies with loyalty and integrity, acting in the best interest of customers while protecting the agency financially and legally.

Customers see empowered employees as people who can actually act on their behalf, fulfilling their requests and solving any problems that arise. For the customer, empowered employees stand above the bureaucratic hierarchy, banishing the "It's not my department" mentality that has become all too common in service industries today.

Travel counselors envision their own empowerment as management's decision to take its professionals seriously, to place trust in their judgment and allow on-the-spot response to customer service challenges without the need to seek permission. Employee empowerment means letting those who know best serve the customer.

Is empowerment a realistic strategy for today's travel agency? It depends on the agency's commitment. These three visions define the goal of employee empowerment: authority through management guidelines to render assistance on behalf of the customer as needed while adhering to clearly defined decision-making, legal and financial parameters.

How can this be achieved? Top-quality service begins in the minds of top management and is executed at the front line. Negotiating the path from visualization to delivering improved customer satisfaction is the art of employee empowerment. The following guidelines may ease the way:

Define the travel agency's vision of top-quality customer service. Does the agency always satisfy customers, no matter what it takes? Does it deliver within certain limits? All of the time? Some of the time? What does "service" mean to the agency? Who renders it — management, employees or both? Talk about it, agree on a definition of the agency's service goals and then find out what it will take to reach them.

Understand the customers' expectations and their current perceptions of the service the agency delivers. Knowing what customers expect in terms of service is critical. Written surveys, comment cards, focus groups, one-on-one interviews, customer panels and studies of important clients are just a few of the tools available to determine what customers need, want and expect.

Provide employees with clearly defined job descriptions and levels of authority. To enable employees to deliver total quality service, each travel counselor must fully understand his or her job and its responsibilities and how each travel counselor contributes to the overall operation of the agency. Ask the best performers in each job classification (entry-level booking agent, senior booking agent, quality control agent, etc.) to outline what they do on a daily, weekly and monthly basis. Categorize the tasks, (greeting customers and establishing rapport, probing for customer needs and expectations, matching product to wants and needs, completing the passenger name records, invoicing the client, etc.)

For each category of tasks, define the actual tasks needed to complete the task. Determine potential points of interaction and communication contact for each category and task. Then, create standards of performance and measurement for each one. Finally, determine the levels of authority for each task category and, if possible, for individual tasks.

Employees need to know what is expected of them. They need a thorough process allowing them to understand management's specifications for service. Defining jobs, detailing all tasks and creating standards of measurement are major milestones on the road to empowerment.

Define potential variables and solutions. What should be done when unexpected or unusual customer needs arise? Anticipating customer service challenges before they happen is imperative for the success of empowerment efforts. Have staff members generate lists of potential "road hazards" and discuss how each could be removed.

Generating "what-if" lists and possible responses involves the staff closest to the problem in its solution and enhances a sense of self-esteem and contribution.

Define the parameters of empowerment. For each of the variables and possible solutions discussed, identify the agency's preferred method for handling the situation. Identify specific steps, outline actions to be taken and determine the limits and the extent of the front-line counselor's authority. Establish an authorized dollar amount, a time frame for resolution and specific follow-up procedures. Some agencies assign a pool of discretionary funds to each agent or department while others set dollar amounts and correlate them to specific problems: $50 for "I'm sorry" flowers, $100 in hotel expenses, $250 credit on next cruise and so on.

In some cases, empowerment may go further. A leading tour operator received a telephone call from a distressed travel agent whose VIP clients had booked a packaged tour with five-star luxury accommodations in Honolulu. However, when they arrived, they were bumped to a lesser property backing the canal.

The distraught agent called the tour operator demanding immediate action on behalf of her clients. The tour operator's service representative offered comparable accommodations on another island, picking up the airfare and providing a limousine for the transfer. The result: satisfied clients, satisfied travel agent, retained relationship.

Was it worth the price? Certainly! Compare the dollars spent on advertising to obtain new customers with the small price paid to keep them. In this instance, the tour operator's service representative was empowered to make a wise decision in the best interest of her company and the travel agent's customers.

Put it in writing, then train, train, train. Outline the program in writing. Conversations won't do. Provide a road map. Provide employees with clear-cut written job descriptions, task details, levels of authority, budget allowances and management strategies for variables. If it's not in writing, too much is left to chance. And point out the gray areas, those situations for which the only reasonable guideline is for the empowered employee to use his or her best judgment.

Make the agency's policy readable and portable. Distribute it widely, so everyone knows what everyone else is doing. Implement a serious training program that conveys the written information and puts travel counselors through their paces.

A major car rental company has undertaken a "Commitment to Quality" program: A mission statement, employee credo and employee empowerment statement are distributed to all employees and customers, too. The employee empowerment statement is posted on the wall of every office and serves as a visual reminder of excellence.

As a result, the employees are viewed as superstars and the company's customers are delighted. When problems occur — as they will in any service industry — the employees are authorized to act. The customer leaves satisfied and ready to do business again with the company that listened to the problem and quickly addressed the complaint.

Report in on a regular basis. Employee empowerment programs live and die by consistent communication and regular reporting between the frontline and management. Travel counselors need to keep management informed of actions taken on behalf of the customer. The empowered counselor doesn't need to get permission before acting, but management must be kept informed.

Regular written or oral reports, simple or complex, keep the process alive and the involvement mutual. Management's role is to listen, support and guide, not to dictate, correct or second-guess the decisions of front-liners.

In turn, regular communication with management does not strip employees of power. If properly handled in an atmosphere of teamwork, mutual problem-solving and a commitment to quality, it actually heightens an employee's sense of contribution and importance. Employees who are trusted and who return that trust can create an environment of team spirit and cooperation throughout the organization.

Equally important is regular and consistent communication with peers. Nothing stalls an organization more quickly than over-promising service and then under-performing, thereby failing to meet its stated commitments to customers.

Monitor and follow-up. Once the front-line agent is empowered, agency management should carefully monitor employee performance through shadow-training, personal observation, one-on-one supervisory discussion and roundtables. As with any other new skill, employees in the initial training phase need consistent positive reinforcement for a job well done and timely guidance on alternative ways to handle less-than-perfect interactions and solutions.

As the travel counselors make progress toward effective employee empowerment, managers can monitor less intensively and rely more upon formal channels of communication and periodic reviews.

Measuring changing levels of customer satisfaction and dissatisfaction after implementation of an empowerment program is a good barometer of its success. However, don't measure too soon. Allow some time for change to occur, then survey the customer base again and compare assessments of service satisfaction.

Ask travel counselors about their feelings regarding the empowerment process. Are they more productive on the job? Do they feel a greater sense of achievement? Has their job satisfaction been enriched? Do they feel customers are more satisfied and are receiving better service? Do they like what they're doing and feel proud to be part of the team? If the answers are "yes," the agency is on the road to personal and professional success, higher profits and customer loyalty.

Case Studies

As a guest at the Newton Marriott in Massachusetts was being escorted to his room, the bellman carrying his luggage accidentally damaged the man's $350 electronic typewriter. Faced with the prospect of an angry guest taking his business elsewhere, the embarrassed bellman and other hotel staffers found a solution — replace the damaged typewriter with an identical machine, free of charge.

At the same hotel, a guest who had checked out of his room complained to the staffer carrying his luggage that his breakfast was prepared improperly. The employee escorted the guest back to the front desk, where the cost of the meal was refunded.

The concept at work here is called "empowerment," and hotel companies are using it to foster repeat business by giving their employees the authority to resolve complaints from guests on the spot and in a way that's bound to satisfy — and be remembered.

Marriott, for example, began testing an empowerment program four years ago; since then it has introduced formal training that stresses how much money could be lost if steady customers become dissatisfied and decide to check in at competitors' properties.

"We have thousands [of guests] who sleep with us more than 75 nights per year," said Roger Dow, vice president of sales and marketing services for Marriott. By estimating that one such customer will spend about $125,000 during 10 years, Dow suggested that if just eight of those guests turn to competitors Marriott loses $1 million in sales.

The idea is "not to [let employees] run loose and do anything they want," but to follow day-to-day ground rules, "building a process where we continually try to exceed [a customer's] expectations," Dow said.

Ray Shultz, president of the Hampton Inn hotel division of The Promus Companies Inc., said empowerment at his company means employees "can do anything that a human being can do for another human being. It really increases your employees' loyalty to you … . It sends a signal we trust your judgment to make decisions based on good common sense and logic."

Clyde Culp, president and CEO of Promus' Embassy Suites hotel division, said training employees to provide better service is the real strategy behind empowerment. "You don't want the customer getting away from you without a satisfactory experience," he said.

In one case, a customer riding an elevator with a bellman at an Embassy Suites property in Washington, D.C., complained about a stay he'd had at another of the chain's properties. The bellman then called that property, and its staff in turn issued the customer a free stay, Culp said.

Employees who are confident they can do a job — and who know their bosses are backing them — will perform better than those who are unsure of themselves, Culp contends. "Customer satisfaction," he added, "is something that has to be measured all the time or you lose sight of it."

Reprinted with permission from *Travel Counselor* magazine, a CMP publication

Chapter 16 — Article Three
Fast Ways to Sidestep Burnout

Maybe you're perfectly happy with your present career path, but workday stress keeps tripping you up. Here are 14 agent-tested ways to make the going easier.

1. Don't suffer in silence. Travel and Transport in Omaha schedules monthly no-holds-barred meetings between agents and management. "The rule is that nothing they can say can be used against them," says president Frank J. Dinovo Jr., CTC. The two-year-old program has already produced changes in compensation plans and staffing. Other agencies use retreats or weekly staff meetings to improve communication. At International Tours and Cruises in Evansville, Indiana, a manager once brought a bottle of wine to a gab session and thus started a now-weekly get-together known as Tradition, where agents exchange war stories. "It's not a meeting," says Charlotte Hatfield, senior vice-president for sales and marketing. "We keep it informal and unregimented."

2. Expand your know-how. You'll gain instant prestige by completing the Certified Travel Counselor (CTC) program run by the Institute of Certified Travel Agents (ICTA), which involves 18 months to three years of study. Or you can earn the right to use the initials DS (Destination Specialist) after your name once you complete one of ICTA's shorter-term geography courses. If you can't commit to extensive study, opt for a weekend Professional Management Seminar, held in different cities throughout the year; they cover such areas as stress management and marketing. Call ICTA at 800-542-4282 (617-237-0280 in Massachusetts).

In cosponsorship with Radisson Hotels International, the American Society of Travel Agents (ASTA) offers one- and two- day seminars on automation, geography, group sales, and more. And just this year, ASTA has introduced KEYS (Keys to Educating Your Staff), four continuing-education modules on such topics such as customer service and problem-solving. Classes are taught in the office by ASTA-trained agency owners. Call 703-739-2782.

If time management is your stressor, the American Management Association (AMA) provides two-day seminars on the subject in major U.S. cities. Call 800-262-6969.

And the Cruise Lines International Association (CLIA) makes the rounds of more than 200 North American cities with its one-day seminars on sales techniques. Call 212-921-0066.

3. Change your workweek. If you need to lighten your load, see if you can work out a flex-time plan with your manager. Darlene Bridges of Brennco Travel in Overland Park, Kansas, says changing to a four-day workweek helped her attitude tremendously. "Now I can combine work and family," she says. "I have that extra day to catch up, which takes off a lot of the stress." Carol Kasper, CTC, general manager of Will Travel in Horsham, Pennsylvania, lets her agents take unpaid leave during slow periods: "They can sit in the sun on a nice day instead of sitting bored in the office."

4. Fam it up. It's educational, and your co-workers will thank you for getting your cranky self out of the office. At Post Haste Travel in Hollywood, Florida, the entire staff flies away for a long weekend once a year, while owner Sylvia Berman, CTC, and the manager mind the office.

If the timing isn't right for the trip, "get away" by watching a video tape of your favorite destination. Or keep a photo of a favorite retreat in your top drawer, and when things get tough, open the drawer and imagine you're there.

5. Work out your problems with a workout. It does wonders for your psyche, says Jacqueline Jamieson, CTC, of the Travel Group in Vancouver, who does aerobics at lunchtime with four other agents. "You come back feeling energized and better about yourself," says Jaimeson. The Travel Group even pays for agents' spa memberships.

6. Dress up — or dress down. At Pennsylvania's Will Travel, each week ends with "Friday Fun Day," in which everybody in the office wears wacky garb. "One Friday, we wore no shoes but instead ran around in crazy socks," says Carol Kasper. "It really helped us relax."

7. Lead a tour instead of booking it. Agents at Farroads International Travel and Tours in San Francisco do. "Not only do they get out of the office," says president David Randolph, "but it gives them better insight about clients and broadens their knowledge of destinations."

8. Plant a surprise. At Atlas Travel in Vancouver, the owner once hired a masseuse, set her up in a softly lit office, and made sure each agent received a 15-minute shoulder massage. And whenever agents book a cruise at Evansville's International Tours and Cruises, they loudly ring a bell to let everybody know of their success.

9. Join a local, state, or regional agent organization. Louanne Keichline, CTC, of Viking Travel in Chapel Hill, North Carolina, belongs to the 400-member Travel Agents of the Carolinas and finds that meetings are a great place to mingle with peers and exchange support. "For a small business that can't afford to attend national organization functions, it's a good way to benefit from a speaker's advice," she says.

10. Get organized. "Try to plan as much of the workday as possible the night before," says Susan Vannesse, CTC, of Travel People Personnel in Boston. "Make a list of duties, and the next day check off each one as it's finished. Prioritize tasks and group similar ones for a certain time of day."

11. Visualize yourself in another line of work. Picture yourself as an emergency-room nurse, a TV-network programming executive, or a hockey goalie. Maybe you'll decide that your own lot isn't so bad. Betsy Welch of Thomas Cook Travel in Cambridge, Massachusetts, has used the technique for years. "Each time I'd reach a career plateau," she says, "I'd envision myself as something else. I'd mentally leave — and come back to my job refreshed."

12. Deal in quality. "Agents have to make promises to clients that someone on the other side of the world may not fulfill," says Scottsdale, Arizona, travel-industry consultant Robert Joselyn. "Sell those suppliers that fix problems and stand behind their product."

13. Don't be a superhero. "If work starts to accumulate, reduce your workload by asking for help," says Howard Lewis, CTC, of Chartwell Travel Services in Inglewood, California. "Admit that there are situations that you can't handle alone."

14. Heed your own advice. You spend all day packing clients off to places where they can recharge while you're running on empty. So why not plan your *own* vacation?

Reprinted with permission from *Travel Life* magazine, November/December, 1991, a publication of Whittle Communications

End of Chapter Review

Name		Date

Directions: Fill in the blanks.

1. What is the purpose of a resume?

    _____

    _____

    _____

2. Name four standard parts of a resume.

    1. _____   2. _____

    3. _____   4. _____

3. List four key items that employers look for on an application or resume.

    1. _____   2. _____

    3. _____   4. _____

4. What two educational programs does the Institute of Certified Travel Agents (ICTA) offer to members of the travel industry?

    1. _____

    2. _____

5. List three intangible skills that are helpful in the job search.

    1. _____   2. _____

    3. _____

Answers to End of Review Questions

1. The purpose of a resume is to introduce applicants to prospective employers through a summary of experience and qualifications.

2. Answers may include: a heading; an objective; an education summary; work experience; other relevant information; references

3. Answers may include: gaps in employment; salary consistency; number of jobs and length of stay; questions that are left blank; incorrect spelling; reasons for leaving a job.

4. The CTC Travel Management program and the Destination specialist program

5. Answers may vary but can include: networking, self-analysis, and perseverance